National Culture and the
New Global System

Parallax  Re-visions of Culture and Society

Stephen G. Nichols, Gerald Prince, and Wendy Steiner,

SERIES EDITORS

National Culture and the New Global System

Frederick Buell

The Johns Hopkins University Press
Baltimore and London

© 1994 The Johns Hopkins University Press
All rights reserved. Published 1994
Printed in the United States of America on acid-free paper

03 02 01 00 99 98 97 96 95 94   5 4 3 2 1

The Johns Hopkins University Press
2715 North Charles Street
Baltimore, Maryland 21218-4319
The Johns Hopkins Press Ltd., London

Library of Congress Cataloging-in-Publication Data

Buell, Frederick, 1942–
    National culture and the new global system / Frederick Buell.
        p.   cm. — (Parallax)
    Includes bibliographical references and index.
    ISBN 0-8018-4833-4 (alk. paper). — ISBN 0-8018-4834-2 (pbk. : alk.
paper)
    1. Literature and society.   2. Cultural relations.   3. Nationalism.
4. Literature—History and criticism—Theory, etc.   I. Title.
II. Series: Parallax (Baltimore, Md.)
PN51.B84   1994
909.82—dc20   94-2076

A catalog record for this book is available from the British Library.

To Jill, Alexander, and Nicholas

Contents

Acknowledgments

THIS BOOK could not have been written without help from many sources. In a number of concrete ways, I am indebted to Queens College and the City University of New York for resources that made my work possible. Queens College provided me with a fellowship leave and course reduction, and PSC-CUNY gave me two summer grants. More important, Queens College's interest in and support for pedagogical innovation was of material help to me, given my interest in globalization and culture. The college, like the borough it serves, has been directly affected by the renewed global migrations of the past several decades: Queens is one of the nation's largest ports of immigration. Work with Queens's international student body has been supported by both the college and outside organizations. I am grateful to the Fund for the Improvement of Post-Secondary Education for three years of support for work with immigrant students; to the Mellon Foundation for three years of support for developing an interdisciplinary world-studies program; and to the National Endowment for the Humanities for supporting two summer institutes in world studies. William Kelly and I led the FIPSE-funded faculty seminar for three years; Morris Rossabi and I directed one of the NEH summer institutes in world studies; and Ronald Waterbury and I directed the final year of the Mellon-sponsored faculty seminar in world studies.

In the course of this work, I benefited greatly from discussions, arguments, and exchanges of information with more people than I can here acknowledge. I am particularly indebted to Barbara Bowen, Françoise Burgess, Matthew Edel, Peter Caravetta, Jacqueline Costello, Joan Dayan, Melvin Dixon, Anne Dobbs, Juan Flores, Lois Hughson, David Kleinbard, Robert Lyons, Charles Molesworth, George Priestly, William Proefriedt, Annabelle Sreberny-Mohammadi, Stephen Steinberg, William Tabb, Amy Tucker, Frank Warren, Gordon Whatley, Edith Wyschogrod, and Jack Zevin. I am grateful to Peter Dreyer, whose careful and exacting reading improved the book greatly. Ronald Waterbury, with whom I taught several world-studies courses, and Anthony O'Brien aided me more than I can say in correlating work on colonialism, postcolonialism, and globalization in the social sciences and the humanities and mapping the new field of global studies. William Kelly commented on sections of this book and was an invaluable partner in discussions about how to redefine American studies in productive new ways. Lawrence Buell, whose expertise includes both American studies and postcolonialism, was unfailingly helpful in discussing the issues involved in this book with me over years. And I am grateful to Sarah Lawall, L. Michael Lewis, Michael Palencia-Roth, and Wayne Bledsoe for instruction and encouragement in my forays into civilizational studies.

I acknowledge my deepest debts, however, in dedicating this book to Jill, Alexander, and Nicholas.

Introduction

The Discourse of Cultural Imperialism

IN 1969 HERBERT SCHILLER voiced what may still seem like a reasonable position when he argued that the "cultural homogenization that has been under way for years threatens to overtake the globe" (1969:112). "The new cultural-ideological structures of an emergent nation," he went on to say, "are no less vulnerable to the glittering socio-cultural products of the already developed world than the new industries of the aspiring states are to the established giant corporations of the industrialized west" (120). Concerned specifically with the development of global media, he advocated a kind of electronic delinking for the sake of preventing effacement of vulnerable cultures. His sense of urgency was fueled by the conviction that "mistakes and failures in agriculture and industry, if momentarily disastrous, are still remediable. Cultural patterns, once established, are endlessly persistent" (110). After 1969 Schiller theoretically retooled his position somewhat by grounding it in the then-emerging field of world-systems theory, but his fundamental polemic remained the same despite this attempt to integrate it into a richer context. And his feeling that the world, especially the weaker Third World, stood culturally in great danger of Americanization expressed not only the position of many media analysts but also the unexamined views of many liberal and left-wing First World critics of First World hegemony.

The enthusiastic endorsement of *Reader's Digest* by David Ogilvy provided a typical example of this gloomy scenario. "The magazine exports the best in American life," Ogilvy wrote. "In my opinion, the Digest is doing as much as the United States Information Agency to win the battle for men's minds" (Schiller 1976:6). Entirely apart from issues of economic exploitation and political repression, Ogilvy's comment evokes a cultural nightmare: a vision of the globe flattened into a low-level monoculture, a gigantic K Mart with no exit. Ogilvy's claim for the ability of *Reader's Digest* to propagate American ideology is essentially similar to the politically quite opposite, but ultimately comparable, analyses of Donald Duck comics by Ariel Dorfman and Armand Mattelart (*How to Read Donald Duck: Imperialist Ideology in the Disney Comic* [1975]) or of the global consumption of "Dallas" by some contemporary media critics. Such analyses emphasize how a dominant United States has achieved "cultural penetration" (Schiller's phrase, 1976:8) of a victimized Third World. The act envisioned is rape, and the result is the effacement of local cultures, thanks to their homogenization by, and assimilation to, American capitalist ideology. This sorry state both follows from and helps further the integration of the Third World into the First World economy as the dependant, underdeveloped periphery of an American imperial center.

Liberal jeremiads against cultural imperialism and its product, global homogenization, have been and still are widespread. But the discourse in which they are usually embedded is anything but as clear and unified as it seems. Indeed, on the face of it, Schiller's language of "cultural penetration," in its unconscious use of gender-significant rhetoric, has uncomfortable overtones. It replicates what it supposedly opposes: it repeats the gendering of imperialist rhetoric by continuing to style the First World as male and aggressive and the Third as female and submissive. In doing this Schiller is not alone; in studying the gendering of the contemporary international system, Cynthia Enloe (1990) analyzes how the inscription of hierarchical relationships between men and women continues in revolutionary nationalism: a male-gendered nationalism seeks to protect a female-gendered cultural whole. As Roland Robertson (1992a:108) has also argued, identification of "the communal essence" of non-Western societies as feminine has been a familiar tactic for marginalizing Third World women.

Second, as John Tomlinson points out, many recent media studies have been dedicated to proving that American popular culture has been consumed globally in a very different way than Schiller suggests. For example, in *Watching Dallas* (1985), Ien Ang notes "the capacity of the audience to negotiate the possible contradictions between alien cultural values and the 'pleasure of the text,'" (Tomlinson 1991:46). Mary Yoko Brannen has startlingly observed of the establishment of a Disneyland in Tokyo that the "exported cultural artifacts are not necessarily imposed onto a passive Other. . . . in fact, the selective importation of Disney cultural artifacts works in the service of an ongoing Japanese process of cultural imperialism" (Brannan 1992:231).

Perhaps most significant are recent developments in the way that television broadcasting has been institutionalized around the globe. Though American and American-style programming still dominates the airwaves, national television broadcasting has commenced throughout the world: national networks appeared, for example, in Thailand in 1955, in Egypt in 1960, and in Papua New Guinea in 1987 (Lila Abu-lughod 1993:465).

More interesting still is the fact that in places like Papua New Guinea and Australia, indigenous programming has appeared, not only on local broadcasts, but also on national commercial networks (Ginsburg 1993; Sullivan 1993). To be sure, some of this activity represents a co-optation and commercialization of indigenous material: Ginsburg sees "commodified images of Aboriginal producers," along with Aboriginal art and music, as "part of the cultural capital on which contemporary Australia builds its national image for consumption and circulation in areas of tourism, political affairs, and the marketing of culture overseas" (1993:562). Other more radical possibilities do exist, however. In Australia, "indigenous production is the focus of events that are constitutive of a global Fourth World / First Nations identity" (1993:562). Either way, nations and groups around the world have shown themselves capable of media production in service of their own national and transnational agendas. Schiller's portrayal of the cultural helplessness of the Third World thus replicates what it opposes: it too readily assumes the imperial viewpoint that Third World cultures are weak and defenseless.

Attributing agency to Third World audiences, rather than seeing them as passive consumers, is an important move. But the image of the Third World's helplessly violated purity has been still more radically undercut by the revelation that such fantasies of preexisting purity, vulnerable to violation, are a fiction—albeit a long-lived one, still widely disseminated. Despite his own later use of world-systems theory, Schiller ignores one of that theory's chief aspects: the Third World has been incorporated into the world system for a long time. It has been "impure" and "penetrated" for centuries, having been shaped and reshaped by colonial circumstances for more than four hundred years. Critics of the American media have, then, shown a remarkable provincialism, forgetting the existence of empires before that of the United States. They have also been infected by the rhetoric and assumptions of the position they condemn, implicitly denigrating the Third World they seek to preserve.

Something of this increasingly compromised conceptual basis for jeremiads against American cultural imperialism has exhibited itself in an extremely interesting way in the jeremiads themselves. Their moral fervor jettisoned, they have become a rhetorical form to be quoted, elaborated, and improved upon. For example, Clifford Geertz (1983:216) characterizes "one of the leading doctrines in contemporary social science" as arguing "that the world is growing more drearily modern—McDonald's on the Champs Elysées, punk rock in China; that there is an intrinsic evolution from *Gemeinschaft* to *Gesellschaft*, traditionalism to rationalism, mechanical solidarity to organic solidarity, status to contract; that post-capitalist infrastructure will soon shape the minds of Tongans and Yemenis to a single pattern." Evoking a notion he then goes on to criticize, Geertz thus turns what was, for those who held this doctrine, a morally earnest critique into a small stylistic tour de force—he is clearly enjoying his own rhetoric. In comments by William Roseberry, the pleasure of evoking the specter of America's cultural transformation of the world is even more obvious:

> We think of office buildings for local outlets of multinationals, of McDonald's and Kentucky Fried Chicken, of shopping malls filled with products carrying labels from U.S. corporations even though they are *hecho in Mexico,* of Exxon and Coca-Cola signs, of television stations carrying Spanish-language versions of "Dallas" or "Dynasty," of mass-market magazines carrying translations of articles from *People,* of stores selling plastic pumpkins and Halloween costumes and children going door to door saying "Trick or Treat, Trick or Treat, ¿ tiene dulces para mí? (Roseberry 1989:81)

Roseberry's comments are less a lament than a stylish recreation of a too-familiar genre: Roseberry intends this effect, inasmuch as he goes on to argue that many of the premises of traditional fears of the homogenization of Latin America are false. In this self-enjoying rhetoric, moreover, a crucial change has taken place: the wealth of detail has become fascinating for its own sake, displayed ultimately as more interesting than depressing. The *ne plus ultra* of this genre is Pico Iyer's *Video Night in Kathmandu,* which records, from a traveler's viewpoint, the way American popular culture has swept through Southeast Asia, with striking impact on a variety of different national cultures. The opening of the chapter on Bali is typical:

> I had come into town the previous afternoon watching video reruns of *Dance Fever* on the local bus. As I wandered around, looking for a place to stay, I noted down the names of a few of the stores: the Hey Shop. The Hello Shop. Easy Rider Travel Service. T.G.I. Friday restaurant. And after checking into a modest guesthouse where Vivaldi was pumping out of an enormous ghetto blaster, I had gone out in search of a meal. I ran across a pizzeria, a sushi bar, a steak house, a Swiss restaurant and a slew of stylish Mexican cafés. Eventually, however, I wound up at T.J.'s, a hyper-chic fern bar, where long-legged young blondes in tropical T-shirts were sitting on wicker chairs and sipping tall cocktails. Reggae music floated through the place as a pretty waitress brought me my corn chips and salsa. (Iyer 1988:29)

At first, it might seem that the East has been homogenized, that the only differences between this Bali and Manhattan's Upper West Side are the relatively higher level of technology and greater felicity of climate available in Bali. But throughout Iyer's book details like these stand out because they are located where they are: exotic Bali very much survives in the context of such descriptions; it becomes the basis for a postmodern carnival of violated boundaries. In Iyer's revision of exoticism, both the inherently bizarre singularity of the imports themselves (the queer exoticism of First World culture, seen from a new angle) and the boundary-violating strangeness of their relocation to Southeast Asia are heightened. Thus, in Nepal, Iyer finds himself "in Eden. The hotel Eden, that is . . . on the intersection of Freak Street and the Dharmapath . . . where Haight-Ashbury meets the Himalayas" (77). In Bandar Sari Begawan, he sees the familiar revealed as the "wonderously exotic" (10) when he watches a Burt Reynolds movie in a shabby guest house. And in Tibet, when unattractive second-generation hippies flock to gawk as buzzards eat the corpses set out for traditional open-air burials, Iyer's portrayal of the conjunction of East and West represents anything but the assimilation of one to the other: it heightens the grotesque peculiarity of each as they jarringly connect.

Is there anything left of the old jeremiad? Horror at impurity and sober social analysis have metamorphosed into stylistic virtuosity, riffled lists of startling examples, not of assimilation—the subjection of one culture to another—but of postmodern boundary violating and syncretistic cultural intersections. Increasingly, stylistic performance is foregrounded and enjoyed for its own sake. In Iyer's book, moreover, a number of underlying reasons for these developments are made visible. The cultural analyses that accompanied Iyer's always-enthusiastic performances move from gestures toward the tradition of lament for lost culture (Bali) and some examples of an anti-American critique of neocolonialism (the Philippines) to more relevant perceptions of how American material is not just absorbed but actively used by different national cultures. The material is used, on the one hand, as a part of people's sometimes limited, but sometimes quite successful, attempts to negotiate and unseat American hegemony, and, on the other, as a part of the formation of a new, syncretic, hybridized media-based global culture. At the beginning of his book, Iyer makes it clear that he is writing, not of the triumph of American power, but of its decline, exemplified first by the Vietnam War and subsequently by the economic miracle of the Pacific Rim.

Change like this has proceeded so far that it seems increasingly intellectually retrograde and naive to evoke the specter of homogenization as the starting point for investigations of global cultural relationships. Indeed, the prevailing current fear is a horror of discordant overabundance rather than of uniformity; Theodor Von Laue, for example, writes deploringly of the fact that the world has become a crammed cultural supermarket, in which people are "challenged but also bewildered by the choices offered and increasingly taxed by the decisions to be made" (1987:339). Charles Bright and Michael Geyer react to this changed situation with neither Iyer's breathless enthusiasm nor Von Laue's saurian primordialist gloom. In such cultural fragmentation, they see the sign that one era is ending and another, ultimately a good one, commencing.

> In this tense and tenuous combination of material integration and cultural fragmentation, we mark the end of the era of purely western domination and the reappearance, in dramatically altered forms, of a world of disparate entities and autonomous regional centers. Women in veils work at computer terminals, dispatching oil tankers to distant markets or military supplies to troops engaged in holy war. This is not Spengler's decline of the West, but the beginning of a global reordering in which the West seeks its place in a world order it must now share with radically different societies. It is the beginning of a truly global politics. (Bright and Geyer 1987:88)

Bright and Geyer represent just one of many competing viewpoints about the nature of this process and the form of the newly emerging global society, but they sound a note of possibility born in disruption that resonates widely today; the underlying cultural, political, and economic order of our world has been changing, and a new, somehow profoundly globalized, era is being born. The world is, many feel, in the midst of a deep sea change in the ways people experience, understand, negotiate, and represent global relationships, a sea change that is reshaping not only quotidian lives, familiar institutions, and local cultures but also ongoing attempts to represent them in fields ranging from sociology, history, economics, art, and literature to science itself. Many aspects of this sea change have had widespread popular play: the debate about the canon and multiculturalism has created bestsellers, and the recent presidential campaign has made the global economy a household word. But change has also unsettled more deeply buried foundations. As I argue throughout this book, dramatic revisions in the way we have mapped global relationships, as we have moved from the breakup of colonial empires to a postwar ecumene of sovereign nations and then to an increasingly globally interconnected world, have helped necessitate many of the theoretical disputes and methodological reappraisals visible in almost every academic discipline over the past twenty years. Much of the theory boom of the past few decades, this book argues, has come in response to underlying global changes, and more specifically, awareness of globalization has recently been prompting individual disciplines to reconceive themselves in light of altering and newly perceived global relationships. Thus, in many individual fields, investigators have, to use the sociologist Roland Robertson's apt phrase, made "concern with 'the world' a central hermeneutic" (1990:19). Similarly, the overall intellectual economy itself—the division of representation of the world into different specialties—has shifted, as boundaries between fields have become blurred or disappeared and varieties of hybrid interdisciplinarity been produced—even become, for many, normative, appropriate for a world of hybrid cultural production.

With a topic that emphasizes change, and, in particular, the assertion that a new era is unveiling itself in the present moment, it is natural to suppose that primary attention will be given to appraisals of recent developments and forecasts of the brave new, globalized world to come. But attempts to understand and respond to globalization have been as retrospective as they are avant-garde. Attempts to understand recent and anticipated events have gone hand in hand with reappraisals of the past, necessitated by our changed awareness of our present state. With Nietzschean pessimism, one might comment that we have been inventing new pasts to serve our altered needs, new narratives (including narratives of the failure of narrative) to tell ourselves the story of how we got to a present different from what was previously expected. Or, more traditionally, one might try to argue that we have only just now begun to understand the way we actually were, something we had hitherto been blind to thanks to the ideological constraints we are only now freeing ourselves from. Writing specifically about the development of global cities in the contemporary world system, Anthony King expresses this double-edged focus of globalization study in noting that "whilst this global *consciousness* is new, the phenomena themselves are not" (1990b:1). Thus, some scholars

> do not see the recent changes . . . as fundamentally new. Rather, trends that have been growing for the last 500 years such as the increases in the internationalization of capital, or in labour productivity, have continued and, due to rapid technological change, accelerated. The system of world cities did not simply appear in the 1950's with cities having been "national" before that time: rather, cities have long performed both national and international functions. (King 1990a:8)

Criticizing Schiller involves, then, not only the assertion that the present has not borne out his direst predictions, but showing how a conceptual framework like his rests, first, on dubious assumptions about the past—the suppression of the previous five hundred years of colonial interconnectedness—and, second, on the largely unconscious use of a conceptual model, or kind of discourse, created to serve interests in that past. For, as John Tomlinson argues, the discourse of cultural imperialism, of which Schiller's work is a part, originated in the West and serves the interests of Western modernity. The threat of cultural imperialism is the basis for a "discourse about other cultures and their rights to flourish . . . that circulates primarily in the heart of the 'imperialist' West. 'Cultural imperialism' is a critical discourse which operates by representing the cultures whose autonomy it defends in its own (dominant) Western cultural terms" (Tomlinson 1991:2). These terms specifically involve a metropolitan-disseminated (although not necessarily metropolitan-originated) notion of national identity, part of the larger discourse of nationalism, which stresses the idea of the endangered cultural identity requiring protection. These national identities are not

> cultural belongings rooted in deep quasi-natural attachments to a homeland, but, rather, complex cultural constructions that have arisen in specific historical conditions. There is a "lived reality" of national identity, but it is a reality lived in representations—not in direct communal solidarity. Furthermore, national identities are, paradoxically, the cultural outcome of the very same processes—expanding capitalism, Western rationality, the breakdown of "tradition," the "mediatisation" of cultural experience—that are said, in other discourses, to constitute cultural imperialism itself! (Tomlinson 1991:84)

Anthony King, summarizing the work of Roland Robertson, a leading proponent of globalization theory, states the issue more sharply, emphasizing its basic paradox:

> What he [Robertson] brings out is that it is crucial to recognize that the contemporary concern with civilizational and societal (as well as ethnic) uniqueness, as expressed via such motifs as identity, tradition, and indigenization, *largely rests on globally produced ideas.* . . . In an increasingly globalized world, "characterized by historically exceptional degrees of civilizational, societal and other modes of interdependence and the widespread consciousness thereof, there is an *exacerbation* of civilizational, societal and ethnic self-consciousness." . . . More recent discussions . . . equally undermine any simplistic assumptions about a general "homogenization of culture." (King 1990b:11)

Elsewhere, Robertson supplies a vivid example of this process that highlights European imperceptiveness of it. He criticizes his own discipline, sociology, for having "played a significant role in the patterning of twentieth-century globalization" but not having focused "analytically and interpretively *on* globalization as an historical phenomenon of increasingly salient contemporary significance" (Robertson 1992:109). Sociology has traditionally focused on social structures in a national, not international, framework; yet what sociologists discovered helped shape nation building throughout the Third World. Noting how Herbert Spencer influenced the development of Japanese and Chinese nationalism, and Emile Durkheim the establishment of the new Turkish republic in the 1920s, Robertson comments that "while Western social scientists, most outstandingly Max Weber, were busy *comparing* East and West as an analytical exercise (with strong political and ideological overtones), the objects of the comparison (more accurately, intellectual and political elites) were busy sifting and implementing packages of Western ideas for very concrete political, economic and cultural reasons" (110).

If globalization in the past has thus covertly produced cultural differences rather than effaced them, these paradoxes continue into the present. The worldwide resurgence of nationalism that has produced outbreaks of violence in places as diverse as Germany, India, and Yugoslavia can be interpreted as a concomitant of intensified globalization. On the one hand, the ideal of national self-determination has continued to filter into the angry aspirations of stateless peoples. On the other hand, it has done so in an era in which peoples have been compressed and connected more tightly together, something that has exacerbated nationalism even as it has produced a new phase of transparent, often explicitly postnationalist, global relationships. Tighter integration has thus paradoxically meant, and continues to mean, proliferation of asserted differences. And a Janus-faced era has thereby been produced, one in which new nationalisms and ethnic fundamentalisms—ones that conceal their global sources—have sprung up side by side with a widespread movement dedicated to demystifying the ideology of national culture and foregrounding the international and intercultural relationships upon which it has in fact erected itself.

Motifs of national, regional, and local identity have thus rested for centuries on global relationships: indeed, they were complexly produced and reinforced as a part of the globalization process Schiller fears, understanding it only as homogenization. Or, to put it more precisely, the Americanizing globalization Schiller abhors is merely the most recent phase of an older, more complex globalization process, one that among other things produced Schiller's own thinking.

If new perspectives on globalization past have opened up, globalization present—a process of volatile uncertainty and rapid change, in which global relationships have grown more visible to many in a wide variety of sites—has received the lion's share of attention. Noting the proliferation of attempts to "map" the globe in the postwar era, Roland Robertson has written:

> "Mapping" the world social-scientifically is, of course, a common procedure, it having crystallized during the 1960s with the diffusion of per-

ceptions concerning the existence of the Third World, on the one hand, and polarized First (liberal-capitalist) and Second (industrializing-communist) Worlds, on the other. Ever since that period—the beginning of the current phase of contemporary, late twentieth-century globalization—there has proliferated a larger number of different and, indeed, conflicting ideological and/or "scientific" maps of the world system of national societies—so much that it is reasonable to say that the discourse of mapping is a vital ingredient of global-political culture, one which fuses geography (as in the sense of North-South and East-West terminology) with political, economic, cultural and other forms of placement of nations on the global-international map. (Robertson 1990:24–25)

The profusion of maps Robertson describes has occurred as a part of a series of rapid changes in global relationships since World War II. The florescence of so many attempts to define not only indicates anxious uncertainty about the nature of what is happening but expresses the growing heterogeneity of the interested parties, as global maps are constructed and inflected in an attempt to construct the world in one's own image. To be adequate, any theory of the present phase of globalization has to come to grips with this volatility and seek to theorize it. The broad outlines of the process are clear: as the colonial era's centered global map of metropole and colony dissolved and a global ecumene of nations was formed from the anticolonialism of the postwar period, interests and positions multiplied, and the three worlds theory (a theory with a number of different versions) was evolved to map and express them. The three worlds theory is perhaps still the basis for our dominant assumptions about geopolitical and geocultural order, but its hold on our imagination and faith is fast passing. In its place, a startlingly different model, the notion that the world is somehow interconnected in a single system, has emerged, expressing the perception that global relationships constitute, not three separate worlds, but a single network. In its originary formulation, many assumptions of the three worlds theory live on: the global system has three (ranked) parts, roughly corresponding to the familiar three worlds. Subsequently, however, the single system has come to be perceived as more and more complex, increasingly centerless, and featuring a multiplication of interacting parts that are increasingly fragmented and unstable. Currently the most innovative forms of global mapping depict a global network in which interests and positions have become paradoxically more tightly knit together and more multiplicitously dissentious than those authorized by the three worlds theory. In these attempts to theorize the present phase of globalization, worldwide interconnectedness does not result in the creation of a "global society." It yields, on the one hand, a decentered set of subnational and supranational interactions—from capital transfers and population movements to the transmission of information—and these interactions help multiply, invent, and disseminate cultural differences, rather than overcome them. On the other, it challenges existing nation-states to reformulate their cultural identities for a more complexly inter-connected era, a process that has been marked by both fundamentalist attempts to reconsolidate borders and new kinds of internationalization that render those same borders startlingly porous.

John Tomlinson's critique of cultural imperialism is poised on the brink of this most recent shift in theorizing global order. The notion of cultural imperialism, Tomlinson argues, can only survive as a legitimate means of representing contemporary reality if it is (paradoxically) detached from the implications of "imperialism" and seen as an effect of modernizing globalization that "weaken[s] the cultural coherence of all nation-states, including the economically powerful ones" (Tomlinson 1991:175). Fur-thermore, this new idea of "globalization" is to be distinguished from the old notion of "imperialism" in that it suggests "interconnection and inter-dependency of all global areas which happens in a far less purposeful way" (175). Tomlinson thus stops where Iyer begins. He saves the notion of cultural imperialism by jettisoning imperialism's centered intentionality, leaving all cultures as victims of a common system. Iyer, by contrast, is relatively indifferent to such last-ditch resistance: he celebrates the vitality of the cultural heterogeneity produced when a postmodernizing globaliz-ation of American commercial popular culture incites cultures and com-munities worldwide to produce a carnivalesque profusion of hybrid forms.

In suggesting this rough outline of the changes this book charts—and in giving the exposition of the changes a narrative form—I do not mean to propose that what has been surpassed is past. Old historical formations seem neither to die easily nor to fade away altogether from our current attempts to form ourselves. As much as we may feel the force of a decen-tered global network in our everyday lives, the legacies of both the colonial enterprise and anticolonial nationalism survive vividly both in many of our necessary interpretations of the world and in the experience these interpretations respond to and perhaps help propagate. Thus Peter Wors-ley, for whom the notion of the Third World seemed "self evident in the 1960s," when he used it with confident referentiality for the title of his book The Third World (1964), has more recently wrestled with the protean indeterminacy of the concept in his subsequent book The Three Worlds (1984). Worsley has graphically recorded the disillusion of his original hopes for postwar anticolonial nation formation throughout the world. At the same time, he has responded to current thought about globalization, and describes important changes brought about by the industrialization of underdeveloped countries and increased integration of the world's nations into a single global system. Even in the midst of outlining these changes, however, Worsley continues to foreground the glaringly inequitable gulfs between nations that gave the notion of three worlds much of its life in the first place. Noting Nigel Harris's contention that Asia's "four little tigers" (Hong Kong, Taiwan, South Korea, and Singapore) represent the future of the Third World, Worsley acidly remarks that "to sustain that argument, he has to ignore most of the Third World, in particular the uncomfortable fact that 'the average rich-world cat consumes around $500 worth of food a year—more than the GNP per capita of the seven poorest nations on earth: Chad, Bangladesh, Ethiopia, Nepal, Mali, Burma or Zaïre'" (1990:90–91).

The result has been that, while the notion of the Third World has been surpassed by globalism for some, for others the concept has not died, although it has lost its former definitional clarity and now survives in the midst of altered circumstances. After debating whether any rationale remained in the post–Cold War era for their continuing alliance, the nonaligned nations decided to focus on the persistence of inequity between countries in the north and south. Others, like the Kenyan writer Ngũgĩ wa Thiong'o, have charted the persistence of the Third World into the era of globalization in a different way. Deterritorializing the category "Third World," abandoning the nation-state as the unit of analysis, and employing the rhetoric of boundary violation, Ngũgĩ has written that the Third World is "all over the world" (1990:972). If the concept of the Third World can be refitted to survive in an era of enhanced globalization, so has the ideal of national culture. The ways in which national cultures have reconceived themselves in order to persist in an era of intensified globalization is one of the recurring themes of this book.

In cultural as well as economic systems, then, older forms and codes have survived despite, among, and also *in* the newer. In this spirit, Anthony King argues that newer global cities were built on the backs of older colonial cities, that colonial history still strongly affects their current development, and that the "geopolitics of history" overrides even "spatial or commercial logic" (1990a:34). From this perspective, complex and messy accretion, rather than teleology or revolution, has characterized the process, and its ruptured narrative has remained inscribed in different ways inside present forms. Given this fact, any narrative structure of development or even change becomes a simplifying expository convenience.

A particular focus of this book is on the fate of the idea of a bounded national culture, and how this notion has dramatically changed in sync with changes in underlying models of global relationships. In presenting a succession of attempts to represent and theorize national culture—and a further succession of efforts to revise or repudiate that enterprise—I examine a variety of literary and theoretical works. In doing this, I attend both to what they assert and the often-unspoken and even unconscious assumptions behind their assertions. Attention to the former will show how producers and students of culture have gradually become aware of new kinds of global relationships and sought, with increasing sophistication, to conceptualize them. Attention to the latter area will show how the "superstructure" of cultural theory and production, every bit as much as the economic "base," is an area in which we can see globalization processes at work. Cultural theory and production, in short, have been deeply implicated in the changes they have only recently explicitly sought to analyze and represent. They provide us with yet another set of symptoms to be studied, even as they seek to furnish us with interpretations of the causes.

Part I

Constructing Tradition
in the Postwar Period

1

The Three Worlds

IN HIS HISTORY of the Third World, *Global Rift,* L. S. Stavrianos summarizes the dramatic change in the global map that followed World War II: "The extent of the global transformation is reflected in the composition of the United Nations, which consisted of 51 member nations when organized in 1945. By 1981, its membership reached a total of 156 countries. The 105 new members consist largely of the Third World states that have emerged from the ruins of shattered empires" (1981:624). The first postwar decade "witnessed the liberation of Asia" and the second the "liberation of Africa," Stavrianos argues (665). From 1947 on, through negotiated transfer of power or armed, revolutionary struggle, countries like China, India, Ceylon, and French-dominated Vietnam achieved independence from the colonial powers that had directly or indirectly ruled them; when the Gold coast became Ghana in 1957, "the colonial dam [was] broken [and] it was impossible to hold back the flood" (667). In the following decade, thirty-two African countries emerged as independent. Similarly, following World War II, when Britain and France withdrew troops from the Middle East, eight states combined to form the Arab League; with Gamal Abdel Nasser's rise to prominence as a regional leader, the "decade after 1956 was the radical decade in the Middle East [and] the Western-backed monarchs of Iran and the Arabian peninsula were on the defensive against Nasser" (648). Attempts to unite in terms of common interests as a nonaligned third force in world politics culminated in 1955 in the conference of twenty-nine African and Asian countries in Bandung. By 1975, with the fall of Saigon, an editorial in Japan's *Asahi shimbun* could assert that "the age in which any great power can suppress indefinitely the rise of nationalism has come to an end" (727).

The reasons for the breakup of colonial empires and the dramatic emergence of so many new independent nations are beyond the scope of this inquiry. They include a variety of structural and proximate causes: the systemic contradictions of what had been a highly successful, worldwide monopoly capitalist-imperialist era, in which 80 percent of the globe had been subjected to European control and conditions created that led to the global revolutionary activity of the twentieth century (according to Stavrianos [437], those conditions included "the uprooting of hundreds of millions of peasants, urbanization without industrialization, environmental degradation and widening income gap between rich and poor nations within Third World societies"); the emergence of Western-trained elites in the colonies; the worldwide dissemination of nationalism as a vital sociopolitical form; the way in which, in World War I, First World powers, in using troops from the Third World, indebted themselves to Third World reform (Johnson 1991:41); the way in which, in World War II, they weakened themselves and provided a training ground for local resistance leaders, who later became leaders in national liberation movements; the increasing prominence of examples of successful anticolonialism (from the Russo-Japanese War of 1904–5 to the independence of Ghana in 1957); and the inauguration of the Cold War era of competition between the United States and Russia (and soon China) for the hearts, minds, governments, and economies of the emerging nations, a competition that gave the latter a new kind of international importance even as it constrained them.

Stavrianos distinguishes three fundamental types of emergent Third World nations: nationalist regimes (for the most part countries that became neocolonies of the West), social revolutionary regimes (from China to Cuba), and "white settler" regimes (Israel and South Africa). In his reappraisal of the Third World from the standpoint of the mid 1980s, however, Peter Worsley emphasizes that nationalism was the common trait among all emerging nations. The Soviet Union, Worsley points out, redefined proletarian internationalism so that "the unconditional defence of the Soviet Union was now the *first* duty of every foreign communist" (1984:277), and in its dispute with the Soviet Union, communist China came to pursue a peculiarly nationalist foreign policy. "The word 'socialism,'" Worsley goes on to argue, "always had a qualifying adjective attached to it: 'African' or 'Arab' socialism or 'people's' socialism, labels which disguised the reality of supremely nationalist regimes to which the class struggle was as threatening as ethnic rivalries" (302). The force of nationalism was so strong that it overcame even the fact that the national entities created were purely colonial constructs, corresponding to no precolonial polity. Thus

> even countries which, on Independence, were to take their names from ancient empires—Ghana, Mali, Zimbabwe—were composed, in fact, of different peoples in different places. Yet the past could be drawn upon

to create ideological resistance to imperialism, by "a certain sort of regression . . . looking inwards, drawing upon indigenous resources, resurrecting past folk heroes and myths," appealing to conceptions of the community which were far "wider, older and superior to . . . a still rudimentary class consciousness." (286)

The nationalisms that spread throughout the Third World were further heightened in the postindependence era: "the nationalist mystique . . . [became] grounded in an institutional practice, that of mobilization for development: 'part', as [Tom] Nairn put it, of the 'great compensatory drive to catch up'" (292).

Worsley's collation of new capitalist and socialist national states is already a hint of the deep disillusionment with the transformative potential of Third World nationalism, a disillusionment that grew during the 1970s and 1980s. Stavrianos struggles to retain the notion of Third World social alternatives outside the system of Western capitalism, trying to retain faith in qualitatively different worlds, but Worsley, in his disillusionment, sees different worlds collapsing into one. Practically speaking, such disillusionment was the result of a number of factors. "By the late 1960's," Worsley writes, "most of Africa had fallen under one form or another of monocentric regimes, either 'no-party', military regimes, or single-party ones" (301). The elimination, save for Tanzania, of radical populist regimes in Africa was also, in part, testimony to the "muscle" applied by foreigners: thus U.S. clandestine services, which "included 'Health Alteration' programs," were funded for "murdering or helping to murder individuals like [Patrice] Lumumba and [Rafael] Trujillo, and attempting to murder Fidel Castro" (304). Similar pressures were exerted by intervention by the Soviet Union, as in the Sudan; but the power of the capitalist world was enhanced by the development of neocolonialism, which subordinated the economies of emerging nations to the global capitalist system. By the 1980s the process had gone so far that many newly independent nations were being styled basket cases of the world economy, a transformation aided by corrupt local elites. Vigorous faith in the doctrine of nonalignment had a similarly brief half-life: writing in 1984, Worsley remarked, "politically today the great majority of the non-aligned are actually *very* aligned" (324).

With these disillusionments came a destabilization of the apparently clear, unitary model for the Third World that Worsley (at the behest of his publishers) had adopted in the mid 1960s, when his book heralded the Third World as a "vital new force in international affairs." As he later wrote, he had then regarded the concept of the Third World as self-evident: "I saw no need to define it any more precisely than that it was the world made up of the ex-colonial, newly-independent, non-aligned countries" (1984:309). By the 1980s, the problem looked much more complex. Well before the recent transformation of the communist bloc, Worsley was wondering "how to reconcile the conception of a *single* world-system with the conception of *three* distinct worlds" (309). At the same time, paradoxically, he was multiplying models of the Third World, pluralizing the concept. Well before the breakup of the USSR, Worsley was arguing that historical, political, and economic models produced different versions of the three worlds. Japan has become a developed capitalist country, yet historically was an object of European colonial pressure (although never a colony); as such, it was for some a member of the Third World, while others dissented from this judgment. Politically, despite the myth of Third World nonalignment, the Third World was split into different camps; similarly, the Second World was also, in the 1980s, anything but coherent, and the First, although more of a bloc, had its rifts. Economically, it has become increasingly difficult to lump together industrialized Brazil and the NICS on the Pacific Rim, oil-rich countries with a restricted interest in modernization, and impoverished nations with tiny GNP's. Similarly, a model that fused political and economic criteria could put the United States and the USSR in the First World as superpowers, Japan, Australia, Eastern Europe, the EEC, and North Korea in the Second, and underdeveloped capitalist and communist nations in the Third. Perspective, as well as ambiguous terminology, adds to the problem, Worsley argues, since global mapping into three worlds is done differently in different parts of the world (the last-cited version being approximately China's).

If disillusionment with the promise of Third World nationalism led Worsley to a deconstruction of the three worlds theory, still another—and quite dramatic—source of instability for the model originated in a different transformation. As noted above, contrary to expectations, traditional assumptions were altered by industrial development in the Third World, a phenomenon that is striking no matter whether it is described as genuine capitalist development or labeled "dependent development," a continuation of the older tradition of subjugation. "Because labour-costs were very low," Worsley writes,

> especially in countries where authoritarian governments kept trade unions firmly under control or actually abolished them, foreign capital flowed in, expecting a far higher rate of return on its investment than it would get in comparable industries in the First World. The textile industry was one of the first to shift its operations to the Third World. Automobile assembly, then automobile production, followed; then shipbuilding. A whole range of new, light but modern, sophisticated

industries, producing transistor radios, plastics, chemicals, cameras, TV sets, components, now employ millions of people in a growing number of Third World countries. (1984:319)

The result was that a number of the strongly etched boundary lines of the three worlds theory were violated: "Poor/rich and industrial/agricultural then no longer overlap" (327). Along with the flooding of the Third World with consumer goods and enhanced intercultural mobility this has meant a drastic alteration in the cultural landscape of the three worlds. Children of the Third World elite and middle class are sent in increasing numbers to Cornell, Oxford, or state universities in the United States for their education. "For the less affluent, the great dream beamed at them night and day on TV" is "to visit the secular shrines of Western culture in person at least once in their lives" (333), thus making a trip to Disneyland the new equivalent of the Muslim hajj. Worsley's rhetoric about cultural developments remains within the cultural imperialist mode of Herbert Schiller, and does not venture into the evocation of postmodern globality Iyer has developed. Nonetheless, the economic and political developments Worsley charts are, as we shall see, crucially important to a more sophisticated globalist cultural remapping of the world than Worsley's, one that the recent transformation of the East Bloc and the USSR has made still more imperative.

Worsley's 1984 discussion of the destabilization of the three worlds theory thus anticipates material to come. For now, we need to return to his earlier confidence about the theory—his feeling in the 1960s that the definition of the Third World was self-evident. Third World nations were then for Worsley "ex-colonial, newly-independent, non-aligned countries" (309). The application of the term "Third World" to a country cannot, however, stop at the borders of history, politics, or economics. The nation-state model disseminated globally from its origins in the eighteenth-century Americas, which first transformed Europe and was then turned to advantage in Europe's other colonies, has a strong cultural component as well. Whether this is foregrounded or mystified, culture has an important sociopolitical role to play; the creation of national cultures has not only legitimized newly formed states but also helped create them in the first place. As a result, it is important to consider some of the cultural consequences, concomitants, or versions of the three worlds theory in its strong, self-evident form as a way of introducing the subject of how global culture is situated in the three worlds theory.

Divisions of wholes into parts—especially threes—form unstable hierarchies. In the heyday of nationalism particularly, the three worlds theory indeed seemed to describe distinct entities; it also seemed to empower the periphery, uniting third World nations into a single bloc and setting them off as an alternative to the other two. However, there were also many ways in which the theory consolidated a hierarchy invidious to the Third World, something that has, in retrospect, become so obvious that the term "Third World" is now frequently avoided because of negative connotations. Even from the beginning, the emergence of a "Third World" from the system of colonial empire was still hedged in, on every side, with ideological, as it was with literal, constraints. Politically, the First World was capitalist and the Second communist; the Third represented the non-aligned nations, seeking, in theory, an independent path. But the term "Third World" "did not originate in the Third World at all but in post-war France" (Worsley 1984:307); it sprang from the noncommunist West, a stratum desirous of "a third way." In the discursive history of its naming, independence was originally conferred upon the Third World from the outside, representing Western dissidents' hope that a future could be read into the peripheries. More important, the name itself invokes a hierarchy it also resists: the French demographer Alfred Sauvy, in an article in *L'Observateur* on August 14, 1952, coined the term as analogous to "third estate"—those who are "ignoré, exploité, méprisé, comme le tiers état" (307). Most important, though, dependency is indicated by the fact that the term is structurally meaningful only with reference to the interests of the other two tiers: the Third is defined as an alternative to the First and the Second, just as it has, in fact, been the bloc the other two have wrangled over.

Economically, a further (and in many ways more inflexible) form of hierarchy privileged the West. In Marxism and developmentalism alike, contemporary national economies are ranked along a timeline that relegates the "less advanced" nations to an "earlier" era than the "more advanced." Thus, if politically the Third World might mean an "advanced" alternative to the First and the Second, economically the three terms are constructed in reverse order temporally: economically, the First, Second, and Third Worlds are differentiated according to the order in which they industrialized. Both W. W. Rostow's *Stages of Economic Growth* (1960) and Marx's *Das Kapital* leave the Third World back in preindustrial times. Rostow's hegemonic theory of developmentalism is notorious on this point; less well appreciated has been the fact that Marxism, as a First World oppositional movement, maintains something similar. Marx and Lenin (the latter except perhaps just before his death) held that revolution in Europe would precede revolution in the peripheries; and in the preface to the first edition of *Das Kapital,* Marx wrote that "the country that is more developed industrially only shows, to the less developed, the image of its own future" (Mittelman 1988:79).

Culturally, there is a still stronger tendency toward hierarchy in the three worlds theory. This cultural hierarchy, however, has proven as brittle as it has been tenacious. Thanks to a vigorous survival of cultural attitudes from the Eurocolonial past, the First World sees itself and is seen as the source of high modern culture and scientific rationality, of universalism and universal literary and artistic genius. Second World culture, by contrast, is seen as a nightmare of arriviste collectivist modernization. State-controlled, propagandistic, and bureaucratic, it represents the triumph of scientism over art: according to Stalin, artists are the "engineers of souls." Third World culture—a category that homogenizes an extraordinary amount of diversity—is depicted, from this hierarchical First World perspective, more schizophrenically. On the one hand, "it" is represented in terms of a deficiency of something the West has in abundance—is depicted as embodying darkness in contrast to the West's enlightenment, as backward and struggling to modernize compared to the West's exceptional and exemplary modernity. On the other hand, it stands in positive contrast to the differentiated, hyperconscious, uprooted, rationalist West and represents *Gemeinschaft* to the West's *Gesellschaft*. As such, it is styled an economy of authentic cultural plenums compared to the deficient, inauthentic West, which is characterized by anomie and lost cultural origins.

In this latter form, Third World cultures are somewhat empowered. They serve the First World intellectual and artistic avant-garde culturally in a way analogous to that in which emerging Third World nations served the noncommunist left politically. They function as repositories of cultural forms and notions about the social and religious functions of culture that First World artists can use to renew their own hyperconscious traditions. But even when (or especially when) so empowered, the cultural plenums of the Third World are kept behind tight conceptual and geographic boundaries. They are restrained, definitionally, as premodern, particularistic, primordialist cultures—firmly bounded, tacit, consensual, apolitical, and set apart from historical change.

Two key components of this theory have proved susceptible to rapid, 360° change. Third World modernization and recent globalization have startlingly undermined the deeply inscribed boundary between the premodern, developing Third World and the developed West. Second, the boundaries that package Third World societies into separate cultures have proved equally vulnerable to the new postnational phase of global integration. Nonetheless, the notions of temporal placement along a developmental timeline and the spatial distribution of the globe into "separate cultures"—notions conceptually foundational to the cultural version of the three worlds theory—have had a vigorous life in the postwar period. They have deep historical roots and are part of the legacy of colonialism, and when Third World nationalism and national liberation movements appropriated many of their assumptions, they came to represent as much a problem as a solution, as critics within and outside the Third World came to recognize. Appreciating the postwar history of these notions requires a series of examples. In the remainder of this chapter, I examine examples of hegemonic portrayals of culture in the Third World illustrative of the two different, even contrary, images of Third World culture described above. Subsequent chapters focus on counterhegemonic versions, portraying how culture is deployed in the service of Third World nationalism.

V. S. Naipaul has perhaps provided hostile critics with the most notorious example of supposed pandering to denigrating First World attitudes about the Third World. Still, a short autobiographical memoir by his late younger brother Shiva more than adequately illustrates hegemonic representation of the Third World as deficiency. In *Beyond the Dragon's Mouth* (1986), Shiva Naipaul vividly evokes this image of the Third World. A pained, and often painful, disgust permeates his nightmarish picture of life in Trinidad, testifying to the fact that he has replicated or introjected metropolitan attitudes about the relationship between Britain and its former colony. Having powerfully evoked these attitudes, Naipaul then takes refuge in a position of frightening, but also self-aggrandizing, alienation and isolation.

A citizen of Shiva Naipaul's Third World inhabits a shabby, disorderly scene, in which the nightmare of *Heart of Darkness* is never far from quotidian experience. Although irony replaces terror, and existential angst largely, but not wholly, displaces nightmare, Naipaul in Trinidad was trapped in a place that horrified and, he felt, degraded him. It was a place of cultural incoherency and illegitimate hybridism, reflected in the indeterminate racial identity and anarchic sexuality of the people. Naipaul not only experienced no sense of belonging, or even place, in Trinidad; he felt as claustrophobically stifled as if he were a British colonialist trapped in the heart of the Africa constructed by European colonial discourse. And the "blackness" of Conradian Africa is not only present in the essay's depiction of nausea at the cultural incoherence of Trinidad, but also, more literally, in its half-concealed representation of blacks and black culture as defective.

The milieu described is thus impossibly "third." It is a "third-rate" environment, in which selves, families, buildings, and institutions are "haphazardly cobbled together from bits and pieces taken from everywhere and anywhere (1986:23). The First World is thus a kind of Platonic model for an impossibly distant Third, which has no other identity than that of a deficient reflection, a reflection that is marred, crude, and expressive of a pathetic, ignorant simplicity. Furthermore, this social and intellectual environment, as well as the self Naipaul so desperately "cobbled together" from (and also against) it, is a "void," a "bubble of inanity," a "no man's land." Weak copies of a distant original, rich in hybrid nonentity, Naipaul's world and his self are always on the verge of becoming uncobbled. The First World, by contrast, is authentic type and presence. Naipaul could only hope to leave the Third for the First on what was at best an "open" and not just a "developmental" scholarship.

In seeking such escape—or in composing a picture that juxtaposes his "father with his glass-doored book-case lined with classical works of literature and philosophy" to "at the other [extreme] . . . the Negro children, running wild and shirtless in dusty backyards, with navels protuberant" and excessive heat, "rotting" fences, "decomposing matter"—Naipaul clearly yearns for the clear, unitary metropolitan original rather than the heterogeneous, distant Third World copy (30). His yearning and his claustrophobia are so great they amount to existential nausea, tinged with Conradian darkness. But escape proves impossible. At Oxford he encounters, in the suicide of a friend, the very void he sought to flee by going abroad: Naipaul replicates, then, not only the experience of the entrapped colonialist, but also what Benedict Anderson (1983) sees as a crucial component in anticolonial nationalism, what he calls the interrupted pilgrimage of the colonial to the metropolitan center. But, like his version of Third World identity, Naipaul's version of the interrupted pilgrimage does not incorporate the critical perspective of political or economic history. It comes, in Naipaul's portrayal, from deep within his own psyche; it does not result from anything so historically caused as discrimination or underdevelopment. If Third World identity is, for Naipaul, the entrapment in an ahistorical "backward culture," the identity crisis of a Third World immigrant to the First is an existential, not social, problem.

Naipaul's memoir—an example of one way in which Third World culture is portrayed in hegemonic versions of the three worlds theory—thus cannot be taken at face value. In a variety of ways, Naipaul's depiction of the Third World is a mystification, because it masks itself as a transparent depiction of a particular cultural universe. Its existential-psychological, culturalist approach omits colonial and postcolonial history. It presents what seems to be a vision of the defective local culture of the Third World by suppressing a host of factors that are not simply local, but blatantly global.

Indeed, a variety of global relationships make Naipaul's apparently local, insider's portrait of Trinidad what it is. Among them are, of course, the factors already mentioned, the ones the Naipauls' hostile critics have singled out. Naipaul clearly had a First World audience in mind and was, hostile critics have maintained, pandering to it. Or Naipaul had so internalized the First World's view of its own superiority that he introjected these attitudes, to his own unhappiness and discomfort.

If Naipaul's work thus paints the Third World through the First World's eyes—if it covertly constructs his view of a local culture according to global influences—it also does so as part of a larger history, the history of the underdevelopment of the Third World by the First. Seeing the Third World as a defective, spurious copy of the First is as old as colonialism. As an English visitor to Istanbul in 1800 wrote,

> Suppose a stranger to arrive from a long journey, in want of clothes for his body; furniture for his lodgings; books or maps for his instruction and amusement; paper, pens, ink, cutlery, shoes, hats; in short those articles which are found in almost every city of the world; he will find few or none of them in Constantinople; except of a quality so inferior as to render them incapable of answering any purpose for which they were intended. The few commodities exposed for sale are either exports from England, unfit for any other market, or, which is worse, German and Dutch imitations of English manufacture. (Stavrianos 1981:134)

Or as the historian K. Onwuka Dike put it, describing the goods shipped back to West Africa in return for palm oil, ivory, timber, and gold, the Third World received "meretricious articles" and did so despite successfully resisted demands, like those of the Old Calabar chiefs, for capital equipment to manufacture their own (1956:114).

Colonial relationships with the Third World thus simultaneously Westernized and degraded the latter; at the same time as they implanted a model to be emulated, they ensured that this model could be only defectively realized in the Third World. What was true of the infrastructure was even truer of the construction of personal and cultural identity. Homi Bhabha has described the complex mimicry involved in the dilemma for colonial subjects of racial and cultural identity; as "not quite / not white" (1984:132), they were governed by models they were only defectively allowed to incorporate. A wide variety of writers, from the Naipauls to Chinua Achebe and Ngũgĩ wa Thiong'o, have described what it meant to be educated in English culture far from England. As Chinua Achebe observes, "winter" was brought to Nigeria in place of the "harmattan" (1973:3), and, as the Naipauls have recorded, schoolchildren in the Caribbean learned from their textbooks to feel English landscapes and manners as more real than their actual surroundings. In such circumstances, local names, identities, histories, cultures, and even ecologies could appear only as defaced, spurious images of what, reciprocally, appeared as valuable metropolitan originals. Deterritorialization of English culture meant its falsification; under Naipaul's construction of "local" Third World culture, then, the invisible (and highly differential) global hand was at work.

If Naipaul's memoir may thus be demystified by what one can best term a postcolonial analysis—by an unmasking of hidden colonial relationships—it can be recovered in a startlingly new fashion by means of a globalist interpretation. Most of the elements of Naipaul's depiction of Trinidad can, with an extremely slight conceptual nudge, be startlingly metamorphosed from a reactionary introjection of hegemonic ideology into something extremely avant-garde. In many ways, contemporary globalization reveals that colonial cultures, rather than being poor copies of a metropolitan original, anticipate the normative image for future worldwide development. I shall be returning to this theme a number of times in this book, and here I shall simply suggest one way this happens. Naipaul's picture of a cobbled-together Third World can be made representative of experience throughout the world, rather than standing solely for the underdeveloped portion of it, if what is essential is not the ideal of a homogeneous national culture but the globalization of culture—the detachment of cultural material from particular territories, and the circulation of it in often blatantly repackaged, heterogeneous, boundary-violating forms throughout the world. In a globally interconnected world of this sort, sites ranging from Pico Iyer's Bali to Manhattan's cable network are all cobbled together out of globally heterogeneous materials; flagrant cobbling together of a variety of sorts becomes, then, a new kind of postmodern cultural project, not a sign of cultural deficiency. In such transformations, the Third World, in a quite different and also broader way than Ngũgĩ had in mind, is discoverable all over the world, and the metropolis will look increasingly to the periphery for its models, rather than the other way around.

As we have seen, three worlds theory generates another, nearly opposite, image of "culture" in the Third World context: Third World cultures are simultaneously depicted by some as defective versions of metropolitan originals and imaged by other observers as premodern plenums. As "local" cultures supposedly still in touch with their traditional roots, they represent the continuation of the past, not the rupture that produces modernity. As a collection of plenums, they represent the many particular, not the universal one. A full-blown description would style them separate, bounded wholes, and each individual culture would appear as consensual, tacit, and enduring in its essence. Crucial to maintaining this positive ideal would be separating the term "culture" rigorously from the vicissitudes, disputes, and disparate interests of present politics and even past history. Such a notion of culture was intimately involved in European nationalism as exemplified in the work of the influential eighteenth-century poet and philosopher Johann Gottfried von Herder. Herder—whom Eric Hobsbawm styles a prophet of what he calls the "transformation of nationalism" from 1870–1918—significantly altered the notion of national patriotism advanced by American "revolutionary-popular" nationalism (Hobsbawm 1990:87). Revolutionary-popular nationalism was based on choice and provided a heterogeneous group of citizens with inalienable rights; the idea of national belonging became more particularistic and explicitly cultural when Herder asserted that each national group had its own *Volksgeist* or *Nationalgeist,* its own language and therefore customs, mores, beliefs, psyche, and worldview. Herder thus valorized a patchwork world of a variety of separate national cultures, and he condemned the imperial civilizations that stamped them out. In so doing, he stimulated the growth of a widespread set of cultural industries—from folklore to philology—dedicated to giving specific shape and content to each individual *Volksgeist* (Brennan 1989:12–13).

Although itself very recent as a historical phenomenon, this brand of nationalism has asserted—and constructed—the ancientness of national cultures. Still, it has been—and continues to be—believed by many, and it seems to provide people with a primordial basis for identity, a sentiment often highly prized in an alienated world. Perhaps the most lucid postwar version of Herder's notion of coherent culture-units—one that applies it to Third World as well as First World sites and meditates on their relationships to their contemporary global setting—is that advanced by Paul Ricoeur in his essay "Universal Civilization and National Cultures." Ricoeur maintains that "as far back as history allows us to go, one finds historical shapes which are coherent and closed"; he asserts that "humanity is not established in a single cultural style" but has "congealed" in "coherent historical shapes" (1965:280). Ricoeur's essay uses these assertions in the service of liberal ends. They form part of a meditation on the challenges involved in encountering and honoring a variety of separate cultures without homogenizing them. Coupling these assumptions with a cautious, limited espousal of cultural relativism, Ricoeur finds the enemy to be Herbert Schiller's familiar bane: the tendency of modern mass culture to homogenize, trivialize, and impoverish the world's ecology of cultures by blurring their coherent historical shapes and swallowing them up in what he calls a "vague syncretism" (282).

A more worthy counterpoint to many traditional cultures, Ricoeur maintains, is modern scientific "universal civilization," which originates, as one might suspect, in Europe, even as debased mass culture is American. Ricoeur retains both this category and his sympathy for cultural relativism by making an important distinction: "The fact that universal civilization has for a long time originated from the European center has maintained the illusion that European culture was, in fact and by right, a universal culture" (277). The notion of a universal civilization is not, for Ricoeur, as it would be for a hardline Eurocentrist, the possession of the particular culture that gave rise to it, but distinct from that culture; indeed, the growth and transmutation of the notion of universal civilization, as more cultures have come in contact with each other in recent history, has "been just as great a test for our culture [as it has been for others] and one from which we have not drawn all the consequences" (277). In line with this distinction, Ricoeur propounds worst-case and best-case scenarios: the best-case scenario envisages some cultures surviving and creatively extending themselves in an encounter with universal civilization, and others falling by the wayside, absent the "capacity for resistance and above all the same capacity for absorption" (281). The worst-case scenario involves the dissolution of the legacy of the closed, coherent cultural shapes into "some vague and inconsistent syncretism" (283).

For Ricoeur, creative encounters between cultures mediated by "a writer, a thinker, a sage, or a religious man" who could "rise up in order to start a culture anew and to change it again with venture and total risk" (281) are the all-important key to achieving the best, not the worst, case. He clearly conceives of this as an apolitical process ("the artist—to take him as one example of cultural creativity—gives expression to his nation only if he does not intend it and if no one orders him to do it" [281]), even as he depicts it as a gendered process that privileges a cultural elite. Such an elite alone can achieve Ricoeur's best case, in which "syncretisms must be opposed by communication, that is, a dramatic relation in which I affirm myself in my origins and give myself to another's imagination in accordance with his different civilization" (283). It is equally significant that the process does not terminate in a homogeneous global culture, but keeps cultural boundary lines firmly in place. Creative encounters update and reinforce old boundaries, rather than effacing them, thereby maintaining the coherent historical shapes of the cultures able to muster such creativity.

Ricoeur's essay is clearly steeped in European romantic nationalism, promulgating romanticism's cult of genius, separating culture from politics, expressing invidious Orientalist and civilizationalist biases (one might suspect, for example, that tribal—African—cultures would be eradicated as incompatible with modernity, whereas the "high" civilizations of the Far East would remain), and privileging male cultural elites. Also, one might suspect Ricoeur's resentment of "vague syncretism" to be part of an attempt, as W. H. Auden (describing the Sphinx) puts it, to "turn a vast behind on shrill America": in this, one might sense not only Eurocentric depreciation of England's former colony, but also some contemporary irritability at America's replacement of Europe as the core culture of the postwar era. Ricoeur can thus condemn aspects of American culture as unattractive while retaining, as more attractive, features of the European tradition. (As we shall see, covert and even overt use of invidious distinctions between European and American hegemony has been a factor often missed or underrated in considering the postwar global map: the First World, in reality, is not as homogeneous a concept as it has often been taken to be, particularly in discussions of culture. Rather than a clear-cut, unitary First World, we have an amalgam of different strata laid down at different times.) Despite these assumptions—the biases of which are glaring to a contemporary eye—Ricoeur's essay is a serious attempt, in cultural terms, to think through the contradiction Worsley points out between separate worlds and the system conjoining them, and it is one of the most elegant restatements for the contemporary period of Herder's notion of national cultures.

Ricoeur's limited cultural relativism thus treats "culture" as the key term for legitimizing the persistence of non-Western societies, but it keeps this enterprise at a safe distance from contemporary politics. Empathy and creative communication between different peoples (a communication that does not, however, endanger that difference with polluting syncretisms) are what is required: both sides are honored, but boundaries stay— have to stay—in place. Although these assumptions have been roundly attacked over the past few decades, they have remained vigorously alive in many quarters and are still, I would argue, the baseline for lay assumptions about culture in many places. For example, a more contemporary, although slightly different, version comes from literature on multicultural pedagogy. Ralph Nicholas argues that bringing anthropology students

> to that moment of understanding another cultural system which enables them—even briefly—to assume the subjective position of a person in another society with another view of the universe and another way of valuing things is a high pedagogical achievement. I sometimes tell students they are like missionaries on a bridge looking down at the poor benighted Hindus bathing in the filthy, contaminated Ganges. The students' task, I say, is to learn to look up with pity at the poor missionaries and imagine them bathing in a tiny tub of wretchedly warm water made

filthy and polluted by their own bodies. Seeing how each might marvel at the misguided idea of purification held by the other is a first step in understanding real cultural difference. (Nicholas 1991:18)

Such a pedagogical technique would appear to be more subversive than Ricoeur's undermining of simplistic Eurocentrism. It postulates no "universal civilization"; indeed, it disrupts Eurocentric assumptions and the privileged viewpoint of the West by asking students to imagine themselves as an "other culture," a particular bounded universe, simultaneously with seeing Hindus that way. It resembles Ricoeur's thesis, however, in that empathetic communication coexists with, even requires, strict enforcement of cultural boundaries: both the Hindus and the American students have complete, closed cultural universes; they each have their own "view of the universe" and "way of valuing things."

[margin note: point: how hard are boundaries?]

But if one interrogates Nicholas' assumptions on a commonplace, practical level, his formulation seems in some ways more illiberal than Ricoeur's, which foregrounds, rather than suppressing, consideration of what yokes separate cultures and civilizations together into a single system. What Nicholas suppresses will come back to haunt him as covert illiberalism. Aside from the question of who is representing whom, there is a sharp, implicit asymmetry between America and India in Nicholas's account: the Americans are students (albeit provincial ones) in a modern university, whereas the East Indians are religious Hindus bathing in the Ganges. The Americans signify the present, the Indian figures the timeless and immemorial past; Nicholas's apparently equal treatment conceals a familiar hierarchical strategy for "othering" the Third World, one explored by Johannes Fabian in *Time and the Other: How Anthropology Makes Its Object* (1983). Fabian criticizes anthropology's construction of its objects as ideologically motivated distancing of them in time and space, a process that subordinates the Third World object of study to the First World investigator. Or, as Arlif Dirlik puts it, "the kind of sympathy that identifies with the Other and yet denies him 'coevalness' (in Fabian's words) is essential . . . to the Orientalizing of the Other" (1991:406).

Keeping the boundary lines in place—keeping the "other" other—is thus an essential part of Nicholas's and Ricoeur's Herderian notions of national culture in the Third World. If one looks closely at the historical background with all of its unregulated messiness, however, these theories seem increasingly like impositions upon, rather than understandings of, that world. Thus, to review Nicholas's confident depiction of India from another angle, we could turn to Anthony King's depiction of the transformation of Delhi by its recent integration into the global economy. We need only

[handwritten note: a dynamic v. bounded view of culture.]

note one small reservation: the fact that Delhi has become an international- al financial and commercial center, and places along the Ganges—like Benares—while connected with these networks, have remained at best regional centers. In Delhi, the old colonial structure of segmented cultures—Old and New Delhi, separated by the "spacious, two-story retail- ing centre of Connaught Circus"—was disrupted, as this "old colonial retailing center" was "ringed by massive high-rise office blocks, a phenom- enon that began by the end of the 1960s" (1990b:47–48). "Redevelopment in Delhi has included huge luxury hotels and supermarket developments. Whilst the old 'Empire Stores' remains, versions of McDonald's have also made an appearance." The colonialists' old bungalow areas have either been designated conservation areas—showing "the degree to which val- ues are shared between the ex-metropolitan (British) and ex-colonial (In- dian) elites"—or have given way to "smaller, more compact modern houses and flats" (49). A short distance from Delhi's International Airport,

> Palam Vihar is developing, according to its promoters, as "the elite neighborhood of Delhi" and "one of the most prestigious localities." Designed for 50,000 residents it has "every conceivable modern facility like schools, clubs, and an exclusive shopping centre." Here are offered "a remarkable range of houses" including "The Continental Villa," "The French Villa," and various styles of "cottages." The Continental Villa has "a European touch of class to it" . . . ; the French Villa . . . "a French flavour in every detail." (50)

Indeed, contemporary with the publication of Nicholas's article, King was noting that "what were once thought of as deep-seated cultural taboos (such as bathing in one's own dirty bathwater in Western-style baths . . .) are being abandoned."

> Three-piece bathroom suites are now manufactured not only with tub baths . . . , but also marketed (by Hindustan Sanitaryware and others) in a range of thirty different colours to provide "a touch of Italian romance in your bathroom." (50)

Boundary lines have not, in fact, remained inviolate, either in the pre- sent or in previous centuries. Americanized simulacra of Europe have en- tered India as merely the latest wave of India's internationalization; India has not remained immune from History. It is interesting that in chronic- ling an interruption in the "long and complex colonial history (not to mention its long and complex precolonial history)" of the "struggle over history in India" (26), Nicholas Dirks (1990) ascribes it to anthropology:

> By the late nineteenth century, Indian history had been effectively eclipsed by Indian anthropology. To understand and to rule India, the

British no longer felt the need to ask historical questions; instead, they thought about India anthropologically. Indians were known by their caste, their character, their custom. And due to a whole complex of conjunctures, Indians lost their history and their historicity simultaneously; their failure to have history was all their own fault. (27)

In the twentieth century, the production of history in India recommenced as a part of anticolonial nation formation, and, with belated recognition of these changes, anthropological discourse, as we shall later examine, has moved beyond Nicholas's cultural relativism to self-reflexive concern with its implication in the history of colonial relationships. And India, which had already had a long history of rapid syncretic absorption of British culture from the colonial world system, and also a very rapid absorption of American culture from the postcolonial world, has established itself in the postmodern cultural economy. After all, India, as Pico Iyer makes clear, not Hollywood, is for a majority in the world the source of silver screen epics.

Lest King's observations seem a validation of Herbert Schiller's fears— lest they portray a globe restructured by an American commercial culture more odious than *Reader's Digest*—I should add that I cite King to show what Nicholas *excludes* from his frame and not to suggest that the new features have erased the old. As King indicates, "versions of McDonald's" have not replaced/effaced "Indian" urban culture, but have been added to and partially reconfigured the hybrid complexities of New and Old Delhi. Indeed, in many ways, recent globalization has intensified the process of differential cultural invention that the era of nationalism commenced, and the "vague syncretism" of the American era that fostered that globalization has proven a lot more vital and interesting than Ricoeur dreamed.

Nicholas's and Ricoeur's uses of the assumptions of the nation-state model for mapping culture globally are thus far from innocent transparencies. They are methods for organizing time and space, cultural maps that construct a particular kind of reality every time they draw a boundary line. Both are devoted, to put it most succinctly, to keeping the "other" other. The two attempts differ in that the global relationships Nicholas suppresses in his attempt to preserve endangered cultural integrity, Ricoeur exposes; Ricoeur creates a more complex scheme, in which the global (universal civilization) and the local (traditional cultures) may interact in a kind of agon, in which victory would mean that both would be reinvigorated, rather than effaced. Ricoeur's conception of culture thus aims to reconcile the conflicting discourses of cultural relativism and cultural imperialism, of traditionalism and modernization. He seeks thereby to ensure both interconnection and integrity globally. Locally, he tries to resolve the Western-originated dispute built into Third World societies in the process of their restructuring according to European nationalism; he seeks to solve the conflict between modern *Gesellschaft* and traditional *Gemeinschaft* (see Robertson 1992a:146–56).

But even apart from the dubious spectacle of a European metropolitan figure imposing European-originated discourses on Third World cultures in the name of preserving them, and seeking, in the process, to keep the "other" other, Ricoeur's theory provides little hope and scant possibility of action. Creative geniuses have always been hard to come by; and the globalizing ministrations of thousands of lesser sorts—from international businessmen to global media employees—have been rather difficult for even the most towering individual (particularly when such an individual is a creative thinker, without political or military capabilities) to resist.

The most damaging objection to Ricoeur and Nicholas is not, however, that their ethical projects are dubious, or that their practical directives are weak. The harshest objection is that their fundamental assumptions— their certainty of the existence of closed historical shapes of separate cultures and civilizations prior to the modern era, in which global forces at last arose to threaten them—are simply wrong.

In later chapters of this book I survey a wide variety of different, often highly politicized, interdisciplinary cultural movements that seek to break down the Herderian cornerstone of Ricoeur's and Nicholas's theories, the notion of cultures as tightly bounded, "closed historical shapes." From this perspective I examine a series of theories of culture that seek, in different ways and from different motives, to redescribe local cultures as, in fact, global constructions, and show that local cultures do not simply exist prior to and apart from global forces, but owe their contemporary existence to them. These cultural theories are spread across a number of disciplines, and many of them are relatively new hybrids of several disciplines; they include decolonization theory, imperial-discourse theory, deconstructionist and poststructuralist literary, cultural, and ethnic theory, the sociology of nationalism, world-systems theory, and globalization theory. Many revisionary theories reach back behind modernization to the origins of European nation building and colonialism; others reach still further back. Some retain a centered global structure, even while criticizing it; others attempt to envision a decentered global ecumene. To anticipate such discussion, it will be helpful, before returning to an analysis of the construction of national culture under the terms of the three worlds theory, to contrast Ricoeur's analysis with the harshly opposite findings of the most influential text of imperial-discourse theory, Edward Said's *Orientalism* (1978).

In *Orientalism,* Said argues that the overall enterprise of constructing the world in terms of bounded cultures is dubious. "The notion that there are geographical spaces with indigenous, radically 'different' inhabitants who can be defined on the basis of some religion, culture or racial essence proper to that geographical space is equally a highly debatable idea," he writes (1978:322). In concluding his highly influential book, he asks what James Clifford (1988:273) calls the most important theoretical question of his study: "How does one *represent* other cultures? Is the notion of a distinct culture (or race, or religion, or civilization) a useful one" (1978:325)? Said's reason for such a sweeping question—and the urgency with which he asks it—comes from his voluminous argument that the notion of "the Orient" is not referential, does not point to something that is objectively "there," but is a European construction imposed on Asia in the process of colonial domination. Indeed, the imposition of a Western-generated notion of bounded cultures on Europe's colonial possessions was one of the most fundamental tools of domination: Orientalists, Said argues, constructed for themselves "a simulacrum of the Orient" and then filtered "it through regulatory codes, classifications, specimen cases, periodical reviews, dictionaries, grammars, commentaries, editions, [and] translations." The result was the construction of *a* culture—a cultural essence seen as somehow persisting apart from history, particularly apart from the history of colonial domination and resistance—that homogenized subjugated peoples by identifying them as "Oriental." By subordinate opposition to an equally homogenized, essentialized "West," the "Orient," then, was defined as a place of "eccentricity, backwardness, silent indifference, and feminine penetrability" (166). Although the specific characteristics of "oriental culture" could and did indeed change with bewildering rapidity (the "Orient" metamorphosed, in a few brief decades, from a place of sexual mystery to a confine of fundamentalist puritanism), the conceptual structure of Orientalism and its role as both explanation of and tool for effecting domination stayed firmly in place.

Clearly, these assigned identities are invidious. They have even resurfaced uncomfortably in both metropolitan anticolonial critiques (as we have seen in the case of Schiller's rhetoric of feminine penetrability) and Third World cultural opposition (as, for example, Wole Soyinka's critique of *négritude* [1975] indicates). More fundamentally, given the fact that the idea of bounded culture was developed in the context of European nationalism, its unquestioned application to other places and times must be revealed as a dubious venture per se. Terence Ranger (1983) gives an interesting example. The African "tribe," he argues, is not African at all, but was invented in Europe: infused with the ideology of the nation-state, Europeans imposed subsidiary versions of this concept on African social relationships, ones that were more complicated, situational, unbounded, and interconnective than this model allowed. They did so, at least in part, because this was the only way that the Europeans could classify and understand the peoples they conquered. Said's particular moral investment in exposing these processes leads him to a harsher judgment than Ranger's. Fundamental to the whole field of imperial-discourse theory is the perception that imposing such a concept of culture is certainly not the use of a neutral scientific tool to reveal Third World cultures as they really are, nor even a haplessly unconscious application of European ethnocentric categories, but an integral part of the mechanism of colonial domination. Knowledge not only follows from power; it is power.

One of the crucial insights basic to imperial-discourse theory, then, is that the term "culture" cannot be separated, as Ricoeur demands it be, from the geopolitics of colonialism. "Culture" is not a term above politics, one that describes mysterious spiritual and psychological boundaries between different peoples, boundaries that remain in place despite politics and history. Indeed, as Said and many others have shown, the very attempt to politically neuter the term has made it more politically efficacious. Even apart from the crasser justifications of European colonialism as a mission to bring higher culture and civilization to the savage world, there were many concrete, practical ways in which separating culture from politics enhanced colonial management. Potential anticolonial opposition from a Westernized native elite (the group providing the leaders of the ultimately successful nationalist movements) was defused by coopting or creating a "native" or "traditional" leader and denigrating the emergent nationalists as "an insignificant minority, with insolent pretensions to speak in the name of 'Nigeria' or 'India'" (Worsley 1984:39). Worsley has further argued that the "liberal" tradition of colonial management, which advocated respect for traditional cultures, provided a basis for such ploys. Thus, in 1920, Sir Hugh Clifford, governor of Nigeria, spoke satirically of "a self-selected and self-appointed congregation of educated African gentlemen who collectively style themselves the West Africa National Conference" and speculated equally satirically on what would happen if "they could be deposited, unsustained by [British] protection among the cannibals of the Mama Hills . . . and there left to explain their claims to be recognized as the accredited representatives of these, their fellow nationals" (Worsley 1964:39). Similarly, Guari Visnawathan (1989) has pointed out how Orientalist sympathy for Indian traditions advanced the colonial project even as Macaulayesque hostility to them did.

Apolitical notions of culture that were in fact anything but apolitical served the colonial project in other concrete ways as well. Perception of, or, indeed, construction of cultural differences among "natives" to be administered enabled colonial powers to use the time-honored device of "divide and rule," a strategy that was enormously effective all over the colonized world. Supplementing original exploitation of cultural divisions at the time of conquest was the enhancement of them in the time of colonial management: if colonized people were fragmented into separate cultures, then the British, for example, could set themselves up, politically, morally, iconographically, and philosophically in India, as in Africa, as the unifying cement without which native societies would fly apart, the universal that held together the many particulars. In this colonial ploy, both the notion of separate bounded cultures and the concept of "universal civilization" both showed themselves to have highly compromised, politicized roots, and the fact that the term "culture" was kept separate from politics allowed the mystification of such outright political domination. In all these ways, culture became, in short, an important strategic component in the construction of global relationships.

To be sure, Said's *Orientalism* has been as controversial as it has been influential. Published in 1978, it was, as Masao Miyoshi remarks, a major restatement of the postwar tradition of anticolonialism. What is most surprising about the book's impact is that it should have taken so many by surprise:

> It is remarkable indeed that Edward Said's *Orientalism* . . . should have had such a great impact on a wide range of disciplines from anthropology, history, and sociology, to literary criticism. Unprepared for the thrust of his argument, which had been unmistakably implied—or even articulated—in anti-colonial liberation ideologies since 1945 and in the civil rights movement at least since the 1960s, the social sciences and the humanities reacted as if caught by surprise, as can be seen in rapid developments in critical anthropology and cultural criticism that ensued. (Miyoshi 1991:191–92)

At the same time, *Orientalism*'s effectiveness as a restatement of postwar anticolonialism obscured a less visible and more contemporary context for the book: a movement toward an awareness of globalization, a movement indicated by *Orientalism*'s demystification of the notion of the local production of culture and its revelation of how individual cultures, along with the idea of "culture," have been produced as part of the construction of geopolitical relationships. Indeed, the history of the book's impact and subsequent influence illustrates the interplay of these two frames of reference, re-enlivened anticolonialism and emergent globalization.

Orientalism was most famously received as an angry anticolonialist tract, one that galled traditional academia, especially by its assertion that a whole variety of scholarly enterprises had been compromised for centuries and were tools of the Euro-imperial project, not objective research. As a summa of anticolonial ire, it was also, however, criticized on the left, as a book that closed off, rather than opened, possibilities of resistance, even as it exposed wrongdoing. The inseparability of political and intellectual developments having been put so squarely on the table that it could not subsequently be ignored, *Orientalism* was then itself found too restrictive in a number of ways.

First, the book seems to depict the global construction of culture in a totalizing manner as a one-way process: the West against the rest. As Homi Bhabha writes, "There is always, in Said, the suggestion that colonial power is possessed entirely by the colonizer[,] which is a historical and theoretical simplification" (1983:200). Colonial power was thus represented, ahistorically, as a completely internally coherent formation, without conflicts, ambiguities, and anxieties. European Orientalism, as critics like Samir Amin (1983), James Clifford (1988), and Robert Young (1990) have also suggested, was not a monolithic structure persisting through all eras, but differed from era to era; furthermore, it was marked by internal conflict, ambivalence, and fear, not self-possessed mastery. To style it as Said does, it has been pointed out, is to give an essentialist portrayal of European Orientalism even as essentialism is being depicted as a bankrupt notion, a villainous European strategy for domination of the Third World. Second, if the West is a monolithic force of such power, there seems to be no way for the Third World effectively to resist it; *Orientalism*'s angry anti-Eurocentrist analysis perversely reinforces, rather than undoes, the power it seeks to attack. Finally, *Orientalism*'s corrosive analysis of how perceptions of other cultures were constructed and infected by power relationships as a part of the process of domination implies, as Said underscores, that the idea of "culture" perhaps has to be abandoned. To Samir Amin, this position disallows all representation of the "other," thereby suppressing dialogue; in contrast, Amin proposes, not a suspension of representation of the "other," but a more widespread, and reciprocal prosecution of it. "Complementary to the right of Europeans to analyze others," he argues, "is the equal right of others to analyze the West" (1983:102). One way of understanding the impact and subsequent criticism of *Orientalism*, then, is to say that Said's book re-enlivened the moral fervor of postwar anticolonialism, while at the same time so embodying the disillusionment with anticolonial nationalism felt strongly by the 1970s that moral condemnation was paired frustratingly with an erasure of viable paths and positions outside the colonialist system. Its globally inclusive drama of illegitimate domination portrays, it seems to its critics, a monosystematic globe.

Subsequently Said (1985, 1993) has responded to some of these criticisms and reinterpreted his own project to make it more clearly an opening rather than a closure, the beginning of a line of postcolonial scholarship, rather than a summa of anticolonial ire. In his recent book *Culture and Imperialism* (1993), in particular, Said comments that "what I left out of *Orientalism* was that response [Third World resistance] to Western domination which culminated in the great movement of decolonization all across the Third World. . . . There was *always* some form of active resistance" (xii). In theorizing this resistance, Said exposes and criticizes essentializing Third World nationalism and fundamentalisms as sharply as he has their Orientalist precursors. In their place, he supports a second-generation opposition, a postcolonial opposition that is not separatist, but seeks to alter the cultural legacy of imperialism from within. In moving beyond the exposure of monologic Eurocentrism and emphasizing what he calls a "contrapuntal perspective" (32), Said seeks to "formulate an alternative both to a politics of blame and to the even more destructive politics of confrontation and hostility" and by doing so reveal "the ways in which a reconsidered or revised notion of how a post-imperial intellectual attitude might expand the overlapping community between metropolitan and formerly colonized societies" (18). Said thus makes it clear that changing world relationships in the postcolonial phase of globalization have a positive side and advances a project for the future: if the imperial past was a monologic yoking of the globe into an oppressively interconnected whole, the present phase of globalization suggests that a new, post-imperial, plurally interactive global culture and system might be born.

In developing his position, Said has moved further across a crucial fault line in postwar thought about geoculture than he did in *Orientalism*. From colonial construction of the other to the mutual determination of all parties thanks to global interactivity was both a small logical step, yet it is also a major conceptual rupture. Said holds to the moral legacy of anticolonialism, even as he steps toward a more uncharted and confusing investigation of global interactivity. As we shall see, others have gone further toward such globalism than Said; other theorists have presented still more radically transformative views of the new global system. Reinterpretation of colonialism as a phase in a much longer history of global relationships —as a step from earlier interregional interactions toward the decentered, yet encompassing, global system of today—has both altered the past and transformatively opened up a future very different from what was imagined mere decades ago.

2

Nostalgic Nationalism in Japan

IN DISCUSSING THE Americanization of the Americas, William Roseberry provides a framework very different from Ricoeur's for thinking of
cultural transactions between the First and Third worlds. Following Eric
Wolf (*Europe and the People Without History* [1982]), who in turn was influenced by Immanuel Wallerstein (*The Modern World System* [1974]), Roseberry argues that "any moment of encounter between a particular agent of
a global economy and a local population, between the 'external' and the
'internal,' will necessarily intertwine with prior and ongoing encounters,
each of which will have its own structure, its own 'concentration of many
determinations, hence unity of the diverse' . . . , its own internalization of
the external" (1989:89). It would be comfortingly simple if this formulation merely described how a "foreign" cultural form was assimilated to
"native" traditions. The problem, however, is that the "native" tradition
in contemporary Latin America was formed as a result of previous interactions with imported forms. Roseberry therefore stresses the odd fact that
laments about the loss of a national culture in Latin America because of
encroachment from the West are really laments about how a culture
formed from previous interactions with the West is being encroached
upon by a later wave of Westernization. Clearly, as one proceeds along
these lines, the search for the uninfected—primordial, bounded, perhaps
essentialized—kernel of "native" culture becomes more and more like
unwrapping an onion: one finds relationships (global, regional) beneath
relationships, not a hard, definite, genuinely local core.

Roseberry's subject, Latin America, provides a particularly rich example, embodying as it does an "ongoing, centuries-long process of the internalization of the external" (91). From it, Roseberry isolates four phases: the
eras of colonial encounters, nineteenth-century nation building, nine-
teenth- and early twentieth-century expansionism, and Americanization
since the 1930s. Even this fourfold layering of global interactions, Roseberry suggests, is a simplified picture of a much more complex sequence. The

number of historical phases could be increased; dealings within any specific period were not large-scale, coherent transactions between national units, but a multitude of larger and smaller, often conflictual exchanges between a medley of different institutions and groups on both sides (from government agencies, for example, to communist and noncommunist labor and evangelical movements of different persuasions). Such complexity is abundant on any national level, and it becomes staggeringly so when the object of analysis is a decidedly nonhomogeneous region like Latin America. Were it possible, unraveling the heterogeneity of international interaction involved in constituting present-day local cultural entities would in any case reveal regional preconquest interactions, not bounded primordial cultures.

In Roseberry's analysis, the global forces Ricoeur confines to two recent historical eras, the spread of universal civilization and Americanization, are greatly expanded. Global interrelationships do not intervene as recent antagonists of older, closed historical shapes, but are foundational to them: they are essential to the production of what appear to be bounded local cultures. Roseberry's formulation is also more daringly globalist than Said's in *Orientalism*. Roseberry attempts to conceptualize global relationships as diachronically layered and synchronically heterogeneous, rather than monolithic; and he analyzes these relationships as transactions between specific social formations and their larger context, rather than coherent, unidirectional domination of one region by another. Keeping Roseberry's version of the construction of culture in mind may be helpful as we now turn to a discussion of Third World attempts to use national culture as a strategic term in a struggle with the West.

Just as Roseberry's vision of global interactions differs drastically from Ricoeur's, recent scholarship on nationalism runs directly against Ricoeur's assumptions about the nature of national tradition and culture. In the history and sociology of nationalism, as well as in world-systems theory, antiprimordialism has become a crucial rallying point. Periodizing the emergence of modern nationalism in four phases (revolutionary-popular nationalism in the United States and France; the transformation of nationalism, 1870–1918; the apogee of nationalism, 1919–50; and late-twentieth-century nationalism), Eric Hobsbawm has shown how, between 1870 and 1918, states and regimes sought to fuse "stated patriotism with the sentiments and symbols of 'imagined community,' wherever and however they originated, and to concentrate them upon themselves" (1990:91). As noted above, this project—on which Herder was an important influence—differed sharply from the revolutionary-popular nationalism of the preceding era. National belonging was no longer based on universalist choice and citizenship but on the myth of belonging to a particular culture. The goal became to "'make Italians' [where they previously had not existed], to turn 'peasants into Frenchmen' and attach all to the flag" (91). Supposedly primordial culture was then invented and elaborated in a variety of ways—for example, through philology (consolidation of national languages), literature (the discovery or forging of national epics), and history (the construction of narratives of the "nation" [Anderson 1983:66–103]). The process was notoriously reinforced by the strong boundary setting of the new pseudoscience of racialism, which, casting aside the older assumption that mankind was divided into a few races according to skin color, now distinguished many, using "race" and "nation" as "virtual synonyms" and "generalizing equally wildly about 'racial'/'national' character" (Hobsbawm 1990:108). Along with this ideological engineering, states increased their involvement in people's lives in a variety of concrete, daily ways to accomplish the same end:

> A family would have to live in some very inaccessible place if some member or other were not to come into regular contact with the national state and its agents: through the postman, the policeman or gendarme, and eventually through the schoolteacher; through the men employed on the railways, where these were publicly owned; not to mention the garrisons of soldiers and the even more widely audible military bands. Increasingly the state kept records of each of its subjects and citizens through the device of regular periodic censuses . . . , through theoretically compulsory attendance at primary school and, where applicable, military conscription. In bureaucratic and well-policed states a system of personal documentation and registration brought the inhabitant into even more direct contact with the machinery of rule and administration, especially if he or she moved from one place to another. . . . inhabitants might encounter the representatives of the state on emotionally charged occasions; and always they would be recorded by machinery for registering births, marriages and deaths, which supplemented the machinery of censuses. Government and subject and citizen were inevitably linked by daily bonds, as never before. (Hobsbawm 1990:80–81)

This emphasis on nations as institutional and ideological constructions typifies the demystification of primordialist nationalism and primordialism that has been important to studies of nationalism in the past few decades. Hobsbawm and Terence Ranger's *The Invention of Tradition* (1983), Benedict Anderson's *Imagined Communities* (1983), and Homi Bhabha's *Nation and Narration* (1990) are but three prominent examples from historiography, sociology, and cultural studies. Indeed, in this wholesale attack on nationalist myth making, what term to use for the process of creating nations has become a matter of some debate. "Nationalism," Ernest Gellner has provocatively written, "is not the awakening of nations to self-consciousness; it *invents* nations where they do not exist" (Anderson 1983:15). Benedict Anderson objects to Gellner's phrasing, not because it highlights the artificiality of nations, but because it backhandedly suggests there might be some other "natural" alternative possible. Arguing that Gellner assimilates "'invention' to 'fabrication' and 'falsity,' rather than to 'imagining' and 'creation,'" Anderson asserts that Gellner misleadingly implies that "'true' communities exist which can be advantageously juxtaposed to nations" (15). In other ways, however, "fabrication" is just the word to use. The term has to be startling to foreground the artificiality, or, better, "artifactuality," of national communities and cultures. Moreover, in a postmodern context, "fabricated" no longer implies a deviation from "true." It quickly becomes a normative term, not a term for violation of a norm.

Together, Roseberry's world-systems analysis and Hobsbawm's history of nationalism paint a picture of the world drastically different from that offered by Ricoeur. National cultures have not only been invented, but invented very recently; furthermore, they have been invented, not locally, but as part of a historical series of global interactions (world-systems theory) or a progressive dissemination of the national form throughout the world (history/sociology of nationalism).

Roseberry's and Hobsbawm's analyses powerfully undercut beliefs about national cultures that had been strongly reinforced and widely held for over a century. Indeed, nostalgic, primordialist nationalism had an extremely vigorous life in the postwar era, and it was not confined to creation of the hegemonic ideologies investigated in the previous chapter. Counterhegemonic, anti-Western forms of nostalgic nationalism were also constructed. In many ways, Japan can provide us with the most interesting and complex example of how nostalgic nationalism was successfully appropriated from and turned back onto the West. Given the existence of a vigorous tradition of nostalgic nationalism in Japan—one that commenced even prior to Japan's reengineering of itself in the Meiji Restoration—an examination of the construction of national culture in Japan will show how Ricoeur's assumptions were manipulated successfully toward counterhegemonic ends. And given the fact that Japan has negotiated a passage from the periphery to the core of the world system, popular versions (or caricatures) of the role its cultural tradition has played in this process have had unusually widespread global exposure.

Japan was both representative of and tantalizingly exceptional in the non-Western world. For a long time, Japan has been ambiguously positioned on the global map: there have been a number of contradictory "Japans". On the one hand, Japan has been seen as the best example of the advantages of staying out of the colonial system. Its retention of its territorial integrity and its successful avoidance of colonization have been crucial to its exceptional status among Europe's other "others." On the other hand, Japan was, of course, forcibly (and traumatically) opened to the outside world by Commodore Perry of the U.S. Navy. It has also been seen as a model for anticolonialism, inspiring Third World anticolonial resistance, a status that it has held, off and on, since its defeat of Russia in 1905. From before the beginning of the century to World War II, however, it has appeared as an imperial power following a First World model, oppressing the Asia it pretended to liberate from the colonial powers. Also, following its reconstruction after World War II, it has emerged as a core country in the current global economy. Japan has thus at different times identified with its Asian context, differentiated itself to identify with various versions of the West, and acted as an imperial power seeking to dominate Asia. Karatani Kōjin has described this contradictory complexity by arguing that modern Japan unfolds in a discursive space that contains four quadrants, which he labels imperialism, Asianism, bourgeois modernization (de-Asianism), and Marxism (1991:199–201). More simply, Ōe Kenzaburō states the problem as a duality, arguing that he can "think of no people or nation as much in need of a clue for self-recovery as the Japanese, neither among first nor third world nations; no other people but the Japanese, whose culture evinces a strange blending of first and third world cultures; no other people but the Japanese who live that reality" (1989:212).

Ōe sees Japan as exceptional thanks to its confusion about its identity. More often, Japanese exceptionalism has been depicted as a part of its overdetermined, dangerous nationalism. Still others have argued that the two images are opposite faces of the same coin, so that persistently exceptionalist Japanese nationalism needs to be interpreted as a reaction formation, an attempt to counteract fundamental insecurity. Either way, the notion of an exceptionalist Japanese cultural tradition was defensively elaborated in opposition to Japanese perceptions of the West's power and as a part of an extremely unbalanced encounter with it. Despite the strongly primordialist, essentialist, and exceptionalist manner in which that cultural tradition has been elaborated—a process that has made nostalgic nationalism, perhaps, a more important component of Japanese ideology construction than in many other sites—its advocates have been often explicit about their importation of Western forms as a means of counteracting Western power. Indeed, a fascinating pattern of the conscious construction of essentialist nationalism as a means of absorbing and negotiating dominant foreign influences has characterized Japan's response not only to two waves of Westernization, Eurocolonialism and Americanization, but, before that, to the centrality of China's Middle Kingdom. Strategies that helped renegotiate Japan's status as barbarian periphery to China interconnected with strategies to deal with, not just *an* encounter with Westernization, but successive encounters with Westernization. Japanese observers from early on clearly differentiated between several forms of Western encroachment and employed fine-grained perceptions of differences within "the West" in forming their ideologies of Japanese culture.

Recently, Western audiences have been most notoriously exposed to the paradoxes of modern Japanese cultural nostalgia by the work and career of Mishima Yukio. His death, like his tetralogy *The Sea of Fertility* and his well-known short story "Patriotism" (1966), was apparently a vivid example of the force of nostalgia in Japanese culture. "Patriotism" dramatizes an event during a 1936 uprising that was hauntingly paralleled by Mishima's own coup attempt in 1970 (assertedly to restore the emperor's prestige), which resulted in the author's bloody seppuku. "Patriotism" is apparently not only a recreation of history, but a nostalgic version of the code of values of the samurai, which enforced unhesitating devotion to the emperor and, to quote Sarah Lawall, united "the 'way of the warrior' (*bushido*) and aesthetic elegance (*yuga*)" (1985:2063).

Mishima called this story of samurai virtue and suicide by Lieutenant Shinji Takeyama and his recent wife a "story of happiness." The label seems, at first sight, as much a sign of its cultural difference as its loving, erotic, and grotesque detailing of the couple's suicide. Perhaps less widely known, as Lawall points out, is the fact that in 1965 Mishima produced a film version of the story, in which the "Liebestod" from Wagner's *Tristran und Isolde* is the only sound track. This explicit influence on "Patriotism"'s love-death story is, however, only one of a number of German and European influences on Mishima, from Nietzsche to Thomas Mann. Indeed, as Lawall notes, "Mishima's chief supporters [in his early period] were academics who followed the 'Nippon-Roman-ha,' or Japanese Romantic School, a movement created in direct and conscious emulation of the 'German Romantic School' sponsored by the Nazis, and whose emphasis on national tradition, Emperor worship, beauty and pure emotions, and the exaltation of death and destruction already coincided with the young writer's tastes" (1985:2064).

That Mishima's Japanese tradition was in large part internationally manufactured has made him seem a special example to many Japanese readers. Ōe Kenzaburō recounts how Mishima once "said that [the European] image of the Japanese is me" and added that this image was "superficial," a "fantasy"; Masao Miyoshi, quoting this comment, adds, "I am curious to know if European and American readers are going to listen at least this once to Japanese views of these foreign views of Japan. It does seem about time" (1991:151). Despite these disclaimers, however, Mishima was far from alone in his attempt to construct, out of international interactions, what Miyoshi has called an "essentialist and exceptionalist posture of mystification" as the heart of Japanese tradition.

Indeed, such attempts date back to well before the Meiji Restoration. In *Anti-Foreignism and Western Learning in Early Modern Japan,* Bob Tadashi Wakabayashi describes this process, beginning with the attempts of Japanese Confucians gradually to revise their position vis-à-vis the Chinese Middle Kingdom—a position that identified Japan as a "barbarian" country on the periphery of the "central" Chinese empire. Tokugawa thinkers sought to drive a wedge into Chinese centrality by claiming "quasi Middle Kingdom status for themselves and their nation. They could acknowledge Japan to be ethnically barbarian, but still declare it superior to Ming or Ch'ing China based on other criteria within the general framework of Confucian values. Civilized life did not require Chinese lineages or inclusion in the Chinese empire; many specific aspects of Chinese culture also were dispensable" (Wakabayashi 1986:23). Jinsai Itō more specifically argued that "the unbroken imperial line signified Japan's superior adherence to a set of values within the Confucian tradition," and that "Japan embodied the hierarchical status order of the Middle Kingdom better than China" (27); Sokō Yamaga "held that Japan was superior to China based on Sinocentric criteria of judgment" (29).

With the rise of the Kokugakusha, or the scholars of Native Learning, in the course of the eighteenth century, this position was attacked in favor of a still stronger one. Instead of constructing Japan as the truest bearer of Chinese values, a primodial Japanese spirit was now invented: "From the late eighteenth century onward, for better or worse, 'the Japanese spirit' . . . would be supreme, would have to be lauded for its own sake. Only then might thinkers supplement it with Chinese or Western 'learning'" (Wakabayashi 1986:40).

For Aizawa Seishisai, the early-nineteenth-century figure on whom Wakabayashi's book focuses, this invention was a conscious reaction to new geopolitical circumstances. Realizing not only that China was geographically not at the middle and did not comprise the largest portion of the earth, but also that the achievements of the Western "barbarians" deserved respect, Aizawa wondered whether the "lowly western barbarians had appropriated the Confucian way and were using it to their own advantage." He argued that Japan should cultivate techniques similar to those of the Westerners. This meant the creation, against the threat from the West, of a Japanese identity or *kokutai*—"the spiritual unity and cohesion needed to make a territory and its inhabitants into a nation" (98). This identity was for tactical reasons to be consolidated around the figure of the emperor.

In this way, Aizawa sought to absorb and outdo Western nationalism. Nationalism was a technique to be appropriated from the Western barbarians, but Aizawa identified it with the prior Japanese internalization of the external, the older Confucian tradition. In turn, the absorption of Western nationalism would lead to an enhanced production of the ideal of a Japanese national essence, transforming and generalizing to the entire citizenry the previous construction of a uniquely Japanese spirit. By the early nineteenth century, then, Japan had a multilayered history of transforming itself from periphery to center by virtue of a paradoxical process—a process in which self-conscious absorption of foreign influences was coupled with the equally self-conscious creation and reinforcement of a myth of primordial national identity. The familiar Japanese slogan "Japanese spirit, Western technique" is deceptively simple; what really happened was the invention of an "ancient Japanese spirit," not the persistence of a mythically preexisting cultural identity that was reinforced by the adoption of foreign techniques.

L. S. Stavrianos credits this tradition with being one of the number of factors that helped Japan resist colonialism and subjugation by the capitalist world economy. "Another factor that facilitated Japan's successful adaptation to the West was her long tradition of borrowing from the great Chinese cultural world," he writes. "This made similar borrowing from the Western world less jarring and painful. Japan had taken selected aspects of Chinese culture with the slogan 'Japanese spirit and Chinese knowledge.' Now Japan borrowed what she wished from the West with the slogan 'Eastern morale and Western arts'" (1981:350–51). In the wake of Commodore Perry's return to Japan in 1854 with the demand for a trading treaty or war, and the significantly named Meiji Restoration in 1866, Japan began a much more wholesale absorption of foreign techniques, which resulted in profound changes in the country. "When Ito Hirobumi, the Choshu official who masterminded the new political system, went on an extended tour of Europe to study the constitutional alternatives, he wrote back in August 1882 that he was rejecting 'the works of the extreme liberal radicals of England, America and France,' and turning to the teachings of

Prussian scholars," Stavrianos notes (356). "I believe I have rendered an important service to my country [and contributed to] the great objective of strengthening the foundation of the imperial sovereignty," Ito said.

Carol Gluck describes the complexity of the transformation of institutions and ideology in the Meiji era in much finer detail than Stavrianos. In the first stage of imitating the West, Japan did a lot of conscious trial-and-error shopping around. In the educational establishment, since the original Education Act of 1872, "administrative and curricular change had been dizzying." Administratively, the highly centralized French model was abandoned first for American-style local control, and then for a "hybrid European statist system which featured German influence." The civil code "went through draft after Napoleonic draft," as debate "pitted French against British concepts of civil law and both against indigenous custom." In 1898, a civil code "now based on thoroughly German models" was put into effect. Similarly, the Japanese Army "moved from a French to a Prussian system" between the 1870s and 1890 (Gluck 1985:19–20). Joseph Tobin describes the extremes to which this emulative tendency could go. In commenting on the Meirokusha group, founded by Fukuzawa Yukichi in 1873, Tobin remarks how

> through their influential *Meiji Six Magazine,* the Meirokusha urged modernization on their countrymen. To them, modernization meant westernization. They advocated individual rights, democratic government, egalitarianism, and universal education and favored Western dress, a Western diet, and Western household furnishings. Some went so far as to question whether the Japanese should give up their feudal and illogical language in favor of the more rational and modern English and whether systematic miscegenation with Westerners might not be the only way to overcome the inferiority of the Japanese gene pool. (Tobin 1992:30)

In internalizing these Western influences and institutions, Japanese ideology performed two very different operations. On the one hand, a tradition of emulative Japanese cosmopolitanism was created as these varied experiments were carried out, and the Western idea of civilization, *bumnei,* was domesticated: "First it acquired the adjectives 'new' or 'Japanese' before it, and then it shed even those. By the end of the period, 'civilization' appeared as an indigenous fact of social life that possessed the same descriptive transparency as any unmodified common noun" (Gluck 1985:254).

The controlling idea behind the essays in Tobin's collection reflects the long life of this strategy: they describe "an ongoing creative synthesis of the exotic with the familiar, the foreign with the domestic, the modern with the traditional, the Western with the Japanese," a process Tobin calls "domestication." In Japanese domestication of material from the West, "Western goods, practices, and ideas are changed (Japanized) in their encounter with Japan. Japan is unmistakably westernized, and yet Westerners who visit Japan do not necessarily find what they see familiar." (Tobin 1992:4).

On the other hand, the notion of Japanese *kokutai*—Japan's special, exceptional identity—was paradoxically also elaborated. Fukuzawa Yukichi argued in 1875 for

> the adoption of Western civilization to strengthen *kokutai*, which he ⟵
> conceived in terms of social, historical, and geographic attributes that
> constituted the essence of a nation—what "in Western language they
> call 'nationality.'" He wrote that every nation possessed a *kokutai* which
> each sought to preserve, and "ultimately the existence of a *kokutai* de-
> pends on whether a nation loses its political sovereignty or not." In this
> usage, *kokutai* was jeopardized from without and would be secured by
> the adoption of Western civilization. In the constitutional debates of the
> 1880s, conservatives like Motoda spoke of *kokutai* as jeopardized from
> within and argued that it must be secured by establishing direct imperial
> rule. (Gluck 1985:144)

The cosmopolitan importation of Western "civilization" was thus para-doxically also a defensive/aggressive strategy to protect and strengthen what was stipulated as being peculiarly Japanese. The idea of *kokutai* was an exceptionally fertile site for ideological production; by 1892, one author "complained that *kokutai* was getting lost among all the new interpretations." But by the end of the 1890s it had been domesticated, and was described "with newly imperialistic journalistic confidence as 'the unique principle of each nation'"; "Japan's *kokutai* was then compared to England's or China's and found by virtue of its immutability to be, as it were, 'more' unique" (145). In many ways, there could be no more interesting illustration of the workings of such a nationalist strategy, the conscious attempt to internationalize the external for the purposes of negotiating passage from international periphery to international core. Absorption of external influences meant the construction, reification, and reinforcement of an idea of national identity; success in this venture meant styling this identity as essentially more "real" than others. As the construction of *kokutai* proceeded in high gear throughout the Meiji period, it resulted in claims that Japanese *kokutai* was "more unique than European versions and that it, in claiming more than 2,500 years of unbroken history, was primordial in the way other nations could not claim." That "there was no nation as old as Japan," Gluck notes, "was alleged and supported with examples of age without national continuity, as in India or China, or national identity without age, as in Germany and Italy" (145).

By the middle of the first decade of the Showa era (1926–89), the cosmopolitan impulse increasingly gave way to the nativist, and, as Japan developed its imperial ambitions on the road to World War II, the ideological production of *kokutai* intensified and became more coercive. Thus, for example, "altering the *kokutai* was first included as a crime against the state in the Peace Preservation Law of 1925. Directed against the Communists and suggesting a meaning similar to that of the word 'un-American' in the United States, its inclusion transformed *kokutai* into a legal term, albeit one that even the drafters of the law had difficulty in defining" (282–83).

As a look at the cultural context of the career of Tanizaki Jun'ichiro shows, Japanese culture continued to be marked by simultaneous cosmopolitan-nationalism and internationalism-nativism. These processes proceeded with different emphases at different periods. In the early part of Tanizaki's career, Taisho (1912–26) cosmopolitanism dominated, as things Western were eagerly sought after and absorbed. In the middle phase of Tanizaki's career, rising nativism made Japanese national identity the dominant concern, and "Japanese tradition" was defined overtly against Western influence. Covertly, however, the construction of "Japanese tradition" continued to be a form of Westernization.

The extent to which Tanizaki's literary career really paralleled these developments has been debated and remains difficult to determine. In his excellent study of Tanizaki's fiction, Ken Ito describes Tanizaki's complex marginality with precision:

> If Tanizaki stood apart from the literary mainstream . . . he did not stand outside of his culture. He situated his fiction firmly in the shifting discourse of cultural identity and cultural alternatives that played so large a part in the intellectual and emotional life of the world around him. During the era of Taisho Democracy, the late teens and early twenties, Tanizaki wrote about the Japanese fascination with the West. From the late twenties through the war years, as Japan embraced the rhetoric of nativism, he showed an interest in Japanese tradition. For this swing of sensibility, Tanizaki has often been cited as one of many writers who lived out a pattern of *Nihon e no kaiki,* or a "return to Japan," whereby a Japanese rediscovers indigenous roots after having once been drawn to things foreign.
>
> Tanizaki's case, however, is far too complex to be subsumed under such a rubric. (Ito 1991:2)

Ito's description of Tanizaki's representativeness, yet haunting marginality, is extremely accurate. Although Tanizaki's fictional meditations are always cast in highly personalized terms—as explorations of characters' erotic fantasies and desires—and although they express their author's highly personal obsession with creating alternative worlds (Ito 1991:29), their obliquity of viewpoint enhances, rather than detracts from, their social significance. Tanizaki's highly personalized fictions engaged Japanese social and cultural debates significantly. Their quietly comprehensive irony ultimately refuses to clearly validate any one position in them. Instead, the novels seem to entertain (and undermine) a bewildering range of those debates' positions and possibilities.

The enthusiastic mass Westernization of the Taisho era provided the background and attitudes for Tanizaki's early fiction. In Taisho Japan, Ito writes, "the 'West' became a mass market commodity," spawning a "proliferation of *bunka* products, such as the *bunka nabe*, the 'cultured pot,'" and the *bunka konro*, the 'cultured gas burner'" as well as the "*bunka jūtaku*, or 'cultured residence,' a moderately priced, semiwesternized house in the suburbs" (68). Taisho industrialization and mass-market Westernization thus represented a significant step beyond the Meiji-era reconstruction of Japan in the image of the West: the cosmopolitan Westernization that had been implemented by the elite of the Meiji era now spread to a wider public and was acted out in the arena of popular as well as high culture, mass entertainment as well as state policy. Meiji cosmopolitanism was, in short, democratized:

> The intellectual historian Ikimatsu Keizō argues that the adoption of the term *bunka* (which in Edo texts had signified the process of enlightenment, but which now was identified with the English "culture" or the German *kultur*) as a key word by Taisho thinkers signaled a major reorientation. It marked a shift in emphasis from the state-sponsored military and industrial ambitions implied by the Meiji term *bunmei*, or "civilization," to the personal, inner stirrings represented by such Taisho ideals as *kojinshugi* (individualism) and *kyōyōshugi* (self-cultivation through education). (Ito 1991:68)

Thus, in Tanizaki's *The Mermaid*, Asakusa, the greatest center for mass entertainment in Japan, contained

> plays of the old style, operettas, plays in the new style, comedies, movies—movies from the West and Japanese productions, Douglas Fairbanks and Onoe Matsunosuke—acrobats balancing on balls, bareback riders, *naniwa bushi* singers, girl *gidayū* chanters, the merry-go-round, the Hanayashiki Amusement Park, the Twelve-Story Tower, shooting galleries, whores, Japanese restaurants, Chinese restaurants, and Western restaurants—the Rairaiken, won ton mein, oysters over rice, horsemeat, snapping turtles, eels, and the Café Paulista. (Quoted in Ito 1991:69–70)

About the time that Tanizaki thus depreciated the Japanese past in favor of a carnival of Japanese simulacra of Western mass culture, he was head screenwriter for the Taisho Katsuei film production company and was characterized by a visitor as a "resident of a California suburb" (76).

As Ito notes, Tanizaki, in the early part of his career, was unusual in his interest in Americanization rather than Europeanizing Westernization: in *Naomi* ([1924] 1985), in which he describes the interior of a *bunka jūtaku* decorated with photos of Mary Pickford, Tanizaki shows himself to be

> one of the few Japanese writers to recognize the growing cultural influ-
> ence of the United States in the years following World War I. The custo-
> dians of high culture . . . inherited Kafū's hostility toward a "mercan-
> tile" America and remained aggressively European in their definition of
> the West. Though Tanizaki's choice of Mary Pickford to represent the
> West of America is not without a certain condescension of its own, it
> does show his understanding of an image of America prevalent in Taisho
> popular culture, that of a younger, more dynamic nation within the
> larger West, a land of industrial wealth marked by an unfettered, if unso-
> phisticated culture. (84)

As Ito sums up the "final paradox" of *Naomi*, however, Tanizaki's attraction to the West was anything but unambiguous: "As much as *Chijin no ai*
[*Naomi*] is a fable of a Japanese dominated by his obsession with the West,
it is also the story of a 'West' that can be manipulated, objectified, and even
consumed. This is a paradox appropriate to the low *bunka* of the Taisho
period" (100). In Tanisaki's version of Taisho cosmopolitanism, then, the
West was being domesticated, or "Japanized," according to the strategy
Tobin describes.

With the advent of the Showa era, nativism began to replace Taisho
internationalism as Japan's most powerful cultural impulse. In the 1930s,
many writers, including some exponents of a short-lived proletarian literature movement, experienced what were styled "returns to Japan," and
the Nippon romanha, the Japanese romantic school, was founded. But as
Tanizaki's *Some Prefer Nettles* ([1928] 1981) reveals, these "returns to Japan"
were perhaps not as simple as they seemed. The depiction of Japan in *Some
Prefer Nettles* is embedded in an extraordinary subtle and ambiguous meditation on the contemporary international and intercultural map. The result was a novel that reveals that "returns to Japan" were actually, au fond,
a stronger form of Japanese internalization of external material than was
the cosmopolitan, consumerist absorption of the West Tanizaki suggests
in *Naomi*. At the same time, recovery of "Japanese tradition" was, in many
ways, a more powerful form of Westernization.

Some Prefer Nettles is the story of a modernized Tokyo couple, Kaname and Misako, who are, thanks to their loveless marriage, considering the (Western and modern) remedy of divorce. Told from Kaname's viewpoint, the novel dramatizes Kaname's conscience-struck inability to act, his perpetual waffling about the idea of divorce thanks to an abundance of sensitivity and scruples. In reality, though, Kaname is torn by his connections with three different women, each of whom represents a significant social possibility for Japan, as well as potential future for him.

Misako, Kaname's wife, is a modernized woman clearly impatient with the nostalgic traditionalism of her father. With Kaname, as Ito puts it, she lives

> as westernized a life as was possible in the Japan of the 1920s. . . . The liver sausages from the German butcher only begin to suggest how much Western products figure in the day-to-day lives of . . . [the] family. Kaname and Misako live in a house with a Western wing, furnished with sofas and chairs; the latest addition to their household is a greyhound . . . called Lindy after [Charles] Lindbergh; and Kaname spends much of his time glued to the [Richard] Burton translation of *Arabian Nights*. (Ito, 1991:144)

In response to the failure of her marriage and Kaname's subtle encouragement, Misako takes a lover; she does so ultimately with autonomous resolve, despite uncertainty about whether divorce from Kaname will lead to remarriage or her abandonment by both men. A second woman in Kaname's life is Louise, a Eurasian prostitute for an English madam. Louise says she was "born in Poland, had been driven from her home by the war, and had lived in Russia, Manchuria, and Korea, picking up new languages along the way" (Tanizaki [1928] 1981:161). She is really, however, "the Eurasian daughter of a Russian and a Korean" (162), and she powders her skin thickly to whiten it. Despite this factitiousness and cultural hybridity, her association with European cosmopolitanism is heightened by the fact that she works for a relic of British colonialism, Mrs. Brent, whose establishment does not admit many Japanese men. At first, the "idea of her Western birth" draws Kaname to Louise with a special fascination: "in that he was no different from most Japanese men" (170). Once he realizes the truth—and becomes aware of the natural golden brown of her skin under the white coating—the fascination remains. He never asks her to take the powder off and always remembers a friend's comment that he would have a hard time finding a woman like her even in Paris. Aware of the deception—aware of the spuriousness of this basis for attraction—he continues finding "something of his longing for Europe satisfied in his relations with Louise" (162).

If the autonomous individualism of modernity (evoked by his wife and associated at other places in the novel with America) and stagey, fictional relics of the colonial system form two of the pillars of Kaname's life and consciousness, the third is "traditional" Japan. This third pillar is embodied in O-hisa, the young mistress of his father-in-law. The latter, despite having himself in his early years "indulged in foreign tastes of the most hair-raising variety" (35), has by the time of the novel established himself like a traditional Edo-period gentleman, with O-hisa as his mistress. Kaname's father-in-law has educated O-hisa as the Genji of Murasaki Shikibu's novel trained his ward. The old man, a connoisseur of traditional puppet theater, has trained his young mistress in traditional arts and decorum, and she accompanies him on nostalgic expeditions to Osaka to see Bunraku performances. Kaname ultimately not only visits Osaka with them at the old man's request; he also goes on a trip to the more remote, rural Awaji, where the ancestor of the Osaka puppet theater is to be found.

Kaname's erotic life, then, expresses the international and interregional sociocultural complexity of cosmopolitan Japan, which contains simulacra of "European," "American," and "Japanese" cultures. More fundamentally, the origin of Kaname's erotic drive also involves an interplay of cultures. Kaname is obsessed with women. He is what the novel calls a woman-worshipper, and this psychological tradition is interpreted as a direct result of his Westernization, his liking for foreign things. To be a woman-worshipper is to deviate from the Japanese patriarchal myths invented during the samurai-militarist periods, which were still very much alive in contemporary Japan; Tanizaki associated his own propensity in this direction with his grandfather's conversion to Christianity and his own early memories of staring at an image of the Virgin and Child (Ito 1991:12). Kaname's woman-worshipping makes him fall away from Japanese tradition. With shallowly modern Tokyo sophistication, he devalues "traditional" Edo culture as vulgar. Edo style—a product of the merchant class Kaname is descended from—repels him. Kaname

> reacted from it toward the sublime and the ideal. It was not enough that something should be touching, charming, graceful; it had to have about it a certain radiance, the power to inspire veneration. One had to feel forced to one's knees before it, or lifted by it to the skies. Kaname required this not only in works of art. A woman-worshipper, he looked for the same divine attributes in women, but he had never come upon what he was looking for either in art or in women. (Tanizaki [1928] 1981:36–37)

Kaname's aversion to Edo culture represents this rejection, thanks to Westernization, of his past in the name of something "higher," but this recourse to the sublime and the ideal is interpreted elsewhere as a result of neurotic fear. Once, as a boy, Kaname had caught sight of the face of a girl whom he had heard singing to a koto:

> His young heart ravished at the sight, he pulled back from the window almost as though he had taken fright at something, so quickly that he retained no clear impression of her features. The attraction was perhaps too slight a one to be called a first love. Still, it dominated his childhood thoughts and dreams for some time after, and it was probably the first sprouting of that woman-worship Takanatsu noted. (116)

Kaname's propensity for the ideal and sublime is thus born as a fearful avoidance response to the experience of beauty enshrined in the "Japanese" tradition of aesthetic elegance. Similarly, his inability to act on his divorce results, the novel hints, from a lack of traditional strength, rather than from an abundance of painful, but praiseworthy, scruples and sensitivity: "The ancients would perhaps have called it girlish sentimentality, this inability to face up squarely to the sorrow of a farewell. Nowadays, however, one is counted clever if one can reach a goal without tasting the sorrow, however slight it may be, that seems to lie along the way. Kaname and Misako were cowardly, and there was no point in being ashamed of it" (104–5).

Tanizaki hints at a final condemnation of Kaname's woman-worshipping. It is not just a sign of his Westernization, but a sign of Westernization of a particularly debased sort. Such a judgment is suggested when the novel contrasts Kaname's woman-worship to the Edo culture he rejects:

> While the dramatists and novelists of the Edo period were able to create soft, lovely women, women who were likely to dissolve in tears on a man's knee, they were quite unable to create the sort of woman a man would feel compelled to kneel before. Kaname therefore preferred a Hollywood movie to a seventeenth-century Kabuki play. For all its vulgarity, Hollywood was forever dancing attendance on women and seeking out new ways to display their beauty. (37)

Unlike Hollywood, Edo culture, which distresses Kaname as "thick, coarse, heavy" (38), has something ultimately more positive in its depths. To be sure, it is distressing: O-hisa's "traditional charms" disquiet him, for, following tradition, her teeth are black, "as if they had been stained in the old court manner," and so crooked that "an eyetooth protruded sharp enough to bite into her lip" (21). Still, in Edo art, primordial depth is still accessible, while the apparent elevation of Hollywood's version of women is shallow: "And yet there was in it [Edo culture] something too of the quiet, mysterious gloom of a temple, something of the dark radiance that a Buddha's halo sent out from the depth of its niche. It was far from the brightness of a

Hollywood movie. Rather it was a low, burnished radiance, easy to miss, pulsing out from beneath the overlays of the centuries (38).

From this perspective, "Americanization" is worse than European Westernization: it is both Western *and* vulgarly modern. Despite his early interest in America, Tanizaki, in his "return to Japan," inscribed something of the majority Japanese view of America in *Some Prefer Nettles,* even as he took America's influence seriously. Specifically, America meant a debasement of the West's own tradition of woman-worship, which was "a long one," for "the Occidental sees in the woman he loves the figure of a Greek goddess, the image of the Virgin Mother" (37). Americanization thus represents the most significant form of Kaname's defection from the Japanese tradition of beauty and courage, while at the same time it is the most vulgarized form of the West's own preoccupation with woman-worship. Urban modernization in its most visible form reveals the full weight of this insight. Americanization appears in stark, distinguishable form in the small provincial centers around Tokyo:

> One might expect . . . [them] to have a patina in proportion as they are old. In fact they are gloomy as though overlaid with a coating of soot. Earthquakes and fires are common, and each rebuilding brings characterless houses of cheap imported woods that might better be used for matches, and shabby Western-style buildings that suggest a run-down, end-of-the-line town in the United States. (130)

The island of Awaji—the end point of Kaname's pilgrimage into nostalgia with his father-in-law and O-hisa—is by contrast, a place where the old patina is still evident: "A modern coating goes no farther than the large cities that are a country's arteries, and there are not many such cities anywhere. In an old country with a long tradition, China and Europe as well as Japan—any country, in fact, except a very new one like the United States—the smaller cities, left aside by the flow of civilization, retain the flavor of an earlier day until they are overtaken by catastrophe" (131). Here Americanization is interpreted as something that is no longer a vulgarization of European tradition. American vulgarity is strikingly distinguished —as in Ricoeur, from the European West—and Japan and Europe are now yoked together in opposition to it. Americanization represents vulgar modernity, in contrast to the yoked traditionalisms of Japan and Europe. The novel's portrayal of Japan versus the West thus becomes first Japan versus two distinct Wests (America and Europe); then it shifts to Japan and Europe versus America.

This quiet complexity distinctly pluralizes and complicates Tanizaki's portrayal of Japanese negotiations with the First World. As Ito remarks, Tanizaki early on recognized the importance of American cultural influence in the post–World War I period. Thus, on the one hand, in *Some Prefer Nettles,* American popular culture (Hollywood movies) and American cultivation of individual autonomy (divorce and Misako's independence) are firmly distinguished from European colonial-cosmopolitan culture (Mrs. Brent, Louise), while both *appear* as alternatives to the "authentically" Japanese (O-hisa, Awaji). On the other hand, as the above description of Awaji suggests, there is, however, a way in which Tanizaki now, like other Japanese, yokes Japan with Europe against America. This alliance, as we shall see, will soon reappear in covert, but powerful, form in the text. We can turn to this, however, only after the overt opposition of Japan to Europe and America has been fully explored.

Kaname's trip to Awaji—his return to Awaji, one almost wants to say—seems at first to Kaname to represent a complete version of a "return to Japan." Kaname simultaneously recovers his partially severed Japanese roots and his own personal past. In Awaji he encounters Edo culture in its purest form; the puppet theater at Awaji is the ancestor of the Osaka theater, and what Kaname has found in Osaka is heightened at Awaji, where he discovers "a low, burnished radiance, easy to miss, pulsing out from beneath the overlays of the centuries" (38). For him, this is no less than the primordial essence of Japanese culture, intact despite the overlay of centuries. In Awaji,

> every detail brought back—how vividly!—the mood and air of old Japan. Kaname felt as if he were being drunk up into the scene, as if he were losing himself in the clean white walls and the brilliant blue sky. Those walls were a little like the sash around O-hisa's waist: their first luster had disappeared in long years under the fresh sea winds and rains, and bright though they were, their brightness was tempered by a certain reserve, a soft austerity. (132)

Not only is the past mysteriously alive in all the reserved surfaces of Awaji, it appears in the continued tradition of the puppet theater, which in turn infuses the whole community with its presence: thus, Kaname sees the world of the theater recreated in the town that hosts its performances.

> Kaname thought of the faces of the ancients in the dusk behind their shop curtains. Here on this street people with faces like theater dolls must have passed lives like stage lives. The world of the plays—of O-yumi, Jūrōbei of Awa, the pilgrim O-tsuru, and the rest—must have been just such a town as this. And wasn't O-hisa a part of it? Fifty years ago, a hundred years ago, a woman like her, dressed in the same kimono, was perhaps going down the same street in the spring sun, lunch in hand, on her way to the theater beyond the river. (132–33)

This mysteriously animate presence of the past makes Awaji a place where, for Kaname, a full-blown version of organicist community is created: art and community, past and present, nature and culture are all fused together in a mythic whole. The "heavy-toned old country plays, in a sense, have in them the work of the race" (143). The theater, correspondingly, "must have been a deep comfort to the farmers," as "how thoroughly the old theater must have penetrated into the corners of the country, one thinks, how deeply its roots must have sunk themselves into the life of the farms!" (144)

If Kaname thus recovers his communal origins at Awaji, he also recovers a lost, buried personal self: it is at Awaji that Kaname remembers the moment of original fear that produced the defect of his later, Westernized woman-worship. Going back to that moment is potentially as therapeutic individually as attending the theater is culturally: an authentic identity that had been repressed is unearthed, made present, restored.

This description of Awaji and Kaname's awakening cannot, however, be taken at face value. It is possible that it is presented with sly, covert irony. Although Tanizaki's elusive elegance and calculated ambiguities make such irony hard to pin down, there are a number of suggestions of it. Suspicious elements include, for example, the persistence of Kaname's conflicts after the trip and the lack of resolution at the novel's end (was the trip to Awaji at all therapeutic for Kaname?); the presentation of all the events of the novel, including the idyll, subjectively through Kaname's consciousness; and the characterization of O-hisa, which suggests ways in which she is not the ideal Edo woman she seems to be (she speaks inelegant Japanese, at times shows a lack submissiveness to the old man, and prefers not to practice her old calligraphy but to read a modern woman's magazine). But the elusive nature of what is restored constitutes a still deeper qualification of the simple drama of cultural recovery. As the novel reveals, O-hisa is an actor, albeit imperfectly trained, and Kaname develops a taste for "people with faces like theatre dolls" and "lives like stage lives"; Kaname's experience may thus not represent an awakening to any genuine Japanese cultural essence, but the experience of a more refined, even exotic skill at simulacra than Hollywood movies, Louise, and Mrs. Brent have to offer. To this apparently decisive demystification of Kaname's idyll, however, there is one important counter, the significance of which we shall explore later. Does the Japanese "essence" perhaps not lie precisely in this capacity for inauthenticity, simulacra, theater? Is Tanizaki perhaps styling "traditional" Japanese culture a culture that made life aspire to the condition of *bunraku?* If so, Kaname's return may paradoxically at its most "real" be a return to simulation.

Given this ambiguity, we must turn to one final, still more fundamental suspicion about the "authenticity" of the idyll. In his discussion of Tanizaki's early career, Ito highlights the personal and artistic influence of Nagai Kafū's theatrical Western cosmopolitanism on Tanizaki. In *Tales of America* (1908) and *Tales of France* (1909), Kafū turns exoticizing Orientalism back upon the West and at the same time deprecates the Orient as mundane: "If, on the one hand, there was the 'West' as 'Orient,' ablaze with color and ripe with possibility, there was, on the other hand, an Orient that was excruciatingly mundane and unyielding to the imagination" (Ito 1991:45). In one returnee story, however, which prefigures his later work, Kafū carries out a more complex maneuver: turning the Orientalist vision back upon the lost Japan of the Edo period, he imbues "with the imaginative hues of the 'West' a Fukagawa that represents the vestiges of the lost world of Edo" (47). Similarly, Tanizaki once wrote of himself, "My fondness for old Japan stemmed from a kind of exoticism, not unlike that which makes foreigners prize woodblock prints by Hiroshige" (quoted in Ito 1991:110–11). As Ito summarizes Kafu's influence and Tanizaki's practice, "When Tanizaki portrays late Edo as the 'other world,' he not only reflects Kafū's reformulation of European Orientalism, but also displays a distinct skill in naturalizing foreign concepts" (55). Accordingly, Ito argues, the portrayal of the Japanese past in *Some Prefer Nettles* ironically presents the construction of Japan in the image of Western Orientalism.

Reinforcing Ito's observation, Kaname's experience at Awaji suggests the quietly ironic presence of a Western model of a more historically specific kind. The description of the idyll at Awaji closely echoes the preoccupations of German romanticism. Indeed, the German terms, later to become notorious, are hard to avoid: Tanizaki portrays the theater as rooted in Japanese *Blut* (the plays embody the work of the race) and *Boden* (the theater's roots are in the life of the farms). The authentic Japan—or even the Japan of exquisite simulationism—is constructed in a German mold. Either way, the construction of "Japanese culture"—even if that culture was one of "lives like stage lives," a cultura of simulacra—is not simply "Japanese."

Such complexity is not specific to Tanizaki; a variety of contemporary examples might be cited. Japanese interest in the German philosopher Martin Heidegger, Neo-Kantianism, and *Kulturwissenschaften* was blossoming then. Naoki Saki has analyzed the Heideggerian influences on Watsuji Tetsuro's anthropology as an "impulse to imitate Heidegger and European philosophy" that "resulted in a desire to react to the West" (1991:178): the process resulted in the explicitly Heideggerian construction of an idea of authentic Japanese national community. More interesting still, Leslie Pincus has described how Kuki Shuzo—the Baron Kuki who conversed with Heidegger—interpreted the structure of Edo style in his book *"Iki" no kozo*. During the 1920s and 1930s, Kuki's analysis of Edo aesthetic style contributed to attempts to "restore Japan to its difference from reigning Western values: by turning *"iki,* an aesthetic style from an era that closely preceded Japan's dramatic encounter with Perry's 'black ships' [into] a privileged signifier of Japanese culture" (Pincus 1991:144). In doing so, "the terms in which he articulated Japan's difference from the West were clearly marked by a long and productive apprenticeship to European letters. It should not be surprising, then, if *'Iki' no kozo* is haunted by the specter of Occidentalism it sought to vanish" (144). Given the fact that "the logic of organicism" (155) of the German romantic and hermeneutic traditions was thus applied to Japan, "the notion of synthesis between method (the West) and matter (Japan) does not adequately describe the transaction conducted in *'Iki' no kozo*. Rather, the concept of an essential Japanese object, of Japaneseness, proves to be the discursive effect of a method [the Heideggerian hermeneutics of ethnic being] with a content all its own" (154).

Just as Tanizaki's fictional returns to Japanese tradition came as the Taisho importation of Western mass culture gave way to the rising nativism of Showa, this impulse to use Edo culture to signify the "eternal landscape of the Japanese spirit" (148) came as a reaction to an era

> where the effects of modernization, initiated by the Meiji transformation and Japan's realignment with the West, penetrated deep into the grain of everyday life. In a transfigured cityscape of streetcars and high buildings, cafes and dancehalls, new social constituencies rose up from below to become active participants in what was dubbed in English "modern life." As if to lure these urban masses into visibility, culture called on mechanized technologies to accelerate and multiply its representations—in motion pictures, phonograph records, one-yen books, and the rhythms of jazz. (Pincus 1991:149–50)

The visible Westernization of Japan—especially the Americanization that followed in the wake of the 1923 earthquake that destroyed Tokyo and Yokohama—was thus opposed, in Kuki's thought, as in *Some Prefer Nettles*, by a covert Germanification that made *iki* the "chosen signifier of Japan, gathering into its interpretive folds attributes deemed representative of Japanese culture" (148). As in Tanizaki, then, the "return" to primordialist Japanese traditions was in reality yet another form of Westernization, covertly mediated by a highly selective, precise use of European models.

Some Prefer Nettles is tinged with the haunting ambiguity that surrounds Tanizaki's work and career. Just as Tanizaki's career seems to parallel the trajectory of Japanese history, but didn't, so his dramatization of different positions may seem to reach some closure, but never does. Is Tanizaki's portrayal of Awaji nostalgic cultivation of Edo culture or a demystification of that nostalgia? Or is its ability to evoke, entertain, and undermine these opposite positions the continuation of a "Japanese" sensibility peculiarly attuned to theater and simulacra? Or does the very construction of the idea of a "Japanese" sensibility not represent a form of Westernization? And, finally, if all of these are to some degree true, doesn't *Some Prefer Nettles*—a book supposedly exemplifying Tanizaki's "return to Japan"— embody a contrary cultivation of cosmopolitan internationalism, in which the nativist impulse is only one of many heterogeneous cultural tendencies in Japan? None of these possibilities are wholly idiosyncratic; as we shall see, they return in debates about culture in contemporary, postmodern Japan. In these debates, Japanese essentialist nativism, conceptions of Japanese culture as a culture of simulacra, references to Edo as a foundational period, and assertions of Japan's cosmopolitan receptiveness to heterogeneous international influence all return as crucial components to be paradoxically reconciled. Of Tanizaki's subsequent career, it is interesting to note that in *The Makioka Sisters* ([1948] 1981), after casting Japan in the image of German romanticism in *Some Prefer Nettles,* he rewrote Japan in European cosmopolitan form via Flaubertian realism.

If, as suggested, the globally mediated "invention of Japan" was not at all a process unique to Japan, but one characteristic of nationalism around the world, neither was the production of images of endangered "indigenous" cultures via the European form of the novel uniquely Japanese. The creation of fiction about endangered "authentic" national cultures by "indigenous" cultural elites has occurred in a variety of supposedly "national" traditions. It is a globally disseminated genre, but one that presents its products as quintessentially local. A subset of the simultaneous dissemination of the discourses of cultural imperialism and cultural relativism, and not simply the product of separate development in local national traditions, it represents a phase in the ongoing process of globalization, not a final elegy for local traditions.

Lawrence Buell (1989) has written of Chinua Achebe's *Things Fall Apart* (1959) as an example of conventions of literary pastoralism that emanated from England to its colonies in America, Africa, and elsewhere—an international, Euro-originated genre that dramatized, however, endangered, supposedly local traditions. Use of metropolitan forms and ideas to dramatize supposedly local primordia has also occurred in other European and also non-European languages. Cheikh Hamidou Kane's *Ambiguous Adventure* constructs an African idyll in French out of European-originated *négritude* romanticism; José María Arguedas's poetry in Quechua about the Peruvian Indians indigenizes Walt Whitman, while his tragically elegiac novel in hybrid Spanish, *Deep Rivers,* translates anthropological knowledge into an avant-garde linguistic form. Timothy Brennan cites Angel Rama's analysis of "transculturation" in the same vein: "Rama notes how in the 1920s and 1930s, Alejo Carpentier rediscovered the African rhythms of the Cuban village by listening to the music of Stravinsky, and how Miguel Asturias learned to marvel at the lyric imagination of Guatemala's indigenous communities by studying surrealist techniques of automatic writing" (1989:59). Christopher Miller (1990) and others have reinterpreted *négritude* generally as French-made. Analogously, the whole American tradition of the search for roots, from Alex Haley's classic (1976) to Maya Angelou's *All God's Children Need Traveling Shoes* (1986) and Michael Arlen's Armenian version, *Passage to Ararat* (1975), has been interpreted by Werner Sollors (1986) and others as less an authentic attempt to recover cultures of origin than an expression of the concerns of American culture. Stavrianos provides an interesting contemporary example: Sandinista attempts to restore Nicaragua's own cultural traditions included, the *New York Times* reported, local poetry workshops that taught "aspiring bards . . . a set of rules—adapted, amazingly from guidance once prepared by Ezra Pound" (1981:483).

Perhaps most comprehensively and challengingly, Mary Layoun, in *Travels of a Genre: The Modern Novel and Ideology* (1990) closely analyzes a series of six novels—two in modern Greek, two in Arabic, and two in Japanese—to show how a European-generated novelistic form was exported to the rest of the world, becoming first an agent for extending the colonial project and subsequently a site for resistance. Thus, the "modern West European novel was apprehended and, at least initially, produced in Greece or Egypt or Japan as the paradigmatic genre of the rational, modern, and democratic West, as an 'advanced' cultural technology" and quickly came to flourish "as the dominant mode in Greece, the Middle East, and Japan" (9), metaphorically " 'colon[izing]' preexistent narrative production" (11). Novelistic colonization was sometimes not metaphoric, but startlingly literal: "in one West African country, colonial officers paid local writers and literate storytellers to write novels in a deliberate attempt to promote the novel over other narrative or poetic forms" (11). Quickly, however, the novel became the site of what Layoun describes as two distinct phases of anticolonial resistance, the first by homologous and the second by counterdiscursive (or, as she calls them, "deformative") strate-gies. The former sought to resist the challenge of Western hegemony by "calling up the 'traditional,' the 'indigenous,' the 'popular,' or the tran-scendent, [while] the latter fiction critically qualifie[d] that proposition" thanks to the insight that "the notions of separate and autonomous devel-opment" (250) on which the earlier novels were based were inaccurate. Layoun's first sort of novels correspond to the fiction of nostalgia as resis-tance that we have been discussing—and that I have redefined as the first phase of globalization in an anticolonial era. Her second variety anticipate developments I shall turn to in the second half of this book—the time when global interconnectedness, not the global fiction of local autonomy, began to emerge as the regnant norm.

Although writers like these have sought to explode the fiction of fic-tions of authentic culture, the tendency to take these productions seri-ously (and realistically) is still extremely widespread. That literary influ-ences do not recognize national boundaries is no news, but that globally disseminated literary forms and influences are used, usually covertly, in the evocation or recreation of endangered traditions and cultures, and that literary production of this sort is not locally determined, but part of the ongoing development of geopolitical and geocultural relationships, is not usually so well attended to or its implications forthrightly faced. In the recent past, and even the demystifying present, many literary investiga-tors have routinely perceived a multitude of influences at work in an au-thor's development and texts, while nonetheless clinging vigorously to the notion that works of art grow out of and participate in traditions packaged in national and geopolitical terms (the "Japanese novel," the "Western tradition"). An unexplored contradiction as sharp as this indi-cates the presence of severe cognitive dissonance, to say the least.

Japan's agonizing reappraisal of its past, during the two decades after World War II produced a sharply critical perspective on many aspects of Japanese nationalism. As Gluck comments, *tennōsei* ideology (the ideology of the emperor system) and the notion of *kokutai* were dismantled with startling speed in the name of democracy (*minshushugi*). Oppositional politics seemed to be a possibility during the initial stages of the postwar attempt to reform Japan in the image of an American democracy; at the same time, a new wave of Japanese cultural cosmopolitanism—this time a decidedly Americanizing one—was breaking. The collection of essays To-bin edited, *Re-Made in Japan,* contains a host of lively, low-culture exam-ples of Japanese absorption of American material from the immediate postwar period to the present. Tobin writes of how the 1980s saw a *nostaru-*

jii būmu (nostalgia boom) that rekindled "consumer desire not for traditional Japanese music and dress, but for the look and sound of the leather-
jacketed hoods and poodle-skirted teenyboppers"—not in fact of the
American 1950s, but of the postwar era in Japan.

> In the postwar era radio and movies played an increasingly important
> role in introducing Western popular and material culture. Elvis Presley
> and other American rock idols became stars in Japan as the American
> Top 40 were broadcast across the country on FEN, the Armed Forces
> Radio. American movies and television along with records and radio
> made American popular culture the rage in Japan in the 1950s. (Tobin
> 1992:14)

Millie Creighton follows Moritsugu Ken in recording how "the first Japanese McDonald's opened in 1971 in a Tokyo branch of Mitsukoshi Department Store with the advertising slogan, 'If you keep eating hamburgers,
you will become blond!'" (46). And Mary Yoko Brannan, in writing on the
Tokyo Disneyland, notes that "many Japanese under the age of forty-five
watched the 'Mickey Mouse Club' on television as children and when
prompted will readily join in a Japanese version of the Mickey Mouse
song" (223).

With the collapse of political dissent by the end of the 1960s and the
great economic growth that followed, ideological construction in Japan of
primordialist exceptionalism and essentialism also recommenced in a new
vein. The models of Japanese imperial historiography (*kōkoku shikan*) resurfaced in the recent "discourse on Japanese uniqueness" (*Nihonjinron*)
(Sakai 1989:101). But the new versions of Japanese exceptionalism and
essentialism have been constructed out of American, rather than European, modernism. Japan's enormously successful self-transformation
into an epitome of late capitalist commodification, a postmodern information society in which commodification includes, not only goods, but
culture, ideas, information, and even critical theory (Ivy 1989), has been
accompanied by a new discourse (at home and abroad) of Japanese identity. In this discourse, Japan's extraordinary technological and organizational achievements have been represented as signs of the exceptionalism
of ancient Japanese tradition. Thus Tetsuo Najita (1989) observes how

> technology came to be ideologized in terms of "culture" to a degree that
> had not been the case before the Pacific War, when, as suggested above,
> culture tended to be appreciated as an ever-shrinking haven within
> which to find creative solace. In the postwar era, and especially with
> high-growth economics, whether the issue was industrial organization
> or the decision-making process of hiring and firing practices or mer-
> itocracy in education or quality control on the production line, techno-

logical excellence and achievement were clothed in traditional cloth—sometimes to the point of absurdity, so that even Westerners have been led to believe that *bushido* is the basis of Japanese technological and entrepreneurial practices. (13)

In this spirit, Prime Minister Ohira Masayoshi argued in 1979 that the time had come for Japan to go beyond attempts to imagine an "overcoming" of the modern. He called instead for "conquering the modern." Japan stood, he felt, at the beginning of an "age of culture" (*bunka no jidai*), in which, since Japan has "already reached a high level of technological and industrial achievement, the 'citizenry should no longer make the modern its goal'" (Harootunian 1989:81). Instead, reflection on the "special quality of Japan's culture" was necessary, or, as Harootunian puts it, the "social imaginary . . . [that, the implication was, had] remained unchanged since the Stone Age" (81). Similarly, Najita notes how postwar Japanese social scientists inverted the essentialism of Ruth Benedict's *The Chrysanthemum and the Sword* by arguing that "it was the very distinctiveness of Japanese vertical or dependent relationships, in groups, and in harmony, that was the basis of sure self-knowledge among the Japanese and that made them effective in the organized processes of high-growth economics" (14). And Marilyn Ivy (1989) analyzes Prime Minister Nakasone Yasuhiro's notorious 1986 speech—the one in which he asserted that the United States contained "many blacks, Puerto Ricans and Mexicans, and on the average America's level [of intelligence] is still extremely low" (22)—as an attempt to link Japanese special identity (traceable back to the time of *Australopithecus* along lines of separate development to a separate genetic origin) with Japanese mastery of the information age. In no other nation, Nakasone said, "does information come so naturally into one's head" (23). Thus, as Ivy comments, Nakasone asserted that the "transparency and consensus of Japanese knowledge allow it to exceed, productively, the heterogenous and racially divided cultural masses of the rest of the globe" (23).

This resurgence of nativist exceptionalism in a new era of Japanese cosmopolitanism is striking because it validates itself in startling new terms. Japan's extraordinarily rapid and complete postmodernization is seen as the sign of its exceptional culture; the paradoxical result is a nationalism that in invoking postmodernization appeals to a condition that, according to most formulations, radically undermines the ideology and institutions of the nation-state. More specifically, in an echo of previous Japanese appropriations of external cultural material, Japan's rapid postmodernization has been interpreted, not as something that has followed a Western developmental timeline, but as the fulfillment of qualities that have always been peculiarly Japanese. Recently, for example, Japan has experienced a popular, not just elite, "boom" in poststructuralist and postmodern theory. But the boom, it has been argued, does not represent an imitative absorption of French originals; instead, French theory has only underscored something that has always—the formulation goes—been peculiarly Japanese. "What meaning does the notion of the simulacrum, the copy, have in a culture where the notion of the origin, it is said, has not existed: where there is no transcendental signified? Where, it is also asserted, literature and art trace the form and flow of sensuous, detached, empty signifiers—rather than fix the meaning of external signifieds; where, in short, there is no logos?" (Ivy 1989:39) Among the many fascinating offshoots of such assertions has been an exchange between Karatani Kōjin and Jacques Derrida, in which the latter cautiously tries to salvage his philosophical movement against Karatani's assertion that deconstruction is not possible in Japan, thanks to Japan's lack of a preexisting logocentric structure (40–41).

To pick just one example of such analyses, "The Postmodern and Mass Images in Japan" (1989), Mitsuhiro Yoshimoto has argued that the construction of a Tokyo Disneyland represents Japan's centrality to the postmodern world system. The Tokyo Disneyland emphatically does not mean the Americanization of Japan. "The Tokyo Disneyland epitomizes the cultural logic of postmodern Japan which has nothing to do with the logic of Americanization" (13). In America, as Jean-François Baudrillard asserts, "Disneyland is there to conceal the fact that it is the 'real' country, all of 'real' America, which *is* Disneyland" (16). The Tokyo Disneyland, by contrast, is not a cheap imitation of an American original, but "takes away from America what makes America unique" (17). Moreover, it turns it to more profoundly postmodern ends:

> The difference between Disneyland in Los Angeles and the Tokyo Disneyland is that while the former produces the imaginary distinction between real and imaginary, the latter exposes the imaginary nature of a distinction between real and imaginary. . . . The presence of Disneyland, which is believed to be something irreproducible, in the vicinity of Tokyo makes us realize that a different type of cultural logic is at work in Japan. The copresence of totally incongruous cultural artifacts in the same space signifies that it is none other than Japan that is Disneyland. . . . Disneyland, which is supposed to conceal the imaginary nature of daily life in the United States, functions in Japan as a carnivalesque celebration of the postmodern imagination permeating every facet of daily life. (Yoshimoto 1989:17)

In Japan, then, Disneyland has proven itself more hyperreal than in America; the result is that Japan, in thus aggressively absorbing American cultural material, has shown that it has moved to the center of the post-modern world system. At the same time, however, Japanese cosmopolitan-ism—Japanese domestication of postmodernism—has gone along with the reconstruction of Japanese tradition. Paradoxically, Japan's post-modern internationalist project makes many again feel the invisible hand of the Japanese spirit at work, and once again Edo culture is invoked as the locus of that spirit:

> Instead of producing the images of our present as the past of some imaginary future society, the postmodern imagination in Japan has "dis-covered" the postmodern in the immediate past of Japanese history. Curiously enough, it is the eighteenth and nineteenth century Edo (present-day Tokyo) society of "floating world," in which, it is often argued, the cultural dominant was characterized by the so-called free-play of signifiers. A vast number of recently published books and articles on Edo culture focus on the native postmodernism preceding the mod-ernization process facilitated by the massive intrusion of the West into Japan since the mid-nineteenth century. . . . the attempt to find some similarities between post-modern commercialism in contemporary Ja-pan and the socio-cultural phenomena of Edo society tends to end up producing a curious conjunction of postmodernism with neo-nationalism or neo-conservatism. (Yoshimoto 1989:19–20)

What was, in short, a buried but distinct possibility in Tanizaki's *Some Prefer Nettles*—the possibility that the Japanese "essence" was a genius for simulacra—has become an overt, exceptionalist claim in postmodern Ja-pan.

Japan has been, as suggested, anything but unique in its strategic internal-ization of the external and manufacture of a notion of national culture. Although the strength of Japan's emphasis on primordialist, nostalgic nationalism has been distinctive, and although its particular negotiations with the West are historically very specific, a number of versions of the strategy of nationalizing/naturalizing diverse cultural material and re-presenting it as part of an ancient, authentic, national tradition can be found in anticolonial nationalisms throughout the world. Similar pat-terns can easily be discovered at other sites in Asia, Africa, and even the United States, in which, in the late nineteenth and early twentieth centu-ries, an Anglocentric strain of nostalgic nationalism was grafted onto its earlier form of nationalism, one Hobsbawm calls "revolutionary popular." If Japan has creatively absorbed foreign material, so has America; if Japa-nese nationalism has been exceptionalist, so has America's; where Ameri-ca, however, has tended, despite Anglocentrism, to emphasize the revolutionary-popular goal of futurity, Japan has invoked primordia, and where America has continued to appropriate the eighteenth-century revolutionary-popular notion of universalism, Japan has appropriated the particularistic European nationalism of the nineteenth century. Perhaps, to do full justice to the commonness of the process I have been describing, we must look at a far greater global-historical canvas than just the period of European colonialism. In a more general sense, cultural appropriation as part of a contest for power has not merely been a feature of nationalism and anticolonialism: it has been a perennial civilizational process. As the global historian William McNeill writes, "Any geographical displacement of world leadership must be prefaced by successful borrowing from previously established centers of the highest prevailing skills" (1990:19).

Such a recognition of the representativeness, rather than (as is customary) of the arcane uniqueness of the construction of Japanese cultural tradition, must raise a final question. The example of postmodern Japan dramatizes the persistence of Japan's yoking of opposites: nationalism is joined to postmodern globalization. But can this *discordia concors* really continue much past the era of global nationalism into the present era? Can the cultural form of the nation, which Benedict Anderson analyzes as a historically specific "cultural artefact" (1983:13), really survive the challenges of the contemporary phase of globalization and the demise of a postwar world order built upon the notion of separate nationhood? Can the artifact of the nation free itself from post-eighteenth-century notions of homogeneity and move successfully in the direction of globalism externally, and (visibly in the case of the United States, if less visibly in Japan) polyculturality internally? Can the effects of modernization on the nation—which Hobsbawm describes as the "homogenization and standardization of . . . [a nation's] inhabitants" (1990:93)—survive in a postmodern world of disaggregated production, global population flows, and heightened international circulation of a smorgasbord of cultural simulacra? The question involves a degree of conceptual aporia, as the notion of postmodern nationalism—a phenomenon sociology now investigates (Kavolis 1991)—is premised, as Roland Robertson has made clear, on the deconstruction of Enlightenment, romantic, and modernist assumptions, assumptions foundational to the national form in the postwar era. Japanese postmodern nationalism has found such a solution, although many observers feel it will be short-lived. Mitsuhiro Yoshimoto has described this attempt to construct a postmodern nationalism as one in which borders are rephrased, selectively, porously, as a strategy for managing information absorbed from the outside, not consolidating territory against outside aggression:

On the one hand, the simulated world inside Japan gives rise to the illusion that Japan has finally opened itself to the outside world; that in the democratic society of a high-tech Japan, the free flow of information is successfully realized; and that what the Japanese can obtain now is not a cheap imitation of the original but the original itself (e.g., the Tokyo Disneyland). On the other, the manageability of free floating signifiers often leads to the erasure of concrete social situations from the outside world, in place of which narrative clichés re-organize signifiers into the master narrative celebrating Japanese uniqueness (*Nihonjinron*). Through the manipulation of mass images, the Japanese have (re-)affirmed their belief that there is something unique about Japan and the Japanese which can never be understood by foreigners (*gaijin*); that the economic success of Japan is inseparable from that unique Japanese essence; and that Japan, as the best country in the world, is taking up the world's central position from Europe and the United States. (Yoshimoto 1989:22)

Joseph Tobin has recounted a number of different examples of this process, noting that

the salience in Japan of the distinction between foreign and Japanese is hard for Westerners to grasp. Japanese things and foreign things are marked as fundamentally different in the way they are advertised and marketed; in department stores' use of separate displays . . . ; in the syllabary used to write about them . . . ; and, most basically, in the way they are categorized by the Japanese language as being *wa* (Japanese) or *yō* (Western). The self-evident power of this distinction between Japanese and foreign goods and practices might be compared to our Western common-sense notion of gender difference: before we can evaluate a person's character or social class, we notice if the person is male or female. (1992:24–25)

Holding cultural boundary lines firmly in place by such techniques, "Japanese" identity has been consolidated even as postmodern cosmopolitanism has proceeded apace. Similarly, Mary Yoko Brannan, although contesting particulars of Yoshimoto's analysis of the Tokyo Disneyland, agrees with him that the way Japanese manage cultural borders means that Japanese internationalism reinforces Japanese nationalism. Japanese Disneyland is structured so as continually to reinforce "the distinction between Japan and the Other" and to keep "the exotic exotic" (1992:227).

Only a minority of contemporary students of nationalism—such as Hobsbawm and John Breuilly (1982)—have argued that nationalism is a waning phenomenon today. Indeed, even Hobsbawm has underscored its recent prominence in places like the countries of the former USSR, Yugoslavia, Germany, and India and an upsurge of xenophobia worldwide; having done so, however, he argues that "nationalism is historically less important" (1990:191) today because the nation-state form "as an operational identity" is in decline before "the new supranational restructuring of the globe" (190). Contemporary nationalism, he concludes, has no historical project; it represents the unfinished business of preceding eras. Roland Robertson has similarly commented that "in the contemporary phase of globalization the concept of the homogenous national society is breaking down, in spite of the reassertion of nationalism in certain parts of the world" (1992a:30). For Robertson, however, this does not sound a death knell for the nation as a social form: "to date there is nothing to suggest that the nationally organized society . . . is about to wither away" (184). Robertson's conclusion is that the nation will still exert an important influence on contemporary globalization: "'internal' features of societies" continue to "greatly affect their forms of global involvement" in an era of intensified globalization, even as they did in the global era of nation building (96). So far, the cosmopolitan-nativist refitting of Japanese identity for the information age, however fragile, has borne this prediction out. Subsequent chapters discuss several different strategies for achieving the same ends.

But how stable constructions like contemporary Japanese cosmopolitan-nativism can be is questionable. Whether the processes of postmodern globalization—for example, the deterritorialization of culture, the internationalization of the economy, the development of communications technology and rapid transport, the heightening of ecological interdependence, and so forth—will undermine political, economic, and cultural borders beyond the ability of even a transformed nation-state to manage the process, and what such a failure might mean, are matters for urgent speculation. Speaking to this point, Hobsbawm, noting the recent resurgence of international migrations, has asserted that "a world of national territories 'belonging' to the natives who exclusively keep strangers in their place" is "even less of a realistic option for the twenty-first century than it was for the twentieth" (1990:182). In only the past two decades, the rate of change has dramatically intensified. In 1960, for example, there were sixty million international arrivals. In 1989, borders became more porous: four hundred million were reported (Urry 1992). Moreover, border crossing has not by any means been confined to people: capital, marketing, manufacturing, and consumption find international boundary lines increasingly porous. Clearly a host of postnational globalist circuits of exchange have developed outside, beside, within, and around the formation of the nation-state, and the extent to which the proliferation of these circuits will affect national structures is uncertain.

Perhaps an anecdote may express some aspects of the problem. In the midst of demonstrators chanting "death to America" in Iran during the Khomeini revolution, Tony Horowitz encountered one man who, when he found out that Horowitz was American, wanted to talk about Disneyland. "It has always been my dream to go there and take my children on the tea-cup ride," he said (Horowitz 1991:27). Does this suggest that even in fundamentalist Iran, the enforcement of national unity is undermined by global dissemination of culture—that even in the most extreme display of national sentiment, global relationships remain in place, not just for an elite, but for common citizens as well? Or does it mean that the two phenomena, nationalism and globalism, can coexist—can persist as two separate codes circulating along coexisting circuits, codes that interact but do not cancel each other out—and thus refigure even fundamentalist nationalism for an era of cultural heterogeneity and multiple subject positions?

3

Constructing a Nation,
Constructing a Narrative

In THE ANTICOLONIAL revolutionary nationalism that followed
World War II, culture played a more complex and aggressively politicized
role than it had in nostalgic nationalism. Nostalgia for a primordial, essentialist, precolonial past was no more than an element in a more complicated process and was finally assigned by theorists like Frantz Fanon to a
compromised early position in the dialectic of nation-formation. In the
process of transforming "culture" into a more aggressively politicized
term, however, contradictions that we have seen to lie at the heart of its use
by nostalgic nationalism—in particular, the participation of global factors
and material in the construction of supposedly local cultures—came more
and more to the fore. The use of "culture" by postwar revolutionary nationalism is an interesting case of a term being advanced more assertively
just when contradictions that formed part of its history were rising to the
surface.

Thanks to the sharp, even absolute, boundary line that anticolonial
nationalism sought to draw, particularly in its revolutionary struggles,
between itself and the colonial powers, the problems of creating a separate
national community were intensified. First, such a community had to be
assembled from the conflicting motives of primordialism and commitment to modernization along either capitalist or socialist paths. In many
ways, nostalgia and revolution stood in opposition to each other, and
Western-educated anticolonial revolutionary elites committed to modernization sharply debated the role of primordialist ideology in the formation of new states. Moreover, if primordialism was rejected or sharply
hedged, as it often was, the problem of detaching modernization from
imitative Westernization remained. As Arlif Dirlik puts it, socialist leadership hoped to create "a new culture which is neither of the West nor of the
past" (1991:400).

Second, in effecting social transformations, there was tension between an elite (or new government) guiding (or constructing) an "authentic" or legitimate narrative of revolutionary development and an elite that proved tyrannical and manipulative, systematically enforcing the false, top-down, invented ideology Benedict Anderson has called "Russifying official nationalism" (1983:104). The extremely precarious legitimacy of "authentic" national narratives could be exposed in the new states either in Soviet-style repression (as in Nuruddin Farah's Somalia) or neocolonial co-optation (as in Ngũgĩ wa Thiong'o's Kenya).

Third, such a community required the construction and maintenance of firm, even absolute, boundary lines between it and the colonial powers, at the same time as it needed to deal with the legacy of a hybrid colonial past. Anticolonial nationalism sought to terminate the legacy of colonialism, but national frontiers were formed by colonial boundary lines that did not reflect precolonial groupings, and the experience of colonialism had irremediably altered precolonial cultural patterns. To establish absolute boundary lines by exorcising the colonial past—to achieve "liberation," an absolutizing term—was a difficult project, given the simultaneous need to internalize the mixed colonial legacy of victimization, accommodation, acculturation, and humiliation, a legacy that was finally not external but internal to colonized states and psyches.

Last, the creation of a separate national community required a strategy for managing contemporary international relationships. Nationalist separatism, the creation of sharply bounded communities, was also very much a part of a world system polarized between capitalism and communism, and these blocs were locked in a struggle over the Third World. In turn, emerging Third World nations saw themselves involved in an international project: they sought to forge a new path, one that would, to paraphrase Fanon's satire of the pretensions of Western humanism, reintroduce mankind into the world. The result of all of these contradictions and stresses was that culture became simultaneously a question and a weapon.

In its ascendancy and decomposition, then, postwar anticolonial nationalism put the assumption that national identity was the most fundamental basis for global cultural, political, and economic relationships to the harshest test. In its eventual failure, moreover, it was prophetic of new, overtly very different conceptualizations of global order and worldwide cultural relationships. In this chapter, we shall look closely at a series of novels, from Southeast Asia, Africa, and the Caribbean, about revolutionary nationalist movements, and at the problematic role played in them by the notion of culture as they dramatize and analyze the struggle for national independence and, in the process, advance their own particular arguments about the complex relationships between revolutionary nation formation and culture.

Kanthapura (1938), Raja Rao's great novel about Indian nationalism, written before statehood, provides an important baseline for highlighting differences in postwar texts. Rao's novel focuses on the formation and temporary defeat of Gandhian resistance in Kanthapura, a village in the mountains of the Malabar coast. Actually, *Kanthapura* is more than that: it is as much an introduction for the Westerner to the civilization and history of India as it is a novel about a particular phase of India's history. Roughly a quarter of the text consists of footnotes by Rao explaining untranslated terms, describing historical events, summarizing philosophical movements, retelling the lives of sages, providing ethnographic material, and recounting traditional tales, myths, and epic narratives. In the author's foreword, Rao writes of how he tried to adapt English to Indian circumstances:

> We cannot write like the English. We should not. We cannot write only as Indians. We have grown to look at the large world as part of us. Our method of expression therefore has to be a dialect which will some day prove to be as distinctive and colorful as the Irish or the American. . . . After language the next problem is that of style. The tempo of Indian life must be infused into our English expression, even as the tempo of American or Irish life has gone into the making of theirs. We, in India, think quickly, we talk quickly, and when we move we move quickly. There must be something in the sun of India that makes us rush and tumble and run on. And our paths are paths interminable. The *Mahabharata* has 214,788 verses and the *Ramayana* 48,000. The *Puranas* are endless and innumerable. We have neither punctuation nor the treacherous "ats" and "ons" to bother us—we tell one interminable tale. Episode follows episode, and when our thoughts stop our breath stops, and we move on to another thought. This was and still is the ordinary style of our storytelling. I have tried to follow it myself in this story. (Rao 1963:vii–viii)

The novel's extensive footnotes form part of the "interminable tale," adding to it episode after episode.

One of the salient features of Rao's comments about the problems of writing his Indian novel in English—something reflected also in the novel's depiction of the village and its people—is the remarkable (and confidently unexplained) coexistence of conscious syncretism and civilizational unity. There is a firmly bounded Indian "we"; indeed, it seems to be a community created by nature, not just mere history; there is something in the "sun" of India that makes Indians act as they do. This community has corresponding cultural coherence and distinctiveness: its great epics govern its folkways, binding it together into a cultural whole, and it has its own distinctive style of narrative art, cultural practices, consciousness, and sensibility. At the same time, Rao's own text is part of an explicitly syncretic literature, and the "we" mysteriously becomes the Anglo-Indian: "the tempo of our Indian life must be infused into our English expression."

Rao saw this duality as inherent in India, not just in his personal literary goals. He found his syncretic literary project difficult, as "one has to convey the various shades and omissions of a certain thought-movement that looks maltreated in an alien language." Quickly qualifying himself, Rao goes on: "I use the word 'alien,' yet English is not really an alien language to us. It is the language of our intellectual make-up—like Sanskrit or Persian was before—but not of our emotional makeup. We are all instinctively bilingual, many of us writing in our own language and in English" (vii). English is alien, yet not alien; indeed, it is part of a tradition of precolonial Indian syncretism, during which India absorbed successive waves of conquerors and languages. Such an essentializing strategy that paradoxically welcomes syncretism, and a process that operated precolonially as well as in colonial times, is close in many ways to patterns in nationalist strategies in Japan. Such similarities, however, evoke differences. Apart from a host of possible historical contrasts, a significant difference in cultural strategy is the tendency in Rao's portrayal of India to fuse tradition with external heterogeneity, in contrast to Japan's complex negotiation of separately held syncretist and essentialist realms. Japan saw itself initially as a "barbarian" country, manipulating the categories of "barbarian" and "middle kingdom" to negotiate a transition between marginality and centrality and constructing, as it did so, the myth of its ancient, unbroken, unviolated tradition to justify this move. By contrast, Rao evokes India's experience as a country whose boundaries have always been violated, a much-invaded land. This porousness, culturally, militarily, and politically, becomes its very strength, making India central rather than peripheral. As a tradition that depicts itself as absorbing conquerors and cultural material from the outside again and again, India has, for Rao, the civilizational complexity to constitute a genuine center. Syncretism, in India, does not just paradoxically reinforce an opposite essentialism, it *is* (more paradoxically still) that essentialism. The only concession to the usual notion of roots is Rao's assertion that the imposed languages of conquerors are rooted somewhat shallowly in their Indian recipients, expressing their intellectual but not their emotional makeups; to this extent only, Rao invokes the notion of an origin apart from syncretism.

The action of *Kanthapura* provides a full-blown realization of a sublime mingling, even coalescence, of the syncretic and the essentialist. The result is that India in the novel fulfills Ricoeur's requirements for a fully civilizational identity. Rao's India shows confidence in a coherence that can best resist effacement by modernism: it clearly possesses a far more finely articulated and deeply rooted identity than (in Ricoeur's terms) mere "national cultures" or "tribal cultures" can muster. Created from an ages-long accretion of heterogeneous material, the composite of contributions from many different eras and cultures, India's civilizational identity is capable of encompassing Western modernism too. And although Kanthapura is only a small village, it is a small *Indian* village, one that is somehow timeless and drenched with the wealth of India's teemingly complex, syncretic-essentialist living past. As Rao writes in the preface,

> There is no village in India, however mean, that has not a rich *sthala-purana*, or legendary history, of its own. Some god or godlike hero has passed by the village—Rama might have rested under this pipal-tree, Sita might have dried her clothes, after her bath, on this yellow stone, or the Mahatma himself, on one of his many pilgrimages, might have slept in this hut, the low one, by the village gate. In this way the past mingles with the present, and the gods mingle with men to make the repertory of your grandmother always bright. (vii)

Steeped in the tones of primordialist nostalgia, such a passage presents a past that is not, however, endangered by modernization, as in Tanizaki, but lavishly alive in the present. Indeed, debate about modernization in India has often differed from debate about modernization in Japan, in that modernization has frequently been styled less as a transformation of the whole society, than as a transformation that has *not* altered the primordial continuums of Indian village life or, more simply, as the addition of yet another cultural element to an already-baffling Indian hodgepodge. Thus, in Kanthapura, characters faced with modern political problems also worship at shrines, tell traditional stories, perform *bhajan* (philosophical hymn singing), attend recitals of *harikathas* (verse narratives extemporized on traditional legends), participate in traditional seasonal festivals, observe the caste system, and honor their local goddess. In the course of these daily events, the past becomes luminously present, and gods enter this world: *Kanthapura* is distinguished by a number of passages of remarkable lyricism.

> Kartik has come to Kanthapura, sisters—Kartik has come with the glow of lights and the unpressed footstep of the wandering gods; white lights from clay trays and red lights from copper stands, and diamond lights that glow from the bowers of entrance leaves; lights that glow from

banana trunks and mango twigs, yellow light behind white leaves, and white light behind green leaves; and night curls through the shadowed streets, and hissing over bellied boulders and hurrying through dallying drains, night curls through the Brahmin street and the Pariah street and the Potters' street . . . and gods walk by lighted streets, blue gods and quiet gods and bright-eyed gods, and even as they walk in transparent flesh the dust sings back to the earth, and many a child in Kanthapura sits late into the night to see the crown of this god and that god. . . . And as they pass by, the dust sinks back into the earth, and night curls again through the shadows of the streets. Oh! have you seen the gods, sister? (81)

In such a wonder-filled version of the Indian "rush and tumble and run on," the village appears to be exactly what Rao's footnotes assure us "the" Indian village has been: "over the centuries . . . relatively unaffected by historical and political changes . . . its cultural continuity intact" (214). This assertion of cultural continuity is still further reinforced by the way the English colonial figures are presented: they remain at the shadowy edge of the picture, masters of the plantation, perceived generically more than individually as the "red-men" (1).

Right in the midst of this uncritically, lyrically evoked, obviously Orientalist, antihistorical cultural primevalism, however—right in the midst of a culture so bounded and coherent that even sanitation, Rao's notes assert, in India is, "like everything, a matter of religion"—the novel dramatizes the beginnings of a modern political movement. But its "modernity" is far from being either monolithic and transformative. As Rao depicts it, rather than Europeanizing and alienating the Indian present from its past, this modernity is almost effortlessly, not only Indianized, but absorbed into the premodern. One stunning short example of the process comes when the narrator—an Indian widow who is described as the "aunt who tells such nice stories" (179)—recounts how one of the local women brought Western learning into the village circle:

Our Rangamma is no village kid. It is not for nothing she got papers from the city, *Tai-nadu, Vishwakarnataka, Deshabhandu,* and *Jayabharatha,* and she knows so many, many things, too, of the plants that weep, of the monkeys that were the men we have become, of the worms, thin-as-dust worms that get into your blood—and give you dysentery and plague and cholera. She told us, too, about the stars that are so far that some have poured their light into blue space long before you were born, long before you were born or your father was born or your grandfather was born; and just as a day of Brahma is a million million years of ours, the day of the stars is a million million times our day, and each star has a sun and each sun has a moon, and each moon has an earth, and some there are that have two moons, and some three, and out there between the folds of the

Milky Way, she told us, out there, there is just a chink, and you put your
eyes to a great tube and see another world with sun and moon and stars,
all bright and floating in the diamond dust of God. (28–29)

As Rangamma related these wonders, Western science ceases to expose
Eastern superstition as primitive, but is absorbed into a more capacious
tradition of Indian storytelling, and the Newtonian mentality that Henry
Kissinger (Said 1978:46–48) once saw as a mark of developed societies is
fully assimilated to premodern wonder, a characteristic, for Kissinger, of
undeveloped cultures. Long before Fritjov Capra (1977), Indian and Chinese cosmologies were made to seem, contrary to the claims of Eurocentrism, not just compatible with, but a more natural locus for modern
cosmological thought than Judeo-Christianity.

The political events of the book also reveal many more examples of
such effortless coalescence. Corner-house Moorthy, the young Gandhian
who radicalizes the village and whom the narrator compares to a "noble
cow" (5), couples politics with traditional religion. It is a vision of convers-
ing with Gandhi that first converts Moorthy to the cause and prompts him
to throw his foreign books out, burn his foreign clothing, and return to
Kanthapura as a Gandhian. When his initial attempts to organize local
protest produce violence, he purifies himself of hatred and anger by fasting
and meditation. Thus, he embodies *ahimsa,* or non-cruelty, an ideal central to Gandhi's spiritual-political campaign of nonviolence. Similarly,
Moorthy's techniques for the political education of the villagers are traditional ceremonies: he arranges a *harikatha* devoted to the story of Gandhi.
Even the village's ruling body, the *panchayat*—so ancient an institution
that glossing the term gives Rao the opportunity to assert that the Indian
village has remained culturally constant over the centuries—becomes, in
Gandhianism, a form of anticolonial organization: Moorthy calls the Congress party the *panchayat* of all India, and forms a local equivalent of it in
Kanthapura. Similarly, newspapers merge with sutras, and the "red-men"
turn into traditional demons: the boundaries between the external and
internal, modern and traditional become completely porous, as the former terms are absorbed effortlessly into the latter.

To stop here, however, would be to simplify the picture dramatically.
This process of Indianization and traditionalization is complicated by the
fact that the novel opposes the invented traditions of Gandhianism to
those "conserved" by a group of "traditional" figures in league with the
colonial powers, although some of them perhaps act out of conscience.
The fact that such an ambiguity exists—that the "traditionalists" do not
appear wholly unambiguously as British-made colonial stooges—means
that it is too simple to say there are two camps, the authentic Indians who

renew their culture (à la Ricoeur) in conversation with modern universal forms and the inauthentic Indians, whose tradition is a creation of Orientalism and colonial management. "Indian tradition" seems indeed to embrace both camps equally warmly; similarly, both seem to be equally syncretic creations.

Thus, Bhatta, a local Brahman who has risen gradually to wealth in the village, loathes Moorthy and all he stands for, even though, as the narrator emphasizes, "there was no money in [that loathing], Sister!" (25) Bhatta's list of complaints includes a variety of ways in which Gandhi's philosophy is a modernizing violation of former tradition: it would abolish caste distinctions and the taboos separating Hindu and Moslem, and encourages women to attend universities and become political agents. Passionately supporting a Swami who, the novel implies, is indeed a tool of the British, Bhatta seeks to have Moorthy named an outcaste, which he subsequently is, horrifying, and ultimately killing, his mother. Even the presence of the British is rationalized, with probably no more of an alteration of tradition than on Gandhi's side. A "toothless old man" mounts the nationalist podium to deliver a tirade:

> "If the white men shall leave us tomorrow it will not be Rama-rajya we have, but the rule of the ten-headed Ravana. What did we have, pray, before the British came—disorder, corruption, and egoism, disorder, corruption, and egoism I say"—he continued, though there were many shouts and booings against him—"and the British came and they came to protect us, our bones and our dharma. . . . For hath not the Lord said in the Gita, 'Whensoever there is ignorance and corruption I come, for I,' says Krishna, 'am the defender of dharma." (88)

Arguing that the "great Queen Victoria" ("may she have a serene journey through the other worlds") had done more to protect that dharma than any Moslem prince had ever done, the old man, in Indianizing the official British line, wreaks no greater change on the "traditional" than those effected by Gandhi's Indianization of anticolonial dissent. More important, the novel does not try to force its readers to make any such distinction between the two practices: it clearly points out the problem, the paradoxical existence of two equally weighted but quite contrary claims, but it does not attempt to enforce a resolution, by seeking, for example, to use a harsh critique of syncretism to promote the creation of "authentic" revolutionary community.

Gandhianism is thus one version of the implementation of profound change, a major act of syncretic creativity; at the same time, however, all such changes are integrated effortlessly into the traditional Indian identity as they alter it. This magical co-enhancement of opposites—essentialism-syncretism, primordialism-modernization—occurs comically and also movingly in the politicization of the town's women. As the political movement gains momentum, and when Rangamma's husband dies, she and Ratna, her widowed, already outspoken and unconventional daughter, become agents to change the roles of women in the community. Rangamma begins to interpret traditional texts in the place of her dead husband, reading them as nationalist allegories; she also begins to teach (storytell) feminist Indian martial history, doing so to transform her peers from Indian wives and widows into Gandhians who will risk their lives alongside the men in protests. When the men object to their women vagabonding about like soldiers, Rangamma negotiates the conflict, remarking, "If we are to help others, we must begin with our husbands" (106). They, she notes, do not really oppose the women's project, but only want to eat on time.

As protests intensify, and the British and their Indian troops and police respond with increasing violence, the women become an integral part of scenes that Rao evocatively describes, scenes of human chaos, astonishing violence and cruelty, and moving communal passion. After nearly being raped, Ratna, rescued by several women (one with a little child), says, when she can speak: " 'Now, sisters, this is no safe place; let us find a refuge,' and somehow we said there's the voice of Rangamma in her speech, the voice of Moorthy, and she was no more the child we had known, nor the slip of a widow we had cursed" (152). In this moment, the spirit passes to Ratna, and she becomes a leader, taking the women to temporary safety.

In thus becoming an avatar proximately of Gandhi and Moorthy, and, more distantly, of Rani Lakshmi Bai, the ancient woman warrior, Ratna is transformed and traditionalized at the same time. The most astonishing of such transformations, however, occurs in the fusion of substance and style in the novel—in a quality that shows especially in the novel's extended depiction of the scenes of disorienting, encompassing violence as the nonviolent protestors are beaten. A brief sample will, however, have to do justice to Rao's style:

> And the Skeffington coolies cry out, "*Mahatma Gandhi ki jai*"; and the coolies of the harvest take it up and shout, "*Mahatma Gandhi ki jai!*" and we are near them and they are near us, and they say something to us and we do not understand what they mutter, and we say "*Mahatma, Mahatma, Gandhi Mahatma!*" and they put their mouths to our ears and say, "*Gandhi Mahatma ki jai!*" and, "Punjab, Punjab!" But our ears are turned to the firing and we strain our eyes to see the coolies on the mound, the coolies of the Skeffington Coffee Estate, but all we hear are shouts and

shrieks and yell. Then, suddenly from the Himavathy bend there is such a rush of more coolies that the soldiers do not know which way to turn, for the city boys are still marching up, and women are behind them, and the crowd behind the women, and there are the coolies across the barricades, and there is such joy that a wild cry of "*Vandè! . . . Mataram! . . .*" gushes from the valley to the mountaintops and all the moonlit sky above us. And the white man shouts a command and all the soldiers open fire and all the soldiers charge—they come rushing toward us, their turbans trembling and their bayonets shining under the bright moon, and our men lie flat on the fields, the city boys and the women, and the soldiers dash upon us and trample over us, and bang their rifle butts against our heads. There are cries and shrieks and moans and groans, and men fly to the left and to the right, and they howl and they yell and they fall and they rise and we rise, too, to fly, but the soldiers have seen us, and one of them rushes toward us, and we are felled and twisted, we are felled and we are kicked, we are felled and the bayonets waved over our faces— and a long time passes before we wake and we find Satamma fainted beside us, and Madamma and I, who were soaking in a ditch, crawl past her. And then there is a shot, and a fleeing man nearby is shot in the chest and he falls over us, and the moon splashes on his moustached face, his peasant blanket soaked in blood, and he slowly lets down his head, crying "Amma, mother! Amm-Amm!" and we wipe the saliva from his mouth, and we put our mouths to his ear and say, "Narayan, Narayan," but he is already dead. (172)

The crowded scene is, of course, reminiscent of Indian temple sculpture overflowing with figural life, with figures pouring beyond any possible frame and giving the impression of abundance of simultaneous motion, rather than construction about a center. Rao's language places the action in an ongoing, unending, perpetual present, into which a phantasmagoria seems free to enter; it dramatizes an event with an abundance of participants and heroes, one in which an excessive, interminable plenitude of particular experience is sustained by a repeated copula expressing the vital, teeming oneness of life. If these stylistic features evoke traditional Indian narrative and plastic arts in a number of different ways, their emotional impact, one of enormous pathos, is also a staple of traditional Indian art. Even the fact that the white men and soldiers are not differentiated in their acts of cruelty—the confusion of cries and howls and blows, rather than pictures of agents performing actions, is typical—helps inscribe them into a traditionalizing portrayal of the oneness of creative-destructive life. These moving tableaux thus recall both Krishna's advice to Arjuna in the *Bhagavad Gita,* legitimizing war because, in the eye of the divine, slayer and slain are indistinguishable, and the story of the demon Ravana that Rao retells in the notes. Offered a choice between ten lives each sweeter than the next, and supreme liberation as a demon to be killed by Siva himself, Ravana chooses demonhood: thus, enemies, under this rephrasing of traditional wisdom via Gandhi's philosophy of nonviolence, may be revealed as anything but that in moments of sublime transformation.

Traditional beliefs and aesthetic forms, in short, are reborn in the midst of depictions of anticolonial protest and the violence that responds to it, even though these depictions are penned in an English conscious of itself as a novel, syncretic style crafted on the peripheries of the British empire. Although the traditional and the modern, the Indian and the English, thus coalesce, Rao retains his clear, critical awareness by showing how their combination can validate very different political positions. It can, as we have seen, validate Bhatta as well as Moorthy, accommodationism as well as resistance. As a result, the novel is not naively nationalist, and the extent to which it endorses the drama it portrays is a difficult question. When Rangamma explicates traditional texts in nationalist terms, she seems to reduce, rather than augment, them; when Moorthy has his vision of the Mahatma, the possibility that the vision has been created in response to his own private psychological needs, rather than being a valid social vision, is definitely suggested. Also, the novel's end displays raggednesses that may mean either the unraveling of the nationalist project or the failure of the traditional fully to absorb the modern: Moorthy abandons the Mahatma in favor of Nehru, as divisions opened up in nationalist unity, and when he returns to a lost Kanthapura, Patel Range Gowda finds his heart wrenched by pangs suggesting that the magical ease with which new and old have coalesced is more fragile a magic than it had seemed. None of these notes goes so far, however, as ironically to sour that magic. The result is the invocation of culture as a strong component in nationalist struggle, while "culture" is simultaneously revealed as a more complex, conflicted, and unreliable a phenomenon than nationalism imagines. Once again, India's civilizational identity looms behind Rao's novel: just as tradition is composed of layer on layer of heterogeneous material, so it can ground—and absorb—a wealth of possible futures.

Indeed, Rao's achievement in the novel is possible thanks to the invocation of just this sort of civilizational identity for India. Civilizational identities (to adapt Whitman, who adapted the *Gita*) are large; they contain multitudes; and they successfully contradict themselves. Such civilizational identity—an identity that can absorb external material and yet retain its boundaries—is, of course, not an internal, or indigenous, creation. It is built upon a history of interaction with Western Oriental studies, an interaction that does not leave India as powerless as Said's *Orientalism* seemed to suppose. Prior to the rise of Indian nationalism, civilizational identity—the strongest form, as Ricoeur makes clear, that a "traditional" cultural identity can take—had built up on collaborative roots. As J. M. Roberts (1976:78) writes,

> British orientalists, at the beginning of the nineteenth century, had begun the rediscovery of classical Indian culture which was essential both to the self-respect of Hindu nationalism and the overcoming of the subcontinent's huge divisions. Indian scholars began to rediscover, under European guidance, the culture and religion in the neglected Sanskrit scriptures; through these they could formulate a conception of a Hinduism far removed from the rich and fantastic, but also superstitious, accretions of its popular form. By the end of the nineteenth century this recovery of the Aryan and Vedic past—Islamic India was virtually disregarded—had gone far enough for Hindus to meet with confidence the reproaches of Christian missionaries and offer a cultural counterattack; a Hindu emissary to a "Parliament of Religions" in Chicago in 1893 not only awoke great personal esteem and obtained serious attention for his assertion that Hinduism was a great religion capable of revivifying the spiritual life of other cultures, but actually made converts.

In Rao's novel, then, civilizational identity provides a strong base for nationalist invention and mobilization of "Indian" culture, while simultaneously offering resources for negotiating the cultural contradictions involved in that project. Discussing post-Orientalist historiography, Gyan Prakash thus dissents from Said's *Orientalism:* although, as he writes, "those inside the structure of Orientalist power [were] allowed little space for resistance," in fact there were "plenty of examples to show that the conflictory economy of orientalism itself provided the basis for challenging colonial power" (1992:179, 180). Prakash then cites nationalist thought in India as an example, arguing that movements like Indian nationalism and "subaltern" resistance struggles "while being constituted by dominant structures, could slip beyond and come back to haunt the conditions of their own constitution" (184). Rao's use of civilizational identity to present India as timeless, bounded, and also syncretically capable of absorbing Western modernity is an example of a strategic use of culture in the manner Prakash describes. Rao used Western civilizational and Orientalist categories to authorize both his stylist innovation and his sympathetic portrayal of Indian nationalism to a Western audience at a time when independence was still an unachieved goal. Orientalism's famous denial of history to the cultures it misrepresented was thus turned, startlingly, to anticolonial ends.

A truly global taxonomy of Orientalisms and of the kinds of resistance their conflictory economies enable has, as far as I know, yet to be written.

V. S. Mudimbe (1988) and Christopher Miller (1985, 1990) have developed an African version of Orientalism, while scholars of (from) Indian and Islamic regions have fleshed out more specific versions for these areas. Miller's *Blank Darkness: Africanist Discourse in French* (1985:16) tries to erect the most comprehensive framework by fitting "Africanist" discourse into an economy with Orientalism:

> the two interlocking profiles of Europe and the Orient leave no room for a third element, endowed with a positive shape of its own; as on a sheet of paper, both of whose sides have been claimed, the third entry [Africa] tends to be associated with one side or the other or to be nullified by the lack of an available slot in our intellectual apparatus. It is Africa that was always labeled the "third part of the world," and Africanist discourse reads as a struggle with the problems inherent in that figure.

Miller thus derives some of the characteristic features of Africa, as rendered by Africanist discourse, from this economy: Africa is, for example, a place of nullity, since, "in the relationship between the self and the other, the third is null." Africans' mental capacities were thus supposed to be null—they became pure human machines "stripped of reasoning faculties and moved only by a blind sensorial *desire*" (18), and the African continent was the unknown, the dark continent. Miller sees "Africanist discourse as an *unhappy* Orientalism, a discourse of desire unfulfilled and unfulfillable" (23).

Miller's work in extending, specifying, and pluralizing the catchall term "Orientalism"—his demonstration that its economy is still more conflictory than we had thought—is important. It provides a different set of distinctions from those of the Marxian tradition as extended by Eric Wolf and Fredric Jameson. They assert that the Third World needs to be differentiated, inasmuch as the expanding capitalist system encountered societies with different social structures and modes of production throughout the world, situations that ranged from the greatest bureaucratic empire of China to tribal societies of Africa. Making such a distinction is different from constructing an economy of colonialisms; it rests on a taxonomy of precontact social forms. Anthony King takes a position similar to that of Jameson and Wolf when, drawing on the work of R. J. Johnston, he uses a slightly different set of criteria to distinguish types of colonized societies on the basis of their social forms when contacted. His categories comprise those that had a highly developed culture and long urban tradition (India, Nigeria); those that had substantial numbers of indigenous inhabitants but few urban settlements (North America); those that had few or no indigenous inhabitants living in an undeveloped social and economic structure; and those that had a sophisticated urban tradition that had declined prior to colonization (the Aztecs) (King 1990a:20–21).

But if Miller's taxonomy of Orientalisms adds an important component to such categorizations and enables a more complex representation of the colonial encounter and subsequent history, one cautionary note must be added. Miller's economy of Orientalisms is too simple and totalizing a schema. It is based on a tripartite division, in which Africanism is the "third" position; but why only three? Why shouldn't there be more? Certainly discourse about the New World represents yet another kind of Orientalism, one that develops into full-blown form sooner, driven by the great opportunities the conquest opened; and shouldn't, moreover, this discourse be divided into at least two parts, one enshrining a construction of "cities of gold" of romance, and the other a "virgin wilderness" pastoralism? Equally problematic, perhaps, is the very attempt to derive differences between Orientalisms from an overall economy—from structural considerations—in place of using the differences of specific histories. Africa is as much indebted to historical circumstances as to its place in a tripartite economy for its enduring identity as the "dark" continent. For example, significant to that "darkness" are the facts that (in contrast to what happened in America) Africans kept the Europeans confined to coastal areas for some time, retaining power as mediators of the slave trade, and disease afflicted the European explorers rather than wiping out the native populations, as it did in America. As Said (1993) has suggested, only a thoroughly differentiated history of Orientalisms would include the wide variety of colonial discourses, from Americanism to Orientalism; would pay attention to the difference between the metropolitan cultures involved, as to the differences of the particular histories of the colonies; and would acknowledge, in each case, the fact that postcolonial knowledge is a contrapuntal phenomenon, predicating an interactive imperial–Third World history and exploring it by means of a dialogue between First and Third World viewpoints. It is, in short, premature for Miller to restrict the economy of Orientalism to three structurally defined parts.

But even if Miller's typology of Orientalisms needs to be made much more complicated, broad contrasts between different Orientalisms can be illuminating. A significant reason for the lack of Third World homogeneity may stem from these sources. The construction of India's civilizational identity that Roberts describes persisted, for example, even when anthropology replaced history as the site of Orientalist construction of India during the nineteenth century (Dirks 1990) and customs such as suttee became the objects of investigation. These customs were studied on the basis of "the fabrication of the lawgiving scriptural tradition as the origins of Hindu customs," Prakash (1992:174) argues, following Lata Mani. Even when India was demoted from being the domain of history and philosophy to being the province of anthropologists, its civilizational identity was preserved; Indian ethnographic "custom" was still embedded in "civilizational" identity.

Africa was not so lucky. In his subsequent study of the relationships of European anthropology with colonial and postcolonial African literature (*Theories of Africans: Francophone Literature and Anthropology in Africa* [1990]), Miller points out the central role played by anthropology in the construction of African identity. Moving from India to Africa involved a relocation from one set of discursive conventions to another—from civilizational studies to anthropology. This made the discursive position of Africans in some ways much more difficult, for in the intellectual economy of the First World, such a change meant moving dramatically downscale. Strongly reinforcing this difference was the way in which the racism inherent in both civilizational studies and anthropology affected the two areas. Whereas racist discourse could, in India, simultaneously privilege the "Aryan" legacy of India, while it demeaned the "Dravidian," in Africa there was no ambiguity to the racial Manicheanism imposed by the colonialists.

Inheriting, politically and economically, a much more balkanized, underdeveloped, and ideologically demeaned area—the site, as Miller puts it, of an "unhappy" Orientalism—African nationalism thus in some ways encountered harsher challenges. At the same time, however, African nationalism had, during its heyday, a far greater impact on the spread of revolutionary nationalism throughout the world than Indian independence did. As the source of the African diaspora, part of the Eurocolonial culture circuit and the New World disaporic circuit, and as the legatee of a colonialism that constructed the most harshly absolute cultural and racial boundary lines, African revolutionary nationalism was in a position to take sharply etched anticolonial positions and spark reactions and imitations throughout the world.

There is potential for opposition in the inheritance in an Africanist version of Rao's nostalgic nationalism—the inheritance in Africa of anthropologically constructed essentialism. This potential surfaced in the *négritude* movement of Léopold Senghor and Aimé Césaire; quickly, however, *négritude* became the subject of heated debate in Africa and was criticized by writers like Fanon, Soyinka, and Ngũgĩ. Senghor's African socialism did not call for independence from France, and *négritude's* interests were judged more cultural than political. More pointedly, its racial essentialism, indebted so clearly (as Miller and Michael Lambert [1993] have shown) to anthropological descriptions of Africans by Europeans such as Maurice Delafosse, Leo Frobenius, and Father Placide Tempels, seemed to continue, rather than rupture, Africa's subordination to Europe. The unhappier Orientalism of Africa seemed not only to have more thoroughly devalued the African past but also to have co-opted more straightforward, culturalist attempts to reverse that devaluation. Criticizing *négritude*, then, Fanon called for liberation in the more complex and conscious terms of political-economy, rather than cultural essentialism; he substituted for the essentialist-culturalist category of blackness the category of the colonized.

Ngũgĩ's novel of Kenyan independence *A Grain of Wheat* (1968) followed Fanon in criticizing the essentialism of *négritude* and presenting a much more demystifying, dialectically historical drama of the struggle for liberation than Rao does. What reinforce each other in Rao—the nationalist movement and primeval Indianness—appear as finally negative in Ngũgĩ. Official nationalism seems fated to turn into neocolonialism and subservience to Europe; and primeval Africanness is revealed as something that has never existed, a myth too easily misused by national demagogues. Instead, true community and culture are, for Ngũgĩ, yoked explicitly to history, and they need to be reinvented within and from it.

In *A Grain of Wheat* no bounded, separate, primordial culture exists in Kenya's present—or ever really existed in its past. True, white characters speak (anthropologically) (Orientalizingly) of "the African." In Africa, Ngũgĩ's John Thompson, the originally idealistic colonialist, changes into a district officer whose cruelty in attempting to repress the Mau Mau rebellion earns him international disrepute and demotion. Thompson first quotes Albert Schweitzer ("The Negro is a child") and then notes, more darkly, "Remember the African is a born actor, that's why he finds it easy to lie" (56). But Thompson is no example to follow: his deterioration in Africa, from idealist to embittered racist, represents an intentionally banalized version of Conrad's Kurtz. Indeed, in meditating on the decay of his original enthusiasms, Thompson quotes with approval Schweitzer's dictum that "Every white man is continually in danger of gradual moral ruin in daily and hourly contact with the African" (56). Thompson's deterioration leads not to metaphysical horror, however, but to a far less stylish, more bourgeoisified set of doldrums: frustrated ambition, misguided cruelty (which he feels is forced on him), marital unhappiness, self-pity, and venal obsession. His fate is similarly devoid of grand theatricality. He fails, leaves Africa, and, persisting in his obsession, prophesies his rebirth as a neocolonialist.

The African characters never use such essentializing language. The novel presents their precolonial past as changing and dissensual, not a matter of timeless essence. The second chapter presents recollections of legendary precolonial history; at various times, men and women have fought each other for power. The English, under Queen Victoria, are then prophetically interpreted as part of that contested history. Similarly, contemporary neo-colonialism reminds Warui, a village elder, of "how people once rose against women-rulers who enriched themselves and forgot the responsibility of their office" (171). More explicit still is the way Warui, in his moments of nostalgia, evokes precolonial tribal conflicts that clearly do not provide a timeless model for anticolonial mobilization. Hearing Lieutenant Koina talk about the hardships of the Mau Mau fighters, Warui bursts in:

> "Cold? I always say this. The young of these days have lost their strength. They cannot resist a tiny illness. Do you know in our days we would lie in the forest nights long waiting for Masai? The wind rubbed our necks. As for our clothes, they were drenched with dew. Yet you would not hear a cough in the morning. No, not even a small one."
> The two freedom fighters looked at Warui. They had been in the forest for more than seven years. But nobody challenged Warui's claim. (21)

On the real social level, as opposed to what is spuriously manufactured in nationalist public rhetoric, no primordial African warrior spirit is reborn in the freedom fighters. Warui's memories are inapposite in that they evoke a very different frame, pitting African against African, contrary to the hopes of anticolonial resistance and nationalist community building. Although his comments are received respectfully, they are absorbed with some detachment: the freedom fighters' silence hints that these memories are perhaps an old man's exaggerated recollections. Just as Githua lies in claiming that his shattered leg is a result of heroic assistance to the freedom fighters—it was broken in a lorry accident—Warui may have distorted memories of his youth. (Of Githuya, General R. remarks, "He invents a meaning for his life, you see. Don't we all do that?" [152]). Most probably, given Warui's status as an elder, the silence following his memories expresses respect given to someone whose status calls for it—respect, however, that masks impatience with his interruption of a conversation the others wish to return to, as indeed they immediately do. Warui's evocation of the past thus does not stand as model for the present; it simply interrupts it.

Sharply contrasting with these openings for primordialism that the novel intentionally raises and rejects is a tradition that is elaborated in detail and presented as vital. This is the tradition of resistance, one that runs from Waiyaki, who was martyred after doing battle with the whites' encroaching "iron snake" (12), through the early reformer Harry Thuku, who was imprisoned, to the Mau Mau, the "Movement" of the novel. This is the lineage of the Movement—the vital force for liberation in the novel, in contrast to the Party that negotiates political independence; the Movement does not predate colonialism, but is coeval with it. Indeed, Ngũgĩ transforms Achebe's nostalgically conceived hero Okonkwo from a protagonist who, for all his flaws, is a tragic hero, representative of a culture erased by the British, into an icon of modern, anticolonial struggle. Waiyaki, the comparable figure in *A Grain of Wheat,* stands for the future, not the past; the novel's epitaph for him echoes its epigraph from 1 Corinthians 15:36:

> Waiyaki's blood contained within it a seed, a grain, which gave birth to a movement whose main strength thereafter sprang from a bond with the soil. (12)

Significantly, where a primordialist would locate a people's foundational bond with its soil in dim precolonial history, Ngũgĩ inscribes it in the beginning of resistance to colonialism.

Ngũgĩ's construction of tradition, then, is an example of what Arlif Dirlik calls "Marxist culturalism," once he has distinguished the latter term sharply from its usual associations. This "culturalism" deploys culture as a liberating practice, criticizing the conventional notion of tradition as "a burden of the past upon the present, an inert legacy that shapes the consciousness of people with its own prerogatives" (1991:407). By contrast, Dirlik shows how Frantz Fanon suggests a very different conception of culture, and Fanon's description was clearly a model for Ngũgĩ's thematization of culture in *A Grain of Wheat.*

> A national culture [Fanon wrote] is not a folklore, nor an abstract populism that believes it can discover the people's true nature. It is not made up of the inert dregs of gratuitous actions which are less and less attached to the ever-present reality of the people. A national culture is the whole body of efforts made by a people in the sphere of thought to describe, justify and praise the action through which the people has created itself and keeps itself in existence. (Dirlik 1991:422)

As Abdul JanMohamed (1983) has shown, Fanon's influence on *A Grain of Wheat* is direct: a "substantial change in Ngũgĩ's style and vision" was caused "in part by his reading of Frantz Fanon's *The Wretched of the Earth*" (209). Generally speaking, Fanon helped Ngũgĩ "subordinate the egoistic messianic fantasies" of his previous characters (and, as James Olney [1973] points out, of the Gikuyu messianic tradition) to "the more substantial economic and political concerns that naturally dominate a colonized society which is fighting to regain control of itself" (222). While Ngũgĩ was deeply influenced by Fanon, however, he modifies or disputes a number of Fanon's key ideas; a variety of specific ways in which he does so will become apparent below.

Thanks to his clear-sighted revision of essentialism and his encounter with *The Wretched of the Earth* (1963), then, Ngũgĩ is able to portray colonial history complexly and seriously. Along with chronicling the rise of the Movement, Ngũgĩ documents oppression and resistance, dramatizing how colonialism reshaped Kenya. Oppression caused shame; colonialism did not remain an external enemy to be driven out by those who drew on the resources of a suppressed, but unpolluted, tradition, but violated and altered people profoundly. Thus Mumbi's father, "once a warrior whose name spread from Nyeri to Kabete, urinated on his legs . . . [and] wept the night long like a child" after he saw Kihika, his freedom fighter son, caught and hanged. The depths and profound implications of such shame—which the book portrays as gnawing at almost every character, no matter how overtly noble his or her actions seem—is perhaps the major concern of the book; shame, not Fanonian violence or nationalist celebration, becomes the chief source of hope for creating a real, not spuriously neocolonial, community out of indepndent Kenya.

A Grain of Wheat contains many resurrections, many instances of the sprouting of the seed adumbrated in the novel's epigraph. Waiyaki is buried and resurrected as the Movement's founder; Kihika's spirit similarly rises again from his crucifixion. This pattern resembles, but crucially deviates from, the logic of Fanon, when he wrote that life could "only spring up again out of the rotting corpse of the settler" (1963:93). For Fanon, the absolute Manicheanism of the colonial situation makes the revolutionary people; revolutionary violence strengthens this strictly demarcated community, as those who commit acts of terrorism erect boundaries between themselves and the colonial authorities, supplementing those the racist authorities have themselves been imposing for years. Thus the rotting corpse of the settler gives birth, via violence, to the revolutionary community. In Ngũgĩ, in sharp contrast, the rebirth comes from the Africans themselves, from what they have suffered and had been tainted by, not their violent resistance. Thus the most deeply inscribed pattern of the novel—the pattern at the heart of all its instances of genuine community formation—is the greater or lesser resurrection of individual characters from their private agonies of shame. These painful rebirths come as a crucial part of a dialectical narrative, and they come, it is crucial to point out at the outset, against the precepts of *both* unreconstructed, superstitious traditionalism and official nationalism. Public rhetoric asks that people not harrow up the painful and guilty past in the new independent Kenya; traditionalism fears exhuming the spirits of the dead from their graves.

Ngũgĩ thematizes his dialectical narrative of revolutionary community formation most clearly and interestingly, perhaps, in his references to the train Waiyaki fights against. The arrival of the train is foretold by a seer and contested by a warrior; it then becomes the pride of the valley (people feel the railway line and train to have "a mystical union with Thabai" [71]) even as it represents colonial underdevelopment and exploitation (in Stavrianos's terms, it becomes a means of turning inner Africa—lands still beyond the embrace of Eurocapitalism—into part of the underdeveloped Third World). Participating in their own domination and forming a syncretic local custom, people make the "railway platform . . . the meeting place for the young"; "love-affairs were often hatched there, many marriages with their attendant cry of woe or joy had their origin at the station platform" (71). Just as colonial development is not harmless, the growing communal, customary importance of gathering at the station becomes something like a drug:

> The train became an obsession: if you missed it, sorrow seized your heart for the rest of the week; you longed for the next train. Then Sunday came, you went there on time, and immediately you were healed.
> From the station they normally went to dance in Kinenie Forest overlooking the Rift Valley. . . . Men bought dances. . . . The conventions governing the dances in the wood were well understood.
> Often the dances ended in fights. (71)

Hinted at here are the simultaneous historical development of colonial assimilation/submission (the railroad becomes central); the colonial invention of "tribalism" (the modern, Western trading center is opposed to the "woods" where blacks now gather for dances and unregulatable conflict); and the divisive impact of capitalism and colonial management by fomenting discord (after they *buy* the dances, they fight with each other).

A turning point in local history comes when Gikonyo and Mumbi make their match, not at the train, but in the forest. On hearing the train approach, Gikonyo and his rival for Mumbi, Karanja, begin a footrace to the station, each man competing for Mumbi. To Gikonyo's chagrin, Karanja draws ahead of both Gikonyo and Mumbi, but Gikonyo is more than rewarded when Mumbi suggests they miss the train. They then go into the forest and make love, Gikonyo removing her clothes "as if performing a dark ritual in the wood" (91): "their breath was now one. The earth moved beneath their body in the stillness" (91).

This union is particularly significant. Mumbi, daughter of one of the great precolonial warriors, sister to the resistance fighter Kihika, "never went to the dances in the forest" but "lay in the sun and ardently yearned for a life in which love and heroism, suffering, and martyrdom were possible. She had fed on stories in which Gikuyu women braved the terrors of the forest to save people, or beautiful girls [were] given to the gods as sacrifice before the rains" (76). Like Kenya seeking independence, her body is pictured as "expressive of a resilient desire for life despite suffering" (136); equally significant is her marriage to Gikonyo, a woodworker whose feel for his craft evoked traditional associations between magic and artisans' craftsmanship ("the touch of wood always made him want to create something. . . . Her [Mumbi's] voice was in the air as he bent down and traced the shape of the panga on the wood. Her breath gave him power" [81]). Their marriage, then, is symbolically associated with Kihika's dream of a Kenya that "belongs to black people. . . . it does not belong to the whiteman. And even if it did, shouldn't everybody have a share in the common shamba, our Kenya? The soil belongs to the Kenyan people. Nobody has the right to sell or buy it" (98–99).

This myth of restored primordialism, however, is also spurious. The significance of the "primordial" forest was manufactured as a part of the colonial era. Furthermore, it is evoked only to be shattered, to die, and be painfully resurrected as something else. At first, though, Mumbi and Gikonyo's forest-based marriage is paired with the establishment of Kihika's forest-based resistance group, and both embody the attempt to make revolutionary use of nostaligic nationalism. Ngũgĩ follows Fanon, at least roughly, in this plotting of revolutionary development: both assign what is valuable in heroic primordialism, a moment they both also see as European-mediated and spurious, to the early phases of nationalist resistance.

At the same time that nationalist resistance locates itself literally and symbolically in the forest, the colonialist side attaches itself more unequivocally to the train. Thus, on finding himself at the train station alone, the disappointed suitor, Karanja, figures out what happened between Mumbi and Gikonyo in the woods and experiences a bitter, harrowing vision: "each man was alone," and men are locked into Darwinian struggle with each other. The content of this vision—the ideology of colonialism in its cruelest, starkest form—is belied by the fact that, when he begins to faint and is about to fall under the wheels of the train, he is rescued by an unknown neighbor; but, false or not, it marks Karanja's future. He goes on to become a collaborator with the British, betrays comrades as an informer, murders and persecutes them as a British-installed tribal headman, and is finally a subservient aide to Thompson, anxious lest his master, like white power itself, leave Kenya at independence. Nationalist resistance was thus born in sync with collaborationists' nihilistic introjection of the oppressor's ideology.

Thus, the train platform and the forest, which were the scenes of the creation of syncretic-colonial "African" traditions, now become the sites of the creation of sharply bounded, separate communities, the community of revolutionaries and the anticommunity of the colonialists and their minions. Revolutionary community, dedicated to the myth of restoring land to its supposedly primordial possessors by means of revolutionary violence, is thereby invented, and "forest" and "train" take on new meanings. The train is no longer associated with African assimilation to colonialism (people "went less to the train" [100]), becoming, instead, the locus for collaborationism; the forest, having lost its genuinely precolonial associations as a place of terrors that "Giikuyu women braved . . . to save people" [76]) and also its colonial associations as the locus of colonialist-manufactured divisive tribalism, takes on the associations of a very different, invented, revolutionary "primordialism."

This revolutionary invocation of primordialism—the claim that the soil belonged anciently to Kenya and has be restored to its proper people in its proper form, as sacred, communal land—is an essential part of Kihika's ideals and, as such, has nobility and power. Their nobility and power, however, simply do not survive the complexities of their success; roughly following Fanon's description of the radicalization of the native intellectual, Ngũgĩ ascribes Kihika's primordialist ideals to an early stage in the revolutionary dialectic. More depressingly, again following Fanon, Ngũgĩ shows how, as independence approaches, their continuation becomes more and more a sham. Public nationalist ceremonies that suppress the real shame and guilt of the colonial past under a veneer of triumph and install a "Kenyan" government that is in fact anything but "Kenyan" (white economic interests are untouched) blatantly uses primordialist symbolism. Such symbolism is a way for the government to legitimize itself and dupe the people. Ngũgĩ portrays this co-optation of primordialism by the national bourgeoisie with Fanonian harshness: the corrupt M.P. who praised Gikonyo's "real Harambee spirit" (60) while, thanks to his connections with the whites and his government office, he is cheating him in a business deal, is one of the book's least attractive characters and symbol of the potential for a profound disillusionment. Postindependence Kenya is *not* returned to primordial owners but handed over, as Fanon describes in a chapter entitled "The Pitfalls of National Consciousness," to the international alliance of bourgeois nationalists, now neocolonial elite, and the former colonialists.

The most moving, and painful, parts of *A Grain of Wheat* explore this disillusionment and the possibility of forming a different, genuinely Kenyan, community not despite it, but *because* of it. To contrast my discussion of *A Grain of Wheat* so far with my comments on *Kanthapura,* it is clear, first, that whereas Rao looks back to timeless cultural essence and a bounded cultural whole in India's past, Ngũgĩ finds this problematic: for the Marxist writer Ngũgĩ, history is real, and culture is part of a process of dialectical invention. No bounded, timeless past ever existed, and the visions of the past are successively reconstructed as present circumstances change. Thus, when Rao shows, magically, the development of political nationalism as a syncretic form, he shows it as something that grafts "English" material onto "Indian" tradition *without,* however, deeply disturbing that tradition. Real change occurs, but the timeless quality of Indian culture remains paradoxically untouched, and Rao's style seeks fulfillment in moments of timeless lyricism or, if action is depicted, the kinetic simultaneity of Indian temple sculpture. Ngũgĩ, on the other hand, dramatizes the attempt to develop a genuine Kenyan community as a dialectical historical narrative, something that proceeds connectedly, and irreversibly, through time.

A second, closely related contrast can now be pointed out, if we examine Ngũgĩ's portrayal of disillusionment with early primordialist ideals. Moorthy is a stronger version of what we find in Tanizaki: a person who, in a visionary moment, finds timeless Indian traditions reborn in front of him. Moorthy encounters them, not solely as a private, nostalgic return to endangered *Boden,* as in Tanizaki, but much more vigorously, as part of an ongoing, public, yet visionary project for the future, and the pathos of Rao's novel is greatest when it mingles present suffering with this intense, visionary hope for the future—a moving populist vision, shared by all involved. In sharp contrast, although almost all of Ngũgĩ's characters experience visions, those visions are *all* thoroughly—painfully and shamefully—denied by fact. The resulting sense of disgrace, mortification, anger, guilt, and failure these messy, painful disillusionments produce, moreover, isolate each character, locking each in a private miasma that the public ceremonies of independence only intensify, as none wishes to reveal his/her past shame and betrayals in the face of such supposedly triumphant solidarity. Only the painful dialectic of digging up of the buried past—a sprouting of a grain of wheat that means the death of one's old self—leads to hope of forming real community in Kenya. Harrowing confession out of the ruin of one's visions and hopes, not passionate, communal pursuit of blessed vision, is what yields community.

In his depiction of this process of community formation by harrowing up the guilt and compromise of the colonial past and years of resistance, Ngũgĩ also most significantly departs from the influence of Fanon. Ngũgĩ's version of the Mau Mau rebellion does not find, as Fanon does, its institutionalization of violence psychologically liberating. Fanon supports what he describes as the Mau Mau requirement "that each member of the group should strike a blow at the victim" because the others can then be "sure of the new recruit . . . [who] could no longer go back into the colonial system" (1968:85). Fanon sees such violence as a means of creating an absolutely bounded revolutionary community, one that inverts colonialism's equally absolute Manicheanism. Such a firmly bounded community, Fanon goes on to argue, forms the basis for the new national community after liberation. For Ngũgĩ's characters, however, violence is not the basis of postindependence community; it results in public vainglory and private, isolating shame rather than communal mutuality. Real community is formed through harrowing confession and exposure of the vulnerability, betrayal of self and others, shame, and guilt that participation in the colonial system and resistance against it inevitably involve.

Each character experiences his or her own vision and, subsequently, his or her own degrading disillusionment. Some of these failures and painful recognitions are presented briefly, some extensively. Lieutenant Koina, for example, has a vision of black power in Africa. As one who is always "demanding his rights" (213), he is kicked out of his factory job, even though he has served the white man during the war and feels this entitles him to more equal treatment. He then works as a servant for Dr. Lynd, whose dog he tends and likes. Worsley's comments about rich world cats have a bitter colonial ancestor in *A Grain of Wheat*: Koina realizes that "the amount of steak the dog ate could have fed a whole family. The amount of money spent on the dog was more than the total wages of ten Kenyans" (213). Joining the resistance, then, Koina comes back and slaughters the dog (which has run to him affectionately) in front of the horrified Dr. Lynd. For Dr. Lynd, this is an experience of Conradian horror, and as staff member under Thompson, she keeps a new dog, one that terrorizes African workers, whom she regards as savages. Koina's Fanon-like vision of liberation through violence is, however, also shattered: it fails when he sees postindependence Kenya still in the power of the whites. Lynd and Koina's nadir comes when they encounter each other at the end of the book; both are deeply shaken. Lynd is filled with terror at being exposed to such monsters in postindependence Kenya, and with his perception of universal vulnerability, Ngũgĩ portrays Koina's reactions as similar: "And there in front of him was Dr. Lynd and her dog. She stood there as if she was mocking him: See me, I have still got the big house, and my property has even multiplied. . . . Doubts stabbed him. It filled him with fear, a kind of premonition. He had tried to share those thoughts with General R., but he could not find the words" (214).

Both Lynd's fantasies of colonial virtue—her pride that she has always treated her servants fairly—and Koina's visions of black power are shattered in mutual humiliation. Each demonizes the other in their later encounter, each sees the other as unaffected, mocking, empowered. And neither expresses that sense of shame. Although Lynd tries to do so with Thompson, he cannot bear to listen to her; and Koina is unable to find the words. The fear and vulnerability they experience remained locked inside them.

Hope of a genuine Kenyan community rests, in fact, not on victory, but on how the failure of dreams is managed. All the English characters are incapable of confessing shame and failure. Thompson's wife, who has an affair with one of her husband's colleagues, never reveals it. Thompson never speaks to his wife of his failure as district officer, and he reacts to independence with renewed fantasies of domination through neocolonial control. Lynd and Koina, obviously, never cross boundaries to speak to each other of their mutual abhorrence and fear. The manipulative triumphalism of bourgeois nationalist rhetoric in Kenya forbids genuine public exploration of the past. The only place where such healing occurs is among members of the former resistance movement and the victims of colonial repression who are willing or forced to explore the shame of their past—a group that does not, of course, include the many collaborationists or neutrals who rush into Kenya's postindependence oligarchy. The specifically Kenyan community that can form, then, is *not* a primordial racial, ethnic, or cultural community. It is a specific subgroup created by a historical dialectic of shame: a group whose spirit, like Waiyaki's, is resurrected from the failure of their hopes, sprouting like the grain of wheat from burial and death.

Two examples of the process must suffice. Gikonyo, who has been arrested as a Mau Mau and sent to detention camp, is able to return years later only through an act of betrayal. Although Gikonyo does not implicate others, he betrays his oath in return for liberation from the camp. He does so because of a vision he has of his home with Mumbi, which is the one thing he has clung to in the prison camp. This is, in turn, humiliatingly frustrated when he finds on returning that Mumbi has had a child in his absence—a child, moreover, by his hated rival, the collaborationist Karanja. Incredulous, then deeply embittered, he takes up life with her again in furious silence and begins a compensatory career as a capitalist entrepreneur. But this career is itself a sour, embittered death-in-life:

"Thabai was just another detention camp" and (echoing the nihilistic vision on the train platform of his enemy Karanja) "to live and die alone was the ultimate truth" (117). Before, when he lived happily with Mumbi, "wealth and power were not important unless they enriched that silent communion from which living things heaved and opened to the sun. The silence which he had now returned to was dead" (116–17). A joyless capitalist, afflicted with a version of Karanja's vision of Darwinian loneliness, Gikonyo is trapped in his private hell.

Mumbi is also trapped in hers. She too has experienced bitter failure, failure of her vision of herself as African heroine. Her seduction by Karanja is nothing near as lurid as Gikonyo pictures it; and her shame, self-mortification, and isolation are, if anything, more intense because of her realization of this. Behind the seduction lies Mumbi's gradual, wearying victimization in the concentration camp Thabai becomes under Karanja's tribal chieftainship. More important, what triggers it is not an act of oppression she could heroically have tried to resist: indeed, she does repeatedly resist Karanja's threatening advances. What leads to the seduction is instead a moment when the boundaries between the oppressor's tool Karanja and the oppressed Kenyan populace temporarily blur. In a moment of kindness, perhaps of renunciation of his lust for Mumbi, Karanja tells Mumbi Gikonyo is to be released from prison. The result is not the prolonged relationship Gikonyo imagines, but a single, confused act of infidelity.

Both Mumbi and Gikonyo dredge up memories in the course of the novel, in painful conversations with Mugo, who becomes the novel's central figure in this drama of confession. At the novel's end, they are ready to begin the process of speaking to each other again and restoring their marriage. An intensely private man who was orphaned and abused as a child, Mugo is hailed, after the rebellion, as a hero: in Thabai, he has defended a woman from the cruelty of Karanja's minions and was subsequently interned and tortured relentlessly, never giving in. In reality, however, Mugo is the novel's biggest betrayer. He was the one who turned Kihika in, who set him up for capture and execution. Mugo's betrayal arises from causes as complex and human as Mumbi's; a recluse with a painful upbringing, he felt Kihika had violated his visionary dream of solitude by implicating him in the Mau Mau resistance. Mugo's ultimate confession is the climax of the novel. Chosen to be the chief symbolic figure—the great hero—of the independence ceremonies, he confesses his betrayal of Kihika publicly on the platform; the depths of the shame of the past are revealed at last, in full daylight, in the midst of the ceremony supposed to celebrate victory. Mugo's indictment of himself saves Karanja from certain death at the

hands of the resistance fighters, who believe he was the one who betrayed
Kihika; it also triggers the final exorcism of the past that brings Gikonyo
and Mumbi to the point of healing and recementing their marriage.

The last chapter, entitled "Harambee," describes this movement toward
reconciliation—a reconciliation that clearly stands as the genuine opposite to the nostalgic nationalist misuse of this term by the corrupt M.P. At
the chapter's (and book's) end, Gikonyo, in the hospital because of an
Independence Day accident, is at last able to envision completing a design
he has thought about for some time: a "wedding gift, a stool carved from
Muiri wood." While in the prison camp dreaming of home, he has tried to
imagine how he wants to style this gift for Mumbi. He has brooded on the
contradictory goals of revolutionary nostalgic nationalism—namely,
carving a "traditional Gikuyu stool"—and revolutionary modernization,
wanting to "carve one which would be different from any others" (109).
Meditating on it for over a year, he is never able to think of a motif. Now, at
the book's end, after this earlier vision has been shattered, and the shame,
anger, and guilt thereby produced dealt with, Gikonyo almost has his
design:

> He would now carve a thin man, with hard lines on the face, shoulders
> and head bent, supporting the weight. His right hand would stretch to
> link with that of a woman, also with hard lines on the face. The third
> figure would be that of a child on whose head or shoulders the other two
> hands of the man and woman would meet. Into that image would he
> work the beads on the seat? A field needing clearance and cultivation? A
> jembe? A bean flower? He would settle this when the time came. (246)

This last uncertainty is resolved in the book's final sentence: "I'll change
the woman's figure. I shall carve a woman big—big with child" (247).

The completion of the design represents persistence and change—a
traditional art renewed—and also the incorporation of colonial syncretism experienced as violation: the child of Karanja, the collaborationist,
links the two adults together. It also expresses hope for a new future: the
woman is pregnant. Gikonyo completes his design at the same time as he
realizes that he and Mumbi will be reconciled; he also realizes, however,
that Mumbi has changed too, into a new, empowered woman, and that "in
the future he would reckon with her feelings, her thoughts, her desires—a
new Mumbi" (247). Thus, the conflictual legacy of precolonial feminism
(the woman rulers and men's opposition to them) is transformed at the
same time as it is continued. Ending in these reconciliations, the novel
does not, however, generalize them finally to all Kenya: Mugo's revelations, his transformation of the Independence Day ceremonies into a moment when real community could be built, leads to his death at the hands

of General R. and Lieutenant Koina, and Gikonyo's private happiness does not do anything to change the fact that Kenya is still in the hands of the neocolonial bourgeoisie.

Both *A Grain of Wheat* and *Kanthapura* consciously examine the processes they dramatize. Both dramatize movements toward the formation of new nations, but both expose conflicts as much as they seek closures. Both portray attempts to re-situate nationalism to the Third World. Rao's novel finds possibilities for opposition in the heart of Orientalist civilizationalism, while Ngũgĩ's draws on the First World counterdiscourse of dialectical materialism to oppose a First World discourse of racist anthropology.

Ngũgĩ's novel is, as we have seen, more painfully conflictual than Rao's, as he negotiates, by means of a dialectical narrative, much sharper contradictions than Rao does between traditionalism and modernization, cultural primordialism and the fabrication of national culture, revolutionary exorcism and syncretic absorption, colonial cruelties and colonial legacies. Unlike Rao, Ngũgĩ cannot invoke tradition and traditional community as a rich given and a resource for action. Africa's unhappier Orientalism—which has constructed its primordial identity via the more harshly racist and downscale "othering" of anthropological discourse—gives vastly less basis for resistance and the formation of new national community than the more complexly ambiguous discourse of Indian Orientalism. Instead, then, Ngũgĩ turns to politics, history, and dialectical materialism, rather than culturalism, as his chief resources. His narrative thus embodies the painful dialectical process of creating an imagined community out of preexisting fragments in Kenya: of creating a separated/separate nation and culture out of the fragments of dissensual precolonial tradition and the fracturing legacy of colonialism.

Although in his perception of vulnerability and shame as the basis of community, and in his detached yet compassionate portrayal of the whites, Ngũgĩ invokes more of the inheritance of Western humanism than Fanon does with his emphasis on the inversion of colonial Manicheanism by violence, the boundary lines both men seek to draw about their imagined revolutionary communities are, of necessity, strongly marked: they have to be, to oppose and exorcise the racial Manicheanism of African colonialism. But there is a price for such intensified exorcism: in an increasingly interconnected world, strong boundary lines are becoming harder and harder to maintain. In sharp contrast to Rao's timeless, porous, syncretic-essentialism, even Ngũgĩ's humanist portrayal of dialectical Manicheanism reveals the difficulty, pain, and above all, uncertainty involved in creating and then policing cultural and social boundary lines.

General R. and Lieutenant Koina execute Mugo even as his confession psychologically liberates Gikonyo, and Mumbi betrays Gikonyo when the boundaries between antagonistic sides momentarily blur. Similarly, Ngũgĩ's optimism about the future is extremely limited. In *A Grain of Wheat*, Ngũgĩ rescues only a small measure of hope for the formation of a separate national community against the increasing threat of a neo-colonialism that undermines the boundaries Ngũgĩ's characters seek to draw between Kenya and the imperial powers. Indeed, as Ngũgĩ's later novels and public career make clear, that hope was ever more severely stressed. But when the failure of such hope becomes an infuriating reality, the disillusionment it produces is also the basis for the development of new models both of culture and of world order.

4

From Three Worlds to One
Two Decades of Rapid Globalization

MICHELLE CLIFF'S *No Telephone to Heaven* (1987) dramatizes the frustrated attempt to form a viable revolutionary nationalist struggle in Jamaica during the period of social upheaval and conflict that came with the unraveling of the leftist program of Prime Minister Michael Manley. The novel thus belongs to the large body of Third World writing about the decay of Third World nationalism and the triumph of neocolonialism, a literature that, like Ngũgĩ's later fiction, depicts the fulfillment of the grimmer possibilities suggested by *A Grain of Wheat*. As Timothy Brennan describes the genre,

> Lamenting the savagery of many states in what should have been the Third World's "springtime" of nationalist idealism is not an activity limited to European sociologists. It forms a major subcategory of Third-World fiction itself, featured in such representative works as Augusto Roa Bastos' *I, the Supreme*, Ayi Kwei Armah's *The Beautiful Ones Are Not Yet Born*, Earl Lovelace's *The Wine of Astonishment*, Salman Rushdie's *Shame* and many others—novels that are really a necessary adjunct to the insurgent and liberationist rhetoric of Frantz Fanon, Amilcar Cabral and their cultural descendants, although in an inverted form: a pointed exposure of what Ariel Dorfman calls the "Empire's old clothes" worn by a comprador elite who, like Chile's Pinochet, Egypt's Mubarak, or Haiti's Namphy, take on the nationalist mantle only to cloak their people more fully with the old dependency. Actually, Fanon himself already diagnosed this same process in his chapter entitled "The Pitfalls of National Consciousness" in *The Wretched of the Earth*. (1989:19)

The book's central character and consciousness is Clare Savage, the light-skinned daughter of Boy Savage (who can pass for white) and Kitty (who is dark-skinned). Having decided to leave the United States, where her family has gone in pursuit of the myth of North American immigrant success, and also to abandon graduate study in England before receiving her degree,

Clare involves herself with an armed revolutionary group in Jamaica: her neocolonial *Bildung* thus not only does not take on her, it radicalizes her consciousness. In quitting North America, she follows her mother, who, appalled at North American racism and culture, leaves her husband and returns to Jamaica, subsequently dying there; in leaving England, she reacts equally strongly against the British colonial legacy, the snobbery of some of her fellow students and the biases of the academic industry. After some travels with a black American Vietnam War deserter, she returns to Jamaica and discovers a role for herself in a national liberation struggle there, offering property inherited from her grandmother to the band of revolutionaries. Although she is light-skinned, of the elite, internationalized in education, and cultural rather than political in her interests, they accept her aid and use her property as a base for mounting an armed campaign.

The novel thus embodies one of its chief concerns in its very plot: the internationalization and heterogenization—perhaps balkanization would be a better word—of the Jamaican national community. The hybrid form of the novel—it is one-third North American immigrant literature, one-third British bildungsroman, and one-third nativist lyric of attempted return to roots—mirrors a hybrid Jamaica set in a hybrid (and hybridizing) world. Jamaica is a land of harsh contrasts. It contains the Dungle, a miasmic slum, comfortable (although walled and guarded) homes for the local elite, North American investment property, including bauxite mines (which cause the rivers to run red and threaten large-scale environmental pollution for Jamaicans), and fancy tourist hotels catering to North Americans, who selfishly and trivializingly see Jamaica as their sandbox. In addition, Jamaicans themselves are split along lines of caste and class: as two crass filmmakers (two white males, one from America and one from England), agree, "They're more English than the English" (203) in terms of maintaining the class system, for class stratification is reinforced in Jamaica by a racial caste system that privileges the lighter-skinned, eliding the *backra-fe-true* (actual white) with the *cuffy-pretend-backra* (upstart, pretend white) (19). Moreover, the elite are thoroughly internationalized, sent abroad for their educations, and perhaps loath to return to Jamaica at all. Classes in the middle are also spread about, as many go to North America to work as servants for the wealthy and watch, from Toronto or New York, the social upheavals under Manley on television, while their white employers remark, "Well I guess that's another place they've ruined for us" (18). The poor are also in many ways fragments of the global ecumene. Just as their shacks in the Dungle are built of pieces of tin, wood, and signboards chaotically recycled from international commerce, their culture is an international pastiche:

Some of them worshipped with their bodies. Rum. Ganja. Music. Water. Vision. Fire. Drum. Stone. They lived amid a commotion of rites. Revival Zion. Convince. Ras Mataz. Shouter. Ras Tafari. Pentecostal. Disciples of Christ. Kumina. Furiously at worship. Trying to make communion with God Almighty. No matter what him name be. What her name be.
    Sasabonsam. Marley. Mighty Sparrow. Garvey. Nanny. Rhyging. (16)

Even the attempts at socialist nationalism under Manley have done nothing to bring Jamaica together as a community. Nationalist politics at best add some international chic to the decadent parties of the children of the elite: "The mother and father in Ocho Rios for the weekend. Buster naked in the pool comparing cocks with his cousin Pedro from Caracas. "We nuh is outstanding cocksmen, bra." Dancing in the chlorinated water arm in arm. Background music. To Be Young, Gifted, and Black finally came to Ja. Reggae-style. Number one on Rediffusion and JBC (20)." At an opposite pole from this easy camaraderie among neocolonials (whose local culture is inseparable from international commercial culture) stand the revolutionaries: they struggle to achieve unity—to create an imagined revolutionary community—out of dispersion:

These people—men and women—were dressed in similar clothes, which became them as uniforms, signifying some agreement, some purpose—that they were in something together—in these clothes, at least, they seemed to blend together. This alikeness was something they needed, which could be important, even vital, to them—for the shades of their skin, places traveled to and from, events experienced, things understood, food taken into their bodies, acts of violence committed, books read, music heard, languages recognized, ones they had loved, living family, varied widely, came between them. That was all to be expected, of course—that on this island, as part of this small nation, many of them would have been separated at birth. Automatically. (4)

The situation in which Jamaica is inscribed is thus extremely different from the one that affects Ngũgĩ's Kenya (which is in turn quite distinct from the circumstances of Rao's India). Ngũgĩ's awareness of precolonial cultural dissensuality and the further fragmentation wrought by colonialism—his awareness of the problematic quality of primordial culture and the difficulty involved in using it as a basis for nationalist revolution—is tame compared to Cliff's perception of the circumstances in Jamaica. In contrast to the dissensual, changing, and increasingly syncretic tradition of Kenya—a tradition that can, however, be organized in a connected, dialectical narrative of the search for a national community—Cliff's novel portrays Jamaica's social background as so thoroughly heterogenized, internationalized, and fragmented that it can only be called a postmodern pastiche struggling to find a narrative.

For one thing, Cliff's Jamaica—like the nineteenth-century Jamaica previously depicted by Jean Rhys (1966)—is a society so fragmented and divided by racial, caste, class, and national factors that it has none of the Manichean coherence that Fanon found in revolutionary Africa. There is neither any single Manichean, black-white boundary nor any dominant tradition of resistance available to help form a revolutionary community. Both have to be manufactured; in its present form, Jamaica is characterized by a multiplicity of fragmented, strained boundaries that do not add up to a stable picture. Second, and equally important, the sociocultural fragments in Cliff's Jamaica are not localized, attached anciently to a specific territory. In an island populated by different, mostly immigrant peoples, the quest for roots leads everywhere, and present-day culture is equally splintered by colonial and neocolonial penetration. For both reasons, there is no bounded site in which to anchor a narrative like Ngũgĩ's; there is, instead, a desperate need to find some ground upon which a narrative might be constructed that can serve as a basis for community. To be sure, what was a defect in an era of nationalism may be completely revalued by a globalist model of world order: the well-known syncretic heterogenization of the Caribbean has led postcolonial literary historians like Bill Ashcroft, Gareth Griffiths, and Helen Tiffin to single out Caribbean polyglossia as culturally exceptional in, and also exemplary for, the contemporary world (1989:39, 44–48). But for the nationalism of *No Telephone to Heaven,* such fragmenting syncretism presents a crucial problem. For Clare even to begin to construct a Jamaica, she not only has to demystify the two cultural and economic systems that have shaped (and are still shaping) Jamaica and unearth an alternate history; she also has to use that history to try to paste fragments together into something common.

Clare seeks to do this ultimately by invoking the name of Nanny, the leader of a slave rebellion who is a prominent folk hero in Manley's Jamaica. The revolutionary group evokes "the name of Nanny, in whose memory they were engaged in this," that "they might move closer" (5). Living together in her name, they uncover something of an "original" place: "they found, in the process of clearing the land, things that had been planted long before—before even the grandmother—which had managed to survive the density of the wild forest. Cassava. Afu. Fufu" (11). Like the syncretic searchers for religion in the Dungle, they manufacture traditions, but ones that, unlike those of the Dungle, can serve as communal bonds, rather than chaotic congruence: "The soldiers smoked ganja only occasionally—and then according to strict tradition" (11). They also return to specific local traditions that persist after all in the rural community where Clare's grandmother had lived: "The rest of the surplus, all that they could not barter, was distributed by Miss Mattie's granddaughter to people around who did not have enough land to support them. It had been a practice of her mother and grandmother" (12). Perhaps one of the most interesting touches in this lyrical search for (and apparent recovery) of personal and communal roots—an experience that virtually incorporates the whole tradition of nostalgic nationalism into the novel—is Clare's repatriation of a cultural artifact that had been removed: "Basket on head, resting on a cotta, bought years ago in Knightsbridge, a gallery specializing in African art, carried as a talisman. Now being put to use, its true properties recognized. It had not been comfortable on a glass shelf; it belonged on a woman's head" (12).

In a later attempt to repatriate what has been internationalized and dispersed, Clare works as a teacher, trying to uncover/recover Jamaican resistance history effaced from official history books. Her icon, in this, is again Nanny, whom she recovers as she radicalizes herself: as both the novel and a memoir Cliff has written about her personal excitement at uncovering Nanny's history describe her, Nanny was the leader of a group of fighters known as the Windward Maroons: an old black woman naked except for a necklace made from the teeth of white men. The novel— perhaps letting us into Clare's deep thoughts, perhaps on its own— invokes Nanny in order to forward a crucial act of recovery:

> They have taken away her bag of magic. Her teeth. Her goat's horn. We have forgotten her. Now that we need her more than ever. The nurses ignore her. The doctors make game of her. The priest tries to take her soul.
> Can you remember how to love her? (164)

The ultimate sign of Clare's communal recovery would be recreating Jamaica in the image of this model of resistance; personally, it would be to recover the language still spoken in the rural area where her grandmother's property was located:

> Coromantee, a tongue barely alive.
> A tongue she could not speak. She who was educated in several tongues, the mastery of which should have kept her from that truck and stifled her longing to know Coromantee. (106)

The lyrical return to her grandmother's property is thus a revolutionary version of Kaname's idyll. To assemble and ground a narrative of liberation would be to build a cultural community that was not just restorative, but revolutionarily transformative. Such an invocation of nostalgia is, however, a bit jarring. On the one hand, Cliff's analysis of Jamaica presents a much more extreme case of syncretic fragmentation than Ngũgĩ's does of

Kenya and reveals a need to reconstruct a narrative and a community from thoroughly heterogeneous, internationalized fragments and expatriated or suppressed materials. On the other, Cliff seems able, much more completely than Ngũgĩ, to indulge in the notion of a return to roots, a restoration of primordial communalism, and a virile revolutionary project. The result is a clash not only of primordialist and postmodern frames of reference—frames with very different assumptions—but of different literary forms: the pastiche in Cliff's novel finally does not hang together and generate a coherent narrative, something confirmed by the ultimate failure of the novel's revolutionary project. The narrative of nostalgia never absorbs the postmodern pastiche of contemporary Jamaica; just as the novel's immigrant narrative, bildungsroman, harsh modernist irony, and lyricism never all cohere. Historically and literarily, Cliff's Jamaica can neither effect the civilizational magic we found in Rao's India nor achieve the dialectical narrative of community-formation of Ngũgĩ's Kenya. Instead, Cliff's revolutionary/nostalgic idyll seems strangely inserted into a wealth of contradictory circumstances and genres.

It is hard, though, to describe precisely in what spirit the novel recognizes and intends Clare's failure to create a local Jamaican narrative and the jarring quality of her insertion of nostalgic nationalist lyricism into a Jamaican pastiche. It is hard to know if the novel dramatizes the failure of a valid revolutionary dream of separate community or if it hints that there is an essentially spurious, simulationist quality to such a dream in an interconnected, postmodern world. Quite simply and baldly, the novel acknowledges the clash of genres and the impossibility of Clare's hopes abruptly and powerfully when the revolutionary group is terminated. Clare and her comrades are wiped out by the Jamaican military. What is hard to gauge is the intent and extent of the irony involved. Does the end of the novel represent a deeply ironic tragedy—the necessary failure of doomed, but valuable, idealism? Or does it hint that both Clare's personal quest and her public project are narcissistic and compromised, and that nostalgic revolutionary nationalism in the more modern, more internationalized world of Jamaica (penetrated by two global systems, unlike Kenya, and up to the moment in fashion and information) is not only an impossibility but self-deception?

At the end of the novel, Clare, machine-gunned where she hides in a bitterbush, experiences a linguistic collage in her fading consciousness: French and English pass by, recalling her earlier remark that she can say "shit" (or be gracious) in five languages (152). But then the list turns to a repetition of "back-raw, back-raw," and the text comments, "She remembered language. Then   it was gone" (208). A succession of further sounds follow; then the novel ends, with the phrase "Day broke" (208). Does Clare plunge to the depths of consciousness and memory and recover Coromantee at last? Is this a victory in tragedy? Or is it a small rush, followed by greater dispersion into fragments, reinforcing her previous dispersion into five languages? Is the apparent recovery only her last, momentarily passing narcissistic self-indulgence? When day breaks, is it light and hope or sobering reality?

Behind all of these questions lies a more basic uncertainty. Do two worlds clash, and does one tragically lose, or has there really only been one all along, one that helps produce the fantasy of an oppositional position, which it then crushes?

To answer these questions, we must disentangle Clare's different struggles and failures. Clare's ultimately failed attempts to demystify official ideology, and thereby construct an alternative world with its own historical narrative, occur on two fronts: against the legacy of the Eurocolonial world system and the pressure of the American neocolonial system. On the former front, the novel explores Clare's attempt to recover some notion of authentic, even primordial Jamaican history from international heterogeneity and colonial/neocolonial domination—specifically through acts of postcolonial, anti-Orientalist scholarship. The first question is whether this activity is radical enough; it seems to be so when Clare sees through the ways in which "Mother" England has appropriated and misrepresented Jamaican culture and history, either by reading through her initial identification with Jane Eyre as a fellow orphan into an awareness of how the book treats Rochester's first wife (a topos, thanks to Jean Rhys [1966] and Gayatri Spivak [1987], of postcolonial feminism) or by encountering the remains of Pocohontas, taken from America, claimed, and reinterpreted by England. Most blatantly, in the British Museum collection, Claire finds a comprehensive revelation of English colonial appropriation of other cultures and knowledges. Recognizing this, Claire reexamines her nostalgia for Mother England: she decolonizes her own mind when she sees through the legacy of associations British literature and schooling have grafted onto her, associations that are not really hers and not even, as she finds in visiting a public school in England, all that true of England either. Shedding these false memories, she readies herself, it seems, for finding a true one.

On the other hand, an extended conversation with a guerrilla fighter from Africa—one who appears to have helped organize the group in Jamaica—indicates that there are some fault lines between this project and that of the guerrillas. First, her interrogator keeps pressing her with the question, would she kill? This discussion indicates that cultural interests are distinct from what is required for political action against oppressors. Claire's *Bildung* through Orientalism and decolonization seems to have been assigned, à la Fanon, to a stage in the political development of the native intellectual, something that means she still has not yet reached full identification with the masses and experienced the transformative, community-building experience of violence. It is possible, then, that Cliff interrogates demystifying postcolonial scholarship—a radical strategy of recent development, one that has blossomed in the wake of disillusionment with Third World nationalism—and finds that it may be, if lingered on, a step back, rather than forward, from the stage of revolutionary nationalism. The implication is that Clare's postcolonial demystification still exhibits uncomfortably close ties to imperial structures; as a result, she has not, perhaps, detached thereby a genuinely salvageable "Jamaica" from the British legacy.

Yet going ahead with revolutionary violence also proves problematic. To be sure, throughout the book, Clare experiences frustrating impotence. Like a number of other characters, she shows herself very good at a kind of sneering cultural satire against Americans. When the guerrillas assemble supplies, they do so by stealing from American kids who are in Jamaica for its dope and reggae:

> The people on the truck did not care at all about these children and had no difficulty stealing from them. They were nuisances, only rarely useful, bodies to be stepped across—should a wallet be visible in the pocket, so much the better. There might be one of Papa's credit cards tucked in, or at the very least a plastic case of American Express traveler's checks. . . . Poor little Americans, after the ad had promised JAMAICA, A WORLD OF CULTURE WITHOUT BOUNDARIES. (6)

At the same time, however, she is still an impotent prisoner of her upbringing, galled, on her trip through Europe, at what the landlady will think of her if she lets a bloodied sheet be seen, and imagining herself saying shocking things to the Queen at a reception, but in reality behaving decorously. The disparity between gesture and murder, sneering satire (with fantasies of invulnerable power) and actual weakness and inner struggle haunt both Clare and the presentation of Clare throughout the novel. But while cultural destruction of the oppressor provides her—and her author—with an enormous wealth of material, political opposition only yields one tragic, Pyrrhic, or merely botched, self-indulgent moment. The book's conclusion raises the question of whether Clare's final act is a martyr's introduction to transformative Fanonian violence or enshrines a critique of it as too crude, and socially and psychologically ineffective, a means of cohering a nation and a psyche so transnationally fragmented. Fanonian violence, in short, perhaps, neither grounds the narrative of a new nation nor exorcises the ghost of the colonial system: that ghost is too deeply embedded, and the existing country and psyches too fragmented, for such magic.

Clare encounters similar problems in struggling against the second form of international penetration of Jamaica. Her attempts to construct a revolutionary opposition—and to make her nostalgic nationalist lyric real—are, if anything, even more frustrated by American neocolonialism than they are by the enduring legacy of British colonialism. If "Mother" England represents a high past to be seen through, America represents an ineffably vulgar present that is, however, ubiquitous, powerful, and dominating. When Clare is placed in school, she and her father are told by the principal that "foreign students begin a year behind so they wouldn't get 'lost'" (97). The principal's condescension is based partly on bigotry, partly on American stupidity. Boy suggests that an "exception might be made for his daughter—after all, she was proficient in Latin and French, was beginning Greek, and had studied algebra and geometry since she was ten. In addition the girl had read many of the classics: Dickens, Shakespeare, Milton" (97). The principal replies in bureaucratese, a parody of déclassé, cultureless American school professionalism, and also of American developmentalist thought. She argues that "children from underdeveloped countries develop at a different rate than American children" (98), and then goes on to raise her eyebrows at Boy's last name (Savage). When told in answer to her question, that Clare's race is "white," she makes innuendoes about color mixing in Jamaica. This is only a more official version of the vulgarity the Savages encounter in southern motels, where they called Jamaica "Jewmaica." The episode is a satire on the unsubtlety of the American either-or view of race in the pre–civil rights era.

America, the land of immigrants, which also excludes and oppresses according to a mindless either-or, is thus perhaps even worse than England, the source of the class and caste system that divides Jamaica. American international commercial culture does to nations what America does to immigrants: it takes them all in and then peripheralizes them. It takes them in by apparent openness and cheap forms of commercialism; the openness is not real, however, and the commercialism manipulates and trivializes. Cultural nationalism is thus co-opted as internationally marketed reggae; Jamaica, the world of culture without boundaries, is trivialized and marginalized into America's sandbox.

This oppression by an American-sponsored global system therefore represents a greater challenge to the revolutionaries—and a greater source of irony about their quest—than the older colonial system does. It governs the present and future, while the other co-opts the past. Crucial to the novel's portrayal of the guerrillas' failure is the suggestion that they are not able to separate themselves from this international system, but are from the start inwardly infected by it. The clothes that, as we have seen, allow the guerrillas to overcome their differences are, in fact, U.S. fatigues, stolen from the childish druggie tourists. Similarly, the guerrillas are killed attempting, not a coup or an outright rebellion, but merely to stop an American film company from trivializing Nanny by making a schlock blockbuster about her. The intolerably crass ("Jamaicans will do anything for a buck" (202) filmmakers are trying to make something of the unlikely topic because it has "lots of action" (205). They plan to cast an "elegant actress" as Nanny and "a strapping former heavyweight" (206) as Cudjoe, and to have these characters speak pidgin Coromantee. The filmmakers are, in short, attempting to transmute the Jamaican oppositional history Clare has painfully assembled into the very different sort of past that Arjun Appadurai argues is typical of the postmodern world. "The past," Appadurai writes, "is now not a land to return to in a simple politics of memory. It has become a synchronic warehouse of cultural scenarios, a kind of temporary central casting, to which recourse can be had as appropriate, depending on the movie to be made, the scene to be enacted, the hostages to be rescued" (1990:4). The threat to Clare's oppositional history is thus its conversion into yet another of these scenarios. Such transformation means not only debasement but also cancellation of all that history's "reality," all its past authenticity and its potential for effecting future historical change. If the filmmakers succeed, it will be that much harder to construct a real/realistic revolutionary narrative and revolutionary community.

But do the novel's guerrillas really occupy a position outside this synchronic warehouse, this North American postmodern system of commodified simulacra? Is the attempt to stop the film by violence, then, a symbolic revolutionary act—part of the recovery of authentic culture, and a revolutionary project against dereifying misrepresentation—or is it itself a film? Are the guerrillas, dressed in U.S. fatigues, themselves playing parts and seeking exactly the same goal the director sets for the actors (without, however, being critically aware, as he is, of its spuriousness): "Let's go, people! Let's make it real!" (206)? From the beginning the book sows this suspicion by asserting the opposite: "Of course," the text comments, the guerrillas' dress is "never only a matter of appearance, symbol. Not at all. They were also dressed—a practical matter, a matter of survival. . . . They were dressed to blend with the country around them" (5). Similarly, Clare's transvestite friend, Harry/Harriet, who becomes a guerrilla, asserts that his early sexual violation by a white man is not symbolic. Intentionally or not, at crucial moments, these assertions suggest the opposite possibility, that the guerrillas have not achieved "reality" but are merely attempting to reify symbols; if that is so, there is no real distinction in kind between the revolutionaries and the movie makers. Both represent attempts to impress their symbolism on reality—to construct culture as a form of hegemony. And both also do this—if the irony is meant to cut this deep—as creatures of a common global system: the localist revolutionaries, clad in U.S. fatigues, may not represent a position apart from the commercial Americanization that trivializes and marginalizes Jamaica, but may (as those who interpret Gramsci pessimistically have suggested) derive from it. They will then have confirmed Fredric Jameson's ironic perception about the postmodern cultural system generally: that it has penetrated and colonized "those very pre-capitalist enclaves (Nature and the Unconscious) which offered extraterritorial and Archimedean footholds for critical effectivity" (1984:87) and that it has totalizingly abolished the possibility of outside positions and demands the "invention and elaboration of an internationalism of a radically new type" (88). Against the force of nostalgic lyricism in the book and the author's clearly expressed identification with it, the novel indeed proceeds to this conclusion, as it portrays only the failed nationalism, and not the invention of a radically new international strategy. And a similar web of irony involves even the author: Cliff acknowledges complex international connections as well as local interests. She is allied with American feminism and conversant with feminist, Orientalist, postcolonialist, and postmodernist scholarship, which she has applied to the Jamaican situation. And she includes in the book her thanks to the National Endowment for the Arts, without whose support it could not have been completed.

Clearly, we have encountered an entirely different frame of reference from that evoked by Ngũgĩ's book. "Culture" has become an extremely problematic term. In Cliff's Jamaica culture is not primordial or associated with particular territory, as it is in Rao, or capable of territorialization by construction of a narrative of separate community, as it is in Ngũgĩ. Instead, the American-dominated global system radically deterritorializes, fragments, and derealizes Jamaica's local culture; furthermore, the novel suggests that, given Jamaica's domination by a previous global system, no genuine local culture has been able to thrive in the past. Instead, Jamaica has been manufactured, under British colonialism, into an ethnically and racially heterogeneous, dependant, peripheral territory. The result is a Jamaica that is indeed "a world of culture(s) without boundaries"—a fragmented, heterogeneous, internationalized, postmodern soup of different groups and codes. Should any genuine opposition form—should any group try to construct a Jamaican narrative that is truly locally, rather than internationally, brokered—the resistance will, it seems, be co-opted by incorporating this narrative into the global system's larger synchronic warehouse of cultural scenarios. The radical legacy of anticolonial nationalism is thus canceled in *No Telephone to Heaven*. We shall later explore, in other texts and analyses, the possibility of that legacy being transformed as a way of negotiating these mutations in the larger global system.

Nigel Harris's brief summary of trends in economic thought during this time forms an interesting parallel to what we have seen happening in fiction, as lyrical continuation of a primordial culture (Rao) first mutates into the dialectical historical narrative of the construction of a separate national community (Ngũgĩ) and then disperses to a postmodern pastiche of deterritorialized international culture (Cliff). Harris records how enthusiasm for import substitution to foster the growth of domestic industries was theorized in the 1940s by one of the founders of development economics, Raúl Prebisch, and subsequently disseminated in the 1950s beyond Latin America. A number of poor countries "adopted programmes of industrialization which depended on limiting imports" (Harris 1987:18) and on providing state support for nascent industries. This represented an attempt to achieve national self-sufficiency against what was increasingly seen as an inhibiting global economic system; Prebisch argued that the orthodox theory of world trade—under which, in an unrestricted world market, each country would specialize in the form of production most efficient to it, thereby gaining a competitive advantage that would ultimately equalize national incomes—did not work for the poor countries in the twentieth century. Although it had, he asserted, been effective in the nineteenth, when Britain's and Europe's imports of raw materials had expanded Latin American economies, in the twentieth century "a changed structure of relationships turned the beneficial relationship into a malign one" (14). The orthodox theory of trade now produced impoverishment in Latin America: as Prebisch wrote, "Reality is undermining the outdated scheme of the international division of labour" (Prebisch 1950:1). Prebisch supplied many reasons for this phenomenon; most prominently, he blamed monopoly control in the core of prices, both of manufactured exports to the peripheries and of imports of raw materials from the peripheries. The faster pace of technological development in the core gave sellers of manufactures monopoly power, and their ability to seek throughout the Third World for the lowest prices for raw materials allowed them to foster an intra–Third World competition that drove down prices.

Prebisch's call for import substitution was directed toward the goal of national self-sufficiency. Soon, however, development economics became a major area of study and application throughout the world. The First World developmentalism of Walt Rostow's *The Stages of Economic Growth: A Non-Communist Manifesto* (1960) agreed that classical theory no longer applied to the Third World and that government action was necessary to break through local rigidities and push Third World countries along the developmental timeline to the point where they experienced industrial takeoff. On the radical side, Prebisch's arguments were extended to support an intensified, radicalized nationalism: import substitution still had not produced stable national economies in the Third World by the 1960s, as Harris summarizes the argument, because

> the existing social structure inhibited the effect of investment. A severely unequal distribution of income cut the size of the domestic market and also skewed it towards upper-income consumption goods. Unequal land distribution severely reduced the capacity of the rural majority to sustain market demand and also reduced the incentives to cultivate more. Import barriers forced foreign companies to make the minimum manufacture legally required in the country (to escape the restrictions on imports), but, because the market was so small, their costs were very high, the product inferior, and increased profits were drained out of the country instead of going to domestic investment. For most countries, the domestic market was too small to support the development of efficient heavy and intermediate industries; for these economic federations were needed—the Latin American Free Trade Area (as also the Andean Pact, the Central American Common Market, etc.). (Harris 1987:22)

Following this line of analysis, a more radical group—one Harris calls the revolutionary nationalists—argued that radical social restructuring had to occur in Third World countries. This was necessary, first, because the existing class structure prevented all necessary change and, second, in order to spread wealth sufficiently to develop a wide-based internal market to consume the products of local industrialization, stimulating it thereby to further local investment. This position represented a more radical assertion of the goal of self-sufficiency and a revolutionary format for the means necessary to get there: Third World societies needed to reshape themselves, André Gunder Frank proposed, and their national economies needed to de-link from the global network.

Frank's proposal derived from a more radical analysis than Prebisch's of the process whereby Third World economies had become impoverished: to quote the title of Frank's famous article (1966), that process was based on the "development of underdevelopment." Underdeveloped economies in the Third World did not represent slow or inhibited progress toward industrial capitalism along a developmental timeline, or, as Prebisch had argued, the blockage in the twentieth century of an international division of labor that had functioned in the nineteenth. They weren't merely *un*developed economies, but actively *under*developed; and this process of underdevelopment—of their exploitation by an increasingly overdeveloped global core—had begun with early colonial plunder and subjection. The past does not create the present, but the present manufactures a false image of the past; and local circumstances are not locally created, but driven by global relationships.

These changing economic theories were not, of course, merely abstract. They formed the underpinnings of concrete political action in the postwar era, ranging from First World anticommunist developmentalism to Third World revolutionary nationalism. In both arenas, the changes saw the intensification of two forces we noted in Ricoeur's cultural analysis: localized, bounded nationalisms and the global system that threatened them, with which they had to cope. From import substitution to revolutionary nationalism, the emphasis on national integrity grew more intense; similarly, the analysis of the factors opposed to it, the global pressures, grew more corrosive and all-encompassing.

An even more interesting parallel to the literature just reviewed is the fact that, as nationalism intensified, global factors were increasingly seen to infect local cultures more thoroughly than Ricoeur's formulation would allow. Increasingly, national unity had to be constructed rather than perpetuated and protected. In the present, radical social restructuring had to take place, and the past was depicted, increasingly, not just as having been disrupted, but as in fact invented by colonialism. What had seemed to be local came to be perceived as the result of a five-century-long global process. With this perception, we have moved even beyond Ngũgĩ's dialectical construction of a communal, historical narrative to Cliff's attempt to create and retroject a narrative into a pastiche of global penetration and fragmentation.

Political, economic, and cultural thought thus became perched upon an increasingly sharp contradiction. Harris expresses the situation well:

> Contradictory imperatives were imposed upon the governments of the newly industrializing countries: on the one hand, a nationalist orientation to reduce dependence upon the rest of the world system and to develop economic and military self-reliance through full diversification of activity; on the other, to expand the income and power of the state and country concerned by increased interdependence and increased specialization. While there were some states that were able to cling to the first perspective (even if with amendments)—such as the Soviet Union—most were bent toward the second by the sheer need for surviv-

al. National economic independence was becoming an expensive luxury few could afford—and the richer they were, the less they could afford it. (168)

Harris is correct in expressing the dilemma in terms of a contradiction: in economics, politics, and culture, nationalism was struggling to pre-serve/create national integrity and also negotiate a global system, increas-ingly perceived as internal as well as external to the nation. With the failure of the era of nationalist hopes, what had seemed to be the solution suddenly seemed the problem, and the existing model turned, startlingly, into what appeared to be its opposite. With astonishing speed, the goal of national self-sufficiency changed into the goal of developing export po-tential for the global economy, and the "gang of four"—Taiwan, South Korea, Hong Kong, and Singapore—became models for Third World devel-opment. And as global interconnections, not national self-sufficiency, be-came the fundamental model, the legacies of import substitution and revolutionary national integration seemed to be the problem, fostering inefficient local industries based on outmoded technologies and an ex-panded state power that had resulted in corruption, not a step toward a solution.

Clearly, these changes dramatically affected not just the Third but also the First and Second Worlds. As the current American obsession with eco-nomic decline thanks to diminished global competitiveness has indicated, they lie behind America's sense of its recent slippage from preeminence, and they were certainly a factor in the still more dramatic breakup of the USSR. In many ways, however, the Third World felt the impact first, in the form of disillusionment with nationalism: revolutions did not realize their populist hopes. Seen from this perspective, neocolonialism in the Third World may not have been based only on the persistence of colonial rela-tionships; it may have been a herald of the globalism to come.

But at the same time as old ideologies and forms were undergoing transfor-mation, a new set were being formed. The attempted supersession of the notion of Three Worlds by a globalist perspective represents not only disillusionment but also the stirrings of something dramatically new and difficult to evaluate. As early as 1984, as we saw in chapter 1, Peter Worsley had noted a significant change, confusing the definition of the Third World greatly: "Poor/rich and industrial/agricultural . . . no longer over-lap" (1984:327). Theorized first by Folker Fröbel, Jürgen Heinrichs, and Otto Kreye (1980) as the "new international division of labor," this development—as Worsley put it six years later—recognized what "earlier generations of theorists on the Left had deemed to be impossible—the

industrialization of Third World economies under capitalism" (1990:88).
The early formulation of the new international division of labor confined
such development to "sectors of obsolete technology the West was happy
to discard" (1990:89); soon, however, with Third World production of
goods ranging from automobiles to semiconductors—and Third World
siting of research and design functions, as well as assembly—a second
stage of "new industrialization" began, disrupting the former assumptions
of a hierarchical global order even more profoundly. Under the first international division of labor, peripheral colonies produced primary products
and raw materials for the industrial core, receiving manufacturing goods
in return; by the end of the 1970s, Harris argues,

> the "less developed countries," as they were now known, were exporting
> more manufactured goods than raw materials, a change producing a
> "spiritual revolution as great as that experienced by economists over the
> age of thirty who were converted to Keynesianism in 1936." By 1980, the
> more developed countries exported 36 per cent more primary commodi-
> ties than did the less developed. From the perception of the 1950s, the
> world had been turned topsy-turvy. (1987:28)

Correspondingly, by the early 1980s, "the majority of exports of the less
developed countries . . . were manufactured goods" (123).

The dramatic success of the Pacific Rim—in particular, of Taiwan, South
Korea, Hong Kong, and Singapore—drove this point home. Many have
looked for cultural reasons for these success stories, but they represent less
individual attainments than "some profound structural change in the
world system" (1987:116). They represent, first of all, the death knell of the
previous era of nationalism: national development under the protective
stewardship of the state has come to seem inhibited, rather than advanced,
and integration with the global system—in some ways nationalism's precise opposite—has become the hope. In terms of U.S. interests, this trend
has been provocatively analyzed and advocated by Robert Reich (*The Work
of Nations* [1991]), who argues that the era of the national corporation, and
national policy based upon the assumed national basis of U.S. corporations, has become a thing of the past; it reached its apex in the decades
after the war and has since declined dramatically in the era of globalization
and multinational diversification. In the Third World, as Harris shows,
attempts to expand domestic markets have yielded to the attempt to expand manufactured exports indefinitely. Fear of foreign capital has been
replaced by efforts to attract it; the public sector has been discredited in
favor of the private, and governments now attempt less to integrate, cen-
tralize, and control the country than to work with industry to develop
strategies for negotiating global commercial relationships. Harris empha-

sizes the fact that this development is driven by the global system, not national policy:

> In sum, then, the process of dispersal of manufacturing capacity is a general phenomenon, not simply something restricted to the Gang of Four. It involved increasingly complex patterns of changing specialization, interweaving different parts of the world unknowingly in collaborative processes of production. If permitted to continue—and it was quite unclear how it could be stopped—it bid fair to end—or at least render very much more complex—the simple picture of industry in more and less developed countries. (116)

Integration into the global economy, rather than enhancement of national economies, now seems the crucial focus for strategies of development. Economic slump and stagnation in more developed countries do not dampen or devastate the economies of the newly industrialized countries, as they might have in the past, but actually increase their exports, as First World enterprises are driven to seek economies beyond their national borders. Similarly, since integration into the world economy is a source of power, and the world economy has become highly diversified, First World governments find themselves very restricted both in their power over their own economies (tariffs are often counterproductive, inducing multinationals to move still more jobs abroad) and in their ability to regulate the world market (boycotts and embargoes have only limited success). Thus, Harris concludes, "the conception of an interdependent, interacting, global manufacturing system cuts across the old view of a world consisting of nation-states as well as one of groups of countries, more and less developed and centrally planned—the First, the Third and the Second Worlds" (200).

The new international division of labor is, however, only one of a number of prominent factors involved in the dramatic shift in perception of world economic, political, and cultural order. As a theorization of the process, it leaves out many highly suggestive details. Itemizing the concerns that became more publicly prominent during the 1980s produces a much more heterogeneous list. The internationalization of production yoked the world together in a producers' network. On the one hand, this meant capacity for dramatic transformations throughout the world, owing to "the ease with which state-of-the-art factories and equipment can be installed" (Reich 1991:209). Astonishingly suddenly, then, the "backward" Third World revealed itself as the site of state-of-the-art computer chip manufacture, and Pico Iyer can write of high-tech, au courant, Americanized popular culture in Third World cities that puts many places in the United States to shame. At the same time, the internationalization of production means the interlinking of diverse places in heterogeneous networks, thanks to the disaggregation of manufacture, whereby "product parts can now be made in specialized locations relatively remote from each other, and the finished product assembled somewhere else" (Harris 1987:193). As Reich's book makes abundantly clear, not only products, but also the "enterprise webs" that make them are "cobbled together" from globally dispersed components (Reich 1991:97).

Such internationalization of production—whereby "American" cars are made in a number of places, a bottle of orange juice is produced jointly in Brazil and Florida, and the latest First World fashions are manufactured by rapidly assembled factories in small Third World nations vying for the global market—is accompanied by the similarly heterogenizing internationalization in many other areas as well. Politically, not only state structures, but also regional and local governments have thus been internationalized. Thus, on the national-state level, integration into international norms and organizations has proceeded to develop. Eric Hobsbawm (1990:181) notes that "the number of *intergovernmental* international organizations grew from 123 in 1951 to 365 in 1984," and the number of "*non-governmental* organizations from 832 through 2,173 in 1972, more than doubling to 4,615 in the next twelve years." Thus, in addition to national arrangements, even sometimes subverting them, sub- and supranational state interactions have dramatically increased, ranging from the direct involvement of local governments in fostering international trade (many local governments have offices in foreign cities [Reich 1991:297]) to collaborative business ventures and sister-city arrangements.

What is true of production and politics is also true of finance, consumption, and population flow. Multinational corporations have become enormously wealthy and powerful: "Today, General Motors spends more than the Japanese Government (and Japan is the world's fourth largest power)," Worsley wrote a decade ago (1984:317). "Nippon Telegraph and Telephone is worth more than IBM, AT&T, General Motors, General Electric and Exxon combined," Miyoshi subsequently claimed at the height of the Tokyo stock market "bubble" (1991:64). Also, with the internationalization of banking and developments in communication and technology that foster the internationalization of capital, a similarly heterogeneous, globalized network of finance has been constructed. Capital began searching out opportunities across national boundaries with dazzling speed and flexibility, spurred by the removal of barriers during the 1980's by a number of different governments, from Japan and England at the beginning of the decade to France and Italy at the end (Reich 1991:138).

Likewise, consumption and marketing are increasingly situated in an international arena, thanks to factors like the development of global brands and products, the internationalization of service functions like advertising and media analysis, and the development of the global media. Thus, when a rural Latin American or Indian village receives global television through its satellite dish, or when brand names are internationalized, people increasingly "dwell" in a global network. As Paul Kennedy writes, "It is a remarkable technical and manufacturing achievement that as the 1980s ended billions of people from the Inner Mongolian plain to the Andean mountains were able for the first time to see the world outside via television" (1993:62–63).

Even more vividly, large populations have come to "dwell" transnationally as a result of the dramatic increase in migration and travel in the past few decades. Thanks to the internationalization of the labor market, the development of global information networks, and increased ease of physical mobility, a new major wave of global migrations has got under way, one that promises to have still more dramatic effects on the global map than the much-studied migrations of the late nineteenth and early twentieth centuries. This has meant not only a huge new influx into the United States and an unprecedented reverse migration from former colonies to Europe, but also population movements within the so-called Third World. As Anthony King has calculated, "in 1979, the USA had some 5 million legal and between 2.5 and 4 million illegal migrants. In 1979, Western Europe had some 6.3 million, and Arab countries almost 3 million migrant workers. . . . developing countries have also seen an increase in the same phenomenon, with 3.5 to 4 million migrants in Latin America and almost 1.5 million in West Africa" (1990a:16). In the large "world cities" King specifically studied, these population flows have occurred both at the top and at the bottom of the socioeconomic ladder: the internationalization of business and finance ensures that the top is heterogeneous, and the dramatic increase in international migrant labor similarly affects the bottom.

Anthony King has become the reigning master of the rhetoric of globalization as a process of recent, but sweeping, epochal change: summarizing many of these trends, King writes:

> Especially in the last two decades, revolutionary developments in communications and transport, including satellite transmission, seven-days-a-week, 24-hour global trading in securities, the burgeoning transnationalization of capital and internationalization of labor, the growing consciousness of global economic, ecological and health concerns and especially the recent immense changes in the world political structure have become part of conventional wisdom. In addition, the steady in-

crease in international organizations, the growing coordination by global communication networks of tasks performed by people worldwide, from international airlines, world news, weather, congresses to scientific research, is matched by the tendency, especially evident over the past decade, for a variety of institutions, groups and individuals (corporations, universities, entertainers, writers or terrorists) to "position themselves globally" whether in relation to markets, media or global cultural politics. (1991:viii)

From this welter of disparate, but interrelated phenomena, King crystalizes the thought of a number of leading analysts of the effect of globalization on culture in the following manner: "despite their different positions, and very different conceptual languages, all share at least two perspectives: the rejection of the nationally-constituted society as the appropriate object of discourse, or unit of social and cultural analysis, and to varying degrees, a commitment to conceptualising 'the world as a whole' " (ix).

Clearly, these developments have had enormous implications for cultural studies and the concept of culture itself. As we have seen, the recognition of globalization has done much to demystify notions of culture generally and specific pictures of individual cultures in the past, as local forms have been revealed to have been created and reproduced in connection with, or even determined by, global factors. As we shall see in the following section of this book, such dramatic internationalization on many levels has resulted in still further-reaching speculation about how hierarchy between the First and Third Worlds has been upset, how culture has been deterritorialized, how local cultures have been heterogenized and international cultures have circulated increasingly heterogeneous material, and how the production of local culture has become more transparently globally mediated. If these areas of concern represent a breakdown in the spatial separation of cultures under the three worlds theory, there has also been a perhaps still more destabilizing undermining of assumptions embedded in that theory about the temporality of cultures. The separation of the premodern precapitalist from the modern capitalist is greatly confused if state-of-the-art production facilities, au courant fashions, and sophisticated information can be globally transmitted with great rapidity, and these contemporary events have reinforced self-reflective critiques (such as Johannes Fabian's intervention into anthropology, *Time and the Other*) in disciplines that have helped construct and police such temporal boundaries.

The cultural hierarchies of the three worlds theory have paradoxically been both tenacious and brittle: they have simultaneously been daringly ruptured and insidiously hard to uproot. Their brittleness can be illustrated by one further look at the three fictions about nationalism examined above. In *Kanthapura*, Rangamma, who is "no village kid" (28), describes Western science to her friends in such a way that modern cosmology merges with premodern religion: the vast stretches of cosmic time find their equivalent in Hindu mythology's "day of Brahma." The scene perfectly exemplifies the confrontation Ricoeur envisions between modern universalism and a traditional civilization rich enough in its resources to be able to incorporate modernism in its own way. The wonder and superstition of the audience, and the quaintness produced by Rangamma's transformation of Western science into what sounds like childlike language all signal India as a premodern civilization; the fact, however, that Hindu mythology is shown indeed to have the conceptual resources to accommodate this Western lore indicates that Indian tradition can achieve a creative encounter with modernity, allowing it to persist, retaining its individuality, rather than being swallowed up in a vague syncretism or simply effaced.

Ngũgĩ also dramatizes the information gap between the sophisticated modern and local cultures; one of Gikonyo's companions in detention tells his mates about "the American War of Independence and how Abraham Lincoln had been executed by the British for leading the black folk in America into a revolt" (107). He also tells a "wonderful story of what once happened in Russia where the ordinary man, even without a knowledge of how to read, write, or speak a word of English, was actually running the government" (108). The portrayal of simplicity might seem the same as in Rao, but the border between the premodern and modern is not so clear for Ngũgĩ as in Rao, and modernizing development from one to the other replaces the paradoxical persistence of the old coupled with incorporation of the new. Gikonyo's companions' comments hold something different from premodern wonder: they do not represent a different culture and mentality, but are the simple result of an information gap produced as one of the many inequities colonialism conferred on Africa. Thus, as the novel's narrative proceeds, such local isolation is replaced by greater and greater awareness of the surrounding world system at work. No premodern sensibility has to be overcome; an increase in information is all that is required.

With Cliff, the local is even less the premodern: indeed, the narrator is depicted, not as suffering from a dearth of information compared to what is available in the First World, but, if anything, from a painful excess of it. She is far more variously globalized than either the novel's bigoted Americans or smug British and is, compared to the Americans, infinitely better educated. Correspondingly, even the cultural limitations of Christopher, the child of the Dungle who murders his neocolonial bosses and becomes a crazed local prophet, are not emphasized. Like the Dungle, constructed out of parts and packaging from international commerce, even he represents, more vividly than First World characters and settings, the syncretic overabundance of the present system, not a different worldview from the past. Paradoxically enough, in the emerging global system, Third World cultural positions can be depicted as, not "behind," but "ahead" of the First World, as sites that reveal what is new about the emerging global system, not what has hung on from the past. What the postmodern "boom" in Japan claims for Japanese tradition has been claimed, in different dress, in different ways, of many other sites throughout the Third World. This dramatic inversion of traditional relationships—this portrayal of Third World positions as au courant and First World perspectives as tradition-bound—occurred even as the promises of national liberation movements, promises of empowerment, integration, autonomy, and the end of colonialism, were not only being repeatedly broken but revealed as illusory.

5

Conceiving of the World as a Single System

IMMANUEL WALLERSTEIN'S world-system theory is perhaps the single most important contribution in theorizing one world rather than three. As embodied in Wallerstein's *Modern World System* (1974), world-systems theory refigures the world as a single capitalist economic system, which, moreover, is not newly created, but has been developing since the sixteenth century. Wallerstein provides both an analysis of this system and an account of its historical development.

In chapter 4, I trace the genealogy for world-systems theory. As Peter Worsley has argued, when colonialism was shattered by Third World nationalism, neocolonial economic control of the new states, not genuine national development, was the result. The non-aligned movement thereupon "shifted from primarily political preoccupations, such as the liberation of the remaining colonies, towards a focus upon economic underdevelopment as the root cause of their political independence" (Worsley 1990: 65). Latin America, a region that had been politically independent for over a century, but one with much experience of economic domination, supplanted the Afro-Asian states in giving primary direction to Third World interests. It was natural, Worsley argues, "that dependency theory should emerge first in Latin America" (86). Soon, however, the conditions that produced dependency theory changed. Both of the choices open to Third World nations under André Gunder Frank's dependency theory—revolution or underdevelopment—were undercut: industrialization spread to the Third World, and disillusionment with revolutionary nationalism grew dominant.

Recognizing the interrelatedness of the First and Third worlds that Gunder Frank had theorized and projected back to colonial encounters, but also responding to disappointment with the notion of alternative systems, Wallerstein "abandoned the idea altogether of taking either the sovereign state or that vaguer concept, the national society, as the unit of analysis. I decided that neither one was a social system and that one could only speak of social change in social systems. The only social system in this scheme was the world-system" (7). If the notion of national society proved inadequate, so did the other familiar units Paul Ricoeur assumed:

> African nationalists were determined to change the political structures within which they lived. . . . What is relevant here is that I thereby became aware of the degree to which society as an abstraction was heavily limited to politico-juridicial systems as an empirical reality. It was a false perspective to take a unit like a "tribe" and seek to analyze its operations without reference to the fact that, in a colonial situation, the governing institutions of a "tribe," far from being "sovereign," were closely circumscribed by the laws (and customs) of a larger entity of which they were an indissociable part, the colony. (5)

From this expansion of reference to colony, Wallerstein moved to an analysis of the colonial system; the complexity of that unit of analysis led him back to European history. At this point, faced with the problem of studying units within units, evolutions within evolutions, he sought some "simplifying thrust" and discovered it when he came to his conclusion that "the only social system in this scheme was the world-system."

In terms of postwar politics, Wallerstein's concept of the unitary world system meant, of course, that he collapsed both the Second and Third worlds into the First. Worsley thus underscores Wallerstein's contentions that " 'socialist systems do not exist in the contemporary world.' The communist state is merely a 'collective capitalist firm as long as it remains a participant in the capitalist market' " (Worsley 1984:312). But such a dramatic revision of Frank's theory and the Marxian perspective and postwar concepts of world order was, to be sure, deeply controversial. As one reviewer of Wallerstein's later book *The Politics of the World Economy* (1984) harshly put it, Wallerstein transformed Frank's theory by "throwing away all that gave Frank's work its political edge, and turning Frank's line of argument into its own antithesis" (Alavi 1986:88). Wallerstein's world system was fatalistically monolithic; Wallerstein's theory, Hamza Alavi argues, is "subversive of all national liberation movements in the Third World," for "only a simultaneous global revolution . . . [can] save the world proletariat" (90).

Wallerstein's concept of the modern world system was so singular and all encompassing, however, that he debated whether it was possible to conduct such an analysis at all, since to do so one would have to formulate "laws about the unique." *The Modern World System* thus emphasized a theoretical issue. "There had only been one 'modern world.' Maybe one day there would be discovered to be comparable phenomena on other planets, or additional modern world-systems on this one. But here and now, the reality was clear—only one" (1974:7). Taking his lead from the science of astronomy—which could only investigate one cosmos—Wallerstein attempted to formulate some of the laws of the modern world system as he traced its origins and charted its development. In doing so, he again emphasized the all-encompassing singularity of his concept of the social system (that is, the world system, not local units like the tribe or nation) by arguing that the social system has to be investigated as a totality:

> Anthropology, economics, political science, sociology—and history—are divisions of the discipline anchored in a certain liberal conception of the state and its relation to functional and geographical sectors of the social order. They make a certain limited sense if the focus of one's study is organizations. They make none at all if the focus is the social system. I am not calling for a multidisciplinary approach to the study of social systems, but for a unidisciplinary approach. (Wallerstein 1974:11)

Specifically, Wallerstein's world system is the modern capitalist system. He notes that "thus far there have only existed two varieties of . . . world-systems: world-empires, in which there is a single political system over most of the area . . . and those systems in which such a single political system does not exist" (348). Of the latter, for which he uses the term "world-economy," and which he sometimes calls the "modern world system," there has only been one instance; all premodern world economies have been "highly unstable structures which tended either to be converted into empires or disintegrate" (348). This modern world system represents a vastly more effective form of economic domination than empire did: it "invented the technology that makes it possible to increase the flow of the surplus from the lower strata to the upper strata, from the periphery to the center, from the majority to the minority, by eliminating the 'waste' of too cumbersome a political structure" (15–16). Moreover, once the state becomes "less the central economic enterprise than the means of assuring certain terms of trade in other economic transactions," the operation of the market creates "incentives to increased productivity and all the consequent accompaniment of modern economic development" (16).

Such a world economy, Wallerstein notes, "seems to be limited in size" (16). Citing Ferdinand Fried, he argues that, just as the limits of the Roman economy were what could be reached in forty to sixty days, so too the developing modern world economy was originally limited in size. In discussing the origins of the modern world economy, Wallerstein thus further specifies his focus as "the 60-day European world economy in the sixteenth century" (17). Crucial to the 500-year survival and stability of this world economy has been the fact that it is not

> a system based on the noninterference of the state in economic affairs. Quite the contrary! Capitalism is based on the constant absorption of economic loss by political entities, while economic gain is distributed to "private" hands. What I am arguing rather is that capitalism as an economic mode is based on the fact that economic factors operate within an arena larger than that which any political entity can totally control. This gives capitalists a freedom of maneuver that is structurally based. (349)

In the very structure of the modern world system, then, one might find multipolar complexity and conflict, as opposed to the centralization of an empire. As we have seen, Wallerstein's world system is all-encompassing and singular. It is also, however, conflictual and complex: the "life" of the world system is "made up of the conflicting forces which hold it together by tension, and tear it apart as each group seeks eternally to remold it to its advantage" (347). Within the singular world system, then, Wallerstein isolates several orders of difference: in his most widely disseminated distinction, he separates the system into a core, semiperiphery, and periphery. In turn, these units are themselves composed of a plurality of "cultural-national" identities. In a passage crucial to understanding Wallerstein's dramatic alteration of the three worlds theory, he writes that

> while, in an empire, the political structure tends to link culture with occupation, in a world-economy the political structure tends to link culture with spatial location. The reason is that in a world-economy the first point of political pressure available to groups is the local (national) state structure. Cultural homogenization tends to serve the interests of key groups and the pressures build up to create cultural-national identities. (349)

Once the bourgeoisie recognized that their interests were linked to national structures, not membership in an international class, this process of nation building began. The results of the process, moreover, reflect the degree to which power has been attained, giving rise to Wallerstein's categories of core, semiperiphery, and periphery. In places where power was more concentrated, coherent cultures and integrated states were developed, whereas in places of geoeconomic weakness, national integration and cultural integrity were lacking. Integrated national cultures were created in

> what we have called the core-states. In such states, the creation of a strong state machinery coupled with a national culture, a phenomenon often referred to as integration, serves both as a mechanism to protect

disparities that have arisen within the world-system, and as an ideological mask and justification for the maintenance of these disparities.

World-economies then are divided into core-states and peripheral
areas. I do not say peripheral *states* because one characteristic of a peripheral area is that the indigenous state is weak, ranging from its nonexis-
tence (that is, a colonial situation) to one with a very low degree of
autonomy (that is, a neo-colonial situation).

There are also semiperipheral areas which are in between the core and
the periphery on a series of dimensions, such as the complexity of economic activities, strength of the state machinery, cultural integrity,
etc. . . . The semiperiphery, however, is not an artifice of statistical cut-
ting points, nor is it a residual category. The semiperiphery is a necessary
structural element in a world-economy. These areas play a role parallel to
that played, *mutatis mutandis,* by middle trading groups in an empire.
(359)

Wallerstein sums up this singular system, operating conflictually through
a plurality of parts of its own creation, as follows: "National homogeneity
within international heterogeneity is the formula of a world-economy"
(353).

Wallerstein's narrative here needs to be supplemented with the burgeoning literature on nationalism and the formation of nation-states,
from theoretical overviews like Benedict Anderson's *Imagined Communities*
(1983), Ernest Gellner's *Nations and Nationalism* (1983), A. D. Smith's *Theories of Nationalism* (1983), and Eric Hobsbawm's *Nations and Nationalism
since 1780* (1990) to specific studies like Eugen Weber's *Peasants into Frenchmen: The Modernization of Rural France 1870–1914* (1976). Wallerstein argues that modern nation building was promoted by the dialectics of the
world economy and differs from analysts who see it as less inevitable and
the product of multiple factors, but these disputes are not relevant here.
What is important for us is the fact that with the rise of the modern world
system, and the flowering of the nation-state as the world's dominant
social form, culture became an increasingly important factor in geopolitical order and an important aspect of the exercise and consolidation of
power; and culture was, in the process, territorialized–attached to territory, given geographical borders—as it had not previously been. The assumptions and attitudes about national culture embedded in three worlds
theory—those I have been deconstructing—were themselves anything
but natural, but were constructed, invented, over the course of the preceding centuries. Thus, what recent centuries constructed, the past several
decades might well deconstruct; indeed, one of the crucial themes of globalization is how the territorialization of culture has been undercut and
even reversed. Particularly thanks to technological developments in travel

and communication, even "national" cultures have come to exist more explicitly across, apart from, and even without territories they possess as their own.

Wallerstein's core/semiperiphery/periphery distinctions sound a bit like a repackaging of the three worlds theory, but there are fundamental differences. First, Wallerstein's system creates its parts, whereas, in the three worlds theory, the system is composed of previously created parts. Thus, for Wallerstein, the content of the elementary parts—the specific "cultural-national identities"—is structurally only secondary, an assertion that sets not only Ricoeur but the whole tradition of cultural nationalism on its head. Second, the cultural content of nationalism is revealed as manufactured, and its manufacture is part of the struggle for position and power in what is (unlike in the three worlds theory) a singular, but (as in the three worlds theory) still hierarchical, world system. Third, the system operates synchronically: parts of it cannot so easily be positioned along a developmental timeline, as they have been simultaneously created. What divides the "modern" from the "premodern" within the system is power more than time; to be "advanced" is to have a coherent cultural-national identity embodied in a powerful state, and is the sign of differential position within the system.

The relational, synchronic creation of both core/semiperiphery/periphery and "cultural-national identities" seems still more radical if one notes that they have intercreated, or interconstitute, each other, and that the system as a whole is therefore an "interactive" creation. Such a rephrasing of Wallerstein's ideas would soon be made, as we shall see, when his theory bred revisionary successors. In Wallerstein's formulation, however, the assertion of a systemic hierarchy highlights inequitable exchanges between the system's parts, thereby suppressing the notion of reciprocality that the word "interactive" stresses. Similarly, Wallerstein's neo-Marxian use of distinctions between capitalist and precapitalist modes of production limits the extent to which his theory destabilizes the timeline implicit in the three worlds theory. Translation of Wallerstein's system into historiography thus typically reimports into historical narrative the somewhat invidious, conventionally Marxian timeline, even though the author's intention may have been different. For example, Eric Wolf's *Europe and the People without History* is a narrative of the growth of the capitalist world system, written with the intention of drawing more attention to the peripheries (the people denied history) than Wallerstein does. Wolf devotes much space to the effect of incorporation into the capitalist world system on peripheral societies, arguing passionately against the legacy of primordialism in what he satirizes as the "billiard ball" school of anthropology—anthropology that investigates Third World and "indigenous" cultures as bounded, "traditional" entities, rather than social forms reshaped by the world system. Wolf demonstrates the interconnections vividly—arguing that "the more ethnohistory we know, the more clearly 'their' history and 'our' history emerge as part of the same history," and that "there can be no 'Black history' apart from 'White history'" (1982:19)—but he cannot escape two invidious forms of temporalization. He stresses the modes of production that characterize the economies of particular societies, pointing out that heterogeneity existed on the periphery, as when precapitalist modes of production coexisted with capitalist ones; in doing so, he subscribes to Marxian historicizing of some as "earlier" than others. Second, he and L. S. Stavrianos—another translator of world-systems theory into historical narrative—historicize development by differentiating between when particular societies were incorporated into the capitalist world system. The result is that when Wallersteinian hierarchy develops its underlying narrative, it does much less to shift emphasis to the peripheries than it claims, but still regulates them narrowly in the terms of the core.

Wallerstein's formulation retains hierarchy in structural analysis and historical narrative, but it links all the parts of the system together. In that respect it is a decentering approach to world order. Anthony King, writing on urbanism, puts this aspect of Wallerstein's thought clearly, in a way that might be generalized to a host of other cultural forms and fields of knowledge. For King, a theory like Wallerstein's shows that "not only can colonial urban development not be understood separately from developments in the metropole but[,] similarly, urbanism and urbanization in the metropole cannot be understood separately from developments in the colonial periphery. They are all parts of the same process" (1990b:7). Studies of colonial urban development thus need to be joined to studies of metropolitan development; economic developmentalism in the peripheries needs to be joined to the economic activity of the core; and, by extension, for example, European literatures (and theories of literature) cannot be understood in isolation from colonial relationships. Such a dramatic rupturing of borders indeed proves to be an opening for a still wider variety of theories of culture and its production, theories surveyed later in this book: the notion, increasingly widely assumed, even when only dimly understood, that the world is a single sociocultural system lies at the heart of much of the astonishing wealth of theoretical dispute about culture of recent decades. Much of this dispute, as we shall see, has focused on undermining several of Wallerstein's essential presuppositions: the hierarchy of the system (its division into core, semiperiphery, and periphery); the notion of the continued manufacture of national cultures as an essential component of it; and the monolithic coherence of the resulting world system. The result, moreover, of undermining these features of Wallerstein's system while retaining the notion of the interactive system itself has been, first, to increasingly decenter Wallerstein's system, and, second, to exponentially augment the amount of difference and plurality generated by the system. I discuss these developments later; here, however, I focus on a few cultural texts and strategies for analysis of culture that utilize Wallerstein's hierarchies.

The film *El Norte* (1983) dramatizes the flight of two Guatemalan Indians—a brother and sister named Enrique and Rosa—from political persecution at home, and their travels through Mexico and illegal immigration into the United States. The film begins and ends with tragedy: at the beginning, the brother and sister flee when their father, who has been trying to organize the Indians to resist exploitation by plantation owners in league with the military, is betrayed and killed, and truckloads of citizens are hauled off by the military, never to return. In the end, Rosa, who, with Enrique, has been horribly bitten by rats as they crawl across the border into the United States through a disused drainpipe, dies of murine typhus, as the weeping Enrique repeats the litany of hopes that has brought them to the United States: we'll have luck; we shall have all we want; we shall return to our village, and people will look on us with envy; things are changing; we must not lose faith. When she dies, Enrique is left with the mockery of all these hopes: not only has he lost Rosa, but, by staying with her at the hospital, he has also lost what is presented as his only chance to make it out of the dead-end situation of illegal laborer and into a decent job and the hope of a green card.

Overtly, the movie is clearly a specimen of the dystopian strain of American immigrant literature/film. Immigrants from a premodern, rural village come to the United States, inspired by its promises of freedom and prosperity, go through great hardships, and encounter tragedy rather than success in the end. The United States does not live up to its rhetoric; it proves to be a land, not of freedom and opportunity, but of discrimination and exploitation. The melting pot does not melt, but exposes immigrants to loss of their culture while keeping them segregated. The vision of immigration as a kind of rebirth, a dramatic transformation of immigrants' lives, proves false. Immigration turns out to be, at best, a loss of roots; at works, of life. Utopian or dystopian, however, this pattern clearly emphasizes the separateness of cultures and the existence of a timeline that distinguishes premodern from modern.

While utilizing this form, *El Norte* nonetheless sets about undercutting its assumptions in a number of ways. The immigrants suffer, but they are not poor, premodern huddled masses discovering an American culture that they can only react to with the awe of Rangamma's listeners. Enrique and Rosa are quick to pick up cultural style and manners as they move from Guatemala to Mexico to the North America, and they emerge, in the United States, as culturally sophisticated as the natives. More important, the considerable differences between cultures—with which the movie has a great deal of fun—are revealed to be differences that mask an underlying monosystematicity. Chased by the soldiers who finally slaughter him, Enrique's father picks up the gun of one he has clubbed, but cannot see how it is used, and is thus killed. At that moment, he seems the culturally limited peasant, incapable of figuring out modern technology, just as the village he lives in is depicted throughout with a loving attention to its primitive-magical-religious culture. Nonetheless, he tells Enrique a truth that applies to the United States as much as to Guatemala, one that the movie presents as essential to all the places on Enrique and Rosa's travels: to the rich, peasants are just a pair of arms to do their work. This bitter truth is emphasized at the end of the movie when Enrique, his hopes and his sister gone, competes with other men to be hired as a day laborer, crying out in the crowd that he has strong arms, will be a good worker.

The underlying common reality is thus economic power, and culture, as in Wallerstein's Marxian system, is only its epiphenomenon. Moreover, cultural difference is presented still more specifically as a textbook illustration of Wallerstein. Enrique and Rosa come from a "traditional" Indian culture; the Indians, however, are a rural peasant group, without a government of their own, exploited by plantation owners and the military government, and their culture helps consolidate them in that exploitation. The Indian who betrays Enrique's father is not only tempted by the overseer with money, but also by the Orientalist assertion that the insurgents do not "respect the old customs." Although the movie dramatizes the characters' deep nostalgia for their Indian culture and fully exploits the emotions associated with nostalgic nationalism, it remains simultaneously clear-sighted about the subordination of culture to politics and economics.

That this economic wisdom about exploitation is not some universalizing principle, true of all places and times, but part of a specifically Wallersteinian system becomes even clearer when the two begin their journey. They travel through a Wallersteinian landscape of periphery, semiperiphery, and core. Guatemala, the agricultural periphery, where indigenous people are exploited by means of military terror and economic peonage, yields to Mexico, a land of constant mobility, travel, and trickster figures, where everyone is in transit, on the make; no one (as Enrique and Rosa's duplicitous coyote tells them) owns anything. Portrayed as a nation of marginal middlemen—for whom every third word is "fuck," and who have a comic charm even when perfidious—Mexico calls to mind Wallerstein's semiperiphery, a place that fulfills a function like the middle trading groups in an empire. A landscape of aging machinery, it also testifies to how underdevelopment impoverishes the people it touches. Finally, the United States is the capitalist core: a place where extraction of economic surplus works most systematically, least individually. The movie, unlike other dystopian immigrant fictions, does not portray cruel exploitation in the form of personal brutality; North Americans for the most part are very nice people, able to be pleasant because their system does the exploitation for them. The wealthy woman who hires Rosa as a cleaning lady and, in a comic scene, explains the complexities of a state-of-the-art washing machine, and the doctor who compassionately treats Rosa when she finally collapses and is taken to the hospital are both kindly and solicitous; so even is Enrique's prospective employer, a Chicago businesswoman who requires him to go to work for her without bringing Rosa along, as families always cause trouble. In its individual representatives, the United States's ethos of individualism and mechanized modernity thus seems benign, but it rests on the systemic oppression of the great majority of people like Enrique and Rosa. As the Mexican-American who rents them a room and finds work for illegals jokes with a colleague, they are, in fact, public servants: the U.S. economy would collapse without the cheap labor they provide.

As an embodiment of Wallerstein's political geography, *El Norte* properly occupies the cleft between traditional immigrant drama and something else. Hierarchy and apparent timeline are present and provide much of the film's pathos; at the same time, systemic global interconnectedness is its underlying message, and culture is ultimately analyzed, against the assumptions that produce the film's pathos, as one of the products of that system. Another device reinforces this interconnectedness in a slightly different way, a device that is similarly used for both nostalgic and demystifying purposes. Frequently, the movie intersperses scenes in the United States with visions from the past, or echoes motifs from the past in present imagery; it also vividly juxtaposes scenes of quiet suburban gardens (void of people, with mechanical sprinklers playing) with the hungry human dynamism of Tijuana. Behind North American values, manners, surfaces, and settings, then, those of Mexico and Guatemala are at times jarringly, immediately visible. These juxtapositions undercut the logic of the territorialization of culture, emphasizing sometimes the characters' nostalgia for home, sometimes the dynamic interconnectedness between the societies, the fact that different regions in fact help constitute each other. The latter sort of juxtaposition thus emphasizes what theorists like Stavrianos, expanding on André Gunder Frank's original formulation, have called the reciprocity of over- and underdevelopment. This concept has proved a more appealing transformation of world-systems thought into historical narrative than Wolf's, and has been provocative in terms of cultural thought as well.

The notion of reciprocal over- and underdevelopment has a longer history as moral critique than it does as part of recent analysis of imperialism. Anticolonial and antislavery rhetoric—dissenting traditions circulating in the core—made use of juxtapositions like those in *El Norte*. In "Free Labor" (1857), Frances Ellen Watkins Harper, an antislavery activist and poet, wrote: "I wear an easy garment / O'er it no toiling slave / Wept tears of hopeless anguish / In his passage to the grave." By implication, women should be aware of their privileges at the expense of others—they are to see tears woven into their slave-made garments. Similarly, Edmund Burke, in the proceedings to impeach Warren Hastings, sought to expose the suffering behind tea imported from India:

> The treatment of females could not be described: . . . the virgins were carried to the Court of Justice, where they might naturally have looked for protection; but now they looked for it in vain; for in the face of the Ministers of Justice, in the face of the spectators, those tender and modest virgins were brutally violated. The only difference between their treatment and that of their mothers was, that the former were dishonoured in the face of day, the latter in the gloomy recesses of their dungeons. Other females had the nipples of their breasts put in a cleft bamboo, and torn off. What modesty in all nations most carefully conceals, this monster revealed to view, and consumed by slow fires. . . . Here Mr. Burke dropped his head upon his hands a few minutes; but having recovered himself, said, that the fathers and husbands of the hapless females were the most harmless and industrious set of men. Content with scarcely sufficient support of nature, they gave almost the whole produce of their labour to the East-India Company: those hands which had been broken by persons under the Company's authority, produced to all England the comforts of their morning and evening tea. (Sulieri 1992:60)

In Wallerstein, such compression of the exploitation of the periphery in the banal, everyday details of the core is implied by the idea that the construction of cultural-national identities is the fruit of power within the system. Anthony King more overtly investigates the reciprocality of un-

derdevelopment and overdevelopment when he shows how such a perspective can be applied to the development of the built environment in
the United Kingdom. Certain segments of it can be seen "not just as the
product of a global economy but of a real international division of labour.
If, 'in a very real sense, the slave plantations of the Caribbean . . . were
part of the social structure of modern Britain,' the vast country houses and
estates such as Harewood, or Fonthill, built on plantation profits, or on
capital accumulated from India were part of an urban system created by
the capitalist world-economy" (1990b:80). King then goes on to single out
two less obvious areas of British urbanization for examination in this large
context: "the rise and subsequent decline of the coastal leisure resort, a
classic case of the investment and circulation of surplus capital, and late-
nineteenth- and early-twentieth-century suburbanization" (1990b:80). In
making this suggestion, King updates Burkean rhetoric for the contemporary suburban mundane; his model suggests how seeing the world as a
single social system must dramatically reinterpret local forms as globally
produced.

Further examples are not hard to find: Cliff's Dungle provides one, and
a 1967 poem by the Guatemalan Louis Alfredo Arrago, quoted by Shiv
Visvanathan (1988) in an article on colonialism and science, is another.
Describing the burial of a dead child in a cardboard box, the poet records
the imprint on the carton: it read "'General Electric Company / Progress
is our Best Product' (261–62). In a still more extreme vein, Frantz Fanon
revised, as Edward Said puts it, "the hitherto accepted paradigm by which
Europe gave the colonies their modernity" and argued "instead that not
only were 'the well-being and the progress of Europe . . . built up with the
sweat and the dead bodies of Negroes, Arabs, Indians, and the yellow races'
but 'Europe is literally the creation of the Third World,' a charge to be made
again and again by Walter Rodney, Chinweizu, and others" (1993:197).

From this perspective, then, First World cultural practices, from customs to literary forms to epistemological assumptions, might be reinterpreted as examples of overdevelopment based on the underdevelopment of the Third World. Benita Parry (1989:52–55) follows Said (1985) in
calling for a reciprocal analysis of the culture of imperialism in the colonial
power along with what has been much more vigorously pursued, the study
of colonialism. Parry cites Said's example of how such an analysis can yoke
Orientalist practice in the colonies with the production of the "sexual,
racial and political asymmetry underlying mainstream modern western
culture." Visible, then, would be the "narrow correspondence between
suppressed Victorian sexuality at home, its fantasies abroad, and the tight-
ening hold on the male late nineteenth century imagination of imperialist
ideology" (54). Ashis Nandy has, in fact, written such a critique in his

sympathetic analysis of Rudyard Kipling in *The Intimate Enemy: Loss and Recovery of Self under Colonialism* (1983). Said goes on, in *Culture and Imperialism,* to present a theory of the English novel as dependent on and supportive of colonialism—as a cultural form that centralized England by rendering it as "surveyed, evaluated, . . . known," as opposed to a vague "abroad" (1993:72), and appropriated, globally, "the capacity to represent, portray, characterize, and depict," which was "not easily available to just any member of any society" (80).

Said sees the development of the novel as in turn part of a larger attempt to make knowledge dependent on the imperial narrativization of history and society—a form of knowledge that suppresses alternative histories and cultural viewpoints. Europe overdeveloped discursive writing in the period of high imperialism by creating the objective European observer, an "invisible scribe" dependent on the transformation of "obdurately material natives . . . from subservient beings into inferior humanity," while a "world universally available to transnational impersonal scrutiny" became "a massively colonized world" (168). In a still sharper vein, Trinh Minh-ha has succinctly satirized Enlightenment assumptions about the First World's quest for knowledge in terms of a pathology of interconnected over- and underdevelopment:

> The idealized quest for knowledge and power makes it often difficult to admit that enlightenment (as exemplified by the West) often brings about endarkment. More light, less darkness. More darkness, less light. It is a question of degrees and these are two degrees of one phenomenon. By attempting to *exclude* one (darkness) for the sake of the other (light), the modernist project of building universal knowledge has indulged itself in such self-gratifying oppositions of civilization/primitivism, progress/backwardness, evolution/stagnation. (1989:40)

In introducing a volume on global cities, King notes that the shift in paradigm, commenced by work like Wallerstein's, became only really prominent in his field in the mid 1980s. This phenomenon poses two questions:

> First, what changes are seen to have taken place in the objective, external world that account for this reorientation in urban research? Second, given that these objective changes have been taking place for at least three decades and, in the longer term, over three centuries or more, why has this theoretical and conceptual understanding of urban development gained currency only from the 1980's and not before? (1990a:4)

As an answer to King's first question, chapter 4 has discussed the variety of factors involved in the contemporary emphasis on globalization: the internationalization of labor, production, consumption and marketing, finance, communications, "dwelling," and population flow. In answer to the second question, King speculates that

> only when the economic base of cities in "advanced economies" in the core was affected, have many urbanists in those countries looked beyond national boundaries to the larger economic system that supported them. Yet the inhabitants of that "external world" have long been aware that their own urban situation has been affected by core societies, except that this was seen as part of a larger process that went by another name—colonialism. Another answer is more prosaic: the academic realization that earlier explanations of urban growth and decline were too parochial and therefore, inadequate: the analysis required a deeper (historical) and broader (geographical) framework that went beyond traditional disciplinary boundaries. (7)

King sees Third World immigration to England, which has made London more and more resemble a city in the former colonies, as an important reason for the boom in global theory of the 1980s; also important was the "Big Bang" of 1980s London, the sudden growth and internationalization of finance thanks to deregulation and the urban building boom that accompanied it, developments that also occurred in the United States during the Reagan era. Conceiving the world as a single social system, then, represents a dramatic alteration in the theoretical paradigm in a core startled by profound changes to itself. These changes emanate both from the center and the margins: they include, for example, the sudden visibility of, and self-representation by, previously distanced or marginalized "others" and a drastic restructuring of international finance.

Looking back at Wallerstein from the perspective of the theoretical boom he helped initiate, King then shows that Wallerstein's world system stands on a particular borderline: the borderline between the anticolonial legacy and the world order that grew out of, yet also transgressed, the assumptions of that legacy. Wallerstein's centered system, based on a structural hierarchy of stronger and weaker, more or less coherent, national units, reflects the anticolonial critique of the worldwide domination of Europe and, latterly, the United States. The new global perspective that Wallerstein's notion of the single system powerfully advances did not, however, remain true to those roots: indeed, as production, consumption, labor, finance, media, culture, and demographics became more and more globalized, the world social system became simultaneously more transparently interactive and complexly fragmented. Thus, King, building on Wallerstein, quickly puts pressure on Wallerstein's concepts of core, semi-periphery, and periphery: in discussing the globalization of London, he argues that "the removal of particular colonialisms from the 1960s

(French, British, and Portuguese) and the general expansion of the world market, though characterized by grossly uneven development, has none the less evened out some of the differences by two processes: the peripheralization of the core and the corealization of the periphery" (46).

To peripherize the core and "corealize" the periphery means the commencement of a movement that may undo Wallerstein's hierarchy. King sees this process, driven by internationalization and immigration, becoming visible in English and European core cities as they come to imitate the segmented colonial city of the periphery. What formerly was confined to colonies (including the United States) appeared in Europe: racial and ethnic separation—colonials versus "natives," as well as the additional segmentation of the "natives" into subgroups that colonial policy enhanced —became the norm in the colonial core. Indeed, King outlines a list of nineteen ways in which the colonial city, not the formerly homogeneous core city, was the precursor of today's world cities (39–45). In doing so, King also reverses the more elusively invidious form of hierarchy that still, as we have seen, lingers about Wallerstein's world system: the idea of a timeline. For King, colonial circumstances represent, in fact, not the past of which the core is the modern future, but a new global future that the core is only beginning to recognize. The peripheries are thus not behind but *further along* the developmental timeline, an argument we have already encountered in surveying Japanese nationalism and shall encounter again, as what was formerly premodern or the underdeveloped, like Japanese Edo culture and King's colonial cities, becomes the herald of the postmodern world system we are now entering.

The remaining chapters of the book explore ways in which the legacy of the colonial center in Wallerstein's classic formulation has been gradually deconstructed in a number of different fields, by a wide range of theorists, including, to a degree, Wallerstein himself, who has recently written about contemporary changes in global order and culture. A key proposition is that as the world draws more tightly together into a single system, it multiplies its circulation of differences. I shall explore the implications of this fruitful paradox for both the production and the conceptualization of culture, surveying developments in a variety of different disciplines.

Part II

Decentering the Core

6

Theorizing Ethnicity in America

JACQUES DERRIDA wrote in 1966 that the science of ethnology was born at a time when a crucial "decentering" had taken place, when "European culture . . . had been *dislocated* from its locus, and forced to stop considering itself the culture of reference" (1978:86). The point of origin of this rupture, this decentering, Derrida located in philosophy, at the moment when the "structurality of structure had . . . [begun] to be thought" and the notion of a "center" that "governs the structure, while escaping structurality" has come to seem illegitimate, a construct deployed in order to make the world thinkable. "Even today," Derrida wrote, "the notion of a structure lacking any center represents the unthinkable itself."

Although a critique of philosophy, Derrida's formulation has great relevance to attempts in a variety of disciplines to theorize world order and culture's place in it. As described in chapter 5, in the field of global mapping, Wallerstein's world-systems theory represents only a partial response to Derrida: although it relieves Europe of the role of culture of reference, and its center does not escape structurality, it does not jettison the notion of center altogether and attempt the "unthinkable." In its later history, however, the formulation of Wallerstein's theory has been attacked precisely for this conservatism. It has seemed to many far too centered to express the changes that have been occurring in the past twenty years. In the next four chapters, we shall look at a series of interventionist cultural movements that have sought to decenter the system Wallerstein describes, often to the point where the "unthinkable" is approached in thought. In this and the next chapter, we shall examine a series of attempts to decenter the core culturally; the subsequent chapters focus on interventionist attempts to decenter relationships between the core and the periphery. For the sake of convenience—and to recognize the fact that the contemporary world is marked by the legacies of two world orders, the Eurocolonial and the American neocolonial—we shall focus on the United States in the following two chapters and on the relationships between England and

Europe and their former colonies in chapters 8 and 9. Cultural relationships perhaps have a much longer half-life than political systems, and
contemporary global culture still circulates material based on the former
colonial-imperial world structure, although dominated by the more recent regime of American commercial culture.

Also, for the sake not just of convenience, but to avoid the well-nigh
impossible task of a short but comprehensive survey of contemporary
cultural disputes, I shall limit my focus to two specific (but high-profile)
areas of cultural interventionism. Clearly, contemporary cultural studies
are marked by an unprecedented heterogeneity of positions, issues, and
approaches. A wealth of work has been done from such perspectives as
race, sexuality and gender, class, and postcoloniality. Furthermore, this
work has been carried out according to a variety of preferred theories and
methods: neo-Marxian, deconstructionist, poststructuralist, postmodernist, subalternist, feminist, new historicist, and so on. And it has centered
about a number of different public issues and points of controversy, such
as multiculturalism, canon reform, the politicization of scholarship, and
anti-Eurocentrism. Although many interventionists write as if in embattled conflict with a much more powerful mainstream, and although the
public hue and cry that neoconservatives have raised has had an astonishingly wide public press and government backing, cultural interventionism has also been appraised, by observers like Elizabeth Fox-Genovese
(1991) and Masao Miyoshi, as having dramatically altered many cultur-
al/intellectual agendas and institutions today. "Evidence of this unmis-
takeable transformation," Miyoshi writes, "can be seen by comparing the
programs of the annual conventions of the Modern Language Association
of 1970—or even 1980—with that of 1990" (1991:193).

From this wealth of heterogeneous but often complexly interconnected
and allied work, I have selected two areas for extended discussion: (1) shifts
in the United States of conceptualizations of cultural identity, as stimulated by and revealed in ethnic and immigrant cultural production and
theory, and (2) the development of counterdiscursive positions in postcolonial cultural production and theory. These two areas—multiculturalism and postcolonialism—are only two of many contemporary movements and concerns, but they are particularly relevant focuses for
revealing relationships between cultural activity and a changed world order. Their very names, in evoking cultural units and colonial relationships,
incorporate the geopolitical boundaries and hierarchies that are now being unsettled and transgressed.

Clearly, much of the public advocacy of, and also alarmed response to,
interventionist cultural theories and movements has come from a sense

that the world order is indeed changing. Crucial has been the perception that the core has been undergoing several transformations: the United States, like England before it, has been losing its hegemony over what appears to be a more plural, up-for-grabs world system, and core countries, internally, have lost their centered coherence. Writing about England, Stuart Hall (1991a), like Anthony King, has underscored factors such as economic decline, internationalization of the economy, and the renewal of global migrations that have reversed the direction of the former population flows by bringing Third World people in large numbers to the former imperial heartland:

> With the processes of globalization, [the] . . . relationship between a national cultural identity and a nation-state is beginning, at any rate in Britain, to disappear. And one suspects that it is not only there that it is beginning to disappear. The notion of a national formation, of a national economy, which could be represented through a national cultural identity, is under considerable pressure. (22)

Circumstances in the United States have been remarkably similar. In the popular media and scholarly analyses, American economic slippage has been mulled over endlessly and has become an important political issue. Immanuel Wallerstein has bluntly written that "U.S. global hegemony, a brief phenomenon, as have been previous such hegemonies, was based on a temporary dramatic edge in the efficiencies of U.S. productive, commercial, and financial enterprises. This period is now over" (19). Culture has been brought into the debate most prominently in tracts like Ezra Vogel's (1979) work on Japanese capitalism, that have sought to explain this decline and locate its causes, at least in part, in culture. Reflecting the same kind of anxiety Hall sees in Britain, neoconservative American prophets of domestic crisis have lamented the supposed loss of common culture in the United States and have equated this with the loss of national power as well as identity. Their target, multiculturalism, has sought, by contrast, to refigure national identity to accommodate the kinds of stresses Hall describes and to pursue in a new form an oppositional ideal that dates back to the early decades of the twentieth century, but flowered most recently in 1960s cultural pluralism. To be sure, a good part of the popular debate may have been motivated by neoconservatives' desire to construct a screen issue for demagogic purposes, a controversy that might distract attention from more fundamental national issues and problems. At the same time, the debate has produced a significant focus of cultural debate in America: neoconservatives and radicals alike have come to assume unquestioningly that culture is deeply political—that it plays a socially transformative role.

This debate has also been part of a larger process. It has come simultaneously as a consequence of, a development in sync with, and an attempt to react aggressively against changes in the surrounding world system. Tracking these developments means circumspectly intertwining local and global narratives, in full awareness that this intertwining will not reveal the simple drama of a nation opening out/in upon the global. What will be revealed is a series of parallel and intricately interrelated transformations in local culture and the global system: the movement from a period of globally disseminated nationalism, which reinforced the construction of national identities as objects of faith and focuses for social organization, to a period of globalism, in which the stereotypical national culture has become increasingly strained, fractured, and demystified, and more complex and heterogeneous forms of local culture have been developed to negotiate the larger system. From a distance, the large-scale pattern has, I believe, indeed emerged, but its "totality" has been built up by a welter of disparate, even conflicting, more and less local and international determinations. A crucial challenge in tracking it is, then, to do justice to often quite separate, historically determined contexts and frames of reference, and the particular, historically determined ways in which a disparate range of factors have interacted.

In America, immigrant and ethnic traditions have been marked by complex relationships between local and global contexts, and the 1960s were, of course, the crucial phase in their postwar development. The 1960s saw a series of crucial turning points: in 1963, Nathan Glazer and Daniel Patrick Moynihan proclaimed that the melting pot had not melted; in 1965, civil rights legislation and an immigration law eliminating national origins as a principle of selection were passed; and in 1966, Stokely Carmichael introduced the slogan "Black Power," leading by the end of the decade to what Thomas Archdeacon calls an "unprecedented consensus" among both militant and moderate black leaders "that they must make the general society conscious rather than unconscious of color" (1983:216). In the wake of—and on the basis of—what Philip Gleason (1980) has called the postwar ideological revival—"the powerful reaffirmation of American ideology as the basis of national identity . . . from World War II to the mid-1960's" (47)—the seams began to split: cultural pluralism emerged as a powerful public issue and force. On the one hand, this represented an extension of the ideologically sacred concept of the United States as a nation of immigrants, a nation of nations; on the other hand, it ruptured these traditions, as analyses of American racism and the failure of the melting pot were supplemented by advocacy of oppositional and revolutionary forms of cultural nationalism. In race relations, in ethnic affairs, and in management of internal borders generally, the boundaries of American identity were being transgressed and shattered.

Focusing more specifically on just one of these factors, the controversy about the melting pot, we can see clearly that what appeared to be local development—the development and rupture of a particular strain of American nationalism, the notion of the United States as the land of immigrants—was a part of global, as well as local, patterns. From the Puritan exodus to Crèvecoeur's celebration of immigrants melting into a new race of men, to the many, differently conceived melting pots of the twentieth century, immigrants have served American nationalism as an important site for inscription of ideology. Indeed, immigrant identity was so valorized that Franklin Delano Roosevelt could provocatively urge the DAR to "remember always that all of us, and you and I especially, are descended from immigrants and revolutionists" (Klein 1981:89), and William Carlos Williams could assert that the source of the American language he so defended was "the mouths of Polish mothers" (229). Margaret Mead could write in *And Keep Your Powder Dry* (1948) that, psychologically, the third-generation immigrant was the archtypal American, and a British observer of America could remark that Americans were a people who were always from somewhere else. Topographically, the United States was held to be the nation of nations, while, developmentally, a familiar trope saw it as completing the westward course of world civilization: both versions, clearly, made America's claim to be a microcosm of the world a basis for America's exceptional national identity.

American exceptionalism was in turn a tool with multiple uses. It was a means of community building in America, and a means of negotiating—or claiming—a position in the world. As such, it has been marked by the oxymoronic doubleness that Michael Kammen (1973) has seen as characteristic of many features of American society and culture: it has had potential simultaneously for imperial and anticolonial uses. On the one hand, it has justified appropriation and settlement of America, masking that as the ethnogenesis of a special people on a virgin land; on the other hand, it sought to unseat English colonial dominance by representing this ethnogenesis as the fulfillment of dreams only glimpsed in Europe. America styled itself variously as the city on a hill, the true church in the wilderness, the true Enlightenment democracy, and nature's society in the new Arcadia. It realized thereby in fact what were, in Europe, ideals, and the result was that Europe would have to look to America for an image of its own transformation. Proclamation of oneself as a city on a hill represented a powerful antidote to fears of vanishing in a wilderness—of disappearing into the merely peripheral—as well as a significant wedge for prying one's way into a core position globally. There had to be a "there" injected into America, unlike Gertrude Stein's Oakland, and, from the beginning, attempts to socially engineer this exceptionalist ethnogenesis were crucial components of American culture. From George Washington's early advocacy of a national university to the common schools movement in the nineteenth century, to the Americanization movement's attempt to manufacture national community at the time of World War I, to the debate about common culture today, participation in an ongoing, anxious debate about American cultural identity, rather than the resolution of that debate, has been what makes one an American. America has been ideologically exceptionalist as the country where a world-significant ethnogenesis is always still *under way,* not one where it has been wrapped up and finally institutionalized.

If the early icons of American ideology—the city on the hill, the virgin land, the melting of peoples into the new figure of the American—were multi-edged tools for community building, appropriating a continent, and negotiating dependent relationships in the colonial-mercantilist world system, later species of American nationalism could be similarly analyzed. There is not time, nor is it appropriate here, to attempt such a global-local history of American nationalism from its beginnings; it must be sufficient to assert that American national traditions were not at any time simply local produce, but remained interactively dependent on the surrounding global system. Just as Japanese nationalism must be reinterpreted in terms of its distinctive styles of community building and negotiation of the world system, American nationalism must be rephrased. Frank Thistlewaite, a pioneer of migration history, has asserted that until recently, thanks to the dominant perception that turn-of-the-century migration meant American immigration, migration history has been like "Andromeda chained to the rock of national history and crying to be freed to become an independent force" (1991:57). This applies equally to the history of American culture and ideology: like studies of migration, it needs to be transferred from a purely American Studies context to a global one (Kaplan and Pease 1993). The postwar period, and developments leading up to it, must supply the chief example of this larger assertion; and the conflict between our two competing notions of ethnic and national identity, the melting pot and cultural pluralism, will reveal itself as, not just a local dispute, but one intricately embedded in global relationships, part of a series of reshapings of the globe that has accelerated as the century has progressed.

Developments in the 1960s played themselves out against well-established traditions of controversy over immigration, ethnicity, and racial identity in the United States, traditions that were, in turn, determined by the interaction of global and local developments. The prevailing localist analysis of American immigrant history has been revised somewhat by Archdeacon, according to whom the so-called new immigration of the 1880s to 1924 was not "a phenomenon exclusive to the United States. The dramatic influx that occurred there formed part of a worldwide movement of people in the late decades of the nineteenth century and the early ones of the twentieth" (1983:113). The drama of Ellis Island was simply America's more culturally heterogeneous, or "ethnically balanced," as Archdeacon puts it, version of push-pull flows that contributed large populations to Canada, South America, New Zealand, and Australia. Similarly, by the fist decade of the twentieth century, in places like Australia, Argentina, Canada, and Chile, new immigrants of disfavored "stock" were, like their counterparts in the United States, being blamed for social problems and screened or excluded according to a racist philosophy that depicted immigrants as biologically and morally inferior to "natives."

To broaden still further Archdeacon's already broadened version, we must place this global migration in two further contexts. First, it occurred as part of the monopoly capitalist/imperialist phase of the world system. At one extreme, it represented a replenishment of pools of exploitable agricultural labor in the peripheral areas in the wake of the abolition of slavery and the destruction of indigenous populations. At the other extreme, in the Untied States, emerging now as a dominant core country, it represented the creation of a kind of internal empire owing to industrialization, urbanization, and the completion of westward expansion. Second, it occurred at the time of a second wave of nationalism in the United States, the time when America's original revolutionary-popular nationalism was supplemented by the Herderian, culture-based nationalism that Eric Hobsbawm (1990) calls nationalism's second global phase. During the latter half of the nineteenth century, Americans absorbed European racialist thought and reconstructed American tradition explicitly in the image of the Anglo-Saxon. As John Higham (1955) and David Bennett (1988) have described, turn-of-the-century America spawned a series of nativist movements based on differences in culture, not religion or political philosophy, as had been the case with previous hostility to immigrants.

In absorbing the new immigrants at the turn of the century, American nationalism developed what was a distinctive internal variation on global colonization, even as, in its traditionally Janus-faced, colonial/anticolonial manner, it was a new alternative to it. It did so to absorb immigrant populations and negotiate a hegemonic place in the world system. On the one hand, immigrants were despised "others," or (in the words of Emma Lazarus, a German-American Jew characterizing later, more exotic Polish and Russian Jewish immigrants) "the wretched refuse of your teeming shore" ([1883] 1987:48). These "others" were socially and economically constrained, ghettoized, and used as exploitable labor for America's capitalist development. William Dean Howells's portrayals of these ghettos in *A Hazard of New Fortunes* (1890) exemplify this enormous social divide: his protagonist observes them as foreign countries within the United States, as picturesque and perhaps more debased than the societies of origin themselves. On the other hand, these same immigrants were promised new lives, and their successes were celebrated as models of the redemptive power of America, which exposed the old world as feudal and oppressive.

The promise to immigrants of transformative inclusion via the melting pot and the simultaneous representation of their identities as alien—a representation that justified their exclusion and exploitation even as it was overtly part of exhortations for their assimilation—displayed the Janus face that, I have argued, was typical of American exceptionalism. Also typical was the implication that, once again, exceptional America was topping the corrupt old country by realizing in fact what in England and Europe were ideal models. Overtly, American took aliens in in all their alienness, and wholly transformed them. American immigration thus promised more than Thomas Babington Macaulay's influential call to form "a class of persons, Indian in blood and color, but English in taste, in opinions, and in intellect" (Stavrianos 1981:477). At the same time, a covert version of outclassing Europe appeared. The vivid realities of a plural-colonial society were institutionalized in Howells's New York, not in Britain; ethnically segmented New York resembled a colonial city, unlike the more ethnically homogeneous European capitals, which were separated geographically from the people they colonized. This appeared first and foremost to people at the time as a critical social problem to be solved, but it also formed the basis of a new, positive, pluralist definition of American identity, a new version of the image of the United States as a nation of nations.

This startling paradox of the era of the melting pot—simultaneous inclusion and exclusion, assimilation and segmentation, nationalizing Americanization and colonial exploitation—marked even American immigrant success stories. Model immigrant success stories, like Mary Antin's at times excruciatingly self-conscious autobiography, were models precisely because they remind us on every page that the author was an "other," while simultaneously celebrating the supposedly complete transformation of that identity. As its critics have long suspected, the notion of the melting pot encoded both inclusion and exclusion, premigration and

American identities, past and present. What it pretended to efface—the latter term of all these dualities—it in fact underscored. As a result, the polemics of contemporary critics of multiculturalism, like Arthur Schlesinger (1991), who have felt that the ideal of the melting pot should not be cast aside and premigration pasts and identities resurrected and explored, rest on a simplified reading of that famous icon. The melting-pot ideal in fact evokes premigration pasts emphatically in its own way, a way that licenses invidious exclusion as well as incorporation.

America's treatment of its immigrants thus involved a variation on the double bind that colonial empires presented their natives with. Worldwide, the assimilated "native" elites could not circulate freely, but ran into discriminatory exclusion when they attempted to make, as Benedict Anderson (1983) has put it, their pilgrimages from colony to metropolitan center. In America, immigrants were blocked at many places on their way out of the ghetto and into the social and economic mainstream, even as the Americanization of particular individuals and the relative success of particular groups were celebrated by both the larger society and themselves.

Against this simultaneously global and local background, the emergence of ethnic pluralism in the United States must be periodized. In particular, America's classical period of immigration (from the 1880s to 1924) and the ideal of assimilation it gave rise to (an ideal most forcefully examined in Jewish-American writing) were a development of and response to the high imperialist era of the larger world system, which Stavrianos dates as 1870–1915. Similarly, the development of cultural pluralism, from Horace Kallen's pioneering article in 1915 to its climax in black nationalism and "new ethnicity" of the 1960s, had its global equivalent in the rise of global anticolonial nationalism, which, according to Stavrianos, began after World War I and reached a peak in the 1960s. Present conditions, I believe, represent a third phase, both in America's development of notions of ethnic and national identity (the local frame of reference) and in the transformation of the capitalist world system (the global frame of reference).

The dynamic center, as Stavrianos puts it, of the "second or unofficial form of cultural imperialism" (477) was the United States. This "unofficial" form was not mediated by direct imperial control, as was the case with colonialism, and it operated in a global order made up largely of separate nations, not of colonizers and their colonies. Whereas, for the first—the imperialist—era, the notion of civilization served a significant mediating role in the realm of culture and ideology, in the subsequent era it was replaced by the idea of the nation. Roland Robertson (1992b) writes:

> The standard of "civilization" arose during the nineteenth century when Asia and Africa "were brought within the compass of the expanding European-centered international system" (Bull 1984:vii). From the European point of view a major issue was that of the conditions under which European states "would or would not admit non-European political communities to membership of the international society they formed among themselves" (Bull 1984:vii). That issue was resolved in principle by the establishment of the standard of civilization. Asian and African "communities" had to meet that standard if they were to be accepted into "international society" (Bull 1984:vii). On the other hand, the ideal of "civilization" certainly acquired a bad name. Even in the nineteenth century, people from such ancient cultures as China and Persia expressed their deep indignation about European arrogance and presumptuousness when the standard was presented to them, particularly when application of it was seen to involve a privileged legal status for Europeans in the form of the right of "extraterritorial jurisdiction." By the post–Second World War period the standard of civilization was, at least in international law, completely dead end, as Bull (1984:viii) remarked, "now appears to us part and parcel of an unjust system of domination and exploitation against which the peoples of Asia and Africa have rightly revolted." Indeed it has by now become a forbidden term in certain circles, a good example of which is the rule that authors of papers presented at meetings of or published in journals sponsored by the British Sociological Association may not use it without heavy qualification. (219–20)

Replacing "civilization" as a juridico-cultural notion for mediating international relationships was the apparently much more flexible and less invidious idea of national "self-determination, strongly (and problematically) advanced by Woodrow Wilson at the Paris Conference following World War I—and then generalized to what became known as the Third World after the Second World War" (Robertson 1992:218). The rise of nationalism led to a new, institutionalized mutation of an interesting phenomenon that Robertson has made a lynchpin of his globalization theory. Nationalism intensified the way that "globalization involves the universalization of particularism, not just the particularization of universalism" (1987:21): "It is crucial to recognize that the contemporary concern with civilizational and societal (as well as ethnic) uniqueness—as expressed via such motifs as identity, tradition, and indigenization—largely rests on *globally diffused* ideas" (1987:21).

Anthony King puts this paradox more strikingly, asserting that "the degree to which cultures are self-consciously 'different' is an indication of how much they are the same" (1991:153). King quotes Richard Handler's

"Heritage and Hegemony: Recent Works on Historic Preservation and Interpretation" to provide a compelling contemporary example of the process:

> Most nation-states (and many "minority groups" as well) now seek to objectify unique cultures for themselves; . . . they import Western (including anthropological) definitions of what culture is; . . . they import Western technical routines to manage their objectified cultures; . . . they promote their "cultural self-images" internationally in an effort to woo the economically crucial tourist trade; . . . in short, everyone wants to put (their) culture in (their) own museums—all this indicates that modernity has not only conquered the world, but has ushered in a "postmodern" global society of objectified culture, pseudo-events and spectacles. (King 1991:153)

To Handler's list of techniques by which nationalism reproduced difference—a list that includes the academic discipline of anthropology, institutions like museums, and tourism—Robertson adds many others, from the globalization of sociology in the nineteenth century to the recent development of a discipline of intercultural communications (1992a: 83–84, 109–10, 172). National self-determination—which, in replacing civilization as the criterion for entry into the world community, seemed and was, to a degree, a dramatic empowerment for non-European peoples—thus also contained a significant amount of covert global regulation and control. This was supplemented by many more overt forms, from foreign investment (U.S. investment abroad quintupled from 1953 to 1973), to developmentalism and foreign aid, political pressure, and even overt use of force.

American hegemony in the postwar period, resting on the advocacy, dissemination, and manipulation of the ideal of national self-determination, thus globalized, in the neocolonial world system, the American Janus face I have referred to previously. Stavrianos calls it "anticolonial imperialism," a new form of domination that sought, in the words of Anthony Eden, to make "former colonial territories, once free of their masters . . . politically and economically dependent on the United States" (1981:626). Stuart Hall characterizes this doubleness as "a form of capital which recognizes that it can only, to use a metaphor, rule through other local capitals. . . . It does not attempt to obliterate them; it operates through them" (1991:28). Clearly, if the United States sought, as Wallerstein says, "to achieve a gradual, relatively bloodless decolonization of Asia and Africa, on the assumption that this could be arranged via so-called moderate leadership" (1991:66), it was a process that nonetheless did involve blood, and operated through many forms of constraint. Such a doubleness—like the very notion of building one's "own" culture in response to considerable constraint by a larger socialization process—should be no paradox to students of American individualism, a phenomenon that has often appeared as conformist anticonformism. Indeed, how else could Walt Whitman be so assertive an advocate of apparently antinomian individualism as (paradoxically) the basis for *the* American type, becoming thereby both rebellious poet and public bard, the Virgil of the American epic tradition? Given all these factors, it should be no surprise that one of the productive conceptual thorns in the side of postcolonial literary scholarship has been the ambivalent position of the United States as simultaneously a neoimperial power and champion of anticolonial nationalism. Even its canonized classics have had to be reinterpreted in a postcolonial, not simply imperial, context, in such a way as to align them with Third World anticolonial, as well as metropolitan-imperial, literature (Ashcroft, Griffiths, and Tiffin 1989; Buell 1992).

America's prominence on the postwar global stage has had internal effects as well. Wallerstein underscores these interlinkages vividly: writing about the identity of the South, he argues that

> when the United States moved into its position as unquestionable world hegemonic power as of 1945, all changed again. It was no longer in the interest of the dominant political forces of the U.S. federal state to have a "backward" geographical zone, just as it was no longer in its interest to have the denial of political rights to minorities such as the Blacks. The homogenization of America was an urgent political (and diplomatic) need of the U.S. federal state. The industrialization of the South and the Civil Rights Act were all part of a larger picture of "cultural" reorganization. The question was only how various subgroups would react to it. Blacks in the U.S. reacted by asserting, in many ways for the first time, their separate "culture." (1991:213)

Wallerstein, with his penchant for totalizing global analysis, is surely wrong in ignoring local narratives, such as the traditions of cultural nationalism among black Americans that significantly predated the 1960s (Van Deburg 1992:33–38). He is correct, however, in seeing the time as a crucial turning point, when cultural nationalism became a prominent ideal and issue for public debate, thanks in part to America's dominant postwar position. The postwar period did indeed give rise to attempts to reengineer the now globally powerful United States which helped produce the countermovement of ethnic nationalism.

This combination of pressures toward homogenization and cultural difference was very complex. It enhanced ethnic consciousness and politics in mainstream as well as radical contexts. As Archdeacon comments,

Cold War anticommunism in the United States had the effect of creating "a bridge of common interests across the broad chasm that had separated most American conservatives from the descendants of the new immigrants." Although "the most strident critics of the Soviet Union continued to be the strongest foes of liberalizing the immigration law . . . , they quickly recruited Americans of eastern or southern European backgrounds for their anti-Communist crusade" (199). In providing a stimulus to bring formerly excluded immigrants into the American mainstream, Cold War polarization only advanced what World War II had begun: in the war ethnic Americans had a chance to prove their patriotism, and fascism had discredited the racialist philosophy applied to immigrants and blacks. Ethnic rivalries were thus not merely acted out in separatist opposition; they also appeared covertly in mainstream controversies. As David Bennett makes clear in recording a fascinating episode in American political and cultural history in his *The Party of Fear,* the McCarthy-era inquisition served covertly as a forum in which these staunchly anticommunist ethnic Americans could turn the tables on the WASP "majority" by arguing that the minorities were the patriots and the WASPS the betrayers. In the speech that catapulted Senator Joseph McCarthy to wealth and power, he asserted that "it has not been the less fortunate or members of minority groups who have been selling this nation out but rather those who have had all the benefits that the wealthiest nation on earth has to offer" (Bennett 1988:293).

But far more prominent was the way Cold War politics served to create separatist opposition to, rather than ethnic negotiations within, the attempted homogenization of national culture. The persistence of prejudice and discriminatory practices toward black Americans provided the most vivid contradiction between America's ideals and practice, something that the position of the United States in the postwar world made intolerable. Gumnar Myrdal's prescient *An American Dilemma* (1944) put the case well: "In fighting fascism and nazism," Myrdal wrote, "American had to stand before the whole world in favor of racial tolerance and cooperation and of racial equality" (Gleason 1980:51). Arguing that blacks were "awarded the law as a weapon in the caste struggle," and that they had "their allies in the white man's own conscience," Myrdal concluded that not since Reconstruction had "there been more reason to anticipate fundamental changes in American relations" (Gleason 1980:52).

These global pressures heightened the internal drama of the black civil rights struggle, a struggle that quickly inspired a wide variety of ethnic groups to imitate it. Crucial to this societywide dissemination of radical opposition was the advent of Black Power and the widespread decision to make society "conscious rather than unconscious of color" (Archdeacon 1983:216), a change that came when black opposition put cultural nationalism prominently on the national and ethnic agenda. Black cultural politics revealed just as firm a syncretism between global and local factors as was evident in official policy: the local African-American narrative knew itself to be not merely local. When "Stokely Carmichael, H. Rap Brown, and Malcolm X called for Black pride and Black power, talked of the creation of a separate black nation in the United States," they did so in the context of a "worldwide struggle by peoples of other colors against the white race" (Archdeacon 1983:216). The insurgency within the borders of the United States occurred in sync with the anticolonial struggles going on outside them; this interrelationship, moreover, had been in place for some time, culturally in the interactions between movements like *négritude* and the Harlem Renaissance, and politically in the involvement of African-Americans like W. E. B. Du Bois in the struggle of African nationalism.

In response to black American leadership in this area, a large number of other ethnic groups within America promulgated ideas of group-formation and political activity in a nationalist mode. Thus, as Archdeacon writes, "emulating their black peers, educated and articulate members of the National Indian Youth Council, including Melvin Thom, condemned 'Uncle Tomahawks' and called for red power" (216). Similarly, Hispanics formed "movements based on ethnic Mexican, or Chicano, nationalism" (217) in the West, as did Puerto Ricans in New York. A striking addition to these movements came from the groups Michael Novak celebrated as the "new ethnics": Novak argued, in *The Rise of the Unmeltable Ethnics* (1972), that the PIGS—Novak's acronym for Poles, Italians, Greeks and Slavs—had, despite their apparent assimilation and often political conservatism, in fact not melted, but both retained their sense of ethnic identity and were subject, like blacks and Hispanics, to discrimination and marginalization by Anglos. Novak saw for these groups a comparable awakening to ethnic identity and political activism, predicting that it would be substantial. Philip Gleason has commented that the movement was "systematically promoted as a way of defusing white backlash" (53)—Novak's ethnics had been among those taunting civil rights marchers in suburban Chicago—but Novak's text is simultaneously more daring and more reactionary than Gleason reveals. It calls, on the one hand, for a political alliance with blacks and others against the Anglos. On the other hand, Novak's comments on black nationalism, and his apologia for Spiro Agnew, uneasily betrays the divisions between "assimilated" white ethnics and black outsider politics, and his book contains momentary flashes, not just analyses, of the raw ethnic anger that publicly took reactionary form.

The black nationalism that emerged so strongly in the 1960s was, to be sure, no single phenomenon, but involved a number of sometimes mutually hostile viewpoints. In his detailed history of the Black Power movement, William L. Van Deburg (1992:132–91) distinguishes three different kinds of black nationalisms from among a welter of black groups and organizations. Singling out territorial nationalism, revolutionary nationalism, and cultural nationalism as the three generic kinds, Van Deburg chronicles the disputes among them, while noting that culture was pressed into service by all three to achieve transformative ends. Of the groups that placed culture foremost on the agenda, the Black Arts Movement Imamu Amiri Baraka spearheaded with Larry Neal was perhaps the most prominent. It adopted a strong nationalist model, incorporating essential patterns from both nostalgic and revolutionary nationalism. Against psychological and social repression, black Americans, as an oppressed group, attempted to recover and create, in revolutionary form, a separate, bounded culture in touch with its origins.

Stephen Henderson's introduction to his tradition-forming anthology, *Understanding the New Black Poetry* (1973), is marked by many of the features of such nationalism. Henderson (whose essay has recently been characterized as having "foundational value" [Bentson 1989:174]), represents the Black Arts Movement as part of a large step for African-Americans beyond the achievements of the Harlem Renaissance, in that

> poets of the sixties were better informed about the true nature of African civilizations and, as a rule, were especially concerned about the political relevance of modern Africa to the rest of the Black World. This obviously has been a result of the emergence of free African states during the past two decades. . . . A further related factor undoubtedly has been the influx of African students into the colleges and universities of the United States. . . . Then, one must consider the Black Power Movement and its extensions in the Black Arts Movement, the national concern with Black Studies and the subsequent reprinting of quality materials on Africa. (24–25)

Black Americans invoked Africa as a model for revolutionary nationalism and a primordial cultural connection. Indeed, Eldridge Cleaver called *The Wretched of the Earth* the " 'Bible' of the black liberation movement," and Bobby Seale claimed to have read it six times (Van Deburg 1992:160). And many black activists linked the rising global interest in Africa to renewed pride in identification with African culture.

Yoking events at home with those in the larger world system, then, Henderson goes on to argue that black poetry incarnates blackness in theme, structure, and saturation: "Since poetry is the most concentrated and allusive of the verbal arts, if there is such a commodity as 'blackness' in literature (and I assume that there is), it should somehow be found in concentrated or in residual form in the poetry" (4). This assertion is more qualified and restrained than many made by Maulana Ron Karenga and by Amiri Baraka under Karenga's influence: blackness also was found in value systems and thought. Henderson's poetics of pressure asserts that the black cultural universe is so bounded that, as Henderson and others maintain, black poetry can "only be properly understood by Black people themselves" (8) and that only blacks can write it: "if a non-Black writer elected to write on a 'Black theme' using a Black persona, and if he were as successful in absorbing Black expressive patterns as some musicians are, then, indeed, there would be real problems. As far as I know, there are no poems written by non-Blacks which have that degree of success" (11).

Such firm maintenance of boundary lines—which were notoriously accepted by white critics like Richard Gilman—illustrates the strong, centering role culture had in 1960s group-formation. An ethnic group's cultural universe, discovered after years of expropriation, could still be fundamentally intact, and it remained so separate that its producers and interpreters would have to be group members. Concomitant with this assertion was the familiar critique (such as Baraka mounted against Phyllis Wheatley) of blacks who didn't promulgate blackness, but were, as the familiar phrase has it, in effect white on the inside. This form of critique—which quickly became part of the political and cultural nationalism of all the ethnic groups mentioned above—accented again the absoluteness of boundary lines between cultures, even as it constrained firmer group-formation.

This strong cultural nationalist position was criticized and parodied by black critics and writers, from Al Young's satires on Black Arts poetry under the pseudonym "O. O. Gabugah" to Ralph Ellison's powerful critique in *Invisible Man* (1952) and Ishmael Reed's portrayal of the Black Arts position in *Mumbo Jumbo* (1972). A more balanced revaluation has come from Henry Louis Gates Jr., who has argued for the "great achievement" of the Black Arts Movement in creating cultural confidence, within which black cultural difference could be explored (1991a:87–88) and also has called for consideration of the "lesson" of Little Tree (1991b), a lesson to be learned from the way the successful practice of ethnic forgery can challenge nationalist assumptions about culture. (Gates wrote the latter in the wake of revelations that the beloved native American autobiography *Education of Little Tree* was written by either a white Ku Klux Klansman or his close relative.) Similarly, Hazel Carby (1987) has opposed essentialisms of all kinds, citing Alice Walker's criticism of a white feminist critic for claiming she was not qualified to theorize black texts properly, because what they represented was beyond her experience, and Kwame Anthony Appiah has analyzed the "invention of Africa" in the mold of European racialism by a Pan-Africanism initiated by two African-Americans, Alexander Crummell and W. E. B. Du Bois. Asserting that the very category "Negro" was a European product, Appiah (1992) has emphasized the continental and international heterogeneity of Africans in place of the homogenizing category of race. And Abdul JanMohamed and David Lloyd, along with many of the contributors to their important volume *The Nature and Context of Minority Discourse* (1991), and Cornel West (1990) have written about the development in America of a postessentialist, heterogeneous, boundary-crossing cultural politics of difference. Again, as with Gates, the most sophisticated of these approaches reinterpret the recent essentialist past as a necessary basis for a further step forward, while criticizing it as a stage that, if stayed within, would mean the reinscription of old forms of bondage.

From a hostile, neoconservative standpoint, Arthur M. Schlesinger, Jr., in *The Disuniting of America: Reflections on a Multicultural Society* (1991), has provided a popularized farrago of insider and outsider critiques of essentialist separatism; like Diane Ravitch's "Multiculturalism: *E Pluribus Plures*" (1990) Schlesinger's book is a labor of aversion, an attempt to discredit contemporary cultural interventionism by focusing indignation and satirical dismay upon an easy target, strident Afrocentrism. Nonetheless, as the Afrocentrist movement has indicated, black cultural nationalism has continued to be an influential position, and, more important, as Gates's, West's, JanMohammed's and Lloyd's critical appreciation has made clear, has established itself as one of the most significant points in postwar African-American and American literary history. It has marked an important shift in thought about and production of culture in the postwar period, a shift with profound consequences and opportunities for both "ethnic" and "mainstream" traditions.

As the era of global nationalism came to an end, the debate about cultural nationalism on the local level in America also began to change. Critiques like those of Gates, Carby, Appiah, and West represented important changes on the local level that have paralleled, reflected, or responded to recent global developments. The rest of this chapter looks closely at a number of different responses to cultural nationalism in ethnic theory, literary history, and the debate about multiculturalism, charting the gradual paradigm change that has occurred in discussions of both "ethnic" identity and cultural tradition and "American" identity and culture. This change, at its most fundamental, represents a shift from the notion of a pluralist society—a society composed of a mosaic of separate cultures—to a view of America as a complex but common social system, one that has propagated and, more strikingly, produced significant cultural differences within itself. Correspondingly, the conceptualizations of ethnicity reviewed represent a movement from nationalist mystification to postnationalist self-reflexivity.

Finally, it will be shown that these local changes occurred in conjunction with a corresponding mutation of the global system. Clearly, as Robertson's, King's, and Handler's comments about the creation of difference in the nationalist era of globalization indicate, local American changes did *not* mirror a simplistic opening out from an era of "national" to one of "global" causation. They indicate instead a development within the ongoing, and quite well-established, process of globalization as it moved from its nationalist to its postnationalist phase.

Werner Sollors's *Beyond Ethnicity* (1986) is one of several ambitious attempts to reconfigure ethnic theory and American literary history. Drawing on Fredrik Barth's *Ethnic Groups and Boundaries* (1969), Sollors argues against the essentialist legacy of cultural nationalism. Barth contends that "when one traces the history of an ethnic group through time, one is *not* simultaneously, in the same sense, tracing the history of a 'culture': the elements of the present culture of that ethnic group have not sprung from the particular set that constituted the group's culture at a previous time, whereas the group has a continual organizational existence with boundaries (criteria of membership) that despite modifications have marked off a continuing unit" (Sollors 1986:27–28). Cultural traditions, in this view, are not legacies from the past but creations of the present. Sollors goes on to note that "Barth's history can easily accommodate the observation that ethnic groups in the United States have relatively little cultural differentiation, that the cultural *content* of ethnicity (the stuff that Barth's boundaries enclose) is largely interchangeable and rarely historically authenticated."

Sollors frequently makes these revelations in the style of a debunking satirist of ethnic cultural nationalist pretensions. Coming to the concept of cultural invention largely from within the narrative of American tradition, and not appreciating its wider historiographic and cultural applicability, he clearly enjoys deflating the "defiant ethnic revivalism and exclusivism" (13) so popular in the 1960s. Describing how "a specialist in ethnic literature" asserted, in effect, that only Italian-Americans could interpret a particular sentence from *The Godfather* (in a speech that, as Sollors acidly puts it, "the ethnic journal MELUS considered worth reprinting" [12]), Sollors remarks that "by the lecturer's own logic, one might assume that Italian-Americans might have difficulties understanding the first sentence of Melville's *Moby Dick*" (12–13). Shortly thereafter, sill focusing on Italian-Americans (one of the groups in fact less affected by the ethnic revival, but a politically safer target for satire than those more affected), he comments that "how an Italian-American academic picks up an Afro-American militant gesture from the 1960s and uses it for his own ends is not subject to scrutiny" (14). Moments like these—in which Sollors's analysis turns to satire and reveals the target of his revisionary literary history—show that Sollors is out to deflate the whole notion of separate cultures and substitute for it a new theory of ethnic cultural production in America.

Following the work of Nathan Glazer (1964), who argues that the unmelted ethnic groups in America have become "ghost nations," Sollors reconstructs his local American narrative by seeing ethnic group reproduction in the United States, not as a continuation of traditions (ethnicity as substance, essence), but as made-in-the-U.S.A. (ethnicity as a symbolic creation that is, in fact, a production of American culture). Sollors cites Fred Matthews's "superb essay," "The Revolt against Americanism": "for American intellectuals, folk romanticism tended to lead not to hatred of 'outsiders' and a lust to purge them from the nation, but rather to a sense of guilt about their own society's exploitation of the strangers, and to the desire to protect them from the aggressive majority. In the American context, alienated romanticism created not xenophobia, but xenophilia" (29).

As an example of cultivation of the outsider, Sollors invokes the "romantic racialism" of Harriet Beecher Stowe's portrayal of Negroes, who exhibit "the highest form of Christian life," as opposed to the Anglo-Saxons, who are "cool, logical, and practical" (29). Examples of such a tradition—a countertradition to America's older racism and more recent antiimmigrant Anglo-Saxonism—could be multiplied. Thus one might also point to Anzia Yezierska, whose Jewish characters often represent passion and poetry, as opposed to WASPS shown as cold and logical. At the height of controversy about immigrants, Yezierska won the Edward J. O'Brien literary prize and had a collection of stories purchased by Metro-Goldwyn-Mayer.

America's cult of the outsider, Sollors argues, underlay the cultural politics of the 1960s, and "self-exoticization . . . has become part of a familiar cultural scenario" (31). The bulk of Sollors's book enlarges on these initial assertions, arguing that a full survey of the American cultural production of ethnicity must locate its topoi in mainstream traditions, in particular the tradition of the New England mind: thus, in *Beyond Ethnicity*, Sollors offers a revisionary literary history of immigrant and ethnic literature *as*

American literature. One question that Sollors asks rhetorically in his first chapter resonates throughout the whole book: "Are ethnics merely Americans who are separated from each other by the same culture?" (35–36). For Sollors, clearly, the answer is yes.

Sollors remains, to borrow Frank Thistlewaite's simile, chained like an Andromeda to the rock of national history. He revises a local narrative in ways that suggest, but do not incorporate, the larger transformations then under way; indeed, at the end of his book, he calls for doing away with naive faith in American exceptionalism, so that America may be reconceived as "a polyethnic nation among polyethnic nations instead of *the* nation of nations" (260). But had he found, rather than merely calling for, a more comprehensive framework than just American literary, social, and intellectual history, he might well have tempered his satire and produced something more than a revalidation of the melting pot in new dress. There is, after all, an abundance of work outside American culture and American ethnic studies that demythifies without dismissing and suggests a more comprehensive framework than the New England mind for the ongoing production of cultural difference. After all, Wallerstein makes almost exactly the same observation about the global construction of national culture as Sollors does about the construction of ethnicity within America, while continuing to take it quite seriously. Wallerstein remarks that the global dissemination of nationalism should "lead us to reflect what pressures exist which cause us to assert our cultural differences and exclusions in such clone-like fashion" (1991:186), but his findings in pursuit of this thought—that these differences are an essential part of the economic relationships of the modern world system—make it clear that the creation of cultural differences cannot merely be stopped by satirical demystification.

While the cultural nationalism of the 1960s was being demystified in this way, the ideal of assimilation and the era it dominated were being reinterpreted. In literary history, the best example of such reconsideration is Marcus Klein's *Foreigners: The Making of American Literature, 1900–1940* (1981). Klein points out, for example, that the Federal Writers' Project of the 1930s was shaped, to a great degree, by "marginal Americans":

> A suggestively large number of the researchers and writers who were engaged (with whatever varying degrees of seriousness and enthusiasm) in the creating of the enterprise called the American Guide Series were immigrants or were the children of immigrants, or were black. . . . Nor was it unlikely that the business of interpreting American culture should have been conducted so largely by, and under the influence of, marginal Americans. By 1930 an approximate one-half of the population of the

United States did in fact consist of marginal Americans, who necessarily were put to the task of discovering a native land from which they might claim rights of nativity. (183)

Klein's comments point toward at least several ways in which "assimilation" was used to encode and manipulate cultural differences. Immigrants manipulated the iconography of America—became the interpreters of the national tradition—thereby altering it substantially. Klein's suggestions about the American Guide Series and the creation of American folklore in the 1930s are echoed by Neal Gabler's *An Empire of Their Own: How the Jews Invented Hollywood* (1988). Gabler chronicles the battle between "the movie Jews" (60) and the Edison trust for control of the industry and the development of film culture as an alternative to WASP genteel culture, emphasizing its development both as a socializing force and a form of insurgency. Perhaps this strategy of manipulation, and therefore control of, American iconography by immigrants is most visibly ideologically realized in the way immigrants like Mary Antin (1912) and the protagonist of Israel Zangwill's *The Melting Pot* (1909) characterize themselves as the true Americans. They claim this status because they have experienced a transformation, as opposed to the descendants of the Pilgrims, who claim national identity thanks merely to birth. Indeed, since status according to birth is an old-world practice that American identity has defined itself *against,* WASP characters like Quincy in *The Melting Pot* are presented, not only as racists, but also as un-American old-world aristocrats. That this represents a genuine dilemma Sollors makes clear when he quotes Barrett Wendell's famous comment on Antin—she "has developed an irritating habit of describing herself and her people as Americans, in distinction from such folks as Edith [Wendell's wife] and me, who have been here for three hundred years." Sollors then adds something usually omitted from Wendell's remark, comments indicating that Wendell is not attacking immigrants but expressing a basic dilemma of American identity (1986:89).

Klein also finds immigrant appropriation of American identity under the guise of assimilation in retrospective autobiography and fiction—in writing that seems to narrativize loss of past and assimilation, but, in fact, Klein argues, grafts immigrant pasts *onto* America. Thus, Klein writes, "the ghetto—Irish, Italian, black, Jewish, and so on—thus could be presented for consideration as a kind of Home Town" (184). In Mike Gold's *Jews without Money* (1930),

one of the great tutelary figures of the East Side is Jake Wolf, the saloonkeeper. Jake Wolf knows English and he has a pull with Tammany Hall, but the most fascinating thing about him is his substantiation of American myth: "The great man is kind to boys, generous with free

lunch pretzels, and full of fine stories. He spent a year in the west in
Chicago, and saw the Indians. They looked like Jews, he said, but were
not as smart or as brave. One Jew could kill a hundred Indians." Where-
fore little Jewish boys with their pale faces were cowboys—and/or
Indians—and are insinuated into America. (Klein 1981:191)

Boundary-violating figures like Jake (who recur in contemporary comedies like those of Mel Brooks), taken seriously, have become material for
contemporary historiography, as witnessed in recent multicultural studies
of the American West that have uncovered Jewish, Asian-American,
African-American, and Hispanic-American cowboys to supplement and
revise the reigning Anglo-Saxon icon. As we shall see in the next chapter,
serious focus on scandalous, boundary-violating figures and a revaluation
of traditions of assimilation has revealed, in Lisa Lowe's words, that "the
most powerful practices may not always be the explicitly oppositional
ones, may not be understood by contemporaries, and may be less overt
and recognizable than others" (1991:29).

Despite Sollors, critiques of 1960s cultural nationalism do not necessarily
have to neutralize the radical political point of that movement. Indeed,
even as a revised view of the tradition of assimilation finds a hidden political and cultural subversiveness, revisions of cultural nationalism have also
taken subversive forms. When Tzvetan Todorov criticized a *Critical Inquiry*
(1986) symposium edited by Henry Louis Gates, Jr.—subsequently published under the title *Race, Writing, Difference*—for manifesting essentialist
and racist attitudes, both Gates and Houston Baker wrote responses that
provide excellent introductions to contemporary transformations of formerly pluralist positions in African-American aesthetics. They called for
the development of black vernacular theories of literature simultaneously
indebted to the tradition of cultural nationalism and critical of it. They
rejected simple classification of their theories as "alternative" voices for
"other" cultures: they were not "ethno-theories" reconstructed out of
separate cultural traditions, available only to those who are "of" them. At
the same time, however, they did not wholly reject these assumptions.
Instead, they fused them with a more demystified radical critique of mainstream knowledge-creation, a critique mounted simultaneously from
within and without. The result was the creation of what we might generically call deconstructionist ethnic theory.

To explain his notion of vernacular criticism, Baker, whose use of the
legacy of militantly revolutionary cultural nationalism is more marked,
evokes the "venerable Western trope of Prospero and Caliban—figures
portrayed in terms of self-and-other, the West and the Rest of us" (190).

Baker is explicit in calling into question the essentializing conceptual framework of "self" and "other," protraying it specifically as an inheritance from Enlightenment knowledge-construction; he deconstructs the trope by taking Caliban's part and reconceiving the world of *The Tempest* according to this perspective:

> A shared nature *as* language—a fruitful ecology of communication— was, thus, subjected to usurpation by men who refused to brook difference. Tyranny demanded self-sameness and subjugation, appropriated labor—even from the seemingly suitable suitor. (Ferdinand becomes the "Other" in the woodpile to qualify as Miranda's groom.) The "tempest," then, is veritably a havoc wreaked by mastery; it disrupts "natural" order, blunts "sounds and sweet airs, that give delight and hurt not" (3.2.134). The Western Renaissance "storm" displaces, in fact, the witch as worker of sounding magic and releases, in her place, the comprador spirit Ariel who aids Prospero's male manipulations. (Baker 1986:193)

Empowering Caliban, in Baker's scheme, does not have to replicate essentialism by either perpetuating or reversing the hierarchy of self and other. Baker scorns the universal humanist move of awarding the colonial subject "the varsity Western W for writing," and he also rejects "the gross polemics of a nationalism that militaristically asserts the superiority of Caliban" (190). Indeed, Baker's analysis of *The Tempest* as a capitalist allegory suggests that (to use a formula Gayatri Spivak applies to the construction of Third World identity) really—in some sense primordially—the "others" are not others but have been "othered."

Baker's alternative—his prescription for disturbing this order—is to urge his Caliban to attempt what he calls "supraliteracy," a gesture that again acknowledges the presence of a common system that constitutes both oppressor and oppressed, rather than claiming a position outside it. "Supraliteracy" is "a maroon or guerrilla action carried out *within* linguistic territories of the erstwhile masters, bringing forth *sounds* that have been taken for crude hooting, but which are, in reality, racial poetry" (195). Guerrilla action is thus likened to gorilla action—the display of gorillas who resist territorial invasion, a display Baker calls a "deformation of mastery" (191).

Baker's Caliban thus refigures the aggressive (male) force of nationalism as guerrilla-gorilla (subversion / aggressive parodic), rather than revolutionary combat, and locates it as a force within, not outside, the system (a Caliban in a Western-authored plot, not an "other tradition"). Caliban uses the language of his masters—but deforms it, both to resist the system and to form a community within it, a community of sophisticated insiders who hear what the rest hear as "crude hooting" as "racial poetry." Such "supraliteracy" both exposes the oppressive system of the masters as itself deformed and provides a basis for building a community of sophisticated insiders within it. In finding this critical sophistication in marginality, Baker echoes the Derridean decentering move, in which the categories of a hierarchy are not just inverted, but the newly inferior term is inserted into the class of the newly superior. The marginalized viewpoint thus becomes the more comprehensive and sophisticated one: it creates an elite community with the completest knowledge of the "systematicity of the system" that constructed all inside it. The outsider becomes insider; the marginalized hold the keys to the construction of both center and margin.

Baker's approach has by now become quite familiar. Distinctions like the one Baker uses, colonized/colonizer—or the equally familiar terms, more appropriate perhaps to national rather than international sites, center/margin—have become staples of radical cultural critique and have replaced the notion of separate, bounded cultures. The "other" has become more clearly "othered," or "marginalized"; and the latter term has been reinterpreted to show that "margins" are not just found on the geographical borders of a social system, but are inscribed everywhere within it. Similarly, a "different culture" has become "cultural difference" as referential identity has been demystified. Identity has been revealed as not referential but constructed, the ideological effect of a process whereby a cultural system perpetually seeks to invent itself by means of the categories of "same" and "different," never managing however to achieve true closure (Parker et al. 1992:5). Finally, revolution in the name of another culture has given way to deconstruction of a system that includes all.

These transformations have all reflected the influence of deconstructionism and poststructuralism, which Terry Eagleton characterizes as "a product of that blend of euphoria and disillusionment, liberation and dissipation, carnival and catastrophe, which was 1968" (1983:143). Attempts to overthrow state power failed; and the old left, perceived as part of the problem rather than the solution, yielded to the creation of a new opposition of "a local, diffused, strategic kind" (142). Although some French poststructuralists flip-flopped from a militant Maoism to strident anticommunism, others, like Derrida, developed deconstructionism as a political practice, substituting subversion from within for revolution in the name of an alternative vision. Much more than Sollors, Baker responds to this larger transformation, which Wallerstein calls global in reach and epochal in significance, rather than merely French. Wallerstein labels it a "revolution in and of" the contemporary world system ((1991:65). Baker's interventions into a local American narrative, then, have global sources and concomitants.

Gates's theory of vernacular tradition is similarly a globally mediated intervention into the local narrative of African-American literature. If Baker's call for "guerrilla/gorilla" practice reevokes revolutionary nationalism's aggressively male force, its drawing of boundary lines, and its attempts to build a separate community, even as it revises the basis for these projects, Gates's theory represents instead a revision of nostalgic nationalism. Gates presents his vernacular theory most fully in *The Signifying Monkey: A Theory of African-American Literary Criticism* (1988), where he notes: "I decided to analyze the nature and function of Signifyin(g) precisely because it *is* repetition and revision, or repetition with a signal difference. Whatever is black about black American literature is to be found in this identifiable black Signifyin(g) difference. That, most succinctly if ambiguously, describe the premise of this book" (vviv).

Gates's study as a whole, however, betrays more interconnectedness between past nationalism and present black deconstructionism than this might seem to indicate. Black Signifyin(g) difference (which deconstructs mainstream culture by repetition with a difference) also operates within African-American tradition and is, moreover, a cultural strategy embedded in that tradition, a result of diasporic culture-diffusion. In this way, Gates imports into his cultural deconstructionism an evocation of nationalist/primordialist roots. Thus, while Gates's above comment suggests that black American literature is American literature repeated with a black difference, Gates also writes that "Afro-American culture is an African culture with a difference" (4) and is the result of the diffusion of one specific trickster figure from Africa, a trickster topos that "not only seems to have survived the bumpy passage to the New World, but . . . appears even today in Nigeria, Benin, Brazil, Cuba, Haiti, and the United States." The topos of this figure (Esu-Elegbara in Yoruba mythology, Legba among the Fon in Benin, Exú in Brazil, Echo-Elegua in Cuba, Papa Legba in Haiti, and Papa La Bas in the United States) "functions as a sign of the disrupted wholeness of an African system of meaning and belief that black slaves recreated from memory, preserved by oral narration, improvised upon in ritual—especially in the rituals of the repeated oral narrative—and willed to their own subsequent generations, as hermetically sealed and encoded charts of cultural descent" (5). In its primordialist—or nostalgic nationalist—mode, Gates's book seeks to reconstruct that wholeness.

In Africa, the trickster figure functions as a part of a divination ritual, specifically as the interpreter of a text given by the god Ifa. Gates draws on "this compelling black figure as the trope of critical activity as a whole" for the construction of his black vernacular theory. In Gates's anthropological analysis of the figure Esu, Esu as interpreter emerges as a "trope for indeterminacy" (39); as the supplement that "'enters the heart of all intelligible discourse and comes to define its very nature and condition,' a role which poststructural criticism ascribes to writing"; and as "the free play or element of undecidability within the Ifa textual universe; Esu endlessly displaces meaning, deferring it by the play of signification. Esu is this element of displacement and deferral, as well as its sign" (42). Esu's indeterminacy "prevents the desired retrieval of one's full, predetermined meaning while on earth" (41). Gates's primordialism is thus anything but a simple attempt to reconstruct a separate tradition; it is a complex and difficult maneuver. Accepting Esu as the trope for black critical activity, as Gates argues on the one hand, is "to ground one's literary practice outside the Western tradition" (xxii); at the same time, the description of Esu as interpreter is drawn from contemporary deconstructionist theory: the non-Western tradition seems startlingly Western, even as it one-ups the West by showing that modern French theory had already been explored and institutionalized in precolonial Africa.

For Esu and his manifestation in black America—both in the repertoire of black vernacular forms, in which Signifyin(g) is the central practice, and in the tales of the Signifying Monkey—have numerous affinities to contemporary literary theory. In naming its most characteristic verbal practice "Signifyin(g)," black American vernacular conducts a "guerrilla action" against the crucial English term "signification" (46). Gates likens the destabilizing black "agnominatio" to Derrida's neologism *différance,* as both are the "repetition of a word with an alteration of both one letter and a sound" (46). Both thereby became illustrations of their own concepts, by resisting self-identical meaning and revealing mutability in the sign. Black Signifyin(g) is thus equivalent to Derridean *différance.* Similarly, after Jacques Lacan, Signifyin(g) represents a return of the repressed: citing Anthony Easthope, who argues that all the "absences and dependencies which have to be barred in order for meaning to take place constitute what Lacan designates as the other," Gates comments that "everything that must be excluded for meaning to remain coherent and linear comes to bear in the process of Signifyin(g)" (50). Signifyin(g) is also, after Mikhail Bakhtin, a "double-voiced word, that is, a word or utterance, in this context decolonized for the black's purposes by 'inserting a new semantic orientation into a word which already has—and retains—its own orientation'" (50). In all of these ways—ways that represent a pastiche of recent literary theory—Signifyin(g) represents more sophisticated, self-aware, fuller use of language than signification; thus, what was marginal becomes central, the key to the nature of the whole system. To pick one concrete example, repetition with a difference means that "the more mundane the fixed text

('April in Paris' by Charles Parker, 'My Favorite Things' by John Coltrane), the more dramatic is the difference" (64).

Given Gates's assertion that he is reconstructing the wholeness of a tradition outside the Western tradition, these coincidences are extremely striking, and Gates seeks to explain his use of poststructural theory to describe black tradition as "analogy," remarking that he delights "in the sense of similarity that discrete literary traditions yield in comparative literary criticism" (xxiv). But Gates negotiates doubleness so persistently throughout the book that this explanation seems more than a bit disingenuous. For example, in the name Signifyin(g), we see "the most subtle and perhaps the most profound trace of an extended engagement between two separate and distinct yet profoundly—even inextricably—related orders of meaning dependent precisely as much for their confrontation on relations of identity, manifested in the signifier, as on their relations of difference, manifested at the level of the signified" (45). "Separate and distinct"—yet "profoundly—even inextricably related": Gates again has it both ways; what Gates in one place calls parallel universes, he later revises, substituting "perpendicular" universes" as "a more accurate visual description" (49). Similarly, in transmitting the tradition, "Black adults teach their children this exceptionally complex system of rhetoric, almost exactly like Richard A. Lanham describes a generic portrait of the teaching of the rhetorical *paideia* to Western schoolchildren" (75). At the same time that they learn this bounded, separate tradition, however, black linguistic sophistication depends also on learning code-switching, "to facilitate the smooth navigation between . . . [the] two realms" of black vernacular and white English. A separate transmission of culture (which maintains bounded community) is thus supplemented by the ability to code-switch (which represents vastly increased sophistication over those whose language is only single-voiced, sophistication that places blacks closer to full awareness of the nature of the social-linguistic system).

The addition of these second to these first frames creates, in *The Signifying Monkey*, a fruitful conceptual aporia, something that results in part from the subtle combination and transformation of two supposedly opposite practices, cultural nationalism and strategic assimilation. We shall explore this intriguing fusion of two opposite traditions more extensively in the next chapter; here, we should note that such negotiations reflect the simultaneous gain and loss involved in the shift in the world system we have been charting, the transformation of nationalism into globalism. As the aggressive strategies of separatist nationalism became more difficult to maintain, their achievements—the legitimization worldwide of new nations and domestically of racial/ethnic groups as actors in the new common system—seeded new forms of cultural/political intervention, forms of oppositional conversations within, rather than against, an encompassing, although complex and finally untotalizeable, global cultural system.

In *Through a Glass Darkly: Ethnic Semiosis in American Literature* (1987), William Boelhower advocates what he calls a semiotic theory of ethnicity in American culture. Like Gates's and Baker's, Boelhower's work is an attempt to reinvigorate American ethnicity in different terms in the wake of cultural nationalism; but Boelhower distances himself more than Gates and Baker do from essentialist concepts of separate ethnic communities and faith in a strongly described "encyclopaedia" of ethnic traits that ground them. Boelhower differentiates the two eras that Gates and Baker strategically combine. He laments the loss of the old (thus proving to be Sollors's successor as critic of immigrant literature, accepting his debunking of cultural nationalism) and yet finds solace in a new, belated strategy (thus countering Sollors, finding continuing strategic possibilities for ethnicity even in Sollors's assertion that Americans are divided from each other by the same culture).

To understand ethnicity in America, Boelhower argues, one needs to return to the circumstances of the original settlement, when Europeans brought a universalizing cognitive system to America and employed it to extinguish Indians' local knowledges. A crucial—and typical—weapon in this effort was the European "map," which traced "the West's radical act of removal, the substitution of a uniform scientific writing in scale for its aboriginal center, the earth" (47).

The result of the contest between Euro-American and Indian knowledge systems was a precariously unstable victory for the former: the creation of a tradition that suppressed cultural difference and created national identity by "ordering American geography into a single semiotic system" (67). The nationalist discourse—"the discourse able to 'make it ethnologically new"—"did not get lost in the gaps and the lacunae thrown up by the world, rather it passed over them" and it did not really succeed in banishing the Indian from its maps. Instead, the Indian reappeared as "a subversive reader in the very text of the map, a principle of disorder. As Michel Serres rightly points out, 'One does not exhaust the real, he covers it. He covers it with letters.' In the blank spaces of the map, where the map is silent, the ethnic factor lurks, and the culture of the map is ineluctably doomed to imperfection" (56).

The Indian—like, later, the ethnic subject generally for Boelhower—thus "imposes or positions itself at all levels of the various cultural systems to which it belongs, either as presence or absence" (37). Homogenization *always* supposes the absence of a presence within the system: the "ethnic" is foregrounded in the presence of an absence within the system. As a result, once one accepts that the "issue at stake here" is no longer "cultural recovery or a literal return to one's ancestors" and that, internalizing Derrida, "if one cannot dwell in the modern world, one can still dwell at the level of interpretation," aboriginal and ethnic difference returns as a feature of the system that tries to efface it: it returns in the strategic production of ethnic signs by agents of multiple identities, a process of creation that is also a process of resistance (143, 133). Boelhower calls this "a weak version of ethnic identity," in contrast to the "ethnic semiosis based on strong sign chains" that occurs when "the ethnic subject is still part of a family, and the family part of a homogenous community" (105). Outside of those communities—be they ghettoes or reservations—weak ethnicity operates; it is as syncretic and subversive a phenomenon as it is in Gates and Baker. It is "exemplified in the Pan-Indian movement, where different tribes have decided to use the stereotypes imposed on them by white Americans in order to create a common political cause. The concept 'Indian' is, of course, a stereotype; no such creature exists in reality. There is really no common Indian identity, culture, or language" (138).

Names imposed on groups by a universalizing system evoke absent presences within that system and can become points of agency: in ever-new contexts, "weak" versions of ethnic identity might seek to destabilize a supposedly universal system by producing the signs of ethnic difference that that system surreptitiously encodes. This would be a creative activity of political and cultural resistance, one that would not seek closure, but would be infinitely productive and invasive everywhere: "Ethnic semiosis, then, is a way of thinking differently by thinking the difference, and in the postmodern American framework this may be all the difference there is" (143).

Cultural difference as conceived by Gates, Baker, and Boelhower is explicitly interventionist. It distinguishes itself, sometimes ambiguously, sometimes sharply, from its own roots in the oppositional cultural nationalism of a previous era. Equally crucial, however, is the fact that it remains oppositional, countering the neoconservative attempt to revive Anglo-centric American nationalism. In its interventions, it seeks to open a closed national system, revealing its complexly plural and untotalizeable systemacity. As Homi Bhabha (1990), writing on the tensions between cultural difference and nation-formation, puts it, the goal is to prevent a system from ever incorporating such difference and thereby retotalizing itself by "dialectical sublation": "In erasing the harmonious totalities of

Culture, cultural difference articulates the difference between representations of social life without surmounting the space of incommensurable meanings and judgements that are produced within the process of transcultural negotiation" (312). As he also puts it more simply, cultural difference refuses to allow knowledge to "add up to" a totalizing generalization; instead, it "add[s] to" knowledges, keeping us aware of the "disjunctive, liminal space of national society" that resists totalization in an oppressive national identity or univocal narrative of its past. The above discussion, I hope has made it clear that although I have described it in terms of the development of ethnic, and thus predominantly local, theory, such a strategy is not solely locally driven. The globalism involved has not just been a result of the dissemination of French critical theory following on, if one accepts Wallerstein's remark, a revolution in the world system. In America, dissemination from Europe has met diasporas from the Third World. Traversing borders between Vietnam, Paris, and San Francisco State, Trinh Minh-ha has written of how the "Third World has moved West (or North, depending on where the dividing line falls) and has expanded so as to include even the remote parts of the First World. What is at stake is not only the hegemony of Western cultures, but also their identities as unified cultures. Third World dwells on diversity; so does First World. This is our strength and our misery. The West is painfully made to realize the existence of a Third World in the First World and vice versa" (Trinh 1989:98).

With Trinh, I anticipate the topic of the next chapter: the way deconstructionist theories of ethnicity are subtly transformed into postmodern strategies of heterogenization. This change reveals itself in shifts in emphasis, in a movement from the language of margin and deconstruction, to that of boundary crossing, hybridization, and heterogeneity, and it reflects an increased awareness of the processes of globalization. Before we turn to considering this further set of strategies, however, we need to supplement our discussion of oppositional cultural interventionism with a look at an important parallel trend: the increasing mainstreaming of multiculturalism.

Albeit with much dispute, interventionist difference has increasingly become a component of America's official, not just oppositional, culture. Whereas oppositional critics have sought to keep the space of national society open, a progressive strain of multiculturalism has attempted to reformulate American national culture for a postnationalist era, to do, in the United States something analogous to what is being done in Japan. In a sense, this has also meant a version of Bhabha's goal of keeping the nation open. Even though it has been aimed at forming a new kind of national civic culture and not, as in Bhabha, an untotalizeable arena of conflicting discourses (a social space that is never allowed to harden into a national identity), multicultural nationalism has constructed itself out of the ruins of the nation-state ideal of homogeneous culture. One of the best indications of such an attempt is the carefully centrist style of the recent report of the New York State Social Studies Review and Development Committee, "One Nation, Many Peoples: A Declaration of Cultural Interdependence" (1991). Not only does it set guidelines for reforming primary and secondary education on the basis of new multicultural notions of how national identity must be refigured for the present era, it shows clearly how its project is wrapped up with the realization that the world has entered a new, globalist phase, a phase for which American nationalism must drastically reform itself.

Two dissenters to the report lamented the passing of previous forms of national identity. Kenneth Jackson and Arthur Schlesinger both voiced an anxiety that has in recent years received at least as much public play as multiculturalism: the fear that the United States has lost its common culture. This fear is driven by the same perceptions that inspire the multiculturalists: perceptions that global hierarchy has come undone and national culture is the core grown more problematic. For Jackson, the common culture America has lost was Anglo-conformity. For Schlesinger, a more liberal version of the melting pot is the norm: while the British legacy is primary, it "has been modified, enriched, and reconstituted by the absorption of non-Anglo cultures and traditions as well as by the distinctive experience of American life. That is why America today is so very different a nation from Britain. Assimilation does not equal Anglo-conformity" (46). Schlesinger, in short, evokes Crèvecoeur's notion that Americans of different origins must be melted into "a new race of men," while Jackson recalls the melting pot featured in the graduation ceremonies of Henry Ford's English school: a large pot into which a variety of ragtag ethnic types descended, to emerge as standardized American workers, dressed in Anglo fashion.

Like two other less and more liberal critics of multiculturalism, Diane Ravitch and Elizabeth Fox-Genovese, both Jackson and Schlesinger evoke a pair of related specters to justify their criticisms and their alarm at the loss of a common national culture. Locally, they interpret multiculturalism, or at least a strong component within it, as fundamentally separatist. This separatism at home is reinforced, repeatedly, by an alarmist appeal to the global picture. As Jackson writes, "the people of the United States will recognize, even if this committee does not, that every viable nation has to have a common culture to survive in peace. As our own document indicates, one need look no further than Yugoslavia, the Soviet Union, or Canada to see the accuracy of this proposition. We might want to add India after the events of the past two weeks" (39). If America gives way to multiculturalism, the extremer dissenters imply, a blood-dimmed tide of ethnic separatism may be loosed on the soil of the United States as well.

The perspective of the majority of the authors of the report is extremely different. Just as assimilation has been socially engineered in a remarkably thoroughgoing manner—through common schools, through the settlement houses, through the activities of a large number of organizations dedicated to Americanization of immigrants—so, the majority of the report's authors hold, multiculturalism must be. The body of the report is full of guidelines for the reengineering of American national identity for a new era. As the introduction puts it, *"if the United States is to continue to prosper in the 21st century, then all of its citizens, whatever their race or ethnicity, must believe that they and their ancestors have shared in the building of the country and have a stake in its success"* (1). Such present urgency, the preamble makes clear, is based on a series of recent developments in America:

> Since the 1960s . . . a profound reorientation of the self-image of Americans has been underway. Before this time the dominant model of the typical American had been conditioned primarily by the need to shape a unified nation out of a variety of contrasting and often conflicting European immigrant communities. But following the struggles for civil rights, the unprecedented increase in non-European immigration over the last two decades and the increasing recognition of our nation's indigenous heritage, there has been a fundamental change in the image of what a resident of the United States is. With this change, which necessarily highlights the racial and ethnic pluralism of the nation, previous ideals of assimilation to an Anglo-American model have been put in question and are now slowly and sometimes painfully being set aside. Many people in the United States today are no longer comfortable with the requirement, common in the past, that they shed their specific cultural differences in order to be considered American. (xi)

The report thus accepts the principle, introduced in the 1960s by black nationalism, that society must be made conscious rather than unconscious of color, as the basis for its reengineering of national identity. It does so, however, as a means toward engineering, not separate cultural identity, but national citizenship. The subtitle of the report underscores this combination of marking ethnic identity with creating a common civic culture: "One Nation, Many Peoples" is subtitled "A Declaration of Cultural Interdependence." Diane Ravitch's arresting formulation—one, however, that she uses with the contrary aim of discrediting radical multiculturalism (Giroux 1992:10–12)—is somewhat similar: America has "a common culture which is multicultural" (1990:339).

This emphasis on heterogeneity is applied in a way that is specifically community building. Although the report does indeed (anxiously) evoke separate descent by saying that each student needs to find "his" or "her" group represented in the curriculum and likewise invokes its opposite, universalism, by worrying about discovering common elements across cultural differences, this familiar language of the particular versus the universal is supplemented by another strategy. The report encourages teaching all students to appreciate the world perspectively. It encourages students to assume each other's perspectives, to explore "all the applicable viewpoints of the historical and social protagonists . . . , paying special attention to the ways in which race, ethnicity, gender and class generate different ways of understanding, experiencing, and evaluating the events of the world" (7). This clearly socializing exercise in perspectivism, moreover, recognizes that individuals have more than one perspective—belong simultaneously to heterogeneously different groupings—and that groups themselves are heterogeneous creations, as "the cultures of all peoples have become intermingled over time" (21). Then, in a move that echoes Bhabha, the report goes on to argue that the ultimate justification for this sort of multicultural education is that its perspectivism reflects, much more than past consensualism, the nature of knowledge itself. "We are beginning to realize that understanding and the ability to appreciate things from more than one perspective may be as important as is factual knowledge" (vii), and that "multicultural knowledge in this conception of the social studies becomes a vehicle and not a goal" (viii). As important as the ability to manipulate perspectives is the fact that knowledge is "socially constructed and therefore tentative" (ix) and is thus misused if totalized. The report thus daringly implies that the need to approach the world perspectively corresponds to a "world"—an object of knowledge—that is itself perspectivist, not referential.

Just as the report's critics make clear that the specter of separatism has a larger global shadow behind it, so the report yokes the reengineering of national culture, not only to maintenance of national strength, but also to participation in the globalist era. It seeks to instil into students a sense of "national competence and world citizenship" (xii) and argues that "beginning in the earliest grade social studies should be taught from a global perspective" (1). Indeed, in a separate opinion appended to the report, Ali Mazrui, the report's most aggressive critic of Eurocentrism and Anglocentrism, ends by emphatically evoking the long tradition of American nationalism (America as the nation of nations, and the completion of the great round of human history) in his support for multiculturalism in a global era, asserting that *"a far bigger question which now arises is how this country, this greatest microcosm of the human race on earth, can also become the greatest epitome of world culture in history. How can the United States succeed in capturing some of the rich cultural diversity of the nationalities represented in its population?"* (43). It is hard, indeed, to tell the opposition from the mainstream in this formulation by the Albert Schweitzer Professor in the Humanities with impeccable Third World credentials.

The report, then, rephrases radical positions in a liberal accommodationist manner by seeking to make society "conscious rather than unconscious" of ethnicity. It does this in an attempt to create a common culture in which multicultural identity is the norm. To be sure, more radical positions might disallow altogether the use of the term "common culture" without necessarily being separatist. As Henry Giroux (1992) has written,

> The attempt to accommodate pluralism to a "common culture" rather than to a shared vision grounded in an ongoing struggle to expand the radical possibilities of democratic public life underestimates the legacy of the dominant culture to eliminate cultural differences, multiple literacies, and diverse communities in the name of totalizing and one-dimensional master narratives refigured around issues such as nationalism, citizenship, and patriotism. (15)

Despite such fears, the report represents, like Giroux's own theory of border pedagogy, an attempt to take back the notion of common culture from the likes of Allan Bloom, Roger Kimball, Dinesh D'Souza, and William Bennett, and it shares with Giroux's theory an emphasis on transgression of boundaries between separate cultures. In their similarity, moreover, both positions seek different goals from pluralism, when it calls for a society that is, at its most harmonious, the sum of separate groups with single authentic identities. And both make relationships between civics and culture explicit and important and reengineer instruction in culture as part of a process of socialization in nonracist, multicultural, postcolonial globalist world.

The emphases in the report and in Giroux's theories, first, on making society "conscious rather than unconscious of color" and, second, on impurity, heterogeneity, boundary violation, and border crossing as an antidote to conventional notions of identity have become a basis, on the one hand, for new radical critiques and, on the other, for transformative formulations of centrist notions of common culture. In the process, WASPs have become an ethnic group, part of a heterogeneity of cultural traditions in America, and scandalous, boundary-violating figures like Gold's Jewish cowboy and Chinese-American Columbuses have become, for some, the models to be aspired to. The next chapter explores one genealogy of these developments in depth. But before we proceed, we should note that they have not only effected some reconfiguration of mainstream American positions, but have been projected far back into history to destabilize the colonial frame of reference—the notion of civilization—as well as the neocolonial frame, the nation-state. They have been used to destabilize the assumptions of Eurocentric civilizationism as well as homogenizing nationalism.

In *Polyethnicity and National Unity in World History* (1985), William McNeill, like Hobsbawm and other recent students of nationalism, has argued that the idea of homogeneous national culture is, in fact, a recent creation. Although McNeill is far from alone in seeing this idea as historically novel, he is extremely provocative in locating it in a revision of the history of civilization, rather than the sociology of nationalism, where it has been more at home. The ideal of homogeneous national community, McNeill argues, was developed in the comparatively barbaric European periphery of the world system of the Middle Ages, the cores of which were the Middle East and China. Thanks to its relative barbarism and isolation, Europe then held the seeds of ethnic homogeneity and stood in sharp contrast to civilizational norms form time immemorial.

To point out the barbarity of medieval Europe goes against the grain of all the assumptions of a Eurocentrism that styles itself the heir to glories of Greece and Rome, but has not been all that unusual in recent world history. Europe has been severed from its chauvinistic taproot in a mythic Greece artificially separated from its Afro-Asiatic context, and Europe has been redescribed as the periphery of medieval Middle Eastern civilization by scholars like Samir Amin (1989) and Martin Bernal (1987). Much more incendiary is to locate polyethnicity—or multiculturalism, given more style by the adoption of a more cosmopolitan-sounding term—as a part of the civilizational norms breached by that barbaric Europe; to then assert that polyethnicity, reinforced by conquest and trade, was a basic concomitant of high civilizational development; and to finish by suggesting that the parochial era of nationalism is coming to an end in the twentieth century, when once again polyethnicity is reasserting itself as a civilizational norm. In such a theory, McNeill, as civilizationalist, has provided an interesting echo of theories, mentioned above, of the postmodernity of premodernity (and vice versa): he has refigured one aspect of postmodern America as a step forward into the foundational past. And he has violated a boundary more blatantly than Ali Mazrui has in fusing radical interventionism with American nationalism. He has urbanely violated what we saw to be the older, European, colonial-era boundary, one that was more genteelly drawn perhaps, but also more absolute. Exploding the civilizationalism that has helped enforce boundaries between the West and the rest of the world, he has refigured civilizationism as a basis of multiculturalism. Great Books, thus detached from the evaluative and interpretative codes of Eurocentric manufacture, would thus become, perforce, the wellspring of radical multiculturalism.

7

The Construction of Asian-American Literature

THE DEVELOPMENT OF what I have dubbed postmodern cultural politics in America, like the evolution of ethnic deconstructionism, occurred within and also against the legacy of 1960s cultural nationalism. A number of the ethnic groups consolidated in the 1960s have recently developed notions of heterogeneity, boundary violation, and border crossing into cultural-political strategies and have done so in loose alliance with each other. In picking just one of these group traditions—Asian-American literature—to show how ethnic nationalism and its successor and revision, deconstructionist ethnicity, have now been further revised, I have responded to a number of circumstantial factors. The most important of these are the recent consolidation and rapid growth of Asian-American literary tradition; its interface with a substantial component of the new immigration, which has in turn been a feature of the new globalist system of porous national borders; and its larger, global background, which has highlighted Asian economic success stories and thus privileged the Pacific Rim in an era of global business as strongly as African nationalism privileged that continent during the era of apparently successful anticolonial nationalism.

Elaine Kim's admirably comprehensive and evenhanded survey of the field, *Asian American Literature* (1982:173–249, 312–13), makes clear how greatly Asian-American literature is indebted to 1960s black cultural nationalism. Asian-American literature was recovered with African-American support and assistance; its reconstruction of tradition followed the example of Black Studies; and an important body of new work was produced under the influence of black nationalist cultural production. Kim documents many examples of this indebtedness, including a wealth of references to black cultural nationalism in Asian-American literature itself. The African-American example—that of another oppressed minority that has, far more harshly than European immigrants, experienced racial discrimination and exclusion—is clearly congenial to Asian-Americans. Since 1790, "free white persons" had been allowed naturalization. An act of 1882, however, forbade the naturalization of Chinese, and it reflected the trend of a series of previous judicial decisions holding that Chinese, Japanese, Hindus, Afghans, Filipinos, Koreans, and Hawaiians were not, in terms of naturalization law, "white persons," while Syrians, Mexicans, and Armenians, for example, were. These determinations were not, in the main, reversed until 1943 for the Chinese, 1946 for the Filipinos, and 1952 for the Koreans and Japanese (Kim 1982:307).

At the same time, the nationalist ethos—its invocation of primordial connections and identity, its use of this identity to build a political community in America on the basis of culture, and its attempt to strengthen that community by proclaiming that it had its own separate, bounded culture—could not work for Asian-Americans as it did for black nationalists. First, it was politically difficult for many reasons for Asian-Americans to invoke the primordial connection. American immigrants from Asia did not have the influence over their countries of origin that African-Americans did as essential players in the formation of African nationalism. As a result of contemporary politics, Asian-Americans were, in many ways, further from, more inessential to, their homelands (as opposed to their villages and families) than were members of the African diaspora, whose temporal distance from actual points of origin was immeasurably greater. These diminished possibilities for asserting primordial connections were much more profoundly disrupted by their contemporary circumstances: Japan's enmity in World War II made it virtually impossible for Japanese-Americans to assert primordial connection as a means of community building in America, and the communist revolution made it almost as difficult for Chinese-Americans. In *All I Asking for Is My Body* (1975), Milton Murayama writes with disgust of the "icky shit-hole" of Japanese-American community, noting that "even if I tried deliberately, every day of my life, I wouldn't be able to produce one-thousandth of the massive shame of Pearl Harbor" (Kim 1982:145–46). And Maxine Hong Kingston shows in *Woman Warrior* (1975:51) how confusing it was to maintain a stable sense of Chinese roots when, under the Communists, the families of the emigrants, better off thanks to money sent back to China, were suddenly reinscribed "not [as] the poor to be championed. They were executed like the [evil] barons in the stories, when they were not barons."

Hisaye Yamamoto's exquisitely crafted short stories (1988) show how tantalizing, but conflicted, an issue primordial identity is. The case of the protagonist of "Seventeen Syllables" (1949), a Japanese-American immigrant who has a brief career as a writer of haiku, subtly dramatizes these conflicts. Winning a prize for her poetry, she is devastated when her husband, angry at her stepping out of her role as traditional wife, smashes her prize and her ambitions. The story seems to suggest that Mrs. Hayashi's poetry is a connection between America and traditional Japanese culture. In the end, however, the story unmasks this apparent traditionalism, as, on one level, made in America. Mrs. Hayashi's poetry represents the syncretic combination of cultural nostalgia with an American empowerment of women, something that in turn comes to grief on the rocks of the more authentic traditionalism of the male prerogative. On a deeper level, though, even this "traditionalism" is deconstructed. Japanese cultural wholes clearly do not exist for Yamamoto's immigrants; what does exist is only the imprinting of particular individual and local pasts on immigrants and their descendants. The end of the story reveals that the source of Mrs. Hayashi's problems is not the reified Japanese tradition but an affair and illegitimate pregnancy in Japan, compensated for by marriage to an immigrant of much lower class and much simpler culture.

If it is difficult to invoke primordial identity as a connection to the past, it is also difficult, for still more compelling reasons, for Asian-Americans to use such identity to support community and culture building in America. The difficulty—better, impossibility—can be put dramatically by saying that Asian-American writers in the post-1960s era had to be simultaneously immigrant writers and ethnic revivalists. The crucial issue was that Asian-American immigrants and the children of Asian-American immigrants were, by the middle of the century, faced with the need either to become American or to assert that they *were* American: the exclusionary bar to naturalization had just been removed for immigrants, and Asian-American citizens, often descendants of many generations of citizens, were sharply contesting their continuing identification as "foreign." Whereas African-Americans had seen the reversal, a century before, of the Dred Scott case, which had denied them citizenship, and, as Gunnar Myrdal shows in *An American Dilemma* (1944), had, in contemporary times, a strong hold on the national conscience, Asian-Americans, at least until midcentury, were not so situated. Asian-Americans were not perceived as having claims on America's conscience or historical roots in America, and Asian immigrants had only recently become eligible for citizenship. With the cultivation of Asian-Americans as a domestic model minority in the postwar period, the assumption of Asian-American foreignness began to be reversed, but Asian-American literature and autobiography still abound with angry stories of fourth-generation Americans being complimented on how well they speak English or told to go back where they belong (Kim

1982:294–95). Intensifying these problems—and adding to the reluctance to use primordial, separate culture as a basis for community formation in the ethnic politics of the 1960s—is the continuing identification of the culture of Asian-Americans as exotic. As Asian-Americans are acutely aware, repulsion from and fascination with the "exotic" serve, among Americans, to exclude or marginalize them.

As a result of both these factors, while it absorbed the exceptionalist nationalism of the ethnic revival, Asian-American literature at the same time made use of the different, even opposed, immigrant drama of Americanization from the preceding era. Two obvious indications of this important, little-noticed fact are that it commenced satirizing the F.O.B. (fresh-off-the-boat) as sharply as assimilationist Jewish-American literature had the greenhorn, and it portrayed the generational conflicts typical of immigrant writing as vividly as Jewish-American writing. In a recent article, Elaine Kim describes a complex oppositional assimilationism as specific to Asian-American tradition: "What Asian American writers express is the desire to remain 'others' by defining their own 'otherness,' not as foreigners but as American 'others.' Our claim on America, then, is part of our resistance to domination" (1991:170).

These changes were under way when the ethnic revival took place. They did not prevent that revival from speaking to what Asian-Americans have in common with African-Americans, a history of racist prejudice and oppression. But they prevented Asian-Americans from simply following the example of black nationalism. Making matters still more complex was an attempt to construct Asian-Americans as a model assimilationist minority, in part to oppose dissident blacks with the counterexample of a "successful" group. This new role was embraced by some and vehemently rejected by other Asian-Americans, but the flip-flop from exotic to model minority produced internal conflict as well as external, interethnic tension.

Kingston's *Woman Warrior* (1975) exhibits these tensions vividly. It is, confusingly, an immigrant novel and a novel of ethnic revival at the same time. Crucial to this (as, indeed, to every) aspect of the memoir is the fact that Kingston poses contradictions that she either does not reconcile or reconciles at different times in different, even opposite, ways. On the one hand, *Woman Warrior* is a story of ethnic revival. Kingston sets herself the task of separating what is merely individual, socioeconomic, or simply spurious from what is "Chinese." "What is Chinese tradition," she asks in a famous question, "and what is the movies" (6)? She initiates this search for a bounded, primordial Chinese culture, moreover, as part of an attempt to heal her own conflicts and to respond to America's treatment of Chinese immigrants: her book crackles with anger and implies the larger project of cultural nationalism. The frequency with which the accuracy of her portrayal of "Chinese culture" has been questioned shows how naively her book has been read as an artifact of this movement: it has been seen as an attempt to represent a separate, bounded, consensual cultural whole.

At the same time, however, *Woman Warrior* is a very different immigrant novel, one that evokes the model of immigrant success and the frustrations and dilemmas of conflicts between second and first generations. Kingston's relationship with her mother is a classic version of these, echoing Anzia Yezierska's portrayal in "The Fat of the Land" (1920) of a heroically ethnic, yet grating, overbearing, oppressive mother. On the one hand, the story of Chinese immigrants to America is thus the typical one of grueling hard work and endurance. On the other, it is the story of a second, Americanized generation that cannot understand its parents; of a mother who imposes Chinese ways on a child agonizingly self-conscious about American responses to them; and a daughter who has to separate herself from her family to achieve her own identity and success as an assimilated American. In short, in *Woman Warrior*, the classic novel of generational conflict and stressful assimilation is wedded to a recent oppositional story of the attempt to recover cultural-national identity, and the two frames of reference remain deeply opposed.

Kingston's text similarly negotiates the equally complex issue of exoticism—which is as much a problem as a possibility for Asian-Americans. A form of exoticism—what Sollors calls the "self-exoticizing" of the ethnic insider—was part of the 1960s ethnic revival: possession of a different culture had cachet and provided a strong oppositional stance. For many Asian-Americans, however, exoticism is an evil: it legitimizes perceptions of them as foreign and unassimilable, and is therefore a mechanism of oppression, not resistance. Frank Chin, a writer who has attacked *Woman Warrior* for pandering to mainstream images of exotic Chinese customs, is intensely critical of any attempt to depict Chinese-Americans in these terms and argues vehemently that Chinese-American identity has been made in America. Chin responds to those who have accused him of rejecting Chinese culture by saying, "the assertion of distinctions between Chinese and Chinese-Americans is neither a rejection of Chinese culture nor an expression of contempt for things Chinese. . . . It's calling things by their right names" (Kim 1982:176).

Contrary to Chin's views, *Woman Warrior* is a fascinating revelation of unresolved tensions about exoticism. On one level, Kingston evokes stories of the suffocation of babies, slave markets, shamanistic exorcism, and eating live monkey's brains—the fascination with the strange and grotesque that exoticism trades on. More compellingly, she embeds these details in what seems an ethnographic presentation of Chinese culture's alien weltanschauung. The portrayal of this weltanschauung is at times quite sympathetic. When, for example, her mother comments that madness represents the inability to achieve variety in talk-story, she expresses what seems a different cultural universe, one that possesses an extremely attractive alternative to the ruthlessly logical Western Enlightenment opposition between madness and reason.

At the same time, Kingston portrays her search for this exotic, bounded, anthropologically constructed cultural identity as conflicted and ultimately frustrated/frustrating. In speculating about her Chinese aunt's illegitimate child and subsequent suicide, Kingston makes up, not one, but too many believable ethnographic possibilities for this enterprise to hang together. Her aunt is the traditionally submissive Chinese woman, giving in to her seducer; she is a covert rebel, breaking the roundness of cultural life in the community; she is an existential victim who falls from that roundness into nothingness; she is a spite suicide who poisons the local wells. This instability not only expresses Kingston's inability to connect with her culture of origin, it also, like much recent theorizing in anthropology, undercuts ethnography's pretensions of depicting bounded, consensual alternative cultural universes. Recent ethnographic self-criticism has found many political and historical justifications for the spurious attempt to create such universes out of fluid, heterogeneous, dissensual, and imperfectly bounded cultural situations; similarly, Kingston offers personal, confessional reasons for criticizing what she is seeking to do, while nonetheless doing it. She explodes the anthropological project by revealing that she is attempting, really, to invent a usable past, commenting at one point, when she rejects a possible identity for her aunt, that "unless I see her life branching into mine, she gives me no ancestral help" (8). Desire, not an attempt to be transparent to an external reality, lies at the root of her constructions of Chinese culture and the past, and Kingston's desires—conflicted, overdetermined, often largely unconscious— are anything but clear.

Similarly, Kingston in other places exposes the fundamental unreliability of what anthropologists call native informants, by noting that her parents, like many Chinese-American immigrants, never explained, and even hid, their traditions from their children, whom they berated as Americanized. Most unsettling, though, are Kingston's occasional revelations that what she has just presented as fact—as memory or ethnography—is actually her fictional invention. She attributes this tricky inventiveness at times to her psychological instability: *Woman Warrior* is an immigrant/ ethnic memoir, but it is also a contemporary confessionalist autobiography, inscribed in a genre that highlights its narrator's unreliability. At times she explains her fabrications as artistry, her imitation of Chinese arts like knot making.

Having thus destabilized the idea of a "Chinese" cultural universe, Kingston gives exoticism an additional turn, reworking it into the locus of still greater cultural destabilization. Along with evoking and deflating it, Kingston turns it around on those who have formerly cultivated it. In a literary version of a movement in anthropology that James Clifford has called ethnographic surrealism (one that was, in turn, inspired by literature), Kingston portrays what she calls "American-normal" reality as just as alienatingly exotic as "Chinese" tradition supposedly is. In the very act of proclaiming that she has left old superstitions behind and assimilated to a new, enlightened American identity, Kingston distorts the new significantly:

> I had to leave home in order to see the world logically, logic the new way of seeing. I learned to think that mysteries are for explanation. I enjoy the simplicity. Concrete pours out of my mouth to cover the forest with freeways and sidewalks. Give me plastics, periodical tables, t.v. dinners with vegetables no more complex than peas mixed with diced carrots. Shine floodlights into dark corners: no ghosts. (104)

American enlightenment modulates sickeningly into the American surreal, then modulates back again. Sometimes each culture seems normative, sometimes both seem abnormal and estranging; and the narrator, even in the act of proclaiming that she has found an identity, has not. Her identity remains fragmented, heterogeneous, composed of opposites that interrupt each other. Even at the book's conclusion, Kingston is, in successive pages, the Chinese woman warrior; an American who shines light in the dark places to exorcise ethnic ghosts; a neurotic American whose fear of phantasmagoria makes her embrace a pathogenic Enlightenment rationalism; and an exile who returns from her barbarian captivity with a new song for her own kind. Kingston has too many personal identities to have a finished "authentic" identity, and she presents too many possible versions of Chinese, American, and Chinese-American identity for the notion of bounded culture to remain viable.

Such considerations raise yet another way in which Asian-American identity cannot fit the mold of black nationalism. Asian-American heterogeneity makes achievement of a separate, bounded cultural identity extremely difficult, even apart from issues of primordialism and exoticism. First, the made-in-America category "Asian-American" is anything but unitary. The term includes Japanese-Americans, Chinese-Americans, Filipino-Americans, Indian-Americans, Korean-Americans, and so on—

peoples, in short, of a wide variety of national origins. These nations of origin, moreover, have historically sometimes been at each other's throats, and the effects of distant conflict are felt in America. Second, the category is temporally quite heterogeneous, since both new nations and very different groupings within older nations (e.g., recent Hong Kong Chinese as well as older Guangdong Chinese) have supplied immigrants to America in the postwar period. Third, these differences based on origin are further supplemented by differences inherent in American experience, from generational and gender conflicts to the development of new class structures and occupational differentiations. Accordingly, Asian-American literature records a variety of clashing types: the model minority figure versus the oppositional ethnic revivalist; the feminist versus the traditionalist; the first versus the second generation. Elaine Kim also documents tension between aristocratic immigrant writers and scholars and Chinese-Americans of rural, peasant origins, and Lisa Lowe (1991:26) analyzes the comedy of internal hierarchies in Diana Chang's "The Oriental Contingent," a story in which women avoid "discussion of their Chinese backgrounds because each desperately fears the other is 'more Chinese' than they are." Finally, the category is riven from within conceptually by the yoking of definition by national identity and racial identity, terms that evoke different traditions of discourse. The category "Asian-American" has remained one imposed by America on peoples self-conscious about their diverse origins; it has not yet become the basis for an ethnogenesis that obscures these roots. Henry Louis Gates, Jr., believes that "African slavery in the New World satisfied the preconditions for the emergence of a new African culture, a truly Pan-African culture" (1988:4), but this has not happened for "Asian-Americans."

The heterogeneity implicit in the category "Asian-American" shows up vividly in the problematic portrayal of the search for identity in Asian-American literature. This problematic has increasingly been turned into an aggressive strategy, and a postmodern cultural politics has emerged in Asian-American tradition, whose difficult heterogeneity has gradually become the basis for something new. In the process, the African-American decision to make "the general society conscious rather than unconscious than color" has here taken on a meaning very different from that ascribed to it by cultural nationalism.

In her story "Seventeen Syllables," Hisaye Yamamoto describes a Japanese-American teenager, Rosie:

> At Japanese school . . . Rosie was grave and giddy by turns. Preoccupied at her desk in the row for students on Book Eight, she made up for it at

recess by performing wild mimicry for the benefit of her friend Chizuko. She held her nose and whined a witticism or two in what she considered was the manner of Fred Allen; she assumed intoxication and a British accent to go over the climax of Rudy Vallee recording of the pub conversation about William Ewart Gladstone; she was the child Shirley Temple piping, "On the Good Ship Lollipop"; she was the gentleman soprano of the Four Inkspots trilling, "If I Didn't Care." And she felt reasonably satisfied when Chizuko wept and gasped, "Oh, Rosie, you ought to be in the movies." (15)

To a detached observer, Rosie's high-spirited mimicry is also sad. Along with a hint of potentially painful self-division in the fact that Rosie performs her American imitations in recess at Japanese school, her friend's spontaneous comment, that Rosie ought to be in the movies, alerts the reader to the fact that, thanks to America's vision of her racial identity, Rosie never will be in them, at least not in any starring role. Her Americanizing assimilation of popular culture simultaneously, then, highlights her Japanese ethnicity and the construction—largely artificial and, as the passage reveals, multicultural—of an "American" cultural identity. The situation is very different from when, say, Mary Antin considers the relationship between George Washington and the Jewish patriarchs: Rosie's Americanization does not even suggest the possibility of the boundaries disappearing and her being transformed into a "real" American. Instead, it reveals more starkly her status as an outsider—a boundary-violating, and therefore boundary-highlighting, hybrid. And it does so despite the additional irony of revealing that what signifies "the American" is itself a surreptitious hybrid of ethnically produced and ethnically marked popular culture.

The protagonist of John Okada's *No No Boy* (1957) is torn by his alienation from his Japanese-American peers by his refusal to serve the United States in the war. Deeply angry at the crazy traditionalist mother who makes him do this, he feels painfully that his fragmented identity is neither Japanese nor American. However, he experiences a small vision of hope, not by resolving his identity contradictions, but by generalizing the agony. He discovers that "maybe the answer is that there is no in. Maybe the whole damned country is pushing and shoving and screaming to get into some place that doesn't exist, because they don't know that the outside could be the inside if only they would stop all this pushing and shoving and screaming" (159–60).

In many ways, Maxine Hong Kingston's recent novel, *Tripmaster Monkey: His Fake Book* (1989) fulfills Okada's prophetic words that "the outside could be the inside." *Tripmaster Monkey* returns to *Woman Warrior*'s theme

of ethnic revivalism in a very different manner. Crammed with polycultural allusiveness, it dramatizes a brief period in the life of Wittman Ah
Sing, a Chinese-American Beat playwright. An outsider painfully conscious of his exclusion, which he feels at every turn, Wittman fights the
thousand secret battles and attempts the thousand secret manipulations
that are the daily fare of an assimilationist like Mary Antin. A prime example of deconstructive ethnicity in action, he both asserts his ethnic identity and inserts himself aggressively into American culture and circumstances.

To fully appreciate how different the deconstructive ethnicity Wittman
represents is from the black nationalist model it supersedes, one further
historical stress involved in the development of Asian-American tradition
must be pointed out: ambivalence about the influence black cultural nationalism had on the consolidation and extension of Asian-American literary tradition in the 1960s. Although black nationalism provided a model
for the recovery of repressed cultures, and although Asian-Americans not
only felt sympathy with, but received actual support from African-
Americans, that very help and influence impoverished as well as enhanced
Asian-Americans. In essays or through the voices of their characters,
Jeffrey Paul Chan, Frank Chin, Maxine Hong Kingston, and numerous
others voice the lament that Chinese-American "identity is yet to be delin-
eated. All we know is what it is not: it is not European, it is not Chinese,
and it is not Afro-American" (Kim 1982:175). Or as Wittman puts it: "So
what do we have in the way of a culture besides Chinese hand laun-
dries? . . . Where's our jazz? Where's our blues? Where's our ain't-taking-
no-shit-from-nobody street-strutting language? I want so bad to be the
first bad-jazz China Man bluesman of America" (27).

One fear, for male writers like Chin and Wittman—who is clearly modeled on Chin—is that the aggressive manhood open to black nationalist
men, and characteristic, as Cynthia Enloe (1989) argues, of the nationalist
ethos, is not open to Chinese-Americans, who are emasculated by American oppression and in American popular culture, depicted not as threatening potential rapists but as sexless Charlie Chans or homosexual Fu Man-
chus. A second fear is that there is no room for Asian-Americans in what
seems a closed ethnic economy. As Wittman laments:

> I can't wear that civil-rights button with the Black hand and the white
> hand shaking each other. I have a nightmare—after duking it out, some-
> day Blacks and whites will shake hands over my head. I'm the little
> yellow man beneath the bridge of their hands and overlooked. (308–9)

As the third term of a triad, Asian-Americans feel themselves endangered:
what Christopher Miller asserts of the Eurocolonial economy of cultures is

perhaps even more compelling when applied to Chinese-American self-perception: "The third entry tends to be associated with one side or the other or to be nullified by the lack of an available slot in our intellectual apparatus" (1985:16). Thus Patricia Mizuhara writes of "play-acting / in a dichotomous world," recording her fear that she will "be caught with any one of my numerous masks off / for fear there'd be *nothing* underneath" (Kim 1982:242). In the same vein, Frank Chin argues that Asian-Americans, caught between black and white, without "something rightly ours" are "hungry all the time . . . chameleons looking for color, trying on tongues and clothes and hairdos, taking on everyone else's, with none of our own, and no habitat" (Kim 1982:242). Just a little of the complexity of this situation can be indicated by saying that Wittman's combination of assimilationism and cultural nationalism can be restated as an assimilationism, not just to mainstream culture, but to a black model of oppositional culture, which, however, rejects assimilationism.

Significant in these comments by Asian-Americans, however, is more than just the fear of nullity, of having no identity. Manipulated by being pulled back and forth between the poles of black and white, and aware of the playacting involved in imitating either model, Asian-Americans couple fear of nullity with an awareness of perpetually inauthentic, heterogeneous role playing: of having too many identities. This dilemma—which, as we have seen, Yamamoto's Rosie experiences, but remains unconscious of, and Kingston's Woman Warrior struggles unsuccessfully to resolve—soon became something Asian-Americans were aggressively conscious of. One of Frank Chin's characters reveals an explanatory virtuosity that might be a resource for coping with this dilemma. Trying to convince a newsman in Chinatown that he is not Chinese, Chin's rebellious Chinese-American protagonist declaims:

> Don't you know there's no such thing as a real Chinaman in all of America? That we are all American Indians cashing in on a fad? . . . No, you're not Chinese, don't you understand? You see it all started when a bunch of Indians wanted to quit being Indians and fighting the cavalry and all, so they left the reservation, see? . . . And they saw that there was this big kick about Chinamen, so they braided their hair into queues and opened up laundries and restaurants and started reading Margaret Mead and Confucius and Pearl Buck and became respectable Chinamen and gained some self-respect. (Kim 1982:184)

In these comments, the Asian-American outsider, deficient in identity in a nationalist mold, shows himself to possess an insider's knowledge of how cultures construct identities, and to be more expert and broadly familiar with the material and processes of American culture than "Americans" themselves are. No authentic member of a separate, bounded, primordial community with definable attributes, the Asian-American (like Gates's and Baker's African-Americans) becomes a deconstructionist master of the American system, unmasked as constructing the very ethnicity it pretends to neutralize in its melting pot. So much for immigrant cultures representing the persistence of authentic roots: like Werner Sollors, Chin asserts that the myth of "roots" is an American act. But like William Boelhower in *Through a Glass Darkly* (1987), Chin's character suggests that this discovery does not neutralize ethnic opposition, but recasts it in a new key. The ethnic who gives up the fiction of "strong" referential ethnicity and realizes that ethnicity is an American act can, perhaps, more radically deconstruct and decenter American culture than someone from a position of revolutionary separatism.

Wittman is the fulfillment of these tendencies. After showing how America constructs its hierarchies by manipulation and suppression of ethnic signs, he then upsets them by inserting himself everywhere as the sophisticated, critical, disruptively culturally different insider. As one who experiences a multiplicity of perpetually inauthentic identities, Wittman is a model figure for a heterogeneously syncretic, multicultural America. Gates's principle of deconstructionist ethnicity is embodied in a Signifying Monkey; Kingston's Wittman is the Tripmaster Monkey, an avatar, not of Esu, but of the Stone Monkey (master of the seventy-two magic transformations) of the classic Chinese novel *Journey to the West*. Indeed, Kingston's deconstruction arguably one-ups Gates's: she admits no legacy of primordialism at all, and she doubtless uses Gates's theory as one of the dazzling wealth of models to which Wittman, imitation of an imitation of an . . . , alludes.

Wittman Ah Sing trips off (or signifies on) many familiar figures and features of American cultural history. He probably trips off Gates. Still more clearly, he is based on Chin, the Chinese-American San Franciscan hippie-bohemian playright. This again is an act of signifying or tripping. Chin was an incensed critic of *The Woman Warrior*: he excoriated it for its feminism and its exoticism, both of which (in rendering Chinese sexism so glaringly and Chinese customs so estrangingly) pandered, Chin felt, to negative stereotypes of Chinese in America. Further, Wittman's name fuses Chinese and American signs (i.e., Walt Whitman's name and his famous line, "Of myself I sing"; "white man"; and Ah Sing, the homely Chinese immigrant laborer). And Wittman's encyclopaedic knowledge of American popular culture and the culture of romantic bohemianism in America (knowledge he uses for his frequent personality changes, from Chinese-American Rilke to Chinese-American Rimbaud to Chinese-American beatnik sage, a role that is in turn an imitation of oriental monks) is supplemented by his status as the well-known master of the seventy-two magic transformations, an incarnation of the Stone Monkey of *Journey to the West*. Indeed, in one of the novel's million and a half hip syncretisms, Wittman is the Stoned Monkey, American tripper (which is, in turn, an echo of Whitman's imitative and inauthentic "trippers and askers").

In creating Wittman's wholly inauthentic composite identity, Kingston heightens awareness of both Chinese and American signifiers as Yamamoto does, replacing assimilationist transformation with an intentionally discordant, hybrid syncretism. In doing so, however, Kingston portrays this syncretism, not as a sign of hapless racial exclusion of which the character is unaware, but as an aggressive tactic that Wittman exuberantly, frenetically uses. This tactic Wittman, following Chin, insists is Chinese-American, not Chinese, thanks to the richness of Chinese-American theatrical tradition (Chinese came to America to play, not work, Wittman asserts, inverting the usual wisdom [250]) and Wittman's own youthful experience in Chinese-American vaudeville.

Wittman is thus an explicitly postnationalist, deconstructive figure: a deficiency of determinable, bounded, separate identity, is both his creative resource and his torment. He experiences his marginalization and deracination most nakedly when he is forced, for example, to confront the strong, referential ethnicity of F.O.B.'s, or the relentlessly stereotypical Chinese-American Judy, who sits next to him on a bus and gradually, hallucinatorily metamorphoses into a blue boar. He is equally at a loss when asked for any flat statement of facts: meeting Tana, to whom he is attracted, and whom he later experimentally marries in a hippie accidental dada fashion, he becomes nervous when she tries to discover his secret name:

> "Do you throw the Ching? My name is number sixty-one, which they translate Inner Truth. You can look it up." I am True Center. Core Truth. Truth is a bird carrying a boy in her talons. She can look it up for herself. He hoped nobody Chinese was eavesdropping. Can't stand hippy dippies who trade on orientalia. (128)

Anything that would threaten to stop Wittman's restlessly nervous flow of thoughts, speech, parodic role playing, perpetual circulation of cultural information, life-styles, signs, is upsettingly dangerous; anything that will tie this continual flow down to some immobile reality is anathema.

Thus, on encountering new immigrants, Wittman recovers himself by casting them, not as painful exponents of given identity, but as people who, on encountering the racism in the American system, have to "tight-en up their act. Turn complicated" (22). As negotiators of culture, they are already actors; ultimately, to quote Wittman quoting Richard Boleslavsky, to act is to become human, for "acting is the life of the human soul receiving its birth through art" (276). Wittman comically levels and universalizes this high romanticism in hip jargon; with his canny wisdom that immigrants have to make their "acts" more complicated, Wittman realizes that to negotiate American culture with any effectiveness, they have to become, like himself, deconstructive sophisticates, embodiments of weak, not strong, ethnicity, highlighting everywhere the ethnic sign, and always deferring closure. When he meets a new immigrant Kung Fu group from China, Wittman is first knocked senseless by one despite his monkey trickery—in other words, he is laid flat by a demonstration of strong ethnicity that he cannot counter by parodically turning it into an act. Immediately thereafter, however, Wittman triumphs, in effect, over them: their spokesman, Siew Loong, reveals they have come to America to try to sell themselves and their idea for a Kung Fu Wild West TV series to Hollywood, an idea (the reader who catches the allusion might ironically note) that did get realized, but with David Carradine, not an immigrant Chinese, as the hero. They are, just as much as Wittman, actors, creatures of a world of socially constructed simulacra; and the more sophisticated Wittman, the dramatist director-actor, quickly incorporates them into his play.

When on the aggressive, Wittman uses his parodic abilities to assume and therefore criticize and expose the smorgasbord of roles that, as Wittman (similarly to Arjun Appadurai) puts it, Central Casting assigns people in America. For example, Wittman works as a clerk in the toy section of a department store. This job is not presented as part of Wittman's personal or social "reality," but is glossed as one of his seventy-two transformations, the lowest of them in fact. Appropriately, Wittman constructs his appearance as a pastiche that calls attention to itself as such. Dressed in the navy-blue pinstripe of "some dead businessman," Wittman sports a green shirt and greener tie (green being a color that yellow-colored people supposedly cannot wear) decorated with orange-and-silver covered wagons and rows of Daniel Boones with rifles; the tie label, moreover, reads, "Wear with brown suit" (44). Violating every boundary he can, and thereby calling attention to the absurdity of naive belief in such boundaries and the constant interpenetration of "fantasy" and "reality," Wittman lives up to the Stone Monkey's Buddhist name, the one Monkey acquires by mastery: "Aware of Emptiness."

Wittman's America is, correspondingly, the postmodern archive of simulations Appadurai describes, a land of Baudrillardean simulacra, an actual Disneyland. As chameleon outsider, moreover, Wittman is its sophisticated insider. Others, who believed in America's actuality, merely have limited imaginations. In his toy clerk transformation, Wittman goes with one of his colleagues to a toy manufacturer's product-line presentation: he witnesses a display, with excruciatingly tacky fanfare, of the new line of Ken and Barbie dolls. At the end of it, "Everybody sang out together like community sing. 'You can tell it's Mattel. It's swell'" (62). Thinking, "Oh god, I don't belong on this planet," Wittman leaves with his colleague, who talks, on the ride back, about "how generous Mattel was to sponsor the do" and what "an excellent presentation it was." Wittman's response is to think, "you have to be dumb to be happy on this earth" (62). Similarly, Wittman deflates the self-deceiving literalism of a Black Muslim as an unconscious construct of the ethnic stereotyping of Central Casting:

> In Berkeley, a Black Muslim spoke about "sanctuary that the Chinese brothers provide one unto another." He had looked right at Wittman, a member of a people with a genius for community. Black guys see too many kung fu movies. They think a Chinese-American can go anywhere in the country and have a safehouse where a stranger can be served a family dinner. (255)

Wittman attacks mainstream America still more directly in two ways. First, he is a consummately acute critic of illusions constructed to marginalize Asian-Americans and enforce American cultural and social hierarchies. A scholar of the Orientalism of domestic popular culture, he comments on invidious ethnic construction in everything from the very Beat movement he emulates to Hollywood movies, artifacts that, as fountainheads of simulacra, attracts as much as incense him. In Hisaye Yamamoto's "Life among the Oil Fields: A Memoir" ([1979] 1988), a Japanese-American narrator interweaves nostalgia for her American and ethnic (not her primordial Japanese) childhood with increasingly harsh ironies, which lead at last to awareness that the very culture she is nostalgic about also encodes exclusionary prejudice. The narrator, at the conclusion, discovers in herself "an anger more intricate" (95) than her parents' literal anger at marginalization. Wittman replicates this love-hate in his characteristically more conscious, aggressive key, and it provides the material for vitriolic anti-Orientalist lectures. Corrosively interpreting popular Hollywood films, he shows how in America race and color are historical constructions falsely rooted in nature, invidious shticks asserted as real.

Second, along with becoming a gadfly critic, Wittman seeks to build, through his postmodern art, a new Chinese-American-brokered multiculturalist community. Wittman's great dream is to stage a Chinese-American drama: he has chosen drama as his form because "by writing a play, he didn't need descriptions that racinated anybody. The actors will walk out on stage and their looks will be self-evident" (34). In a play, then, Wittman can foreground the ethnic sign (make society conscious of color) without doing so in a nationalist—or racinated—mode: it can be foregrounded as part of an extravagantly hybrid spectacle. The more artful, sophisticated Disneyland that Wittman thereby creates not inappropriately, echoes Mitsuhiro Yoshimoto's analysis of Disneyland in Japan: if Japanese culture claims centrality for itself in the postmodern world of simulcra thanks to the culture of its Edo period, *Tripmaster Monkey* suggests that Chinese-American culture can press similar claims. For example, Chinese-Americans' mastery of artifice can be related to their tradition of theater generally, and to devices like the "memory village" (a model immigrants memorized in order to deceive the immigration authorities) specifically. In this act, both American lives and Chinese pasts became fabrications necessary for negotiating the present system. Chinese-Americans become foundational virtuosi, like Edo-period Japanese, of the process of building life upon invention.

True to the pattern of ethnic group formation laid down in the 1960s, Kingston locates these postmodern aptitudes in Chinese-American tradition. It is important to add, though, that similar abilities to see through mainstream culture as a falsely naturalized construction have been claimed, from early on, by a variety of immigrant cultures in America: Abraham Cahan's David Levinsky achieves this competence in dealing with American businessman, Gates's account of the Signifying Monkey attests to just this sort of competence, and even Michael Novak, exponent of the more conservative ethnic groups, styles immigrants as cunning disbelievers manipulating alien norms. Wittman is, in short, a more explicitly oppositional version of what was, in its earliest forms, an old assimilationist tradition: he is a product, once again, of transformations of both cultural nationalism and assimilationism.

Wittman's great accomplishment, then, is staging his drama, which turns out to be a postmodern, carnivalesque spectacle of hybrid Asian-Americana. Passionately upset by a review that claims "East meets West"— a quotation from a review of Kingston's *Woman Warrior* (Kim 1982:xvi)— Wittman asserts the hybrid, Chinese-American basis of the whole production. Indeed, in presenting heterogeneous material (from Chinese myth to an unclassifiable variety of Asian-American circumstances) in heterogeneous modes (from burlesque to the epic), the play does foreground a heterogeneity of types. Asian-American multiplicity is represented, as actors include Nanci Lee (a well-to-do amalgam of the model minority and Chinese-American princess types); Judy (the representative of raw Chinese-American ethnicity); the new Hong Kong immigrants of the

Kung Fu group; Wittman's parents and aunts, representatives of the scandalously hybrid tradition of Chinese-American vaudeville; and the stereotypical early generation of sojourner Chinese-Americans, the "old futs" who run the society where the play is staged. Further Asian-American heterogeneity is represented in Wittman's Japanese-American friend, Lance Kumiyama; "white" Americans participate as well, including Tana, Wittman's wife, and a Yale Younger Post Wittman has uncovered working in the stockroom at the toy store. (Wittman wants to include a Barbie from the Mattel show as well; although he doesn't manage this, he does get Leroy Sanchez, his Mexican-American counselor at the unemployment office, to participate.) Reinforcing this carnivalesque heterogeneity of deracinated cultural signs is the fact that actors cross boundaries to play each other's ethnic parts: not just Asian-Americans but Americans play Asian characters. The ultimate import of the spectacle is to create a new kind of imagined community: a community of marginal figures, rebellious outlaws of all descriptions (301–2) who will not be confined to the theater but disseminate out to infect and alter "real" America, which is also, as we have seen, a form of theater. Rather than the homogeneous "imagined communities" of nationalism analyzed by Benedict Anderson, Wittman's version of "making society conscious rather than unconscious of color" highlights differences within a single system, which is shown, thanks to the exposure of its racism and the recovery of repressed subjectivities and pasts within it, to be more complex and heterogeneous than anyone had thought. Wittman does not, as a cultural nationalist would, try to construct a position apart from that system. Convinced that "community is not built once-for-all [but] people have to imagine, practice, re-create it" (306), Wittman seeks to define a new community, and his goal is the same as that of American multiculturalists: engineering a new kind of society that represents a radical transformation of previous notions of national community and culture.

Wittman's efforts are, to be sure, affectionately mocked by the narrative voice at the end of the book. Wittman is prophetic, but also extravagant, perhaps clownishly foolish, and not fully effective. In the end, not only the reviewers, but his own community misunderstand him, and clearly his experimentalist theater does not end America's problems. Even he, after staging a theatrical event in which Gwan Goong, the Chinese god of war and poetry, figures prominently, realizes he has partly missed the mark. Especially for his feminist author, evoking the god of war and poetry too closely represents the nationalist yoking of cultural identity and rediscovered warlike manhood. The book underscores this illegitimacy in that it is set during the Vietnam War era, and Wittman, at the end, suddenly becomes a pacifist. Perhaps this is a commentary on both Wittman and the 1960s in San Francisco, echoing how the Stone Monkey, who tries rebelliously to upset Heaven (read America) with his magic powers, is overcome and punished by being buried under a mountain. Or perhaps Wittman resembles his forebear Monkey in a different way: perhaps he is the accomplished trickster who leads a much less conscious company toward enlightenment and the attainment of the true scriptures. That duller company would include Piggy—perhaps Judy, the unconscious Chinese-American stereotype who requires nationalist awakening before a further transformation to hybrid heterogeneity—and Tripitaka—the too-human larger American society, which lags cravenly behind Wittman's vision. In this reading, the "West" of Wittman's journey would represent that as-yet-unreached goal of both traditional and multiculturalist American nationalism, the closure of the great round of civilization by the construction of a "nation of nations."

If the end of *Tripmaster Monkey* can be read in this fashion, Lisa Lowe's (1991:24) analysis of "heterogeneity, hybridity, multiplicity" in recent Asian-American literature, like Amy Tan's *Joy Luck Club* (1989), and film, like Peter Wang's *A Great Wall* (1985) suggests that Tripitaka-America has advanced since the time of Wittman's play, the countercultural 1960s. Arguing that Amy Tan's *Joy Luck Club* poses "an alternative to the dichotomy of nativism [nationalism's affirmation of the separate purity of ethnic culture] and assimilation by multiplying the generational conflict and demystifying the centrality of the mother-daughter relationship" (37), Lowe pays close attention to the heterogeneous definitions of Chinese-American the novel's four separate stories of mother-daughter pairs represent. Similarly, she focuses on how the film *A Great Wall* delineates differences between Chinese and Chinese-American cultures when a Chinese-American family visits relatives in the People's Republic. In both cases, what for Wittman was deconstructive and experimentalist is now normative for, and domesticated within, American society and the world system: hybridity and heterogeneity are assumptions behind cultural identity in these systems, replacing the nationalist assumptions of separate purity and authenticity of culture.

Lowe's analysis wisely depicts the present stage in America, not as the supersession of the nationalist era, but as transformative growth from it. She argues that the essential oppositions of the nationalist era are being decentered by the use of heterogeneity as a strategy: dominant America's strategy of inscribing Asian-Americans as a homogeneous group is being disrupted, which then allows Asian-Americans further to decenter American society as, no longer a construction of majority versus minority, but a "multiplicity of various, nonequivalent groups" (30). More variously than when Kingston exoticized the "American-normal," present ethnic cultural politics make sure that no aspect of American culture will be free of an ethnic sign. "Anglo" culture will be a particular tradition within American culture, not the mainstream majority to which minorities must conform or against which they must rebel. Such a strategy of heterogenization, Lowe argues, opens up a further possibility:

> Asian Americans can articulate distinct group demands based on our particular histories of exclusion, but the redefined lack of closure—which reveals rather than conceals differences—opens political lines of affiliation with other groups (labor unions, other racial and ethnic groups, and gay, lesbian and feminist groups) in the challenge to specific forms of domination insofar as they share common features. (30)

Lowe's construction of oppositional politics for an era of postmodern heterogeneity is, as we shall see, a strategy that is anything but confined to American ethnic politics: it has been formulated as an essential strategy of postmodern politics (Laclau and Mouffe 1985; Jameson 1991:319ff.) and as a globalist strategy for dealing with a decentered world system. Once again transformations in local American and global concepts of culture and cultural production have occurred in sync with each other. Moreover, this linkage has been made, much more emphatically than it was in the nationalist era, fully transparent, as American multiculturalists and global postcolonialists have explicitly drawn upon and contributed to work in each other's fields. Lowe herself acknowledges her indebtedness to Trinh Minh-ha and Nancy Fraser: Trinh locates the strategy of heterogeneity in postcolonial global-local circumstances, and both Trinh and Fraser develop it in the context of feminist theory, which has itself become the basis for an imagined community that cuts across national borders.

Although the postmodern politics they describe represent a stage beyond ethnic and cultural nationalism and incorporate a sharp critique of its assumptions, Lowe is explicit about how the nationalist legacy nonetheless lives on *within* the newer, postnationalist forms. "The very freedom, in the 1990s, to explore the hybridities concealed beneath the desire of identity," Lowe writes, is "permitted by the context of a strongly articulated essentialist politics" (39). A substratum of essentialist boundaries is, quite simply, required to give meaning to their violation by the postmodern cultural politics of heterogeneity and hybridity. Also, the retention of the nationalist category "Asian-American" as the basis for cultural-political activity represents not only a base for present departures, but a possible basis for organization and action: as Gayatri Spivak describes it,

oppositional cultural politics can make "strategic use of a positive essentialism in a scrupulously visible political interest" (Spivak 1987:205). The
conscious use of what is fictional—a nationalist concept of ethnic group
identity—may yet serve to ground oppositional political action. Such
strategies have been advocated also in larger contexts than American ethnic politics. Terry Eagleton has advocated the development of "ironic nationalism" (1990). Bill Ashcroft, Gareth Griffiths, and Helen Tiffin (1989)
have interpreted postcolonial literary study as genealogically dependent
on the creation of national traditions in Third World anticolonialism,
paralleling Lowe's description of contemporary American ethnic cultural
politics as dependent on 1960s cultural nationalism. Amanda Anderson
has analyzed a wide variety of "double gestures"—political practice that
works "through what are ultimately dangerous fictions"—as strategies of
postmodern politics (1992:63–80). In these accounts of genealogy, as well
as descriptions of the styles of oppositional politics, movements on the
local level in America transparently mirror and make overt use of developments in the larger global arena.

The resurgence of immigration since the 1965 liberalization of immigration law provided an important new force for change in notions of cultural
identity in the United States. An America redefining itself encountered in
this immigration an important aspect of the new stage of the capitalist
world system that was then emerging. For the new immigration was new
in its form and style, as well as its numbers: it brought a decentering Third
World influx into colonial and neocolonial cores, and it was part of a larger
movement toward the globalization of many areas of economic, social,
and cultural life, a process that includes the deterritorialization of culture
and the globalization of "dwelling."
      The immigrants the new global migration has brought to America are
different from their predecessors in a variety of ways. One of the most
significant differences between older and newer immigrants lies in their
concepts of home; this difference, in turn, is located in crucial changes in
the overall world system. Put simply, memory in the contemporary global
system is no longer what it used to be. A classic trope of traditional immigrant nostalgia can be found in Asian-American literature in Carlos
Bulosan's lyrical narrative *America Is in the Heart* (1943). In it, Carlos, still a
child in the little farming town of Binaloan in the Philippines, witnesses
his brother's return from World War I. Leon arrives as his father is plowing.
His father's face breaks "into sudden gentleness"; then Leon hoists Carlos
on his back, and "with an affectionate glance at the animal, he took the
rope from my father and started plowing the common earth that fed our

family for generations" (4). Bulosan's important successor, Bienvenido N. Santos, records an unsettling transformation of this idyll of wholeness and reconnection with family and primordial *Boden* (soon to be painfully shattered by Carlos's emigration first to town, and then to America). As a writer of stories about Filipinos, Santos found himself troubled by "the new breed of Filipino immigrants, professionals and businessmen who lived in mansions on hills above the babel of the narrow streets, or in the exclusive residential sections away from the smell of the harbor and the fish markets" (Kim 1982:271). They are callously upscale:

> No nostalgia for the new breed. The talk closest to home revolved around the current peso-dollar exchange, tax exemptions, loopholes in the tax laws and proven ways of circumventing them. New car models. At the last party I attended, they were comparing the relative power and clarity of their C.B. radios and how to keep them from being stolen. (Quoted in Kim 1982:272)

Santos depicts the new immigrants as global cosmopolitans; disquietingly, they show no nationalist nostalgia. Revising still another of the time-honored tropes of traditional American immigration experience is the fact that the transformation of the homeland effaces, not just national, but temporal boundaries. In the global "American century," immigrants are not only already "Americanized" before arriving in the United States, they no longer move forward in time from a premodern to a modern society. Traveling to America no longer means traveling into modernity, and returning is no longer like going back in public and personal time. If Sollors, Chin, and Wittman after him deconstruct the myth of premigration roots as a made-in-America fantasy, the transformed world system reveals it as a curious relic of past assumptions and ideology. Thus, when Leo Fang's Chinese-American family encounter their Asian relatives in *A Great Wall*, heterogeneity meets heterogeneity, and the two are subtly differentiated as aspects of the same time frame. As Lowe comments:

> The film contains a number of emblematic images that call attention to the syncretic, composite quality of all cultural spaces: when the young Chinese Liu finishes the university entrance exam his scholar-father gives him a Coca Cola; children crowd around the single village television to watch a Chinese opera singer imitate Pavarotti singing Italian opera; the Chinese student learning English recites the Gettysburg Address. (1991:38)

It should come as no surprise when the image of homecoming from *America Is in the Heart* surfaces, in parodically changed form, as one of the images flickering through Wittman's stream of conscious in the process of his perpetually deferred self-construction from an encyclopaedia of cultural models. Steering his just-recovered grandmother (who has been granny-dumped in Las Vegas) across a crowded street, Wittman suddenly transforms himself into Bulosan's "manong pinoy come home from the city to take the reins of the carabao from the old mother's brown hands, and plow the wet rice field" (263). Wittman flashes on this image as he decides not to rush his grandmother across the street ("let the fucking honkers run over the both of them"); reunited with his grandmother, Wittman momentarily reenters premodern time and sentiment for the space of a paragraph or two, thereby repeating, albeit with substantial difference, Bulosan's text.

Bharati Mukherjee, a new immigrant from India, but also a global cosmopolitan who had studied and taught in both Canada and the United States long before her naturalization, faces the issue of nostalgia in the transformed, globalized world squarely. Her short story "Nostalgia" presents a dramatically revised vision of America, the world, and the new immigrants: in what appalls Santos, Mukherjee finds possibility, and what Wittman tries to lead his ignorant land to see, she displays as the staple of daily life, these days, in globalized America. The story chronicles a day in the life of an East-Indian-American psychiatrist, Manny Patel. Patel's New York milieu is heterogeneously multicultural: it is not a centered system that the story deconstructs, but an already thoroughly decentered system of circulating differences. It is the New York that a recent Russian immigrant, quoted by Annelise Orleck in Nancy Foner's *New Immigrants in New York*, describes as a confusingly culturally centerless place: "Where are all the Americans is all I want to know. . . . I haven't met any yet" (1987:295). Manny's milieu is clear from the beginning of the story, when, with the help of an African-American guard, several Jamaican nurses, and a Korean colleague, he subdues a mental patient, the descendant of eastern European Jews. In his madness, the patient imitates Noël Coward; in an exquisite English accent, he villifies Patel in British working-class slang as "Paki scum" (1985:98). Mukherjee's New York thus fits Fredric Jameson's description of postmodernity, in which "the advanced capitalist countries today are a field of stylistic and discursive heterogeneity without a norm" (1984:65). The city is a syncretic cultural and linguistic hodgepodge. The heir of Russian-Jewish immigrants speaks exquisite English to an audience that contains no Anglos; he inveighs, in America, against East Indians in low-class British invective spoken in an upper-class accent he has taken, nostalgically, from yesterday's popular art. In such a New York, unstable cultural heterogeneity and inventive syncretism, not Anglocentrism or its heir, oppositional ethnic politics, are the deepest norms. Even Manny's

American wife is portrayed as an ethnic type: Anglos too have become "others," and the society of outsiders of which Okada dreamed is mainstream America.

The overt action of the story is Manny Patel's attempt to return from a position of apparent assimilation (he is so Americanized he votes for Ronald Reagan, marries an American, and burns his India Society membership card) to connection to his own culture—to enact the ethnic nationalist model fully—by picking up and sleeping with a young Indian woman, Padma. At the peak of his infatuation, he is drenched in nostalgia: he wishes he had not married an American or left India, and that "he were in his kitchen, and that his parents were visiting him and that his mother was making him a mug of hot Horlick's and that his son was not so far removed from him in a boarding school" (111).

His nostalgia is, however, gross self-deception—like, Mukherjee implies, the model of cultural nationalism that underlies it. There are many false notes in the story: that mug of Horlick's, an English brand in a colonial culture, undercuts nostalgia for a separate, bounded, cultural universe just as strongly as the similarly nostalgic memory of a drink taken in neocolonial, pre-Castro Cuba does for a Cuban-American. The Cuban drink turns out to be Hershey's chocolate, but the memory of it haunts Hector in Oscar Hijuelos's *Our House in the Last World* (1983) until he at last realizes the truth. These examples of the duplicity of memory exhibit the ways two different world systems construct memory; and the ironies in each case undercut the politics of memory, even as they signify on Proust's madeleine. Still more disquieting is the fact that Manny comes from a family that had already undergone modernization in India; his father had blackened teeth, but operated a movie house in Delhi, which he staffed with poor cousins; Manny himself went to Delhi Modern School and eventually Johns Hopkins. In New York, he only confirms a process begun in India, working as a psychiatrist and routinely receiving inside information about Wall Street from a former classmate from Delhi who works for Merrill Lynch.

Still more outrageous is the way Manny's "Indian identity" and his "return to his roots" are both, the story underscores, made in America. When he takes Padma (who wears a "Police" T-shirt with navy cords) to an Indian restaurant, Manny fantasizes that "the old assurance, the authority of a millionaire in his native culture, was returning" (109). But he has, in fact, only become a millionaire in America. Similarly, when he pays for a hotel room for the two of them, registering under the name of Dr. Mohan Vakil and wife, 18 Ridgewood Drive, Columbus, Ohio, he feels he has "laid claim to America" (110): his nostalgic return to India via an affair with

Padma is thus also the embodiment of Americanization. Manny's nostalgia, in short, leads him to return to a land that never was, created through the circumstances and the culture of the land of which he is now a part.

Manny's utterly spurious return explodes in his face when the fling turns out to be a set up. Padma turns out to be prostitute working for the restaurant maitre d', and Patel has to bribe his way out of the fix when the man enters his hotel room and claims she is underage—his sister's youngest daughter. Reinforcing the fact that Patel's nostalgia is utterly solipsistic is the fact that Padma, she tells him, cannot have an orgasm: "You won't have to worry about pleasing me" (110) she says, and it enhances Manny's pleasure.

It might seem that all this irony makes the story a rehearsal of classic immigrant fiction like Anzia Yezierska's "The Fat of the Land," in which assimilation heightens the pain of culture loss. Manny's story might be a bitter tale of Americanization that prevents him from ever going home again. The story is, however, a replication with a difference. After the predators have gone, Manny squats over the sink "like a villager . . . the way he had done in his father's home" and defecates, then uses the shit ("it felt hot, light, porous, an artist's medium" [113]) to write WHORE on the mirror and floor. In the abrupt deflation of his nostalgia, he achieves, in a sense, an authentic return at last—and one, moreover, that is secretly gratifying. His shit is an artist's medium, and he returns to the India of public elimination that so disgusted V. S. Naipaul, as well as the India in which he was not a millionaire, but a villager, as his father had originally been. In addition to this irony, the story undermines the usual assumptions of dystopian, "you-can't-go-home-again" nostalgia by having a happy end. Manny's tempest departs as quickly and completely as it came. Indeed, when Manny leaves the hotel the next morning, he discovers his Porsche has not been vandalized, and he interprets this to mean that, despite his brush with the deities (specifically, the goddess Padma incarnates), he has somehow been spared.

Not only does the story thus show the failure of nostalgia to not be terribly traumatic, but only a little ripple on the surface of his love and marriage, it also hints that Manny has never really assimilated, in the traditional sense, in the first place. The fact is that Manny continues to have an unconsciously porous selfhood, one that readily—effortlessly—absorbs American material, customs, cultural knowledge, and family, and simultaneously floats all this side by side with a number of Indian traits and beliefs. Thus, Manny gets his job and stock tips in America easily (the latter from an Indian network), and he transposes his Indian family feeling onto his wife Camille's mother and their son. In his bond with Camille's mother, moreover, Manny's cultural difference is again underscored by the fact that he embraces her warmly, while Camille, a typical American, rejects her to pursue a liberal yuppie life-style. More marked still is the fact that Manny carries the Goddess—Parvati, who arranged his birth to a forty-three-year-old mother—with him. He "couldn't pretend he had been reborn when he became a citizen in a Manhattan courthouse" because "rebirth was the privilege of the dead, and of gods and goddesses, and they could leap into your life in myriad, mysterious ways"—as, indeed, Padma comes to test him. Crèvecoeur's picture of becoming American as a form of rebirth thus never applies to Manny; his old Indian piety stays in place. Thus, while Manny's national- ist nostalgia is utterly deflated (Padma is a whore), Padma paradoxically remains an agent of the goddess, and Manny's identity is, at the end as at the beginning of the story, equally porous to American and Indian mate- rial. Manny is, to put the matter most accurately, fully bicultural in this porosity: he is as absorptive of global cosmopolitan heterogeneity as America is of immigrants and Indian cosmology is of shape-changing deities and incarnations. In Patel, then, American and "foreign" material commingle, and assimilationism coexists thoroughly comfortably with retention of cultural difference.

In making Patel so labilely bicultural, Mukherjee gives her protagonist the sort of cultural identity Rao ascribes to India: in his Indianness, he absorbs all. Such porous selfhood has continued to seem hauntingly Indi- an, as a recent comment by Amitav Ghosh indicates. Writing on diasporic Indians, Ghosh maintains that Indian emigrants remain connected to India differently—and more completely—than members of other diaspo- ras to their homelands:

> It is impossible to be imperfectly Indian. . . . Were it possible to be an imperfect Indian, everybody in India would be. This is not merely be- cause India has failed to develop a national culture. It is not a lack; it is in itself the form of Indian culture. If there is any one pattern in Indian culture in the broadest sense it is simply this: that the culture seems to be constructed around the proliferation of differences (albeit with different parameters). To be different in a world of differences is irrevocably to belong. (Ghosh 1989:77–78)

In Ghosh's updating of Rao's civilizational Indian identity—his recasting of it in the poststructuralist language of cultural difference for a world in which nationalism has been undercut—India stays culturally whole in a heterogeneous world paradoxically because it has never had the whole- ness of a national culture. Ghosh's formulation thus less erases the legacy of Indian nationalism than reinscribes it for a postnationalist, globalist era. In this reinscription the cultural and intellectual possibilities of Rao's civilizationalism—Indian tradition's ability to absorb the cultures of India's many conquerors—are refigured in fascinatingly avant-garde ways. Indianness in Ghosh (as it does also in Salman Rushdie's *Midnight's Children* [1980]) thus becomes the best preparation for conceiving a postmodern polyculturality that seems to burst apart a national frame.

Mukherjee has clearly drawn on some of these resources in her mastery of the discourses of American ethnicity and immigration. As she writes in the preface to her collection *Darkness*, she sees her Indianness as "a set of fluid identities to be celebrated" and thus reinterprets it as "a metaphor, a particular way of partially comprehending the world" (1985:3). Such positions are part of contemporary postnational or globalist cultural politics; cultural hybridity, as we shall see, has been adopted widely in America and the world as a progressive program. Writers like Ghosh, Mukherjee, and Rushdie are participants in this new global/globalist movement more visibly than they are inheritors of a national tradition. Still, the forms of their participation, their peculiar inflections of the larger enterprise, bear the marks of an older national formation. Although this book contains no chapter on transformations of Indian nationalism in the gloablist era to parallel those on developments in Japan and America, the alert reader will find, scattered throughout, a variety of material by diasporic and non-diasporic Indian-born writers and theorists with which to begin assembling such a narrative.

In a final turn to "Nostalgia," Mukherjee also invokes an American trope to ground ideologically exactly the same phenomenon. If Patel's unconsciously porous bicultural selfhood seems "Indian," Mukherjee implies, the glaring stress Patel's New York puts on cultural heterogeneity is profoundly American—the form American nationalism takes in the new world system. Manny, the well-paid psychiatrist, feels himself indebted to America for its wealth, not of money, but of madness. America's streets of gold have become streets of crazies, who find their equivalents, on deeper levels of the story, in New York's riot of boundary-violating, boundary-crossing hybrid cultural forms. A carnivalesque version of several famous tropes of American ideology—America the nation of nations, America the land with gold-paved streets—has, the story implies, become a new basis for exceptionalist American identity in a globalized world.

A story from a subsequent volume, "Orbiting," illustrates a second aspect of Mukherjee's portrayal of the intersection between the new global immigrant and American society. It dramatizes what happens when new immigrants encounter, not a repetition with a difference of the melting pot, but a landscape of ethnic cultures. If Mukherjee locates her transformation of the image of the melting pot in cosmopolitan New York, she places her exploration of American ethnic pluralism in provincial New Jersey. American ethnic culture, in the story, is not only downscale, compared to the new immigrants, but has modeled itself so completely on American small-town provincialism that it has lost its international connections. Thus, when a political refugee from communist-dominated Afghanistan meets Rindy, daughter to a North Italian–American and a Calabrian raised in Italy, an important conflict and revision of assumptions results.

Although Mukherjee's New Jersey reveals an ethnic America conscious of its pluralist organization into separate groups, a more heterogeneous ethnicity is, in fact, to be found everywhere. Italian-Americans are Italian-American, but scratch the surface and fissures appear. The story explores differences between father and mother (Rindy's dad makes it sound "as though Mom was a Korean or something" [1988:59]), and it supplements these intraethnic differences with still further ones produced by exogamy: Rindy's sister has married Brent Schwarz, né Schwartzendruber, son of an Amish farmer in Iowa. But masked as American pluralism, this heterogeneity seems anything but avant-garde: it appears in relentlessly unsophisticated and downscale American forms. Rindy's previous boyfriend, for example, leaves her for cosmopolitan travel, telling her

"You know, Rindy, there are *places*. You don't fall off the earth when you leave New Jersey, you know. Places you see pictures of and read about. Different weathers, different trees, different everything. Places that get the Cubs on cable instead of the Mets." He was into that. For all the sophisticated things he liked to talk about [like the ying and yang, and commercialized orientalia] he was a very local boy. (63)

Similarly, Rindy's whole family, although immigrants and children of immigrants, are extremely local: in them, the assimilationist strategy Marcus Klein has found in previous immigrant fiction, that of locating an ethnic hometown in America, works entirely too well. Even Rindy, with her fake zebra-skin cushions, futon, and lasciviously tangled satin sheets, is local-downscale in her attempts at stylishness; Brent, owner of a discount camera and electronics store, and sporting an obvious hairpiece and gold chain, is even more so.

When Ro, the Afghani refugee, enters Rindy's life, the encounter is very different, then, from the classical drama of premodern immigrant meeting the modern, Anglocentrist American. That drama is turned on its head, refigured as global cosmopolitan meeting ethnic localist in an America that has become, in fact, much more bewilderingly culturally decentered than its downscale ethnic pluralist ideology allows its people to realize. Rindy's father, an arch–American conservative and yet looking "funereal like an old-world Italian gentleman because of his outdated, pinched dark suit" (70), is provincially shocked at meeting Ro, an obvious Third World foreigner. When Ro moves to greet him, resorting to his "Kabuli prep-school manners," the father is astonished. "I can almost read his mind," Rindy thinks, and immediately records his reaction to Ro: "*He speaks*" (68). Amazed that Ro, given his origins, is capable of human speech, Rindy's father and Brent are further set on their heels when Ro reveals his cosmo-politan experience (he "skied in St. Moritz, lost a thousand dollars in a casino in Beirut" [72]) and, even more, when he narrates his suffering as a political prisoner. Rindy's father's American provincialism and chauvin-ism make him equate stories of political terror with communism, al-though Ro is an anticommunist; and Ro's experience with torture, with real pain, make Dad and Brent abashed of "their little scars, things they're proud of, football injuries and bowling elbows they brag about" (74).

What happens then, in this encounter between a decentered localist ethnic America and the new global migrant, is that the more sophisticated, the global-cosmopolitan overwhelms the provincial-local. In the process, the latent, bewildering heterogeneous cultural hybridity of America—symbolized by the fact that the gathering Ro comes to is an ethnic-American Thanksgiving dinner—is brought at last to full visibility, break-ing apart the pieties of ethnic pluralism's separation of ethnic identity according to groups. America is more complicated and intermarrying than it allows itself to realize, and this complexity is heightened when it en-counters a still more sophisticated, complex global heterogeneity in Ro. Such an encounter, the story implies, can be good for both sides: Ro, who is ashamed that he comes "from a culture of pain" (74), can leave that shame behind in America, and American multiculturalism can profit from a new hybrid strain, brought by the new immigration, one that will ease it out of its provincial blindness into greater sophistication for a globalist era. Lov-ing Ro raises Rindy's consciousness from a local to a global perspective; at the same time, it makes her feel a resurgence of American ideology ("Ro's my chance to heal the world" [74]). Ro, in turn, is simultaneously the bearer of new kinds of difference, new kinds of knowledge, and the truest version of the American hero, the "real" "Clint Eastwood, scarred hero and survivor" (75). In being so commodified, turned into a sign, the shame of his culture of cruelty (a strong, referential culture) is left behind.

Mukherjee underscores the haphazard, comically decentered nature of such contemporary syncretism by the story's conclusion. Rindy smiles suddenly, to her mother's surprise, when she realizes Ro is the only circumcised man she has slept with. Part of the comic vagaries of unpredictable desire, this moment suggests the topsy-turvy nature of experience in a culturally decentered America and world: given the American secular (cultural?) norm of circumcision, Rindy has, to use the phrase of Orleck's informant (1987), at last met a "real American," who turns out to be an immigrant Afghani Muslim. In Mukherjee's postmodern immigrant America, global and local enhance each other and prove increasingly interchangeable, each term revealing the other in its core, even as multiculturalism, not ethnic pluralism, becomes the staple of mainstream identity. Mukherjee's revelation of cultural heterogeneity as an American norm does not form the basis of a countercultural attack on a repressively centered cultural system, as with Wittman Ah Sing's deconstructionist cultural politics. By now it *is* the norm of an already-decentered system. An ethical project in Mukherjee's immigrant tales is to make fully transparent the way an awakened, multicultural America can reflect a polycultural globe.

Mukherjee has written of a variety of immigrants, both educated and uneducated, upscale and downscale in origins, but the notion of the immigrant as global cosmopolitan, come to add a new, transformative element to American multiculturalism, has been one of the most effective themes of her work. Such global cosmopolitanism, in a figure like Ro, is complexly inventive. First and foremost, it depends, as L. Michael Lewis (drawing on William McNeill) has noted, on the fact that, in the context of globalization and Third World international migration, polyculturality has increasingly become the civilized norm. We have had to revise our "conventional notions of the cosmopolitan and parochial" (Lewis 1991:8) by relocating the cosmopolitan tradition from a now more monocultural First World to the more mobile and heterogeneous Third World. First World explorers, colonialists, and travelers have lost their identification as globals in a world of localist Third World cultures; the Third World has become the source of the new cosmopolitans.

By far and away the fullest analysis of the new Third World literary cosmopolitanism, however, has been made by Timothy Brennan. He locates Mukherjee among a "grouping" of Third World writers who have emerged, globally, in reaction to the previous era of Third World nationalism. Brennan's list includes Salman Rushdie, Vargas Llosa, Isabel Allende, and García Márquez. His "grouping" of these writers, he adds, is

> not an attempt to fix Rushdie and the others into a spurious "school" or common style, but to suggest a creative community, international in scope, that the publishing industries have actually unified in the minds

of the Western public. Even politically, they certainly do not share the same positions on the contentious topics of socialism, NATO or the debt crisis. But for all their differences, they seem to share a harsh questioning of radical decolonisation theory; a dismissive or parodic attitude towards the project of national culture; a manipulation of imperial imagery and local legend as a means of politicising "current events"; and a declaration of cultural "hybridity"—a hybridity claimed to offer certain advantages in negotiating the collisions of language, race and art in a world of disparate peoples comprising a single, if not exactly unified, world. (Brennan 1989:35)

Brennan's attitude toward these writers is deeply ambivalent. He argues or implies repeatedly that they have been co-opted, or have conspired in their own co-optation, by Western constituencies. True, their longing for Western values and culture cannot be transparent or unambiguous: V. S. Naipaul cannot be included in this category. But the West is nonetheless dominant in their institutionalization, as they are not a self-made "grouping" but have been made into one by publishing industries for the Western public. Moreover, in their work, they do not appropriate the role of cosmopolitan for the Third World as a part of a progressive project, but regress to an older tradition of European cosmopolitanism as a way of distancing themselves from the "sacrifices and organizational drudgery of actual resistance movements," while at the same time remaining "horrified by the obliviousness of the world toward their own cultures" (27).

But behind Brennan's ambivalence is the fact that his ideological commitments are retrospective. Brennan counterbalances these media-created Third World cosmopolitan "celebrities" (as he calls them) with the tradition of anticolonial nationalism. In summarizing the political aesthetics of Antonio Gramsci and Carlos Mariategui, Brennan writes that they focused "on a decisive valorization of 'the people' and an insistence on the fact that culture itself is meaningless if not considered 'in its national aspect'" (1989:16). Although Brennan invokes Bakhtin to develop a much more complex, transnationally mediated aesthetics for the postwar novel "in its national aspect," he retains nationalism as the only basis for contemporary political and cultural opposition: "It is not that people, or the artists who speak for them, can imagine no other affiliations [than to the nation-state], but that the solutions to dependency are only collective, and the territorial legacies of the last two hundred years provide the collectivity no other basis upon which to fight dependency" (20).

In an increasingly global system, righteous polemics like Brennan's, his thinly veiled charge of selling out, may be a thing of the past, arising from disillusionment with revolutionary nationalism. More important, Brennan ignores how, in the wake of that disillusionment, cultural opposition of many kinds has been shifting from homologous strategies of cultural nationalism to counterdiscursive reappropriations of the colonial legacy. Although Third World cosmopolitanism is indeed politically ambiguous, it does not represent a reversion to European attitudes, but an attempt to appropriate the legacy of the First World. It is, in short, part of the postnational process of decentering.

In another way as well, Mukherjee's appropriation of cosmopolitanism is not a return to Europe. It is complicated by the fact that, if it is a Third World appropriation of cosmopolitanism, it is also an intervention, in several ways, in the discourses of American nationalism. Most clearly, Mukherjee uses her global cosmopolitanism as a means of transforming American attitudes toward immigrants and the conventions of immigrant literature. In her recent fiction, Mukherjee is well aware of the cachet that the culture of the older colonial core still has for its former colony, and, in depicting Ro's cosmopolitanism, she attributes to him a classy European chic, something that a member of the international Third World could be supposed to have more of than a citizen of the United States. Perhaps Mukherjee's sense of authority in doing this is enhanced by her own elite status as Brahman intellectual from the jewel in the crown of the former British Empire, the only place, some English pundits have asserted, where English culture can still be found; but perhaps it is also heightened by the fact that, in the period after the 1960s, until recently, some three-quarters of the immigrants to America from India were men and women with advanced degrees. Both sorts of cosmopolitanism connect with old American preoccupations: the relatively long-term political independence of the United States has been coupled with a persisting sense of cultural inferiority and awkward provincialism, a tradition that has run smoothly from the anxieties of the early Puritans to nineteenth-century outrage at Mrs. Trollope's rendering of American manners (Conrad 1980:30–38) to the present century's self-critique of ugly Americanism.

Casting immigrants as global cosmopolitans has thus been an old American tradition and strategy, dating back at least to Hjalmar Boyesen ([1877] 1969) and Abraham Cahan (1898). The latter, no ordinary immigrant himself, was a Russian Jew who had absorbed high European culture in Russia; as such, in writing about immigrant Jews in America, he was writing about an ethnic culture he really only came to know there. Cahan's short story "Circumstances" makes clear not only how some immigrants' lives in America meant downward mobility for them, but also how writing about immigrants meant a revision of high literary expectations downward to a lower stage of action. Cahan's immigrants in "Circumstances" are more nearly his own class than most of his subjects: they are a married pair of intellectually avant-garde Russian Jews who face a life of downward mobility and grinding constraint in sweatshop America, gradually losing their capacity to appreciate higher culture, and their marriage, to America's grimly pragmatic necessities. The upshot of the story is the failure of their marriage thanks to the attraction that springs up between the wife and a more successfully Americanized lodger with good prospects, whom they are forced to take in. The literary reference behind the action is Tolstoy: Cahan worked to rediscover a constricted version of *Anna Karenina* in—or perhaps more accurately, despite—the crabbed American circumstances and dress of Howellsian realism.

We saw something similar in Clare Savage's encounter with a stupidly racist American educational bureaucracy in Michelle Cliff's *No Telephone to Heaven*. Clare, the gifted product of an elite colonial-British education, is treated as a disadvantaged student in America. In Mukherjee's fiction, however, immigrants' global cosmopolitanism has changed dramatically. From a minority tradition, expressing the lot only of an overprivileged few and overshadowed by a mainstream honoring of upward mobility and success, it has developed into something central to the experience of a wide variety of new immigrants. Thus Mukherjee sees herself, as a writer, attempting to transform a tradition of immigrant literature that was "déclassé," and to do so without adopting the aristocratic hauteur of the "émigré" or "expatriate." As a self-declared practitioner of this American genre, Mukherjee has sought to remove the genre from its second-class literary citizenship by representing immigrants in a new way and using them to redeem America from provincial narrowness. Similarly, Mukherjee depicts immigrants as sophisticated presences in a globalist era, in which Eurocolonialism retains its cultural cachet even as it yields to an American-dominated world system, a system that in turn has been increasingly transformed by empowerment of the Third World, first through nationalism and then, more important, through globalization. Mukherjee describes her colleagues at the naturalization ceremony as follows:

> The old pieties of immigration no longer hold. A Norman Rockwell would have been hard-pressed to find the immigrant-icons of an earlier era—the hollow-eyed and sunken-cheeked were not in evidence. There was a notable lack of babushkas, with wrinkled, glistening cheeks. (Their closest ethnic embodiment, a beautiful Russian woman sitting in front of me, was reading Nabokov's "Speak Memory" during the long waiting period.) A Dominican man next to me joked as we sat down after pledging allegiance, "Hey, now we can make a citizens' arrest!" Behind me, Chinese teen-agers passed copies of The New Yorker. (1988a:1)

But Mukherjee's immigrants are not just upscale; they also become the normative Americans. In short, Mukherjee uses her appropriation of cosmopolitanism to intervene as well in the larger debate about American cultural identity. In her depiction of an immigrant-transformed America, in which cosmopolitan-globalism meets and further hybridizes local American pluralism, she contributes to multiculturalism's attempt to refigure American national identity for the globalist era, an era to which the cultural homogeneity of post-Enlightenment nationalism is no longer applicable. The attempt to craft such a postmodern nationalism is, moreover, in Mukherjee's fiction, as in much of the academic debate surveyed at the end of the last chapter, a confusing fusion of radical and mainstream traditions, of the legacies of assimilation and pluralism, of the melting pot and politicized ethnicity. Mukherjee's stories might equally well be seen as an extension of radical valorization of minority positions and a celebration (in a new form) of the melting pot. She moves further beyond the legacy of essentialist cultural nationalism into an exploration of heterogeneity greater than even Lisa Lowe would allow, for she constructs a postmodern alliance of, not just oppositional, but oppositional *and* mainstream positions.

Mukherjee's combination of radicalism and centrism is visible in her sharp criticism of nostalgia in "Nostalgia." It is more overt still in comments she has made about her particular "school" of immigrant writing.

> I would rather we all cashed in on the other legacy of the colonial writer, and that is his or her individuality. From childhood we learned how to be two things simultaneously: to be the dispossessed as well as the dispossessor. In textbooks we read of "our" great empire and triumphs (meaning British), "our" great achievements in the arts (meaning the Moslem Moghuls) and "our" treachery in the Sepoy Mutiny (meaning "native" troops). History forced us to see ourselves as both the "we" and the "other," and our language reflected our simultaneity. In time, after independence, the Mutiny became the first great patriot uprising, a war of liberation. Mahatma Gandhi, always suspect in the Bengal of my childhood, was simultaneously the Great Soul beloved of the West and the scruffy low-caste politician who permitted the dismemberment of India. (It's the privilege of the once-ruled to change their history and nomenclature. There are no absolutes, only correct contexts.) Perhaps it is this history-mandated training in seeing myself as "the other" that now heaps on me a fluid set of identities denied to most of my mainstream American counterparts. The training in our ethnic- and gender-fractured world of contemporary American fiction allows me without difficulty to "enter" lives, fictionally, that are manifestly not my own. (1988a:29)

Although this portrayal of her early readings echoes Shiva Naipaul's
description of his schooling, it does so in a radically altered fashion.
Naipaul's cobbled-together heterogeneous education made him subservient to a pursuit of mainstream models, which were not cobbled together;
the fractures that appalled Naipaul and violated his implied model of
coherent national cultures empower Mukherjee, who cheerfully takes
them as the key, now, to the postmodern world system. Mukherjee thus
brings her Third World experience with fractured identity and "otherness"
—her ability to see truth and identity as context-defined—to the Western
radical tradition, which, after the "revolution in the world system" of
1968, has come to emphasize ethnic- and gender-fractured identities. And
what Mukherjee brings is something beyond these movements in the core:
not the "genuine ethnicity" of Third World nationalism, but a more historically realized and also *more complete* fracturing. Specifically—and very
unsettlingly for radical critique—her fractured experience involves not
just the historical experience of being dispossessed, but also that of dispos-
sessing; not just that of being defined as "the other" but also that of speaking in other contexts as the "one." In this self-analysis, the coherence of
heterogeneous radical coalitions Lisa Lowe advocates has been undercut,
not because Mukherjee opposes Lowe's radical narrative, but because she
extends it to include dominant as well as oppositional positions in her
notion of heterogeneous identity. In short, in her comments, Mukherjee
combines the legacy of 1960s cultural radicalism with the legacy of official
nationalism. At the same time, she converts Fredric Jameson's analysis of
how postmodernity has decomposed national cultures ("the advanced
capitalist countries today are a field of stylistic and discursive heterogeneity without a norm" [1984:65]) into a reaffirmation of American nationalism for the globalist era.

To explain Mukherjee's enhanced problematizing of identity—her extension of heterogeneity to encompass politically opposite positions—
one might speculate that what we have traced as the Japanese-American
and the Chinese-American traditions of belonging to / being torn between heterogeneous categories might be still more richly heterogeneous
in an Indian-American. While Chinese- and Japanese-Americans have
been cast as racial "others" and model minorities in different periods,
Indian-Americans had already crossed racial boundaries before the removal of racial categories from naturalization law in 1946. As people of "Aryan" descent, a number of Indian-Americans had been granted citizenship
in the early part of the century; in 1923, the U.S. government cancelled
their citizenship, under the rationale that the term "white" in naturalization law related, not to scientific terminology, but to the terms of the "man

in the street." Although approximately seventy naturalized Indians had their citizenship cancelled, one, Dr. Sakaram Ganesh Pandit, a lawyer, appealed his case to the Supreme Court and won (Bagai 1967:30–32). But at least as important as this Indian-American heritage is Mukherjee's identity as diasporic Indian. As with Amitav Ghosh, a reinscription of Indian nationalism may reinforce her transformation of American multiculturalism; similarly, as we shall see in the following chapters, postcolonial scholarship from an Indian site has emphasized both the porousness of boundaries between colonialist and colonial subject and the way native elites absorbed colonial strategies of domination even as they fought for liberation from colonialism. And to these factors we must also add the fact that Mukherjee is also responding to a larger globalist movement that cuts across national boundaries even as it interacts with national legacies, taking on different inflections at different sites. Typical of this movement has been the cultivation of hybridity as a cultural strategy suitable for negotiating the postnational, postmodern world. Derek Walcott, for example, writes that "revolutionary literature is a filial impulse"; Mukherjee would agree with what he went on to maintain, "that maturity is the assimilation of the features of every ancestor" (Brennan 1989a:53).

And indeed, along with all these other ancestral features, Mukherjee also affiliates herself clearly with American ancestral roots. She ends her comments about the legacy of radical anticolonialism with a statement that sounds hauntingly like assimilation to the legacy of a canonized white male American author. She enters lives manifestly not her own: she is large, she contains multitudes. Walt Whitman, whom we have just seen turned into a nervous, experimental Chinese-American playwright, has now become a much more secure and confident East Indian immigrant author of fiction. Or can this be put thus, so abruptly? Whitman, after all, constructed himself and his vision of America by Americanizing Indian philosophy.

Asian-American literature provides only one skein of examples in contemporary American cultural politics of the development of postmodern ethnic strategies—the development of boundary violation, heterogeneity, hybridity, and border crossing as means for transformation of ethnic and national identity in globalist America. As we saw in chapter 6, official multiculturalism incorporates these strategies to a degree; they have also been disseminated widely through a variety of other ethnic traditions formed in relationship with black cultural nationalism. Hispanic-American and native American, as well as a new generation of African-American writers and intellectuals, have also developed a postmodern cultural politics of boundary violation, heterogeneity, and border cross-ing. Abdul JanMohamed and David Lloyd (1991) have collected work in a variety of ethnic and postcolonial traditions under the rubric of minor literatures, a rubric constructed by Giles Deleuze and Felix Guattari (1983). They have done so, moreover, in the attempt to construct alliances and dialogue between a heterogeneous variety of oppositional positions.

JanMohamed and Lloyd encountered resistance to their enterprise when the National Endowment for the Humanities rejected their proposal for a conference. The reason given was that a collection of "Chicano, Indian, Pacific Island, Aborigine, Maori, and other" ethnic literary special-ists would be "diffuse" and become "an academic Tower of Babel" (1991:3). Against this opinion, JanMohamed and Lloyd argue that no such Babel would be presupposed if Europeans came together to discuss their national literatures; that the marginalized indeed have a lot in common; that their alliance might indeed be as dangerous as the NEH reviewer doubtless felt it would be; and that the rejection followed in a long line of attempts to keep minorities from communicating with one another. Sim-ilarly, many of the theorists in the book that resulted from this conference conceive of the present as a "post-ethnic" moment similarly to the way Lowe depicts it; contemporary ethnic theory is built upon the gains of, while critical of the assumptions of, cultural nationalism. And it is com-mitted to the maintenance of "multiple identities" that are "neither reduc-ible nor impermeable to one another," as well as the perception that there is "no sphere of universal or objective knowledge or purely instrumental rationality, that what is worked out in one sphere can be communicated in another, and that institutional boundaries will always need to be trans-gressed in the interests of political and cultural struggle" (15).

Particular emphases have thus emerged in differently inflected ethnic enterprises, which, in turn, have a larger family resemblance. On African and African-American tradition, JanMohamed follows Fanon in empha-sizing the Manichean construction of cultural and social boundary lines and the counterstrategy of "negating the negation as a form of affirma-tion" (1983, 1991); Kim argues for the unique Asian-American strategy of oppositional assimilation; and Renato Rosaldo emphasizes Chicano histo-ry as distinct from "the history of immigration and displacement" (whites were the recent immigrants, not the Chicanos), arguing for deadpan humor and bilingual border crossing as oppositional strategies. Similarly, Gloria Anzaldúa, in "*La conciencia de la mestiza*: Towards a New Conscious-ness" (1987), theorizes mestiza identity—or, more particularly, radical les-bian feminist mestiza identity—in the Southwest as a complex construc-tion of crossed borders, incorporating, among other identity positions,

Mexican, indigenous, and white identities. For her, replacing oppositional ethnic politics with the attempt to construct a complex cultural identity that combines antagonists opens up a variety of political and cultural possibilities that could either transform the mainstream or lead to new oppositional perspectives. An ethnic

> counterstance refutes the dominant culture's views and beliefs, and, for this, it is proudly defiant. All reaction is limited by, and dependent on, what it is reacting against. Because the counterstance stems from a problem with authority—outer as well as inner—it's a step toward liberation from cultural domination. But it is not a way of life. At some point, on our way to a new consciousness, we will have to leave the opposite bank, the split between two mortal combatants somehow healed so that we are on both shores at once and, at once, see through serpent and eagle eyes. Or perhaps we will decide to disengage from the dominant culture, write it off altogether as a lost cause, and cross the border into a wholly new and separate territory. Or we might go another route. The possibilities are numerous once we decide to act and not react. (378)

For Anzaldúa, psychic integration/liberation precedes social:

> The struggle is inner: Chicano, *indio*, American Indian, *mojado*, *mexicano*, immigrant Latino, Anglo in power, working class Anglo, Black, Asian—our psyches resemble the bordertowns and are populated by the same people. The struggle has always been inner, and is played out in the outer terrains. . . . Nothing happens in the "real" world unless it first happens in the images in our heads. (385)

To achieve this, however, Anzaldúa, whose language and attitudes remain strongly oppositional and deeply indebted to cultural nationalism, echoes language that the conservative assault on multiculturalism has made popular: "Other than a common culture we will have nothing to hold us together. We need to meet on a broader communal ground" (385).

If a wide variety of ethnic traditions have been thus refigured under the pressures of a postnational era, so have migration studies. In "Mexican Migration and the Social Space of Postmodernism" (1991), Roger Rouse has argued that notions essential to traditional studies of migration—the notions of migrating between coherent, separate, "communities" and the familiar opposition of "center" and "periphery" both regionally and globally—increasingly need revision in light of present realities. In particular, the assumptions of accounts that emphasize "a unidirectional shift" and argue that "immigrants . . . move between distinct, easily demarcated communities and, in the long run, . . . [are] capable of maintaining involvement in only one of them" (12) have proven quite false. Global communications and the ease of transportation permit dwelling in several communities at the same time, and the communities themselves have been culturally and demographically heterogenized by global capitalism.

As a result, assimilation has given way to multiple sociocultural identities, as transnational migration has brought "distant worlds into immediate juxtaposition [and] their proximity has produced neither homogenization or synthesis" (14). People have interpreted "their current lives and future possibilities as involving simultaneous engagement in places associated with different forms of experience" (14). And these places themselves have been pluralized. Thus, rural Mexican villages are now tuned in to American culture via satellite dishes, even as their economies are increasingly determined by global capitalism. And by the mid 1980s in Los Angeles, "75% of the buildings were owned in part by foreign capital, and as much as 90% of new multistory construction was being financed from abroad" (16). Correspondingly, on the bottom of the social ladder, the Third World was in America:

> ways of life commonly identified with the Third World are becoming increasingly apparent in a country often treated as the apogee of First World advancement. Extreme poverty, residential overcrowding and homelessness, underground economies, new forms of domestic service, and sweatshops exist side by side with yuppie affluence, futuristic office blocks, and all the other accoutrements of high-tech postindustrialism. (Rouse 1991:16)

In the words of the *Los Angeles Times,* "squalid, plywood-and-cardboard hooches sit in the shadow of million-dollar mansions, where the BMW and Volvo sets rub elbows in the supermarkets with the dusty migrants fresh from the fields" (17). Like King, Saskia Sasson-Koob has called this process "peripheralization at the core" (1982:17).

Multiple hybrid identities, composed of crossed and recrossed boundaries, have thus become, according to Rouse, the contemporary global as well as American norm. Rouse quotes Guillermo Gómez-Peña, a writer who has lived "two histories, languages, cosmogonies, artistic traditions, and political systems" (15):

> Today, eight years after my departure, when they ask me for my nationality or ethnic identity, I cannot answer with a single word, for my "identity" now possesses multiple repertoires: I am Mexican but I am also Chicano and Latin American. On the border they call me "chilango" or "mexiquillo"; in the capital, "pocho" or "norteño," and in Spain "sudaca." . . . My companion Emily is Anglo-Italian but she speaks Spanish with an Argentinian accent. Together we wander through the ruined Babel that is our American postmodernity. (8)

In a recent article on contemporary global postnationalism and ethical projects suitable for such an era, Arjun Appadurai sought to come to terms with the conflict between "the difference between [America's] being a land of immigrants and being one node in a postnational network of diasporas" (423). Like Rouse, Appadurai argues that "diaspora runs with, and not against, the grain of identity, movement, and reproduction" (427). The United States is thus "no longer a closed space for the melting pot to work its magic, but yet another diasporic switching point, to which people come to seek their fortunes but are no longer content to leave their home-lands behind" (424). Indeed, in the increasingly postnational world being formed, which Appadurai proposes as a basis for transforming the bloody, racist, exclusionary legacy of territorial nationalism, diasporic identity has gotten even more complex than Rouse allows:

> For every nation-state that has exported significant numbers of its popu-lation to the United States as refugees, tourists, or students, there is now a delocalized *transnation,* which retains a special ideological link to a putative place of origin but is otherwise a thoroughly diasporic collec-tivity. No existing conception of Americanness can contain this large variety of transnations.
>
> In this scenario, the hyphenated American might have to be twice hyphenated (Asian-American-Japanese or Native-American-Seneca or African-American-Jamaican or Hispanic-American-Bolivian) as dia-sporic identities stay mobile and grow more protean. Or perhaps the sides of the hyphen will have to be reversed, and we can become a federation of diasporas. (424)

More daringly than Mukherjee, Appadurai tries then to reclaim an "Ameri-can" identity in a new way that is explicitly postnational. The United States might "come to be seen as a model of how to arrange one territorial locus (among others) for a cross-hatching of diasporic communities" and be "a sort of cultural laboratory and a free trade zone for the generation, circulation, importation, and testing of the materials for a world organized around diasporic diversity" (425). Paradoxically, America would then be a postnationalist nation: a nation that provided a model to the globe for the development of a truly "postnational imaginary" (428).

The developments I have been tracing have occurred most dramatically at the top and the bottom of the social structure. Mukherjee's depiction of immigrants as global cosmopolitans makes her most clearly an exponent of the upscale side of contemporary global migrations; Anzaldúa has shown that the same perspective can operate among more ethnically mar-ginalized and economically impoverished groups. And Rouse, studying rural Mexican migrants, has come to similar conclusions. The same hour-glass shape—globalization at the top and bottom—has been observed in Europe. As Anthony King (1990a:41) has pointed out, contemporary internationalization in London has been characterized by internationalization at the top and at the bottom.

As we have seen, these changes at the top and bottom, and in ethnic and immigrant cultures in America, have substantially affected overall definitions of national identity. And behind this development lie, more transparently than ever before, the mediations of the global system. The subject population of Rouse's study—like Mukherjee's immigrants—did not move along the circuit of the centered colonial world order, from preindustrial village to colonial capital, periphery to core; instead they moved from one place to another in a world system whose centered structure and internal boundaries have broken down. This breakdown affected migrants' places both of arrival and origin: thus they moved to a foreign-owned Los Angeles from villages reshaped by telecommunications networks with American programing. Both migrants' "home" and "abroad" were constructed through the mediation of transnational, not national, capital: migration took place now between differentiated points in the same system rather than from one bounded world to another. Similarly, American ethnic debates have increasingly occurred in reciprocity with developments in other frames, such as postcolonialism and contemporary theories of nationalism. More and more immediately and transparently, then, the global has overtly penetrated the local, in America and abroad: points everywhere throughout the world have become composed overtly and simultaneously of global and local factors.

In the preceding chapters, we have gradually shifted from analyzing the decentering of the culture of the core under the interplay of two distinct and multifactoral narratives, one global and one national-local, to a perception that transformations in the core have been increasingly directly driven by, and interlock with, changes in the overall fabric of core-periphery relationships in the world system. The global mediation of local forms has become increasingly direct and transparent. At a later point, we shall examine how a variety of formulations both within and outside the tradition of world-systems thought have been evolved to try to account for and systematically describe this decentering of the overall global system. But before we look at changing opinion about the nature of the system as a whole, we must examine a second significant form of cultural interventionism. From considering the fragmentation of the American core, we shall turn to the problems and possibilities involved in disruption of relationships between the former colonial core and its periphery.

8

Postcolonialism

MULTICULTURALISM'S politics of identity have also been advocated outside the United States. The great Nairobi literature debate at the University of Nairobi described in Ngũgĩ's *Decolonising the Mind* (1986:89) sounds hauntingly like canon reform in the United States. More provocatively, Stuart Hall's analysis of cultural interventionism in contemporary Britain overtly connects itself to American debates. Hall charts a similar emergence of politics of difference and heterogeneity from the disrupted legacy of essentialism. What was it like, he asks, "to really begin to recover the lost histories of Black experiences, while at the same time recognizing the end of any essential Black subject"? (1991b:57). More challengingly, since "Black identity" in the 1970s included people from the "Caribbean, East Africa, the Asian subcontinent, Pakistan, Bangladesh, from different parts of India, . . . all [of whom] identified themselves politically as Black" (55), the next generation of oppositional politics decomposed "Black political identity" into considerable heterogeneity. This heterogeneity further pluralized itself, as in America, by the exploration and privileging of multiple identities, and a "politics . . . increasingly . . . able to address people through the multiple identities they have" was born: "Out of that notion some of the most exciting cultural work is now being done in England. Third generation young Black men and women know they come from the Caribbean, know that they are black, know that they are British. They want to speak from all three identities. They will contest the Thatcherite notion of Englishness, because they say Englishness is black" (59).

Like the Anglos in America, the English were thus turned into an ethnic group in England, setting the stage for the surprising cultural reversals Pico Iyer wittily chronicles. In Hanif Kureishi's screenplay for Stephen Frears's *My Beautiful Laundrette* (1985), "every white is on the dole and every Black is on the rise"; in Timothy Mo's *Sour Sweet* (1985), "a Hong Kong Chinese family settles down in a London so cantonized—and Cantonized—that throughout the novel's 278 pages of English life, not a single Englishman is named"; and in Lady Antonia Fraser's *Oxford Blood* (1985) "the ultimate upstanding Englishman . . . just happens to be Chinese, and the proverbial Scottish nurse . . . just turns out to be West Indian" (1988:359).

What is distinctive about Hall's position is that he asserts that current English cultural ferment is rooted in the American-dominated global system. He argues that the present ferment arises from the replacement of an era of globalization based on the nation-state by one that goes "above the nation-state and . . . below it" (1991a:27)—an era of globalization to which responses go "global and local in the same moment," in which "global and local are the two faces of the same movement" (27). This "new kind of globalization," Hall argues, is "not English . . . [but] American" (27). Key to its creation is the development of "global mass culture" (27)—in particular, global commercial culture, a mass culture "dominated by television and by film, and by the image, imagery, and styles of mass advertising" (27)—and the global dissemination of American ethnic opposition.

To be sure, Hall has been accused before of excessive generosity in ascribing the development of the cultural studies movement in England to external influences, not internal sources. Patrick Brantlinger calls Hall's 1976 survey of the movement a "history of British cultural studies as a sort of French dependency" (1990:63). Still, the politics of identity Hall describes are doubtless "American" in both, or at least one, of two senses. Although the British cultural studies movement has strong roots in the work of Richard Hoggart, E. P. Thompson, and Raymond Williams, and, more generally, in the tradition of English Marxism and a larger tradition of class awareness, the politics of identity Hall describes involves something different: these identity politics draw on contemporary American influences and descend from the upheavals of the "American" era of postwar revolutionary nationalism. Thus, for example, as the new global migrations of the postwar period have confronted England with a domestically polycultural population—an ethnic population—concern with race relations similar to America's has become part of England's cultural landscape, taking the form, as it does in the United States of aggressive cultural nationalism. Only subsequently, as Brantlinger notes (148), were these issues added to the concerns of British cultural studies.

As the previous chapters should have made clear, Hall's periodization of the American global system and its influence on England is slightly different from the one I have been using. The American global system, I have argued, actually preceded contemporary globalism: I have styled America's replacement of England as the cultural core of the world system as crucial to the postwar phase of anticolonial nationalism, an era the United

States sought to dominate and manage, and more recent globalization as being as much a challenge to U.S. hegemony as it is an extension of it. To the challenge of lost control of an emerging world order, American multiculturalism is, I have argued, a proactive response. Hall, by contrast, privileges America as the herald of the current postnationalist/globalist world system, deemphasizing consideration of America's role in the previous era of national independence movements.

Whether or not contemporary global culture represents American decline, not dominance, however, and whether or not Anthony Smith is right in styling contemporary global mass culture as different "from earlier cultural imperialisms" in that "they were extensions of ethnic or national sentiments and ideologies" while that of the present has become "by definition and intention 'supranational'" (1990:176), I would agree with Hall that what he describes is an outgrowth of U.S. hegemony. As Hall argues, that hegemony embodies a new capitalist strategy recognizing "that it can only, to use a metaphor, rule through other local capitals, rule alongside and in partnership with other economic and political elites. It does not attempt to obliterate them; it operates through them. It has to hold the whole framework of globalization in place and simultaneously police that system: it stage-manages independence within it, so to speak" (29).

This accurately described America's strategy for managing nationalism throughout the world. The more recent legacy of that strategy has been, both Hall and I would argue, the production of two tiers of cultural phenomena in the globalist era. Having learned that, at a certain point, "globalization cannot proceed without learning to live with and working through difference" (31), the new global culture has produced a kind of commercialized, pleasure- and consumption-oriented cultivation of difference:

> Advertising produced the image of the post-feminist man. Some of us cannot find him, but he is certainly there in the advertising. . . . In England it is these new forms of globalized power that are most sensitive to questions of feminism. It says, "Of course, there'll be women working with us. We must think about the question of creches. We must think about equal opportunities for Black people. Of course, everybody knows somebody of different skin. How boring it would be just to know people like us. We don't know people like us. We can go anywhere in the world and we have friends who are Japanese, you know. We were in East Africa last week and then we were on safari and we always go to the Caribbean." (32)

Calling this the "world of the global post-modern," Hall argues that contemporary globalization has conversely produced new kinds of oppositional movements that are localist responses to globalization—"anti-systemic" movements, in Wallerstein's terminology, that have been dialectically produced by the system. They clearly have Hall's sympathies: he finds the multiculturalism described above primarily in the West ("when I speak about the exotic cuisine, they are not eating the exotic cuisine in Calcutta. They're eating it in Manhattan" [33]) and sees it as "just another face of the final triumph of the West" (33). (Pico Iyer would, however, explode the claim that Calcutta has no global exotica and does not participate in the global consumer culture. Hall's conflation of American cultural imperialism with globalism, his attempt to attach contemporary global culture to the neoimperial center of the West, necessarily leads him to retain some of Herbert Schiller's assumptions about the Third World, styling it as a less-globalized, potential victim of metropolitan cultural aggression.) For Hall, by contrast, localist opposition represents the development of a different and progressive form of multiculturalism: "The emergence of new subjects, new genders, new ethnicities, new regions, new communities, hitherto excluded from the major forms of cultural representation, unable to locate themselves except as decentered or subaltern, have acquired through struggle, sometimes in very marginalized ways, the means to speak for themselves for the first time" (34). This progressive multiculturalism led to the "politics of multiple identity" described at the beginning of this chapter.

Although this represents a genuine resistance to the West—or, as Hall also puts it, to capital's attempt to "get hold of everybody, of everything, where there is no difference which it cannot contain, no otherness it cannot speak, no marginality which it cannot take pleasure out of" (33)—it is of the "same moment" as the former. Hall thus holds asunder the oppositional and official components of American multiculturalism even as he yokes them. His formulation suggests that today a whole spectrum of positions are available. I showed, in chapter 7, how the two strands can be interwoven, although there are also many who distinguish sharply between reactionary and progressive forms of cultural postmodernism. The striking feature of Hall's argument is that however the two movements are related, both hegemonic and oppositional American cultural strategies have been globalized: multiculturalism and postmodern commercialism have become international phenomena.

Hall states clearly that in Britain this American-disseminated cultural ferment succeeded and replaced older cultural assumptions. The era of a very different sort of cultural politics—the "Cartesian certainties" of a strongly centered imperial and national identity that was always "negotiated against difference" (22) and always "placed *everybody* else" (21)—has definitely ended. For Hall, it was a British era. Michelle Cliff's symbol for this now-surpassed previous cultural form is the British Museum, an appropriative collection of the cultural artifacts of "everybody else," a dis- and then re-placement. It organized the peripheral, non-English differences about an English core, which, it in turn thereby helped to define and firmly bound, and it then spoke (in English) for that Third World, subjecting it to English taxonomies, English systems of judgment. The British Museum, then, is in effect the symbol of how the colonized world was known—which means represented and constructed—by a firmly bounded colonialist core, and Hall and Cliff see this knowledge as neither genuine representation nor a transparent window on reality, but as a construction both embodying and advancing unequal relations of power.

The cultural decentering of the centered world system I have been charting has, however, fostered a second widely disseminated movement. Postcolonialism has returned to the legacies of British imperial nationalism and colonialism, legacies that are not as passé as Hall seems to indicate. Indeed, the force of this older legacy has been so strong that postcolonial studies have become at least as prominent a feature of the contemporary cultural map as multiculturalist studies.

In practice, as in theory, the two movements have interlocked significantly with each other, postcolonialism influencing multiculturalism and vice versa. Although for many the two fields now so overlap that it is hard to extricate them from each other, they originally disseminated across the Atlantic in opposite directions. Whereas Hall argues that British cultural studies have absorbed American cultural strategies, Robert Young claims that postcolonialist ideas, originating in France, entered the United States with Edward Said's *Orientalism*. Previously, American intellectuals' appropriation of French theory was

> marked and marred, by its consistent excision of Eurocentrism and its relation to colonialism. Not until Edward Said's *Orientalism* (1978) did it become a significant issue for Anglo-American literary theory. Two years earlier Said had complained quite justifiably that "the literary-cultural establishment as a whole had declared the serious study of imperialism off limits"; it would not be too much to suggest that *Orientalism* broke that proscription, and as such cannot be underestimated in its importance and in its effects. Nor would it be overstating the case to say that much of the current pressure for the political, particularly in the U.S. where there is no recent substantial tradition of political criticism, has followed from the work of Said. (1990:126)

To this description of how the concept of postcolonialism spread internationally, we should add a consideration of a different sort to explain the overlap between postcolonialism and multiculturalism and the dissemination of both movements internationally. In today's globalist world, neither intellectual movements nor national cultures stay within geographic boundaries. Territorially "improper" locations for cultural movements (and their exponents) have come to express how aware we have become of interconnectedness in a globalist era: physical re-siting can be seen as both an expression of globalization and an actual strategy, part of current cultural resistance to centered notions of official or oppositional nationalism and a component of the contemporary politics of marginality and, subsequently, heterogeneity. Multiple sites may provide privileged perspectives in the globalist era. Thus, Hall is a Jamaican migrant to England writing, in the articles I have cited, about its Americanization; Gayatri Spivak is Indian-born, teaches in America, and writes about, among other things, postcolonial literature and history, French theory, and American multiculturalism. Spivak has, moreover, argued provocatively against the nostalgia for lost origins of "indigenous" theory, in favor of using the whole spectrum of what "one has." "To construct indigenous theories," she comments, "one must ignore the last few centuries of historical involvement" (1990:69).

Although the two movements are difficult to extricate from each other, multiculturalism has, generally speaking, reflected a fundamentally nationalist American emphasis in its concentration on the politics of cultural identity—its attempt to generate a radical critique of the idea of national (racial, ethnic) identity with the aim of dismantling it and reconceiving it for the present day. It has decentered the core from within and seeks to do the same globally by transgressing national/ethnic/cultural boundaries and cultivating notions of heterogeneous identity. Postcolonialism, by contrast, focuses on the disruption of an earlier, more centering sort of boundary line: the distinction between colonial power and colony. As we have seen, this latter boundary line culturally invokes more absolute and centering civilizational differentiations, whereas the former mobilizes and transforms the more varied and flexible notion of national unity and culture.

In invoking this more absolute boundary, although it has also been concerned with the politics of identity, postcolonial scholarship targets broader and more basic issues than multiculturalism. It seeks to reevaluate the ways in which we have sought, and are still seeking, to know and represent the world—the ways in which we have constructed it in knowledge and art—by examining the roots of a variety of academic discourses, from anthropology to history to literature, literary history, and theory. In the following, I focus specifically on its critique of what Cliff embodied in her

depiction of the British Museum—its disruptive, political use of genealogical analysis of cultural representation and knowledge construction.

Postcolonial scholarship attacks what Paul Ricoeur calls the "universal
civilization" and "universal science" invented in Europe. It does this by
tracing a wide variety of specific colonial genealogies for, on the one hand,
the development of cultural and aesthetic forms (ways of representing the
world that claim to be universally human), and, on the other, the elaboration and institutionalization of "objective" and "scientific" disciplines
(ways of representing the world that claim to be disinterested and true).
These colonial genealogies seek to reveal several things. First, they attempt
to show that particular discourses of knowledge or art are neither objective
nor universal, but were constructed out of and in service of the project of
colonial domination. Second, they seek to reveal that these forms of representation are thus not specifically "European" in origin, but the creations
of colonial interactions. Postcolonial studies thus seek to refute both aspects of Ricoeur's analysis of the notion of universal civilization and its
apparent implications:

> The fact that universal civilization has for a long time originated from
> the European center has maintained the illusion that European culture
> was, in fact and by right, a universal culture. Its superiority over other
> civilizations seemed to provide the experimental verification of this pos-
> tulate. Moreover, the encounter with other cultural traditions was itself
> the fruit of that advance and more generally the fruit of Occidental
> science itself. Did not Europe invent history, geography, ethnography
> and sociology in their explicit scientific forms? (Ricoeur 1965:277)

Universal civilization—even in Ricoeur's formulation, in which it transcends the Europe that gave it birth—is thus neither universal nor even,
properly speaking, European-originated. Instead, to quote Said's comment about knowledge-construction in the era of high imperialism again,
there is a conjectural fusion between "the historicizing codes of discursive
writing in Europe, positing a world universally available to transnational impersonal scrutiny, and . . . a massively colonized world" (Said
1993:168).

Concentrating on the postcolonial critique of historicism, Robert Young
argues that postcolonialism developed from a number of different sources.
On the one hand, it is a self-critique by the First World, a critique of
knowledge and representation that is as peculiarly French as the concerns
of the Frankfurt School were peculiarly German. In the Frankfurt School,
the key text was

> obviously Horkheimer and Adorno's *Dialectic of Enlightenment* of 1944.
> The date, and the exiled place of composition of its authors, suggests

tellingly that the situation with which it attempts to deal is the phenomenon of fascism which seemed to have stopped in its tracks the long
march of the progress of reason, and its liberating enlightenment ideals,
of which Marxism was the fullest political development. Horkheimer
and Adorno therefore pose the question: how has the dialectic deviated
into fascism? Why has History gone wrong? (Young 1990:7)

By contrast, the French

> have never regarded fascism as an aberration, concurring rather with
> Césaire and Fanon that it can be explained quite simply as European
> colonialism brought home to Europe by a country that had been de-
> prived of its overseas empire after World War I. French poststructuralism,
> therefore, involves a critique of reason as a system of domination com-
> parable to that of the Frankfurt School, but rather than setting up the
> possibility of a purged reason operating in an unblocked, ideal speech
> situation as a defence against tyranny and coercion in the manner of a
> Habermas, it reanalyses the operations of reason as such. (8)

In the postwar period, the Algerian war of independence further reinforced this anticolonial perspective. As Young comments, "It is significant
that Sartre, Althusser, Derrida and Lyotard, among others, were all either
born in Algeria or personally involved with the events of the war" (1).

Young outlines how the French reanalysis of reason sprang from a number of roots: the phenomenological tradition of Husserl, Heidegger, Le-
vinas, and Derrida; the failure of Sartre's subjectivist-humanist and Althusser's objectivist attempts to retheorize Marxism (after which "no one
has attempted a new theorization of a Marxist history" [63]); and work
done on the history of science by Gaston Bachelard, Georges Can-
guilheim, and Jean Cavailles, work largely unknown outside France. The
crucial target of these reanalyses is the way Hegelian and also Marxist
histories represent attempts to write historicist master (universal) narratives: these grand narratives of History as an expressive totality parallel
and were implicated in the colonial projects of Europe. Young summarizes
the criticisms:

> Such knowledge is always centered in a self even though it is outward
> looking, searching for power and control of what is other to it. Anthro-
> pology had always provided the clearest symptomatic instance, as was
> forseen by Rousseau from the outset. History, with a capital H, similarly
> cannot tolerate otherness or leave it outside its economy of inclusion.
> The appropriation of the other as a form of knowledge within a totaliz-
> ing system can thus be set alongside the history (if not the project) of
> European imperialism, and the constitution of the other as "other"
> alongside racism and sexism. (4)

In this vein, Jacques Derrida has described his critique of logocentrism as "above all else the search for the 'other' " (16). As we saw at the start of this section, Derrida articulates the "philosophical category of the centre . . . with the problem of Eurocentrism" (18). Similarly, Foucault, even if he did not write the "ethnology of Western culture" (74) that some admirers have claimed for him, deeply influenced the anti-European critiques of knowledge of Edward Said and Gayatri Spivak—writers who have criticized Foucault for his Eurocentrism.

Young finds a second source for contemporary postcolonialism in Third world anticolonial writing, especially the work of Frantz Fanon, which Sartre described as "the striptease of our humanism" (121). In writing about the hypocrisy of European humanism, Fanon produced a scathing indictment of its universality: in the conclusion of *The Wretched of the Earth,* Fanon castigates "that same Europe where they were never done talking of Man, and where they never stopped proclaiming that they were only anxious for the welfare of Man: today we know with what sufferings humanity has paid for every one of their triumphs of the mind" (1961:251). Said (1993) emphasizes Fanon's importance to the process of deconstructing imperial culture and knowledge much more strongly than Young. He finds political activity in the peripheries, not the philosophical self-deconstruction of the colonial powers, to have been the most important source of postcolonial critiques of knowledge. In the colonizing nations, Said argues, there was "no overall condemnation of imperialism until—and this is my point—*after* native uprisings were too far gone to be ignored or defeated" (241); "only after nationalists first took the lead in the imperial territories, then expatriate intellectuals and activists, did there develop a significant anti-colonial movement in the metropolis" (242). Correspondingly, Said argues that, before that time, metropolitan opposition movements—such as workers and women's movements—accepted, rather than opposed, their nations' imperial ambitions.

These different developments have resulted in a critique of modes of knowledge and representation. According to this line of argument, the supposedly peripheral phenomenon of colonialism was actually central to "the fundamental structures and assumptions of Western knowledge," and that therefore "the legacy of colonialism is as much a problem for the West as it is for the scarred lands beyond" (Young 1990:126). This profoundly interventionist critique seeks first to undercut Ricoeur's faith in the "universality," "disinterestedness" and "objectivity" of a wide variety of First World cultural, intellectual, and scientific discourses—from history to anthropology, from literature to science—by investigating their (buried) colonial genealogies. In so doing, postcolonial analyses also deny that these discourses were locally formed in Europe: that is, they reject the localism of cultural nationalism. Rather, they assert, such discourses were created as part of a common system of highly differential relationships between colony and colonizer.

Although uncovering the colonial genealogies of academic discourses, in "their explicit scientific forms" is clearly a profoundly political act, the theoretical insight that informs it is anything but confined to the arena of postcolonial political scholarship. The notion that universal laws no longer apply, and that what have been taken to be such are the product of evolutionarily developing systems and local circumstances—the notion that natural "laws" are not "natural" but evolutionary-historical constructs that require contextualization—has been essential to the present ferment in theoretical physics, from cosmology to chaos theory. Indeed, the required contextualization has been twofold: the cosmos is evolving, and with it the "laws" that govern its operation, laws that have only local rather than universal applicability; and our means of representing the cosmos in knowledge have likewise been historically produced, requiring, in turn, social-historical contextualization (Kuhn 1970; Sheldrake 1989; Lyotard 1979). Given the latter of these two processes, it should be no surprise that, as well as an explicitly postcolonial historiography and anthropology, we now have work that identifies itself as postcolonial science (Nandy 1988).

But as much as postcolonialism is dedicated to a refiguration of the past, it decenters present cultural politics. As Timothy Brennan argues,

> the wave of successful, anti-colonial struggles from China to Zimbabwe has contributed to the forced attention now being given in the English-speaking world to the point of view of the colonized—and yet it is a point of view that must increasingly be seen as part of English-speaking culture. It is a situation, as the Indo-English author Salman Rushdie points out, in which English, "no longer an English language, now grows from many roots; and those whom it once colonized are carving out large territories within the language for themselves." The polycultural forces in domestic English life have given weight to the claims of the novelists and essayists abroad who speak more articulately and in larger crowds about neocolonialism. And, in turn, such voices from afar give attention to the volatile cultural pluralism at home. The Chilean expatriate, Ariel Dorfman, has written that "there may be no better way for a country to know itself than to examine the myths and popular symbols that it exports to its economic and military dominion. And this would be even true when the myths come home." (48)

This description shows how the legacy of revolutionary nationalism has developed in postcolonialism, as in multiculturalism, into something

new and quite different: challenges from the outside, from "another culture" or an "outside position," have yielded to attempts to reappropriate
what is more and more clearly a common, but heterogeneous, system.
What Rushdie asserts of the English language could be applied to almost
any cultural and scientific discourse. Contemporary intellectual discourses have increasingly grown from many roots as former colonial subjects have carved out large territories in (or recolonized) them. Familiar
First World discourses (such as "English literature" and the European-
originated disciplines "in scientific forms" from historiography to sociology) have increasingly been contested, retheorized, and practiced by a variety of players. New methodologies, new forms of practice, have evolved to
match new globalist geopolitical conditions, just as intellectual and cultural practices interacted with geopolitical circumstances, albeit in a very
different way, in the colonial era. Further, as Dorfman's comment reveals,
postcolonialism has not only reappropriated the cultural possessions of
the core, it has sought to provide a privileged point of view on the workings of the system as a whole: increasingly, a crucial key to the self-
knowledge of the core has been found in the peripheries. Thus, as postcolonialism has recolonized First World discourses, it has also, in one
formulation, sought to decolonize not just the Third but also the First
World.

Postcolonial literary studies are one of the many possible illustrations of
this complex process. Ania Loomba's intervention in *Gender, Race, Renaissance Drama* (1989) draws, in turn, on the work of Gauri Visnawathan
(1989) and Chris Baldick (1983) on the remarkable Anglo-Indian genealogy of institutionalized English literary studies. Essentially, Loomba asserts
that the humanist claim of universalism for the great texts of English
literature—best exemplified in the elevation of Shakespeare to imperishable greatness—is not a testimony to literature's separation from politics
and history, but, in truth, the opposite, a particularly mystified and powerful way of making literature serve political ends:

> English literary study was shaped by the same processes in which it
> actively participated. In other words it did not have some inherent claim
> to, but *was invested with* humanistic and moral attributes. The history of
> this investment is interlaced with what Chris Baldick has called the
> civilizing mission of English literature in relation to various subordinate
> classes and groups. (Loomba 1989:11)

As has become commonplace in contemporary literary-political disputes,
Loomba has responded to the charge the oppositional readings of literary
texts are political by pointing out that apparently "universalizing" or "aes-

thetic" conventional readings of those texts are just as deeply political—or perhaps more perniciously so, as they mask their ideological commitments.

Loomba and Visnawathan show how the politics of humanism and the academic discipline of English studies were deployed and even formed in Anglo-India. Visnawathan's *Masks of Conquest: Literary Study and British Rule in India* (1989) is an extended study of the surprisingly non-local origins of English literary study: "The amazingly young history of English literature as a subject of study (it is less than a hundred and fifty years old) is frequently noted, but less appreciated is the irony that English literature appeared as a subject in the colonies long before it was institutionalized in the home country" (3). It was, moreover, institutionalized as part of the process of social control, as part of the colonial project. Subsequently, what had been tested in India was adapted to and applied in England. That this was not a monolithic, unilateral process is clear from Visnawathan's discussion of the many disputes and different positions involved in the construction of English literary study in India, and from Loomba's account of how it has lived on, surprisingly, as a component of Indian nationalism, surviving even into the postindependence era. Loomba quotes Jasodhara Baghi, who points out how in Bengal "the evocation of the Hindu Brahaminical golden age was conducted within the protective umbrella of English literary values. . . . When the theater moved out of the household of the aristocracy onto the public commercial stage, Girish Ghosh . . . (showed) the glory of a Hindu heroism alongside his adaptations . . . of Shakespeare" (1989:22). In more recent times, the universal validity of Shakespeare has continued to be political resource for the Indian elite, marking and legitimizing their differences from Indians who are not literate in English: "The editor of a volume examining Shakespeare in India puts it plainly: 'The England of trade, commerce, imperialism and the penal code has not endured but the imperishable empire of Shakespeare will always be with us. And that is something to be grateful for'" (22).

Having outlined the colonial genealogy of English literary study and argued that the attribution of universal greatness to literature like Shakespeare's plays is part of a politically interested use of that literature, Loomba goes on to provide counterinterpretations of Shakespeare. She attempts what she calls a postcolonial "appropriation" or "reappropriation" of Shakespeare. If literary criticism has "lost its innocence" by revealing its inescapable involvement in politics and history—if it has revealed the "worldliness" of its texts, as Said might say—then "our own reappropriations . . . need not be apologetic about their partisanship" (7) In attempting these, Loomba evokes her own identity-position as a hermeneutic tool:

> The female reader in the sub-continent is the recipient of texts that are the products of another culture and employed in the service of colonial and neo-colonial attitudes; written by men and made to speak on behalf of anti-feminism; brought in for specific purposes but projected as universally valid and true. But precisely these alienations, as I hope to show, can be useful in formulating an alternative reading and teaching practice. (Loomba 1989: 6)

Loomba thus becomes a practicing example of the postcolonial intellectual Said describes:

> Many of the post-colonial writers bear their past within them—as scars of humiliating wounds, as instigation for different practices, as potentially revised visions of the past tending towards a future, as urgently reinterpretable and re-deployable experiences in which the formerly silent native speaks and acts on territory taken back from the colonialist. And, for the first time, these writers can read the great colonial masterpieces that had not only misrepresented them, but had assumed their inability to read and respond directly to what had been written about them, just as European ethnography depended in very real measure upon the natives' incapacity to intervene in scientific discourse about them. (Said 1986:55).

Loomba's subsequent interventions in Shakespearian criticism—her specific reappropriations of it—are in this vein. They represent first, an expansion of what is actually in the text: for example, she explores race, gender, and class issues in *Othello* and *The Tempest*, recapturing both as politically charged documents from readings that would universalize the former play as a tale of jealousy, not race, and the latter as a fable of the artist, not the colonialist. Second, Loomba refuses to limit herself "to the spaces allowed by" the European text; she extends her critical analysis to the historical contexts of the texts and "the economic, sociopolitical, and institutional realities in which our academic practice exists" (158). "We must [Edward Said more specifically comments] . . . read the great canonical texts, and perhaps also the entire archive of modern and pre-modern European and American culture, with an effort to draw out, extend, give emphasis and voice to what is silent or marginally present or ideologically represented (I have in mind Kipling's Indian characters) in such works" (1993:66). In thus reconceiving Shakespeare, Loomba is not acting alone: her chapter on *The Tempest*, for example, is an addition to an already impressively large body of work, including commentaries by Aimé Césaire (1969), George Lamming (1960), and Roberto Fernandez-Retamar

(1989), in which the play becomes a colonial fable and the potential and limitations of Caliban's perspective are explored.

Such intervention and reappropriation is obviously something profoundly different from an "ethnoperspective" on Shakespeare. A comparison with older assumptions can, however, be illuminating. Laura Bohannan's witty, but uncomfortably patronizing, portrayal in "Hamlet in the Bush" (1966) of African elders interpreting the plot of Hamlet wholly differently than Bohannan does, and then generously explaining it to her, evokes a separate hermeneutic universe brokered by a First World anthropologist. Although the point of the piece is an endorsement of cultural relativism, the empowerment of the "other" is clearly limited and the boundary lines between native and Westerner are firmly drawn, keeping hermeneutic systems separate and keeping the "other" "other." Although a "native" culture might be dignified by such relativism—it might be represented by ethno-theorists as sophisticated in the image of a First World academic curriculum, possessing its own ethno-aesthetics, ethno-psychology, ethno-philosophy, and so on—it is still typically brokered by a First World researcher and imaged in terms of First World disciplines. Postcolonial Shakespeare, by contrast, has left the bush, has been conducting its work in both Western and postcolonial academies, and has been dedicated from the start to criticizing and refiguring the discourses of those academies. It seeks, in short, to transform and pluralize common discourses, not inhabit separate universes; and it uses its Third World positionality as a privileged site within those discourses rather than privileging them as a site apart. Postcolonial interventionists have thus been decentering a common world; however much they have made use of Third World perspectives as hermeneutic positions, they have crossed boundaries: they have not been kept in the bush.

Postcolonial literary scholarship thus reveals a past in which supposedly universal, First World–originated discourses are in fact neither universal nor made in the First World and advocates a present project in which Third World actors seek to reappropriate the discourses they helped create. In the process, the colonial past has rapidly shed the totalizing narrative of domination that Said's *Orientalism* has been criticized for propagating. Its narrative has been rewritten to emphasize interaction as well as domination.

As we have seen, Said reconceived his project in the wake of such criticism. The colonial encounter, he has written, could be "a mutual experience . . . [in which] true there has been a principal and a subordinate, but there had been dialogue and communication" (1986:62), and in *Culture and Imperialism* (1993), he describes how the imperial past has been and can be further reformulated in many fields by "contrapuntal" analysis. Thus, the genealogy of cultural and scientific discourses reveals, not just totalizing European knowledge-construction in the service of totalized power, but a "much more varied and intertwined archaeology for knowledge" (1986:64). The colonial subject is present, then, not simply as victim, but in a variety of ways for a variety of postcolonial theorists: as the presence of an absence ("the holistic, representative vision of society could only be represented in a discourse that was *at the same time* obsessively fixed upon, and uncertain of, the boundaries of society, and margins of the text" [Bhabha, 1990:296]), the absence of a presence ("master texts need us in the construction of their texts without acknowledging that need" [Spivak 1990:73]), and an as-yet-undiscovered presence ("the extraordinary dependence—formal and ideological—of the great French and English novel on the facts of empire has never been studied from a theoretical viewpoint" [Said 1986:59]). In the process of finding stronger roles for the colonial situation and even subjects in the construction of First World *epistēmē*, colonial power has come to be seen as less monolithic, but rather as riven from within, operating through conflictual mechanisms in non-synchronous fashion, and even deeply concerned with and shaped by its own impotence and vulnerability, not power.

In this passage from domination to interaction, and from what Said (1986:46; 1993:18) calls the politics of blame to a more complex politics of secular interpretation, Homi Bhabha is a pivotal figure, and Sara Suleri's *The Rhetoric of English India* (1992) reaches a kind of high-water mark. Robert Young traces how Bhabha opened up Said's totalizing picture of the West's Orientalist domination of its colonies: Bhabha's concern was "to demonstrate an ambivalence in colonial and colonizing subjects by articulating the inner dissension within a colonial discourse structured according to the conflictual economy of the psyche" (145). Bhabha undoes the apparent totalization of colonial power in a variety of ways. Turning Freud on his head, he finds in colonial stereotypes of the "other" that Europeans, not "primitives," practiced a kind of fetishism, predicated as much on "anxiety and defence" as on mastery (1983:202), thereby empowering assimilation as a site of resistance; he analyzes the menace in colonials' mimicry of their "masters" (1984); he describes colonial hybridization as a process whereby colonial power repeated itself with a difference in exporting itself to the colonies, threatening its own legitimacy and opening up sites for opposition (1985a); and he reconfigures colonialism as an interplay between narcissism and paranoia (1985b).

Young observes that, in the process, Bhabha "certainly develops Albert Memmi's argument that there is never a simple distinction between colonizer and colonized," adding, however, that "this only prompts the question of whether there can be such categories in general" (1990:151). Such questioning reveals the limits of postcolonial positions: in detotalizing and heterogenizing the identities of both the colonized and colonist, in seeing both positions as constructions of a common, complexly interacting system, and in joining First World self-critique to Third World critique of First World knowledge, postcolonialism has poised itself on the brink of a metamorphosis. Anticolonialism has almost shifted into interactivity; oppositional analyses have almost shifted into analyses of mutuality; and corrosive deconstruction has nearly become polyglossic conversation.

Young describes the change of enunciatiative position between Fanon and Bhabha extremely well. He cites Sartre on Fanon: Fanon, writing in elegant French, overtly addressed a separate, bounded Third World community while simultaneously communicating harshly with, by coldly ignoring, his European audience. As Sartre comments, "his work—red-hot for some—in what concerns you [Fanon's European readership] is cold as ice; he speaks of you often, never to you" (155). Bhabha's texts, by contrast,

> are not directed towards any specific addressee; nevertheless he manages to produce a comparable sense of discomfiture and disorientation. . . . in the opacity of his discourse, his descriptions of slippage and ambivalence begin to seem equally applicable to the rhetoric of his own writings which reproduce the forms and structures of the material he analyses and thus simultaneously assert and undermine their own authoritative mode. To his reader, as he enacts what he describes, at times Bhabha's discourse becomes as incalculable and difficult to place as the colonial subject himself. (156)

If Bhabha has become a placeless, subversive voice in contemporary theory because he is in so many places, he has spoken for a contemporary world of crossed boundaries and composite selves as much as Fanon's voice strikingly represents both the "anticolonial" and "national" frames of anticolonial nationalism.

More recently, Suleri has crafted an enunciative position and cultural/historical analysis that still more clearly are products of a mobile, interconnected, but differentiated and interactive, global system. In *The Rhetoric of English India,* she focuses on how

> colonial facts are vertiginous: they lack a recognizable cultural plot; they frequently fail to cohere around the master-myth that proclaims static lines of demarcation between imperial power and disempowered culture, between colonizer and colonized. Instead, they move with a ghostly mobility to suggest how highly unsettling an economy of complicity

and guilt is in operation between each actor on the colonial stage. If such an economy is the impelling force of the stories of English India, it demands to be read against the grain of the rhetoric of binarism that informs, either explicitly or implicitly, contemporary critiques of alterity in colonial discourse. The necessary intimacies that obtain between ruler and ruled create a counter-culture not always explicable in terms of an allegory of otherness. (Suleri 1992:3)

Suleri replaces Said's early paradigm of colonialism as a master-slave relationship with "a figure of colonial intimacy" (23). Mixed heterogeneous identity—"the imbrication of our various positions and presents, the ineluctable relationships of shared and contested meanings, values, material resources" (15)—has become the necessary substitute for "alterist" readings. In Suleri, then, oppositional reappropriation has shaded into interactive mutuality and colonial discourse generates "a new idiom of cultural compassion, as it studies the commonality of loss" (15). Behind these sorts of shifts in the representation of the past, the notion of a changed present has clearly been crucial. Anticolonial nationalism has passed; and with an increasingly subtle and thoroughgoing perforation of its strongly marked boundary lines, a new discourse of present and retroactive mutuality for the globalist era has been forming.

As important as these recastings of colonial history and uncovering of colonial genealogies for intellectual and cultural discourses have been, postcolonialism has not only constructed itself from critiques of past and present imperial formations. It has also constructed itself by critically examining its own tradition of anticolonialism. It has, in effect, studied its own genealogy. In doing so, as Young points out, it has attacked not only Hegel, but also Marx, challenging not "just the politics and institutions of the right but also the politics and theoretical systems of the left" (Young 1990:2); along with criticizing the metropolitan opposition, it also has mounted a sharp and scathing critique of Third World nationalism and fundamentalism. Thus, postcolonial critics like Gayatri Spivak have been "constantly vigilant with respect with the hidden ways in which nominally radical, or oppositional historians [like First World feminists and Third World essentialists] can often unknowingly, or even knowingly, perpetuate the structures and presuppositions of the very systems they oppose" (162). Postcolonialism, then, is as self-consciously a part of the revision of previous European oppositional politics in the wake of May 1968 as American multiculturalism was a self-reflexive, post-1960s revision of the previous assumptions of black nationalism and the new ethnicity.

Specifically postcolonial positions thus distinguish themselves from their own roots in prior oppositional movements, while practicing their critique and transformation of the legacy of colonialism. Like that of contemporary American ethnic theory, this internal critique is complex. For example, the construction by nationalism of a variety of bounded, separate, and even supposedly essentialist and primordially rooted national traditions is a legacy that remains very much alive, even as it is criticized, in both postcolonialism and multiculturalism. Although postcolonialism has mounted a harsh internal critique of both traditional oppositional politics and cultural nationalism, it has also built upon the achievements of the oppositional Marxism and nationalism of this era. Thus, for example, in a recent attempt to survey postcolonialism in literature and literary theory comprehensively, *The Empire Writes Back* (1989), Bill Ashcroft, Gareth Griffiths, and Helen Tiffin argue, analogously to Lisa Lowe on American ethnic politics, that without the "development of national literatures and criticism," and "without the comparative studies between national traditions to which these lead, no discipline of post-colonialism could have emerged," and that "all post-colonial studies continue to depend on national literatures and criticism" (1989:17). These intellectual and institutional continuities coexist with differences. The development of postcolonial literature and theory reveals that

> profound interaction and appropriation has taken place. Indeed, the process of literary decolonization has involved a radical dismantling of European codes and a post-colonial subversion and appropriation of European discourses.
>
> This dismantling has been frequently accompanied by the demand for an entirely new or wholly recovered pre-colonial "reality." Such a demand, given the nature of the relationship between colonizer and colonized, its social brutality and cultural denigration, is perfectly comprehensible. But, as we have argued, it cannot be achieved. Post-colonial culture is inevitably a hybridized phenomenon involving a dialectical relationship between the "grafted" European cultural systems and an indigenous ontology, with its impulse to create or recreate an independent local identity. (Ashcroft, Griffiths, and Tiffin 1989:195)

Postcolonialism, in this reading, not only involves and practices cultural syncretism between Europe and its former colonies, it also encourages it between the "postcolonies" themselves, promoting the interaction of different, recently created, or consolidated national traditions. It seeks, in short, to build a transnational oppositional alliance. Mapping this heterogeneous alliance has, however, proved rather difficult. Ashcroft, Griffiths, and Tiffin survey a considerable variety of attempts to structure the postcolonial alliance, discussing racial and diasporic formations, groupings thanks to victimization by colonialism, and a variety of other orderings implied in such terms as "Third World," "terranglian," and "Common-wealth." In their own survey, they distinguish between three kinds of postcolonialisms, linked to areas according to historical and cultural criteria: they see a monologlossic postcolonialism emerging from former white settler colonies, like the United States, Canada, Australia, and New Zealand; a diglossic variety emerging from societies in which bilingualism was institutionalized, like India, Africa, and the South Pacific; and a polyglossic form emerging from polydialectical communities like those of the Caribbean. Given their emphasis on the emerging heterogeneity and syncretism and postcolonialism, they see the Caribbean as the crucial model for the future; it embraces the most complex forms and possesses "the greatest potential for abrogating Eurocentric concepts" (117). Overall, they argue, postcolonialism enshrines syncretism and hybridity. It must have "the ability to include, for example, the English literature of the Philippines or of the United States as well as that of "pakeha" (white) or Maori writing in New Zealand, or that of both Blacks and whites in South Africa" (24). Ashcroft, Griffiths, and Tiffin envision this as ultimately part of an ethical project of decentering cultural globalization:

> The post-colonial world is one in which destructive cultural encounter is changing into an acceptance of difference on equal terms. Both literary theorists and cultural historians are beginning to recognize cross-culturality as the potential termination point of an apparently endless human history of conquest and annihilation justified by the myth of "group purity," and as the basis on which the post-colonial world can be creatively stabilized. Nationalist and Black criticisms have demystified the imperial processes of domination and continuing hegemony, but they have not in the end offered a way out of the historical and philosophical impasse. Unlike these models, the recent approaches have recognized that the strength of post-colonial theory may well lie in its inherently comparative methodology and the hybridized and syncretic view of the modern world which this implies. (37)

Benita Parry (1989), previously surveying theories of colonial discourse against the background of Frantz Fanon's advocacy of revolutionary opposition, differs strongly from Ashcroft, Griffiths, and Tiffin's ethical vision. Clearly valorizing Fanon's writings for the way they intercede "to promote the continuation of a political conscious, unified, revolutionary Self, standing in unmitigated antagonism to the oppressor, occupying a combative subject position from which the wretched of the earth are enabled to mobilize an armed struggle against colonial power" (31), she criticizes

Spivak and, to a lesser degree, Bhabha, for their revisions of Fanon's revolutionary intransigence. She considers that Spivak's criticisms of "nostalgia for lost origins as a basis for counter-hegemonic production" and Bhabha's excoriation of the "self-righteous rhetoric of resistance" extend "to a downgrading of the anti-imperialist texts written by national liberation movements" and have "obliterated the role of the native as historical subject and combatant, possessor of an-other knowledge and producer of alternative traditions" (34). Parry is, moreover, highly suspicious of affirmations of syncretism as an attempted "harmonization of alterities," an underwriting of "the goal of a cultural esperanto assembled out of existing modes" (50). Such inclusive apolitical humanism only enhances the muffling and muzzling of Fanon she perceives, even as Bhabha's and Spivak's reinterpretation of colonialism mutes his call for a combative subject position antagonistic to the whole realm of colonial practice and discourse.

Parry's strongly etched analysis of postcolonial theory is accompanied by a rereading of Fanon and a sophisticated theoretical rephrasing of revolutionary opposition for an era in which naive nationalism has been deconstructed. Clearly, the paradoxes we saw in our discussion of Mukherjee and multiculturalism apply also to work in postcolonial theory. Just as recent transformations in radical positions about American ethnic and national cultures have so complicated the notion of cultural identity that it has become increasingly difficult to separate the opposition from the center, so transformations in the radical analysis of colonialism have distanced it confusingly from its passionately anticolonial origins. In both cases, moreover, the result has been an increasingly subtle differentiation of positions; in both controversies, critics like Parry and Brennan have sought to revalorize anticolonial cultural nationalism and preserve what they consider genuinely radical positions from what they see as a drift back to neocolonial co-optation. Despite their critiques, however, a development hard to reverse, one that raises new possibilities and responds to new conditions, has taken place. There has been a transformation from speaking against to speaking with and to; from a sense of cultural communities as separate to an awareness of their complex interlocking; from a cultivation of opposition to a grappling with the possibilities and limitations of interaction. Clearly, Parry would be sharply critical of Suleri's "new idea of cultural compassion." At the same time, perhaps, Parry's attempt to maintain so absolute and global a boundary line as that between the colonial and the anticolonial risks becoming an exercise in anger that enforces a Manicheanism in the past where it never successfully existed (Fanon's predications that revolutionary violence would forge absolute boundary lines between colonialist and colonized did not come true) and in a present where such a boundary is increasingly unclear, blurred, and difficult to police. One of the fascinating things for a reader of Said's *Culture and Imperialism* is tracing the ways in which he tries to bridge both positions, advancing, for example, his vision of a vehemently antinationalist, yet ardently anti-imperialist, Fanon for the present era, and eschewing a "politics of blame," advocating compassion, and seeking to forge "new alignments . . . across borders, types, nations, and essences" (1993:xxiv–xxv) at the same time as he writes an extended indictment of imperial culture.

9

Postcolonial Dialogism

IN THE DEVELOPMENT OF decolonization theory, as in the elaboration of postcolonial literary theory and history surveyed above, the emergence of "counterdiscursive" postcolonial strategies (strategies that contest, or recast and reappropriate, a common discourse) from the
"homologous" strategies of nationalism (strategies that replicate a First
World form in a Third World setting) has been clearly visible. This development is yet another example of the sort of transformation Benita Parry
resists.

Published fourteen years after *A Grain of Wheat*, Ngũgĩ wa Thiong'o's
Decolonising the Mind (1981) is an attempt to re-theorize resistance in the
wake of still more complete disillusionment with the new Kenyan nation
than the novel, already gloomy, reveals, although, like *A Grain of Wheat*,
it is deeply indebted to Franz Fanon's *The Wretched of the Earth* (1963). In
both books, Third World oppositional cultural movements have two great
tasks. First, the process of cultural alienation produced by colonial education has to be reversed. (As Ngũgĩ writes, "to control a people's culture is to
control their tools of self-definition in relation to others.") This cultural
alienation was accomplished originally by "The destruction or deliberate
underdeveloping of a people's culture, their art, dances, religions, history,
geography, education, orature and literature and the conscious elevation
of the language of the colonizer" (Ngũgĩ 1981:16). For the victims, this
meant "seeing oneself from outside oneself as if one was another self," and
it did "not matter that the imported literature carried the great humanist
tradition of the best in Shakespeare, Goethe, Balzac, Tolstoy, Gorky,
Brecht, Sholokhov, Dickens. The location of this great mirror of imagination was necessarily Europe and its history and culture and the rest of the
universe was seen from that centre" (18).

Reversing this process is inseparable from the second great task, the
creation of a decolonized society. For both Fanon and Ngũgĩ, one aim of
cultural decolonization is to create a literature not meant "to be read

exclusively by the oppressor," or even by a native comprador elite. The goal is to become a "native writer" who "progressively takes on the habit of addressing his own people" (Fanon 1963:240). But Ngũgĩ faced a very different intellectual climate from the revolutionary nationalist optimism that inspired Fanon, and his versions of these goals—culturally delinking from Europe and aiding in the creation of a decolonized society—also differ in important ways. For Fanon, the possibility of a culture that progressively takes on "the habit of addressing its own people" is present in the creation of national cultures. Sharply criticizing *négritude*'s cultural essentialism as the reverse of colonial oppression, easily manipulated by a corrupt emerging bourgeois elite, Fanon saw it as an incomplete step in a greater, more truly dialectical revolt, the goal of which is to create "a fighting literature, a revolutionary literature, and a national literature" (1963:223). The key to this process is "the fight for national existence which sets culture moving and opens to it the doors of creation" (244). By comparison, *négritude*'s dreams of pan-African and diasporic racial identity as the basis for "progressive" cultural production are vain:

> There can be no two cultures which are completely identical. To believe that it is possible to create a black culture is to forget that niggers are disappearing, just as the people who brought them into being are seeing the breakup of their economic and cultural supremacy. There will never be such a thing as black culture because there is not a single politician who feels he has a vocation to bring black republics into being. (Fanon 1963:234)

Thus, while culture is a crucial tool in the political process, Fanon is clear that it follows as well as forwards history; it is the offshoot of sociopolitical formations. As we saw in analyzing *A Grain of Wheat,* these are not primordialist, but created by a dialectical historical process of boundary creation and community building. A social unit is thus necessary to ground the ongoing elaboration of revolutionary culture. Said (1993:267–74) attempts to emphasize Fanon's harsh critiques of national independence without social revolution, to the point of styling Fanon as postnationalist, but, on the contrary, Fanon pinned his hopes for the future on an antinostalgic conception of the nation:

> Culture is first the expression of a nation, the expression of its preferences, of its taboos and of its patterns. It is at every stage of the whole society that other taboos, values, and patterns are formed. A national culture is the sum total of all these appraisals; it is the result of internal and external tensions exerted over society as a whole and also at every level of that society. In the colonial situation, culture, which is doubly deprived of the support of the nation and the state, falls away and dies.

The condition for its existence is therefore national liberation and the renaissance of the state. (Fanon 1963:244)

Having committed himself to the cultural and political form of the nation, Fanon envisions an international alliance: "Though there is no common destiny to be shared between the national cultures of Senegal and Guinea," he wrote, "there is a common destiny between the Sengalese and Guinean nations which are both dominated by the same French colonialism" (234).

Fanon warns eloquently and prophetically against the dangers of African nationalism—the possibility of its neocolonial co-optation—but his faith in the nation as a basis for genuinely revolutionary cultural, social, and political transformations was well suited to his times, since revolutionary nationalism in the Third World seemed to be a force that could create an allied, empowered Third World and therefore a new geopolitical map. In retrospect, however, even Fanon's critically alert advocacy of revolutionary nationalism seems indebted to faith in what was, every bit as much as the essentialism Fanon deprecates, a reformation of Africa according to a model disseminated from Europe. This faith is just one of the aspects of Fanon's theories that have been criticized for replicating colonial practices. Indeed, ferreting out homologies in what has proclaimed itself to be oppositional has been one of the most widespread techniques for qualifying and refiguring cultural nationalism. Always more complicated than his detractors tend to allow, however, Fanon was not just a theorist liable to such attacks, but one who mounted them himself. What has been turned against him is no less than his own critique of *négritude*.

Ngũgĩ belonged to a subsequent generation that saw the failure of those revolutionary nationalist hopes. In *Decolonising the Mind* he came to locate hope for a "progressive" culture in a different social formation, communities of speakers of the same language. Language, for Ngũgĩ, came to represent an essential, prior unity, out of which progressive social formations and progressive cultures could be constructed:

Language carries culture, and culture carries, particularly through orature and literature, the entire body of values by which we come to perceive ourselves and our place in the world. How people perceive themselves affects how they look at their culture, at their politics and at the social production of wealth, at their entire relationship to nature and to other beings. Language is thus inseparable from ourselves as a community of human beings with a specific form and character, a specific history, a specific relationship to the world. (Ngũgĩ 1981:16)

From this position, Ngũgĩ seems to extend Fanon's critique of *négritude* as dialectically incomplete, indebted to the colonial source it resists, to cover the "unique literature" (which he follows Janheinz Jahn in calling "neo African literature") Africans have recently given the world: "Novels, stories, poems, plays written by Africans in European languages, which soon consolidated itself into a tradition with companion studies and a scholarly industry" (12, 20). This literature, initially part of a worldwide democratic revolutionary movement, remains, Ngũgĩ argues, indebted to European roots and a European audience, and it became a tool by which the neocolonial, metropolitan bourgeoisie in Africa consolidated its identity and its power.

In thus more radically localizing the sociocultural basis of political and cultural activism, Ngũgĩ rescues Fanon's project and terminology from the disillusionments of an era in which the nation-state lost much of its legitimacy and power as a transformative social form. Ngũgĩ's attempt to bridge these two worlds—the revolutionary nationalism of the 1960s and what one might call globalizing postnationalism—creates problems, however, that make *Decolonising the Mind* an interesting, uneasy document. To contemporary ears, its comments on culture sound simultaneously more atavistic and more relevant than Fanon's.

On the one hand, in his thorough disillusionment with national independence, Ngũgĩ locates the basis for cultural action in language communities; in doing so, he both returns to the mystifying, romanticist, Herderian theory of national coherence and appeals to the past ("language as culture is the collective memory bank of a people's experience in history") much more strongly than to the future ("an invitation to action and a basis for hope") (Ngũgĩ 1981:16; Fanon 1963:232). *Decolonising the Mind* is at times precariously essentialist, and Ngũgĩ seems to have dedicated himself to the survival of the primordial while simultaneously advocating the innovative-progressive. Ngũgĩ thus produces rhetoric that rejects the impure, the hybrid; he criticizes literature in foreign languages as "not African literature" but "another hybrid tradition" (26). Such phraseology implies, of course, that by contrast there is a nonhybrid, genuinely African sort, and Ngũgĩ writes of his theatrical experiments at Kamĩrĩĩthũ as such a literature, an "attempt at reconnection of the broken roots of African civilization and its traditions of theater" (42). Further, he describes himself, in contrast to Fanon's assertion that the native intellectual, "after having tried to lose himself in the people and with the people, will on the contrary shake the people," as learning "anew the elements of form of the African theatre" from the peasants he worked with and for in his theatrical productions (Fanon 1963:222; Ngũgĩ 1981:45).

Ngũgĩ nonetheless also eschews nostalgic essentialism. He continues to echo Fanon's assertions that revolutionary action produces culture, and

42   Decentering the Core

that all culture is future-oriented, writing that "the real language of African theatre is to be found in the struggles of the oppressed, for it is out of these struggles that a new Africa is being born" (61). And he reiterates Fanon's caution that "the struggle for freedom does not give back to the national culture its former value and shapes . . . [and] cannot leave intact either the form or content of the people's culture" (Fanon 1963:246). But more radically than Fanon, Ngũgĩ advocates the synthesizing of African cultures out of and via globally disseminated materials. He has no difficulty fusing the "elements of form of the African theatre" he has learned from the peasants with elements of the modern avant-garde theatrical tradition (and the theory that sustains it). Following Brecht, he incorporates slides into a theatrical production, and he quotes Karl Marx in theorizing about African drama. Despite his efforts, the distinction he wishes to maintain between "authentic" African literature and Afro-European literature as another "hybrid creation" thus becomes increasingly precarious. And in fact, for both forms and methods, from its management of community-based co-authorship to its actual theatrical devices, his Kamĩthĩĩrũ theater project was indebted to the infusion of globally disseminated left-wing avant-garde techniques and forms. In *Decolonising the Mind*, then, Ngũgĩ attempts to fuse, or alternate between, first, the language of primordial continuity and transformative future projects, and, second, the rhetoric of authenticity and the practice of eclectic innovation.

The only reconciliation of these opposite polemics Ngũgĩ's theory allows lies in the concept of indigenization. Ngũgĩ seeks to show how a language community can by hybridized, yet remain culturally coherent and continuous at the same time, and, in doing so, he urges African artists to become a version of Ricoeur's cultural geniuses. Rather than pluralizing English, as Salman Rushdie advocates, Ngũgĩ envisions transforming Gĩkũyũ and other African languages by indigenizing globally disseminated information:

> Why, we may ask, should an African writer, or any writer, become so obsessed by taking from his mother-tongue to enrich other tongues? Why should he see it as his particular mission? We never asked ourselves: how can we enrich our languages? How can we "prey" on the rich humanist and democratic heritage in the struggles of other peoples in other times and other places to enrich our own? Why not have Balzac, Tolstoy, Sholokhov, Brecht, Lu Hsün, Pablo Neruda, H. C. Anderson, Kim Chi Ha, Marx, Lenin, Albert Einstein, Galileo, Aeschylus, Aristotle and Plato in African languages? And why not create literary monuments in our own languages? Why in other words should Okara not sweat it out to create in Ijaw, which he acknowledges to have depths of philosophy and a wide range of ideas and experiences? (Ngũgĩ 1981:8)

Similarly, on a more mundane, but equally vivid, level, Ngũgĩ remarks:

> Since the new language as a means of communication was a product of and was reflecting the "real language of life" elsewhere, it could never as spoken or written properly reflect or imitate the real life of that community. This may in part explain why technology appears to us as slightly external, *their* product and not *ours*. The work "missile" used to hold an alien far-away sound until I recently learnt its equivalent in Gĩkũyũ, *ngurukuhĩ-*, and it made me apprehend it differently. (16–17)

Ngũgĩ's project is, then, to empower the local by indigenizing, or internalizing in a primordialist manner, the global. Ngũgĩ's ability to sound essentialist in one sentence and globalist and postcolonialist in the next stems from this strategy of globalist indigenization. The terms point in opposite directions, but there is really no clear dividing line between indigenization and the apparently opposite formulation that argues that local identities are constructed out of globally disseminated material. Should we regard indigenization—or, more terminologically blatantly, *re*-tribalization or *re*-traditionalization—as conservative or avant-garde? Are they present processes or continuations of the past? Do they point backward or forward? The ambiguity is apparently unresolvable.

The only possible answer to this aporia is that such projects are global versions of what we have examined in American ethnic cultural politics. They are versions of what Gayatri Spivak (1987) and Amanda Anderson (1992) have called "strategic" essentialisms, ones that make use of the notion of primordial continuity to create and mobilize a community. Furthermore, like Lisa Lowe, Ngũgĩ is seeking, not just to mobilize the Gĩkũyũ language community, but to construct a heterogeneous global alliance of different groups. Ngũgĩ ultimately calls for the global dissemination of "indigenization" as a basis for a new, heterogeneous alliance of African peasant/language communities with "all the other peoples of the world . . . the peoples of Asia, South America, Australia and New Zealand, Canada and the U.S.A." (30). Eschewing Fanon's notions of international alliances, Ngũgĩ seeks, by appealing conservatively to language communities worldwide, to operate at a level simultaneously above and below the nation—to refigure "native" opposition in a localist-transnational fashion.

But Ngũgĩ's strategic essentialism does not admit it is strategic, and his project clings to the old nationalist rhetoric of primordialism. As a result, in *Decolonising the Mind*, Ngũgĩ remains committed to utilizing two languages—the older language of cultural nationalism and the newer one of postnationalist globalism-localism—interruptively, without acknowledging that he is doing so. The result is a powerful polemic; at worst, it is a mystification; at best, a postnationalist strategy.

What Ngũgĩ suppresses, Ashis Nandy attempts to foreground in his intricate revision of decolonization theory. In the first two essays in *Traditions, Tyranny, and Utopias* (1987), Nandy compresses and advances the argument of his *The Intimate Enemy: Loss and Recovery of Self Under Colonialism* (1983). As the title of the earlier book indicates, Nandy's concerns are those of the tradition of decolonization we have been examining. He writes in the introduction to *The Intimate Enemy*, of a

> second form of colonization [that] at least six generations of the Third World have learnt to view as a prerequisite for their liberation. This colonialism colonizes minds in addition to bodies and it releases forces within the colonized societies to alter their cultural priorities once for all. In the process, it helps generalize the concept of the modern West from a geographical and temporal entity to a psychological category. The West is now everywhere, within the West and outside; in structures and in minds. (Nandy 1983:xi)

Nandy's vision of the colonized might seem at first identical to Ngũgĩ's, but the concluding sentence shifts the emphasis significantly. The omnipresence of the West is extremely different. It is deterritorialized, more like a universal malaise that afflicts us all than a specific intersocietal oppression (the West versus the rest). And indeed, Nandy's version of decolonization is distinct from Ngũgĩ's and Fanon's in the extent to which territorial, cultural, and historical boundaries are repeatedly and intentionally transgressed. Their violation is central to both Nandy's analysis of the effects of colonialism and his proposed remedy for them.

Perceiving that the "West" is now omnipresent, Nandy dramatically extends Fanon's original critique of the homologous—of movements, like *négritude*, that replicate what they think they are resisting. For example, in criticizing Fanon, Nandy argues that Fanon's vision of the cleansing role of violence sounds alien to many Africans and Asians because it is insensitive to the more subtle kind of cultural resistance that seeks liberation, not only from colonial violence, but also from the anticolonial legacy of violence; not only from the external aggressor, but the aggressor in oneself:

> Fanon admits the internalization of the oppressor. But he calls for an exorcism in which the ghost outside has to be finally confronted in violence, for it carries the burden of the ghost within. The outer violence, Fanon suggests, is the only means of making a painful break with a part of one's own self.
> If Fanon had more confidence in his culture he would have sensed that

his vision ties the victim more deeply to the culture of oppression than any collaboration can. Cultural acceptance of the major technique of oppression in our times, organized violence, can but further socialize the victims to the basic values of his oppressors. (Nandy 1987:33–4).

Though this psychological-political critique of Fanon is couched in terms of the nationalist inheritance in decolonization—in terms of liberation from an oppressor and an appeal to confidence in one's "own" culture—it finally employs very different terms and appeals to different assumptions. Exorcism is not only not enough, but bequeaths a heavier set of chains; likewise, the aggressor is within as well as without, not so easily separable from oneself. Having thus blurred the boundary lines between aggressor and victim, Nandy then locates the wisdom that blurs such distinctions between cultures paradoxically, provocatively, *in* Third World cultures. Third World cultures tended to be nondualistic, as "many defeated cultures refuse to draw a clear line between the victor and the defeated, the oppressor and the oppressed" (33).

Nandy therefore rejects nationalism's rejection of awareness of the liberated victim's co-optation. Thanks to nondual cultural traditions, the colonized subject can accept compromise and hybridity, as the nationalist Fanon could not, and Nandy readily allows himself to be infected by what Fanon suppresses: "Let us not forget that the most violent denunciation of the West produced by Frantz Fanon is written in the elegant style of a Jean-Paul Sartre. The West has not merely produced modern colonialism, it informs most interpretations of colonialism. It colours even this interpretation of interpretation" (1983:xii).

Having thus made boundaries porous, Nandy proceeds to reap all the benefits he can. As with revaluation in America of assimilation as a source of more subtle oppositional strategies, Nandy finds positive (oppositional) value in strategies that range from apparent collaborationism to utilization of the mutuality of oppressor and oppressed. A striking example of the latter is Nandy's analysis of Gandhi's manipulation of connections with the oppressor, rather than exorcism of those bonds. Citing Father G. Gutierrez's comment that one must love one's oppressors by liberating them from their inhuman condition as oppressors, Nandy remarks that it "almost inadvertently captures the spirit of Gandhi":

> The two-tier identification with the aggressor, which Gandhi so effortlessly made, is the obverse of the identification with the victim which allows a freer expression of aggressive drive. The Gandhian vision defies the temptation to equal the aggressor in violence and to regain one's self-esteem as a competitor within the same system. The vision builds on an identification with the oppressed which excludes the phan-

tasy of the superiority of the oppressor's life-style, so deeply embedded in
the consciousness of those who claim to speak on behalf of the victims of
history. (1987:35)

Identification as a source of liberation, and greater confidence in one's
own culture as a prerequisite for acknowledging relatedness, participation
in a common system: Nandy's version of decolonization strategy erects
itself on these paradoxes.

Crucial to these strategies for liberation is the notion of dialogue—a
dialogue, as Nandy frequently puts it, between the visions of different
civilizations. This dialogue is, however, anything but an exchange between clearly (territorially, culturally, socially) differentiated entities. As
Nandy repeatedly emphasizes, for the dialogue to be genuine, it needs to
make a number of crucial insights fully operative.

First, the conversation partners in a dialogue are not historically distinct. Indeed, they must implement the notion that there is "continuity
between the victors and the victims" (26) and that, although "the subtler
and more invidious forms of oppression" are those "which make the victims willing participants and supporters of an oppressive system" (27), to
react by trying to erase this legacy binds one to it all the more. Rather than
becoming aware of the colonization of one's mind as a possession of oneself by something alien, Nandy makes the chief task of decolonization the
recognition that, in a culture of violence, there is "continuity between the
victor and the defeated, the instrument and the target, the interpreter and
the interpreted. As a result, none of these categories remain pure" (38). The
possibility of Gandhian, as opposed to nationalist, liberation is thus open:
a liberation that involves liberating even the oppressors from their inhuman condition as oppressors.

Only with such a recognition does dialogue—which Nandy sees as a
much more complex relationship than interchange between fundamentally separate entities—become possible. A dialogue between different societies' "utopias" embodies the exchange of mutual criticisms, the ability
to hear each other's criticisms and apply them to self-examination, and a
capacity to be self-reflexive about one's own criticisms of the other:

A utopia must be able to take criticisms from other utopias as if the
criticisms were partly undetermined by social, political and psychological forces. And it must be able to view its own criticisms of other utopias
and visions as at least partly determined by interests and/or drives. I like
to believe that this principle is Gandhian. In the 1920's, when feelings
were running high in British India because of the freedom movement,
Catherine Mayo wrote her savagely anti-Indian and pro-imperialist trea-
tise, *Mother India*. Gandhi called the book a "drain-inspector's report"

but added that every Indian should read it. While Mayo's critique of
Indian culture was blatantly prejudiced, he seemed to imply, Indian
culture should have the self-confidence to put her criticism to internal
use. (8)

Correspondingly, it was an advantage, rather than a sign of colonial domination and dependency, when Indians, as colonials, were forcibly, offen-
sively informed about metropolitan cultures and history, and not vice
versa. "While even the 'universal' Western visions of a good society do not
have to include India except peripherally as an object of study, charity or
experimentation," Nandy writes, "even the more parochial Indian visions
have to include some version of the West, either as internal ally or critic"
(6). What was traditionally a sign of the peripheral—lack of cultural coherence and autonomy, penetration by outside cultures—is in fact, once the
continuity between oppressor and oppressed is accepted, an advantage to
the postcolonial side when it comes to establishing dialogic relationships.
India's awareness of past interactions and present mutuality can then be
vastly richer than the West's. From this perspective, even the most corrosive postcolonial critique of the relationships between colonialism and the
construction of Ricoeur's universal scientific discourses can be a gift from a
more abundant "periphery" to a core victimized by its own colonial legacy, and not the blame of an oppressor by a victim.

Dialogues carried out in this way will, Nandy argues, enrich and change
both sides. Liberation will become as deterritorialized as Nandy has argued
the concept of the "West" is. In dialogue, neither side will be able to
totalize knowledge; no real dialogue will exist if one side commands "the
framework, tool or theory for understanding the other," and the other
serves "as the object of interpretation and as a reservoir of implicit or latent
insights which could be useful or enriching for the former" (14). Rather, a
dialogue "is supposed to involve parallel but interrelated processes of self-
confrontation in each culture or faith participating in it" (15). In this
respect, Nandy's faith in dialogue goes beyond mere relativism:

> It is easy to leave other cultures to their own devices in the name of
> cultural relativism, particularly if the visions of the future of these other
> cultures have already been cannibalized by the worldview of one's own.
> It is less easy to live with an alien culture's estimate of oneself, to inte-
> grate it within one's selfhood and to live with that self-induced inner
> tension. It is even more difficult to live with the inner dialogue within
> one's own culture which is triggered off by the dialogue with other
> cultures because, then, the carefully built cultural defences against dis-
> turbing dialogues—and against the threatening insights emerging from
> the dialogues—begin to crumble.

> Thus we come full circle. A dialogue of cultures—or of utopias, visions and faiths—is a dialogue within each participating culture among its different levels and parts. (17)

Just who/what the participants are in such dialogues, however, shifts unsystematically in Nandy's writing. In different places in his work, the different conversation partners are cultures, civilizations, premodern versus modern societies, or even the formerly colonized Third World versus the former colonial core. This slipperiness occurs even in the essay entitled "Towards a Third World Utopia." By far and away the bulk of Nandy's examples of fruitful dialogue are, moreover, Indian, and they equally evoke conversations between premodern and modern, East and West. When Nandy argues that the nondualism of Third World cultures allows them to abrogate the boundary line between oppressor and oppressed, he ascribes a prominent feature of Indian philosophical tradition (nondualism) to the whole Third World, explaining it as the result of a common historical experience of colonial victimization. A varied historical alliance, one suspects, is thus covertly appropriated by the ghost of Indian civilizational nationalism. With this warning, we can now proceed to put some flesh on Nandy's argument by citing a few examples of alternative visions that Nandy's premodern and/or civilizational partner could bring to its dialogue with the West.

The first element of the vision, which "many major civilizations in the third world have protected with care," is "refusal to think in terms of clearly opposed, exclusive Cartesian dichotomies" (31). As opposed to Fanon, Gandhi is thus a "non-player," not a "counter-player," in his anticolonialism (34). Second, while Western society mainly emphasizes productivity, and therefore establishes hierarchical relationships between the genders and between age groups, "many of the major Eastern civilizations, in spite of all their patriarchal elements, saw a continuity between the masculine and the feminine, and between infancy, adulthood and old age" (38). Reacting against the hypermasculinity inherent in the code of the colonizer, and likewise in the Indian nationalism formed in opposition to / imitation of that code, Gandhi thus posited "two alternative sets of relationships against the imperial ideology and its native versions. In one, masculinity was seen to be at a par with femininity and the two had to be transcended or synthesized for attaining a higher level of public functioning. . . . Gandhi's second model saw masculinity as inferior to femininity, which, in turn, was seen as inferior to femininity in man. (39)

A third example is the "non-dual vision of 'positive freedom': the cultural refusal in many parts of the savage world to see work and play as clearly demarcated modalities of human life" (42). Premodern cultures are often stigmatized as consisting of "indolent shirkers who could not match the hard work or single-minded pursuit of productive labour of the colonizers" (42). Nandy does not reject this stigma in favor of gestures of oppositional revolt, à la Fanon; instead, he finds oppositional strategy in such noncooperation and shirking. This practices the wisdom of the venerated *Bhagavad Gita:* "Who dares to see action in inaction / and inaction in action / he is wise, he is yogi / he is the man who knows what is work" (44).

A fourth example is the way "some third world societies" "resisted the oppression which comes as 'history'" (46). Western historiography, according to Nandy, depends on repression: the separation of acceptable historical narrative from unacceptable memory, and the repression of the latter. By contrast, Nandy remarks that

> the burden of history is the burden of such memories and anti-memories. Some cultures prefer to live with it and painfully excavate the anti-memories and integrate them as part of the present consciousness. Some cultures prefer to handle the same problem at the mythopoetic level. Instead of excavating for the so-called real past, they excavate for other meanings of the present, as revealed in traditions and myths about an ever-present but open past. The anti-memories at that level become less passionate and they allow greater play and lesser defensive rigidity. (47)

This position, Nandy goes on to note, collaborates (as indeed do all his positions) with contemporary Western self-critique:

> In their scepticism of history, the ahistorical cultures have an ally in certain recessive orientations to the past in the Western culture, which have re-emerged in recent decades in some forms of structuralism and psychoanalysis, in attempts to view history either as semiotics or as a "screen-memory," with its own rules of dream-work. As we well know, the dynamics of history, according to these disciplines, is not an unalterable past moving towards an inexorable future; it is in the ways of thinking and in the choices of present times. (48)

Finally, Nandy argues that even "the so-called dependency syndrome in some third world cultures" in fact represents something positive, in contrast to Fanon's and Césaire's criticism of Octave Manoni for "'dressing up' the old stereotype of the Negro as an overgrown child" (49–50). Indeed, instead of the independence Fanon would insist on,

> to the extent Manoni imputes to the Madagascan some degree of anti-individualism, to the extent the Madagascan is not a well-demarcated person, he unwittingly underscores the point that modern individualism

—and the insane search for absolute autonomy it has unleashed—
cannot be truly separated from the thirst for colonies, *lebensraum* and
domination for the sake of domination. In an interdependent world,
total autonomy for one means the reduction of the autonomy of others.
(50–51)

The fact that all of these positions—these examples of the visions of
other civilizations or premodern societies—are also First World self-
critiques is, for Nandy, no accident. It exemplifies his concept of dialogue.
These positions are not voices from an "other" but allies in the First World
"struggle for self-discovery," thus pairing intersocietal with intrasocietal
dialogues (55). Or as Gyan Prakash puts it in "Writing Post-Orientalist
Histories of the Third World" (1990), Nandy is one of a number of post-
Orientalist historiographers who speak

> within and to discourses familiar to the "west" instead of originating
> from some autonomous essence. . . . [This] does not warrant the conclu-
> sion that the third-world historiography has always been enslaved, but
> that the careful maintenance and policing of East-West boundaries has
> never succeeded in stopping the flows across and against boundaries and
> that the self-other opposition has never quite been able to order all
> differences into binary opposites. The third world, far from being con-
> fined to its assigned space, has penetrated the inner sanctum of the first
> world in the process of being "third-worlded"—arousing, inciting, and
> affiliating with the subordinated others in the first world. It has reached
> across boundaries to connect with the minority voices in the first world:
> socialists, radicals, feminists, minorities. (403)

What Nandy conceptualizes as dialogue, Prakash sees, in terms of the
sociology of knowledge, as indicating that the "formation of third-world
positions" in contemporary discourse represents "engagement rather
than insularity" (403).

Nandy's appealing vision of a world interconnected in dialogue with itself
depicts a synergism that resists zero-sum thinking. Each partner becomes
the other's ally in its "struggle for cultural self-discovery," and the "chilling
[because homogeneous] concept of One World which nineteenth-century
European optimism popularized" is avoided. Nandy's version of this process is doubtless too detached from ongoing geopolitical and economic
struggles to suit most as truth: it is, as he himself makes clear, a utopian
vision of a dialogue between utopias. Paul Ricoeur and others have argued,
however, that utopianism is necessary if we are to envision viable social
alternatives and counter Karl Mannheim's contention that it is impossible
to have a theory of ideology that is not ideological, to establish a counter-

position that is not part of the dominant game (Brantlinger 1990:83). Nandy's open-eyed analysis is thus an act of strategic fictionalizing.

Nandy does not, however, examine the terms that constitute his dialogue partners—civilization, culture, premodern society, Third World— very closely, and his shiftiness in not doing so allows him to suppress history. On the one hand, he makes Indian tradition and history the representative postcolonial norm, thereby suppressing present historical heterogeneity; on the other hand, he avoids seeing how the formations that constitute his dialogue partners are themselves historically constructed entities, the products of relationships of power. Also, although Nandy is extremely sensitive to what unequal or spurious dialogue sounds like, he does not link the production of true dialogues to the acquisition of geopolitical power by the partners. Indeed, he cannot, given his desire not to replicate Western hierarchies in his decolonization theory. On this point, Gyan Prakash's terminology seems much more subtle, although less utopian: Prakash describes the "formation of third-world positions" as part of a contest over knowledge, something that makes it clear that the construction of the conversation partners is itself a strategic construction, part of those relationships of power. Nandy is clear about how history has shaped what is spoken back to the West; he is not clear about how history has likewise shaped who (or, better, what entity) does that speaking.

Although Nandy explicitly distinguishes himself from Fanon, and is much more astute than Fanon in his criticism of homologous practices, he ultimately shares with both Fanon and Ngũgĩ a discourse built on an unresolved internal tension. From Fanon through Nandy, decolonization theory involves a covert tension between appeals to continuity with the localist past and the construction of new kinds of social forms and international communities for the future. Decolonization has remained a modern movement—sometimes an explicitly modernizing movement—even when it claims the authority of continuity with the past; its "neotraditionalism" exemplifies the same doubleness we have seen in "re-traditionalization." In decolonization theory as a whole, this ambiguity is vastly less a mystification than it has been in contemporary religious fundamentalism, or even much recent ethnic activism and nationalism. Traces of this mystification remain even in so critically self-aware a theory as Nandy's, however, and they mark the less self-aware conceptions of Ngũgĩ much more prominently. Prakash's contention that contemporary Indian historians are engaged in constructing "third-world positions" as a strategy in post-Orientalist historiographic discourse is more clear-sighted than Ngũgĩ's or Nandy's formulations. But, as Prakash's Foucaultian terminology shows, his version is influenced by a different conceptual model.

At the same time, there are significant changes in the course of this succession of theories. First, in moving from Fanon to Nandy, cultural nationalism's assertion of the separateness of separate cultures yields to a vivid perception of how cultures interact; revolutionary separatism is renounced in favor of dialogue—the maintenance of different positions by self-differentiating entities in a common discourse. Second, totalizing narratives of domination mutate slowly into awareness of reciprocity and possibilities for resistance in the colonial system. Self and other, or the One and the Other, systems of binary opposites, yield to a more complex awareness that each term is shaped by and helps shape the other. Third, the transformative analysis of domination/liberation and possession/ exorcism is changed into analyses of strategic maneuvers seeking to contest or productively alter an increasingly mutual discourse. Ngũgĩ's strategy of a heterogeneous alliance of embattled localisms is a conflicted, last-ditch attempt at maintaining the strong, separatist boundaries of cultural nationalism in an era of globalism. Nandy's call for dialogue represents a newer transgression and strategic crossing of boundaries, an approach as heterogenizing as it is heterogeneous, and one more sanctioned by the globalist present.

Nandy's dialogue does not go as far as other strategies do. It enforces, even as it transgresses, familiar Orientalist and anti-imperialist borders, by mobilizing unexamined terms like "culture," "civilization," "premodern," and "Third World" as signs of persisting cultural wholes. In now turning to a genealogy of postcolonial scholarship in ethnography, we shall examine a cultural interventionist movement that does not simply mobilize those terms but comes to see them as Prakash does: first, explicitly as historical constructions, the result of relations of power, and, second, as plural entities with chaotic borders, dissensual constructs not susceptible to totalization as wholes.

Patrick Wolfe's "On Being Woken Up: The Dreamtime in Anthropology and in Australian Settler Culture" (1991) is a handy starting point in a short narrative of postcolonial anthropology. The article gives a clear example, in anthropology, of the limitations of Said's *Orientalism* as it was notoriously first read—as an inherently pessimistic, totalizing narrative of colonial domination. Wolfe's critical description of Australian ethnography seeks to show how primordial connections in the colonial world were severed by colonialism, then utterly reconstructed in the anthropology colonialism brought with it. Further, Wolfe traces how recent indigenous cultural politics descend from and, unhappily, unconsciously continue that process of domination.

Wolfe begins by invoking notions of discourse and discursive formations to analyze, in new terms, the drama of cultural transformation and loss. He traces how the Australian aboriginal concept of dreamtime—a sign for many of a remarkable cultural survival, from which the First World, especially the New Age First World, can learn much—was really a creation of imperial anthropological discourse, an invention of the colonizer. The invention, moreover, served the colonizer's ends: in granting aborigines the parallel Australia of their supposed "dreaming," it licensed the colonialists' appropriation of the real one. The cycle has not subsequently been broken, Wolfe goes on to assert. The aboriginals today, he argues, have attempted (as Boelhower depicts American Indians doing) to deploy this construct in their own behalf, but have met with little success in their attempts at resistance, community building, and empowerment. In making these observations, Wolfe's analysis does not perpetrate the ambiguity we have seen in decolonization theory: he is clear throughout that contemporary resistance is resistance in the name of a culture that is already a hybrid creation, structured in large part on the basis of the interested interpretations of the colonial masters.

In Wolfe's pessimistic view, then, even the hybridized resistance of the aboriginals' anthropology-constructed "indigenous movement" fails. Worse, it is doomed to failure:

> [The] Kooris submission to anthropological language was the result of invasion rather than of cultural selection. With the spread of settlement, settler and Koori discourses merged. It follows that the isolation of anthropology for discrete analysis can only be a heuristic device. For as part of the discourse of colonial power, anthropology becomes an object of contestation for the colonised, who seek to appropriate it to their own advantage by turning it back upon their expropriators. In the process, however, the colonised acquiesce in the terms encoded within that discourse, whereby their collective self-assertion finds expression as a species of nationalism, which, in turn, encodes the progress-based rationale for colonisation. Thus the collective unity underlying the Koori (or "pan-Aboriginal") identity is itself the product of colonial conquest, which installed the prerequisite of a generalised other. More specifically, however, in adopting the twofold discursive structure of the Dreaming complex [which distinguishes origin—precontact idyll—and present circumstances—the continuance of present, dreaming aborigines in a ritual space that does not conflict with white settlement], Koori ideology recapitulates the familiar mythology of the nation state, which has an origin but is eternal. The irony of Koori's adoption of the Dreaming complex is, accordingly, a symptom of the containment, or relative powerlessness, of their discourse. (216)

In attempting to contest the dominant discourse, then, the Koori proceed according to assumptions that marginalize them; they thus cannot succeed with their project. Wolfe's analysis is an updating of Said's Orientalist domination for the era of ethnic resistance: even in it, anthropological discourse remains monolithic and monolithically allied to nationalism. It thus completely controls the Koori resistance, even as it completely reshapes that resistance in its image.

Others might respond that the Koori need to be more involved, not less, in anthropological discourse. The Koori's attempt to contest their oppressors' discourse is frustrated, not only by inequity of power, as Wolfe argues, but also (as Wolfe presents it) by a relative theoretical blindness and simplicity. Accepting what Nandy calls a nondialogic situation, they try to use what is imposed on them to resist, but in an uncritical way. They do not theorize the process of the imposition and the limitations of the imposed form. They remain trapped in homothetic opposition. Correspondingly, postcolonialism would argue that what they need is to develop counterdiscursive strategies. A Koori who participates with Wolfe on the level of theory—who mounts an Orientalist critique of anthropology in relation to Koori culture—would thus be another matter: he or she would be empowered within anthropological discourse, not haplessly shaped by it. Wolfe's pessimism depends, then, on the maintenance of the boundary lines of a familiar colonial intellectual economy: material for analysis is drawn from the periphery but manufactured into contemporary discourse in a closed conversation in the core.

Revelatory of this is the fact that Wolfe presents his analysis as the completion of a project begun by Talal Asad in "The Concept of Cultural Translation in British Social Anthropology" (1986). Although sharply critical of anthropological discourse and the falsely apparent neutrality of its concept of cultural translation, Asad's essay is, however, much more optimistic about the possibility of contesting discourse than Wolfe's. And it advocates a possibility that Wolfe does not consider—namely, incorporating the colonial subject into the anthropological conversation. Asad starts out with the same critique Wolfe makes: anthropology's translation of cultural matrices (matrices that are, as part of this act of translation, conceptualized as "implicit" or "unconscious") ignores the inequities of power between the First World of the investigator and the Third World of the native, and anthropology's complicity in them. The notion of cultural translation masks the assumption, by the translator, of "power to create meanings for a subject through the notion of the 'implicit' or the 'unconscious,' to *authorize them*." Furthermore,

> it remains the case that the ethnographer's translation/representation of a particular culture is inevitably a textual construct, that as representation it cannot normally be contested by the people to whom it is attri-

buted, and that as a "scientific text" it eventually becomes a privileged element in the potential store of historical memory for the nonliterate society concerned. In modern and modernizing societies, inscribed records have a greater power to shape, to reform, selves and institutions than folk memories do. They even construct folk memories. (Asad 1986:163)

For Asad, however, this critique does not portray a hopeless situation, but suggests a project. Asad is quick to point out the conditions necessary for genuinely critical analysis. The purpose of criticism is to "further a collective endeavor. Criticizing 'savages who are after all some distance away,' in an ethnographic monograph they cannot read, does not seem to me to have the same kind of purpose. In order for criticism to be responsible, it must always be addressed to someone who can contest it" (156). Self-reflexivity within anthropological discourse is necessary to alter it; the nonreciprocality between anthropological discourse and its objects of study is odious. Asad opposes a concept of translation from Walter Benjamin and Rudolf Pannwitz to the process of "forcible translation" anthropologists employ:

Our translations, even the best ones, proceed from a wrong premise. They want to turn Hindi, Greek, English into German instead of turning German into Hindi, Greek, English. Our translators have a far greater reverence for the usage of their own language than for the spirit of the foreign works. . . . The basic error of the translator is that he preserves the state in which his own language happens to be instead of allowing his language to be powerfully affected by the foreign tongue. (157)

Conventional anthropology thus parallels bad literary translation, in that "as social anthropologists we are trained to translate other cultural languages as texts, not to introduce . . . cultural capacities, learnt from other ways of living, into our own" (160). The distinction is between a monologue apart and a conversation with—between subjugation of the other's knowledge system and pluralizing one's own.

James Clifford has perhaps had the greatest visibility as a critic of ethnographic monologism. Linking such practices with colonial origins, he explores ways to push ethnography in new directions. In analyzing how ethnographic authority has recently been problematized, Clifford charts a series of developments in ethnographic writing, by invoking the theories of Mikhail Bakhtin:

A fundamental feature of the genre [of the novel], he [Bahktin] argues, is that it represents speaking subjects in a field of multiple discourses. The novel grapples with, and enacts, heteroglossia. For Bakhtin, preoccupied with the representation of non-homogenous wholes, there are no integrated cultural worlds or languages. All attempts to posit such abstract unities are constructs of monological power. A "culture" is, concretely, an open-ended, creative dialogue of subcultures, of insiders and outsiders, of diverse factions. (1988:46)

By putting "culture" in quotes, Clifford, who has also written about the way modern travel and electronic communictions have broken down international barriers, recognizes that the "cultures" are constructed from within and without, locally and globally; their construction is undertaken by insiders and outsiders, "natives" and "ethnographers," and is dissensual and dialogic. Representing a "culture," then, demands new techniques, and Clifford presents a series of these, such as the representation of culture dissensually through multiple informants; its representation through dialogue or a presentation of findings as the result of a process of dialogue between anthropologist and informants; and its representation by means of an expansion of the role of the native informant to the point where he or she became co-author of the ethnography. The result, for Clifford, is that ethnographic texts seek to become not just dialogic, but, like the "cultures" they study, polyphonic creations. Furthermore, as authorship is complicated, so must the implied reader be:

> It is intrinsic to the breakup of monologic authority that ethnographies no longer address a single general type of reader. The multiplication of possible readings reflects the fact that "ethnographic" consciousness can no longer be seen as the monopoly of certain Western cultures and social classes. Even in ethnographies lacking vernacular texts, indigenous readers will decode differently the textualized interpretations and lore. Polyphonic works are particularly open to readings not specifically intended. Trobriand readers may find Malinowski's interpretations tiresome but his examples and extended transcriptions still evocative. Ndembu will not gloss as quickly as European readers over the different voices embedded in Turner's works. (52)

Trinh Minh-ha's essay "The Language of Nativism" in *Woman, Native, Other* (1989) presents a still more corrosive and polemical analysis of the monologic authority of anthropology. The "science" of ethnography, she asserts, is "gossip," "a conversation of 'us' with 'us' about 'them' . . . in which 'them' is silenced. 'Them' always stands on the other side of the hill, naked and speechless" (67). To those who argue that anthropology is a part of an oppositional movement in the First World—a "noble defence of the native's cause" (57)—Trinh responds that "the Great Master [Bronislaw Malinowski] has made it clear: anthropology is a question of paying off old scores between white men" (57). What has "been written never addresses the Yellow, the Black, or the Red" (57). The "ideal set up by the Great

Master" is based on this monologism: it is, Malinowski wrote, "to grasp the native's point of view . . . to realize *his* vision of *his* world" (73). Drawing implicitly on *her* Third World identification, Trinh thus purports to voice the standpoint of the "native" (female) left out of this venally appropriative conversation. She finds contemporary attempts to refigure the discipline wanting: quoting Clifford Geertz's call to make anthropology "converse with them," she comments that one can see this as a refutation of the Great Master's ideal "if one turns a blind eye to the self-congratulating, patronizing (but refined) tone of this claim for a *conversation with them*" (73).

Trinh fuses the call for dialogue with self-reflexive criticism: contemporary postcolonial exposure of the colonial roots of ethnography with the perspective of the native answering back. She both answers and alters ethnography from within; her back talk as Third-World-identified writer is also ethnography's self-reflexive critique. Nowhere does this happen so effectively as when she turned what ethnography traditionally ascribes to the Other back on itself—and does so from a point not wholly apart from, but within the context of, ethnography's self-critique. The Great Master's ideal of grasping the native's point of view, not the peoples anthropologists describe, is cannibalistic and primitive: "Keeping such cannibal-anthropological rites in mind, one can only assent to the following remark by an African man: 'today . . . the only possible ethnology is the one which studies the anthropophagous behavior of the white man" (73). After casting the white man in the role of cannibal-subject and practitioner of rite, not science, she continues her satire by suggesting an interesting perspective for contemporary critiques of ethnography. The very lack of critical self-consciouness that produces traditional ethnographic authority—its faith that it, as master of "universal" scientific discourse represents reason and self-consciousness, investigating, in turn, "tacit" cultures incapable of self-conscious analysis, and its refusal to see these assumptions as a part of power relationships—means that ethnographers, not "natives," are the blind inhabitants of a tacit, unexamined culture. The pressure of the language of anthropology, she writes, lies "not so much in its systematization and argumentation as in its unconscious 'stickiness'" (76).

In place of such ethnography, Trinh advocates the development of a dialogic perspective, which would lead to an altogether new notion of knowledge. Monologic knowledge is an impossibility, for "how can he, indeed, read into the other knowing not how the other read into him?" (76) Trinh thus proposes a mode of "knowledge" that transcends the present "scientific" framework: "the other is never to be known unless one arrives at a *suspension* of language, where the reign of codes yields to a state of constant non-knowledge." As is characteristic of her counterdiscursive, but not separatist, opposition, she constructs her vision out of sources that range from Buddhist to (more usually) contemporary French theory. She acknowledges contributions, for example, even from "a thoughtful white man" (74), Roland Barthes.

Trinh's empowerment of herself as participant in current anthropological theory and critique, as well as as a "native" answering back, can be made even clearer when we realize her criticism of Geertz has been voiced as well by a "non-native," Paul Rabinow. Like Trinh, Rabinow criticizes Geertz, and also Clifford, for "failing to use self-referentiality as anything more than a device for establishing ethnographic authority" (1986) and for being insufficiently dialogic in their own practice. This criticism has prompted Christopher Miller to add that "dialogism as a mere *style* of representation must not be mistaken for genuine dialogue itself" (1990:28). The polycultural cosmopolitan Trinh thus consciously writes within the theoretical discourse of the West that attacks its roots at the same time she writes against it: indeed, she does the former so provocatively because she constructs the latter position so effectively. What she does *not* do is write as a ghettoized junior partner in a Western-refereed enterprise. She is referee as well as player.

Anthropology, Edward Said (1989) has argued, has been a particularly troubled site thanks to postcolonial awareness of historical relationships and disciplinary genealogies. This uncomfortable theoretical reappraisal is made in highly visible books like James Clifford and George Marcus's *Writing Culture: The Poetics and Politics of Ethnography* (1986) and Marcus and Michael Fischer's *Anthropology as Cultural Critique: An Experimental Moment in the Human Sciences* (1986), as well as in work by Johannes Fabian, Talal Asad, and others. Anthropology's "enabling moment," Said remarks, was the "ethnographic encounter between a sovereign European observer and a non-European native occupying, so to speak, a lesser status and a different place" (1989:205). Against this, Said calls for what Trinh Minh-ha enacts, an awareness of "Who speaks? For what and to whom?" (212). Similarly, Roland Robertson cites Geertz's recent (and rather more traditionally cultural pluralist) "conversion":

> Having been so influential with respect to the "thick" study of "the local" [Geertz 1983], Geertz now emerges as an advocate of a much more subtle and demanding practice. He speaks of the necessity to "enlarge the possibility of intelligible discourse between people quite different from one another in interest, outlook, wealth, and power, and yet contained in a world where, tumbled as they are into endless connection, it

is necessary to get out of one another's way" [Geertz 1988:147]. (Robertson 1992a:180)

But although anthropology has been an especially troubled discipline, the evolution of these strategies is by no means unique to it. Clifford's notion of representing culture polyphonically; Aschroft, Griffith, and Tiffin's celebration of Caribbean polyglossia; Michael Palencia-Roth's (1992) reinterpretation of civilizational encounters in Bakhtinian terms; and post-Orientalism's decomposition of monolithic colonialism into dissensual, heterogeneous, and nonsychronous activities at many sites all bear a family resemblance to one another, revealing important trends in postcolonial cultural studies today: the program of highlighting and transgressing cultural/intellectual boundaries, and the corresponding refusal of analytic totalization, of retotalizing culture in a new way.

World-systems and globalization theories, as they have moved from Wallerstein's centered system to theorizing a decentered global ecumene, have responded to both these currents in cultural study. Indeed, they have been challenged to do so by several sharp criticisms. Although he does not reproduce his criticisms of Wallerstein in *Culture and Imperialism*, Said has, in recent comments, been negative about world-systems theory, and an analogous critique has been made by John Tagg. In positively appraising the heterogeneity of post-*Orientalism* scholarship, Said writes that recent revisionary works are "valuable because they get beyond the reified polarities of the East vs. West kind, and in an untotalizing way they attempt some grasp of the heterogeneous and non-synchronous developments that have eluded the so-called 'world-historians' like Wallerstein, as well as the colonial Orientalists" (1986:63).

Elsewhere, Said surprisingly characterizes world-systems theory as productive of a new kind of essentialism (1990). He thereby misses the fact that Wallerstein is as relentless a critic of culturism and essentialism as he himself is. But Said's more searching criticism of world-systems theory as an analytic generalization that threatens to narrativize, and therefore totalize, the untotalizeable specificity of different cultural and historical interactions is articulated in more detail by John Tagg, who writes:

> I would still be resistant to the view that it is only empirical research that stands between us and a comprehensive account [of the dissemination globally of the particular cultural form of photography]. Quite bluntly, I would suggest that the very desire for such an account is tied to notions of social totality and historiographical representation that are untenable. If we are to talk of global systems, then we shall have to ask whether concepts of globalization can be separated from theoretical totalizations. (1991:156)

Tagg goes on to outline the untotalizeable complexity involved in the development of amateur photography as a discourse: one has to consider a welter of global and local factors, from the increasing integration of capitalist production to local copyright law, to technological, economic, and cultural upheavals, to the reconstitution of the family and sexuality, all of which can be regarded as constitutive conditions for its emergence. A localized (geographically, institutionally, disciplinarily, etc.) cultural practice, such as amateur photography in Japan, was, then, created from a heterogeneous variety of locally (nationally, regionally, etc.) and globally circulating (and interacting) political, economic, and cultural discourses. The global discourses, moreover, often circulate in a highly differentiated and nonsynchronous manner. Any attempt to construct a cultural world-systems map from this complexly unchartable, unpredictably mutating interactivity appears more and more to be futile.

As world-systems theory has been developed and changed to describe an increasingly less-centered global system, however, many of these criticisms have been acknowledged and incorporated. Certainly, the center of the world system has not held. More recent analyses of contemporary global interactions have narrated, not the consolidation of a hierarchical world system about Europe and then America, but the dispersal of such a system. Globalism has seemed increasingly differentiable from Eurocentrism or Americanism; globalization increasingly distinct from Westernization. But, more daringly, recent attempts to theorize the decentered world system have reconceived the notion of "system" altogether: they have attempted to describe a specifically "chaotic" order, one that is, in a strict sense, not totalizeable.

Antitotalization has become an issue in world-systems and globalization theory. Roland Robertson recently made one response to such critiques by trying to draw a fine line between the retention of a conceptual narrative and homogenizing totalization. His globalization theory he argues, describes the "exacerbation of collisions between civilizational, societal and communal narratives" that occurs as global compression increases. While postmodernism asserts an end to the notion of the master narrative and describes cultural and epistemological fragmentation, Robertson's globalization theory seeks to account for "heterogeneity, without reducing it to homogeneity" (1992:156). Arjun Appadurai, on the other hand, more fully incorporates postcolonial and postmodern knowledge-critique by arguing that the contemporary (postmodern) system has become so decentered it is no longer totalizeable in any conventional sense, and that the attempt to recount its narrative must, like Jean-François Lyotard's *The Postmodern Condition: A Report on Knowledge* (1979), present the case of a narrative of the evolution of circumstances that have meant the end of the production of stable, singular master narratives.

Recent thought in the tradition of globalization and world-systems theory has thus responded so significantly to Said's more recent formulations, for example, that it seems at times to provide precisely what he has lately called for. In the context of arguing against essentialisms of all sorts, Said calls for violation of the logics of borders, acknowledgment "of a world map without divinely or dogmatically sanctioned spaces, essences, or privileges" (1990:11) and argues that, as exile teaches, "literary [and cultural] experiences" overlap "with one another and [are] interdependent despite national boundaries and coercively legislated national autonomies" (14). To then recognize how history and geography have been "transfigured into new maps, new and far less stable entities, new types of connections" (14–15), Said calls (1990:16; 1993:318) for "a global and contrapuntal analysis" that is not "modeled (as earlier notions of comparative literature were modeled) on the notion of a symphony; rather we have more to do with atonal ensembles, and with such special or geographical and rhetorical practices as inflections, limits, constraints, intrusions, inclusions, prohibitions, all of them tending toward elucidations of a complex and uneven topography" (16). Said has thus come to offer a suggestive sketch for precisely the sort of contemporary transnational image or map that world-systems and globalization theories, in their sophisticated postnational phase, have sought to develop more fully. Indeed, they have gone disruptively further than Said, with his still-incensed appreciation of the continuing power of imperialist ideology and practice; they have attempted to theorize a world system so fragmented, on the one hand, and so complexly interactive on the other, that even Said's anticolonial, anticentrist critiques seem too centering, too indebted to the colonial narrative of boundaries between the West and the rest.

In the following two chapters, I discuss the short, but quite abundant, history of attempts to conceptualize the ongoing process of world interconnectedness in the past four decades systematically, focusing on the way these theories describe world culture. World-systems theory and its offshoots began with the centered world system of Wallerstein, but it soon strove to represent a more and more complexly decentered world. After Wallerstein's initial formulation, some, like Janet Abu-Lughod (1989), William McNeill (1990), and, most daringly and programmatically, André Gunder Frank (1991), have tried to read the concept back into premodern world history; correspondingly, others—including Wallerstein himself— have sought to revise his original world-systems theory to suit contemporary history. The result is that a plurality of world systems have been described. In the following chapters, then, I trace developments beyond *The Modern World System,* showing how a depiction of contemporary culture that violates most of the familiar postwar geographical, theoretical, and disciplinary boundaries has begun to emerge.

Part III

Culture in the Contemporary Global System

10

The Marxian Tradition

WHEN WALLERSTEIN FIRST formulated his world-systems theory, he revised the Marxian tradition in several ways. Compressing three worlds into one and disparaging the effectiveness of communist alternatives to the capitalist system, he created a theory of global capitalism that acknowledges nations and regions as important factors in the worldwide accumulation of capital. Other neo-Marxian globalist approaches have also been developed, so I begin my survey of conceptualizations of culture in the global system with an examination of neo-Marxian theory.

In his recent work, Wallerstein has elaborated on his earlier concept of the capitalist world system in several important ways. First, he focuses more explicitly than before on the role culture plays in the world system; second, he speculates about the present state and future prospects of the system. In "Culture as the Ideological Battleground," an essay in his *Geopolitics and Geoculture* (1991), Wallerstein applies Marx's famous distinction between base and superstructure, between "the material transformations of the economic conditions of production" and the "ideological . . . forms in which men become conscious of this conflict and fight it out" (Marx 1904:12) to the world system. Wallerstein argues that "culture" is a crucial ideological battleground for the modern world system. To conceptualize this process, he isolates two different definitions of the term: (1) "culture" meaning what distinguishes groups like nations from each other, and (2) "culture" meaning what creates distinctions within groups. Peoples have particular "cultures" (1); within one people, some, the elite, enjoy "culture" (2).

These two usages, Wallerstein argues, have no objective, material reality, but are "the consequence of the historical development of [the capitalist world] system and reflect its guiding logic" (1991:32). They serve to mystify people about the real nature of the system's contradictions and thereby help keep it firmly in place. Wallerstein shows how this process operates by charting the way two particular ideologies, the "ideologies of

universalism and of racism-sexism," work in the world system. These ideologies use the two notions of culture to keep the underlying system intact. Universalism serves as a "palliative and deception" to mask the "hierarchy of states within the interstate system and a hierarchy of citizens
within each sovereign state" (43). It simultaneously holds out the false
promise of equality for all and validates those at the top of the hierarchy as
the possessors of the "universal" culture. Correspondingly, racism-sexism
legitimizes inequality and hierarchy by creating invidious group distinctions on the interstate and intrastate levels that rank groups and classes
within societies and national cultures globally.

To these purely system-created differences, Wallerstein adds another
order of system-created difference, which we shall examine shortly: that of
"antisystemic movements" that are also "a product of the system" (51).
Both systemic and antisystemic deployments of culture are thus, first,
products of the overall system and, second, processes that tend toward its
increasing differentiation. What is crucial is that Wallerstein conceptualizes the world as a single system that does not homogenize, but systematically produces a number of orders of cultural difference, laying the cornerstone of contemporary thought about globalization's effect on culture,
not as the effacement of separate cultures by a homogenizing hegemony,
but as the manufacture of new orders of cultural difference by a system
that has already included everyone.

Wallerstein's vision of this process can serve as a baseline against which
to assess more radical conceptions of culture in the world system. First,
Wallerstein sees culture as an essential element in the traditional world-
systems tendency toward totalization in a centered hierarchy; the mystifying, but essentially differential, process of culture works to mask and maintain the hierarchy of a system that has a core, a semiperiphery, and a
periphery based on economic power. Second, Wallerstein puts fundamental emphasis, globally, on national culture: just as the "political superstructure" of the world system is "the network of 'sovereign states'" (1991:107),
so the basic cultural units that the system constructs and deploys are
national. Finally, for Wallerstein, culture is superstructural: it is produced
by and a handmaiden of the system. As we survey the development of
counterpositions to Wallerstein and the privileging of decentered, fragmented, postmodern heterogeneity encountered in cultural studies, we
shall find all three of these propositions attacked. The global cultural system appears more and more decentered and untotalizeable; a welter of
other units than nation-states significantly mediates culture; and what
Janet Wolff has called Wallerstein's (and other globalists') "pretheoretical" status with regard to developments in cultural theory is sup-

planted by conceptions that stress "culture as *representation*" and more clearly foreground "the *constitutive* nature of [such] representation" (Wolff 1991:170, 171).

But it would be grossly unfair to portray Wallerstein as blind to these various challenges to his theorization of the world system. Indeed, he has recently been extremely responsive to the many changes in the global system—and the cultural ferment they have produced, or been produced by—that cultural analysts focus on. He accommodates these changes by attributing them to a break in the history of the world system, which, in an optimistic reading, may both foretell and mediate its end. The totalizing system we have known since the 1500s may well be drawing to a close, and Wallerstein (writing at times with a hint of a prophetic ardor, a significant change from the dense empirical texture and apparent fatalism of *The Modern World System*) sees some possibility of dramatic positive change, as well as of disaster, in the approaching end. The messianic aspect of Marx that he has been criticized for excluding from his former systematization of the world has resurfaced in his drama—grander than Marx's because more genuinely global—of the end of the world system.

Wallerstein asserts resoundingly, to start with, that "U.S. global hegemony, a brief phenomenon, as have been previous such hegemonies, . . . is now over" (20). In this process, Japan appears "to be playing the same role today *vis-à-vis* the United States that the United States played *vis-à-vis* Great Britain" (20). This mutation of the system has occurred via three cyclical shifts. First, there has been a shift in the location of "core-periphery links in commodity chains": in these chains "corelike processes" were partial monopolies and "peripheral processes" were "ones in which market competition is maximal (and profit levels low)" (39). Second, a shift from an A- to B-phase in the Kondratieff long wave has occurred in the present era: markets have become saturated with too much competition and capital accumulation rates have fallen, and everything has pushed "toward contraction but also, of course, towards the search for the creation of new monopolistic centers" (40). In a middle-run perspective, Wallerstein argues that these new centers will involve "microprocessing and all its potential product packaging, biogenetics, and new energy sources" (43). These will breathe new life into the old system for a while. The third cyclical shift has been between "moments of hegemony in the interstate system and periods of rivalry. . . . True hegemony is the achievement by one strong state of a high concentration of economic monopolies, which then undergird other kinds of power" (40). Wallerstein predicts that as new attempts at hegemony form, the United States will align itself with Japan and Asia (increasingly as a junior partner to the former) and a united Europe will align itself with the countries of eastern Europe and the former Soviet Union. This new form of hegemony will not, however, allow for the "Europe-based universalistic ideology" culturally that accompanied British hegemony in the nineteenth century; it cannot, because "the very point of this civilizational reassertion [the reassertion of non-European civilizations] is its multiplicity . . . [which] has been part of interstate relations since the conference of Bandung" (45).

Wallerstein thus seems to forecast the emergence of a new cultural hegemony, the global capitalist culture of consumer-oriented multiculturalism that Stuart Hall has described. Wallerstein suggests, moreover, that this culture might be grounded, not in American neocolonialism, but in its decay and the emergence of a new geopolitical order that promotes the violation of old cultural as well as political boundaries. But Wallerstein does not pursue these speculations, because he is really much more interested in the other side of Hall's coin, the new oppositional culture produced by contemporary globalism. The reason for this interest is that in *Geopolitics and Geoculture,* Wallerstein is vastly less concerned with the middle-run prospect of changes within the capitalist world system than he is with the forecastable transformation of the overall system into something else. In this the crucial issue is "not the decline of the West following its rise; it is the transformation of our current world-system into a different form (or forms) of historical system" (45). The new oppositional cultural movements ultimately provide the best index of such an epochal change.

This transformation is foreseeable because, thanks to changes in the economic base, the present system will soon exhaust the mechanisms it needs to resolve its periodic crises. The system cannot, structurally speaking, survive. Although in the past it has overcome economic downturns by the creation of new monopolistic sectors—made possible by increased commodification—this process cannot go much further in an almost completely commodified world. In the past, the system overcame divisions between classes by increasing contractualization of political processes "as democratization, and as the strengthening of state structures within an ever more codified interstate system," but with the end of nation formation and the achievement of state power by Marxian and nationalist opposition movements, it has exhausted these resources; it can no longer use such "progress" any longer to cope with or mask the increasingly polarizing inequities of capitalist exploitation. Wallerstein also occasionally mentions ecological limitations as a similar factor: his point is that the world system's mechanisms for crisis-resolution can no longer keep the system going.

This analysis underlies Wallerstein's interest in the current generation of oppositional movements, which, he feels, are more radically anti-systemic than earlier movements that dreamed of consolidating state power. Like traditional Marxism and revolutionary nationalism, the newer generation of antisystemic movements were produced by the system, but they can never, like their predecessors become merely "part of the cyclical renewal of the capitalist world-economy" (42) by temporarily resolving its contradictions. The new generation of leftist movements—which formed itself as much against the older generation of the left (styling that generation as part of the problem, not the solution) as it did against the system itself—will not only never serve, as previous opposition did, to resolve the system's contradictions; it may just hold the promise of something new.

In describing the variety of the new movements (only some of which are postmodern), Wallerstein casts his net at least as widely as Hall, Lisa Lowe, and Abdul JanMohamed and David Lloyd do in their descriptions of heterogeneous cultural alliances between oppositional groups. Born in the events of the 1968 "revolution in the world system" (Wallerstein 1991:65–83), the new movements have developed from the groups that old class- and nation-based oppositional politics attempted to marginalize and told to wait for their revolution. They include "the unfulfilled nationalities for socialist movements, women for both kinds of movements, and any other group that could lay claim to political oppression" (72); the reform and extra-party movements that have more recently emerged in socialist countries like Russia and eastern Europe; issue-based movements like ecological activists; and groups advocating the resurgence of civilizational or even fundamentalist religious identity. In not seeking power through state structures, and in their very heterogeneity, many of these represent something new and unpredictable. Indeed, Wallerstein's vision of their yoked heterogeneity is so boundary-violating, it includes, as Lowe's, JanMohamed's, and Lloyd's alliances perhaps would not, groups traditionally seen as being on the right.

Wallerstein's version of the postmodern politics of heterogeneity fuses traditional messianic hope with postmodern uncertainty. The end of the system may yield atomic devastation or transformation into a new system or multiplicity of separated systems at least as exploitative as the old; it may also initiate the creation of a juster and more humane system. Wallerstein formulates a characteristically historicist answer to the disputes raging in cultural studies. To describe the end of the existing world system and the birth of a new era, he draws on the new science of chaotics and relegates traditional Marxism to a previous period, styling it part of the cultural logic of the capitalist system. He thereby incorporates the theoretical ferment of contemporary cultural study into a particular historical phase of the decline of the capitalist world system. Following Ilya Prigogine and Isabelle Stengers (1984), Wallerstein sees the capitalist world system as leaving a phase of relative stability and approaching a bifurcation point. Prigogine and Stengers argue that chaos theory introduces "*history* into physics and chemistry" (234). "Scientists are saying today that systems move away from equilibrium states and that, when they do, bifurcation replaces linearity, bifurcation being defined simply as 'the appearance of a new solution of the equations for some critical value'" (234). Natural laws, and the equations that embody them, are thus historically produced and historically changed; and the regularities of a state of equilibrium are neither "natural" nor universal. Chaos is the more fundamental norm. Wallerstein locates this drama in his world system by arguing that its approaching bifurcation point will produce a similar crisis, change, and revelation; as the systemic crisis—bifurcation point—approaches, the false equilibrium on which conventional visions of order have been constructed will vanish, and chaos, the more fundamental "structure," will be revealed. The crucial human concomitant to such moments is that in them, at last, "human will has wide scope and therefore historical choices are real and not manipulated" (48). For this prophetic translation from the "natural" sciences, Wallerstein looks to the new antisystemic movements, which are the harbingers of the bifurcation point.

Wallerstein's appeal to chaotics is no more singular or idiosyncratic than his version of the postmodern politics of heterogeneity. Indeed, in her book *Before European Hegemony* (1989), Janet Abu-Lughod reads interest in decentered world systems back into the medieval period, seeing that era as revelatory of the fact that "no system is fully integrated" and therefore totalizeable:

> Instead, the theories of chaos (recently described by [James] Gleick) may be more pertinent. In world systems, as in weather systems, small localized conditions may interact with adjacent ones to create outcomes that might not otherwise have occurred, and large disturbances may sometimes flutter to an end while minor ones may occasionally amplify wildly, depending upon what is happening in the rest of the system. (369)

Wallerstein rescues his centered, Euclidean description of the capitalist world system by seeing it as a local historical equilibrium, governed by the Newtonian laws it has created, and revealing, in its end only, the strange, exciting, non-Euclidean possibilities chaotics describes. Abu-Lughod more radically theorizes these chaotic properties as a part of *all* world-systems, taking her more obviously decentered medieval world system as the norm. This is not surprising in a world-systems theorist responding still more strongly than Wallerstein to the ferment of contemporary cultural studies. We shall later encounter a highly sophisticated version of this approach in Arjun Appadurai's theorization of the contemporary global cultural economy. What Wallerstein defers to the prophetic future and firmly distinguishes from middle-run developments, Appadurai locates in the increasingly decentered, globalized present; what Wallerstein requires his system to end to get to, Appadurai and Abu-Lughod see as features of ongoing world orders.

Before we reencounter these questions, however, we should spend some time looking at the ways in which a second extension of the Marxian tradition conceptualizes global culture. Again, we encounter an ultimately centered and totalizing theorization of culture in relation to the present world system, but one that is more subtle than Wallerstein's can be in its ability to describe specific cultural products.

Fredric Jameson links his analysis of postmodern culture directly to the Marxian master narrative: postmodern aesthetic style is the cultural dominant of a new phase of capitalism. In a short talk on cognitive mapping, Jameson juxtaposes literary modernism's relationship to the colonial world system it was embedded in to postmodernism's relationship to the contemporary world system. Modernism's attempt to deal with the scarcely representable realities of the imperial system—the colonial system in which the truth of "limited daily experience of London lies, rather, in India, or Jamaica, or Hong Kong"—meant developing figures, like the relativization of character's consciousness, to try to represent the unrepresentable "absent cause" of imperial social experience (Jameson 1988:350). Postmodernism, by contrast, faces

> The moment of the multinational network, or what [Ernest] Mandel calls "late capitalism," a moment in which not merely the older city but even the nation-state itself has ceased to play a functional and formal role in a process that has in a new quantum leap of capital prodigiously expanded beyond them, leaving them behind as ruined and archaic remains of earlier stages in the development of this new mode of production. (1988:350)

This new stage of capitalism has been accompanied by a sea change in literary representation, the development of postmodernist style. Jameson describes its peculiarities as

> symptoms and expressions of a new and historically original dilemma, one that involves our insertion as individual subjects into a multidimensional set of radically discontinuous realities, whose frames range from

the still surviving spaces of bourgeois private life all the way to the unimaginable decentering of global capital itself. Not even Einsteinian relativity, or the multiple subjective worlds of the older modernists, is capable of giving any kind of adequate figuration to this process which in lived experience makes itself felt by the so-called death of the subject, or, more exactly, the fragmented and schizophrenic decentering and dispersion of this last (which can no longer even serve the function of the [Henry] Jamesian reverberator or "point of view). (1988:351)

On the one hand, then, postmodern style represents radical, postnational decentering. "The unimaginable decentering of global capital" is visible in it. The new world system produces a "fragmented, heterogenous cultural style" assembled from the circulation of decontextualized cultural fragments, pried loose from their origins and derealized, and creates equally decentered, fragmented subjects. As Jameson puts it in his essay "Postmodernism, or, The Cultural Logic of Late Capitalism":

If the ideas of a ruling class were once the dominant (or hegemonic) ideology of bourgeois society, the advanced capitalist countries today are now a field of stylistic and discursive heterogeneity without a norm. Faceless masters continue to inflect the economic strategies which constrain our existences, but no longer need to impose their speech (or are henceforth unable to); and the postliteracy of the late capitalist world reflects, not only the absence of any great collective project, but also the unavailability of the older national language itself. (Jameson 1984:65)

On the other hand, this fragmentation and decentering is a result of the capitalist system having entered a new stage, marking a "dialectical expansion over the previous stage"—in other words, an increase in the systematicity of the world (1984:78). Jameson cites Ernest Mandel's description of three eras of "technological revolution within capital itself":

The fundamental revolution in power technology—the technology of the production of motive machines by machines—thus appears as the determinant moment in revolutions in technology as a whole. Machine production of steam-driven motors since 1848; machine production of electric and combustion motors since the 90s of the last century; machine production of electronic and nuclear-powered apparatuses since the 40s of the 20th century—these are the three general revolutions in technology engendered by the capitalist mode of production since the "original" industrial revolution of the later 18th century. (1984:77–78)

Jameson then related these stages to three "fundamental movements in capitalism, each one marking a dialectical expansion over the previous stage: these are market capitalism, the monopoly stage or the stage of imperialism, and our own—wrongly called postindustrial, but what might be better termed multinational capital" (1984:78). He goes on to describe this new stage in terms of the extension of the capitalist system and the elimination of enclaves within it:

> I have already pointed out that Mandel's intervention in the postin-
> dustrial involves the proposition that late or multinational or consumer
> capitalism, far from being inconsistent with Marx's great 19th-century
> analysis, constitutes on the contrary the purest form of capital yet to
> have emerged, a prodigious expansion of capital into hitherto uncom-
> modified areas. This purer capitalism of our own time thus eliminates
> the enclaves of precapitalist organization it had hitherto tolerated and
> exploited in a tributary way: one is tempted to speak in this connection
> of a new and historically original penetration of Nature and the Uncon-
> scious: that is, the destruction of precapitalist third world agriculture by
> the Green Revolution, and the rise of the media and the advertising
> industry. At any rate, it will also have been clear that my own cultural
> periodization of the stages of realism, modernism and postmodernism is
> both inspired and confirmed by Mandel's tripartite scheme. (1984:78)

In *Postmodernism, or, The Cultural Logic of Late Capitalism* (1991), a significant expansion of the argument of his earlier essays, Jameson develops
and further specifies his stage theory in several ways. First, Jameson rephrases and reemphasizes his argument that the new stage of capitalism
that has produced postmodernism eliminates enclaves of precapitalist organization. Modernism arose in a time of incomplete modernization, a
time when "realities from radically different moments of history" coexisted (Jameson 1991:307). With the advent of late capitalism and postmodernism,

> the survival, the residue, the holdover, the archaic, has finally been
> swept away without a trace. In the postmodern, then, the past itself has
> disappeared (along with the well-known "sense of the past" or historici-
> ty and collective memory). Where its buildings still remain, renovation
> and restoration allow them to be transferred to the present in their
> entirety as those other, very different and postmodern things called
> *simulacra*. Everything is now organized and planned; nature has been
> triumphantly blotted out, along with peasants, petit-bourgeois com-
> merce, handicraft, feudal aristocracies and imperial bureaucracies. Ours
> is a more homogeneously modernized condition; we no longer are en-
> cumbered with the embarrassment of non-simultaneities and non-
> synchronicities. Everything has reached the same hour on the great
> clock of development or rationalization (at least from the perspective of
> the "West"). This is the sense in which we can affirm, either that modern-
> ism is characterized by a situation of incomplete *modernization,* or that
> postmodernism is more modern than modernism itself. (1991:309–10)

Second, Jameson makes it clearer than ever before that postmodernism
is probably a transitional stage between two larger eras:

The postmodern may well in that sense be little more than a transitional period between two stages of capitalism, in which the earlier forms of the economic are in the process of being restructured on a global scale, including the older forms of labor and its traditional organizational institutions and concepts. That a new international proletariat (taking forms we cannot yet imagine) will reemerge from this convulsive upheaval needs no prophet to predict: we ourselves are still in the trough, however, and no one can say how long we will stay there. (1991:417)

In their book *The End of Organized Capitalism* (1987), the economists Scott Lash and John Urry follow Jameson, making use of his work, but presenting a somewhat different, more complexly multifactoral economic, political, and cultural analysis of the decentering of the First World from within. Rather than extend the Marxian narrative by arguing that it has continued into a new, more comprehensive phase, they describe the changed present as a crucial rupture within that narrative. They argue that the era of what they call "organized capitalism"—capitalism that fits the Marxian model and produces organized forms of economic and political control and an organized class structure—has given way to what they called "disorganized capitalism." They describe the process as follows: "Toward the end of the nineteenth century, organization—via the concentration of capital—in the economy occurs, followed rapidly by the organization of classes and their interest organization in civil society; organization of the state follows much later, typically between the two world wars" (7). Subsequently, in the First World, capital, civil society, and the state have become progressively deorganized, thanks to a variety of factors, ranging from the dispersion and deindustrialization of First World economies and the rise of the service class to "an increase in cultural fragmentation and pluralism, resulting both from the commodification of leisure and the development of new political-cultural forms since the 1960's" (6–7). Globally, these developments are abetted by factors like the increase in the number of nation-states implicated in capitalist production, the growth of a world market that has meant that "national markets have become less regulated by nationally based corporations," and "increasing independence of large monopolies from direct control and regulation by individual nation-states" (5).

Lash and Urry's analysis of the disorganization of capital thus revises the Marxian master narrative differently than Jameson and Mandel do. Although their analyses echo each other in many ways, Lash and Urry's emphasis is on decentering fragmentation in the structure of the economic system, as well as social and cultural systems, rather than increasing coherence in the economic system accompanied by social and cultural fragmentation. But in describing culture, Lash and Urry ground a presupposition of Jameson's theory of postmodernism even more specifically than Jameson does. Postmodern culture is not the dominant of a new phase of global capitalism; it is, in Lash and Urry, more specifically than in Jameson, a First World phenomenon, attached, moreover, to a particular class. As regards the economic base, Lash and Urry argue, "the spread of capitalism into most Third World countries" was founded on "the basic extractive/manufacturing industries (such as steel, coal, oil, heavy industry, and automobiles," which "in turn has shifted the industrial/occupational structure of the First World economies toward 'service' industries and occupations" (6). This service class, created now, not by the development of underdevelopment in the Third World, but by the exportation of a surpassed stage of First World development to it, has, Lash and Urry argue, become the locus of postmodern culture.

Relying explicitly on Jameson and Jean-François Baudrillard for a description of postmodernism, Lash and Urry contend that it is simultaneously embedded in the underlying structure of the service class, consumed by it, and part of its hegemonic enterprise:

> Our central claims in this section will be that it is the developing service class which is the consumer *par excellence* of post-modern cultural products; that there is a certain "hegemonizing mission" of the post-modern tastes and lifestyle of significant sections of this new middle class; and that there are certain structural conditions of the service class that produce a decentred identity which fosters the reception of such post-modern cultural goods. (292)

Using Pierre Bourdieu's schema, Lash and Urry argue that this class has a preeminently "destructured and decentered habitus" (296); it is, therefore, part of the disorganizing forces of contemporary capitalism, not consolidatable into a class in the traditional sense of a bounded group with common interests and identity. Television, for example, undercuts both grid and group (common classificatory schema for and boundaries to distinguish what is internal from what external to a collectivity) by minimizing

> the importance of these separate and distinct information systems both through exposing individuals of all groupings to the general information system and through giving each age, gender, class grouping a chance to see the intimate spaces of the lives of other groupings, a chance which otherwise would not have been available. In addition of course, isolation in one's living room will have a negative effect on the solidification of collective identity. (297)

In invoking Bourdieu, Lash and Urry's analysis is not only an extension of Marxian economics and adaptation of postmodernist cultural studies, it also incorporates the rapidly growing field of the sociology of postmodernization. Drawing on a wide spectrum of work by analysts like Bourdieu, Charles Jencks, and Mike Featherstone, Hans-Georg Betz has recently surveyed existing theories of the postindustrial, or information, society. Betz underscores, in a slightly more globalist vein, the symbiosis between economic and cultural disorganization. Noting that Charles Jencks was one of the first to try to conceptualize postmodernization and culture comprehensively, Betz summarizes Jencks's theories:

> He saw the most important characteristic of the postmodern world in a shift from industrial to post-industrial/information society and in the cultural shift from modernism to postmodernism. Among its main characteristics he saw a movement from centralized mass production to decentralized individualized production, from integrated mass cultures to a myriad of "taste cultures," from national consciousness to a mixture of global consciousness and regional identification, together with the "revolutionary growth" of a new class of white-collar workers, occupied with the generation, management and control of information. (Betz 1992:98)

Although Lash and Urry describe the development of the new phase of capitalism differently than Jameson, and although they place postmodern culture more specifically in this new system than Jameson, their description of the postmodern cultural style itself derives in great part from Jameson. Moreover, they follow him in seeing postmodern culture as constitutive of social relations in a way that culture previously was not. The awareness of the constitutive power of culture that Janet Wolff (1991) finds lacking in Wallerstein is thus foregrounded and seen as the product of a recent historical development. Jameson argues that the new multinational phase of capitalist production has colonized the unconscious and nature, thereby encompassing enclaves previously defended from it. Lash and Urry add that

> with the sea change in modern society, in which large organizations, workplaces and cities are of diminishing significance for each individual, the processes of forming, fixing, and reproducing "subjects" is increasingly "cultural," formed of available "life-styles" not at all based on where one lives or whom one knows, that is, on those who are immediately present. (15)

Yet in all these versions, from the perspective of a student of globalization, postmodernism is surprisingly traditionalizing in a number of ways. To so specifically locate postmodernism in a service class, which is itself located in the First world, is, paradoxically, to center postmodernism's decentering: it centers postmodernism globally, for it shows how, in culture, as in economic development, the First World is a step ahead of the Third on the developmental timeline. Although Jameson has been a sharp critic of both postmodern culture and late capitalism, he makes this implication similarly inevitable. In seeing postmodern culture as the dominant for an emerging new phase of global capitalism, and in his emphasis on postmodernism as depending on completed modernization, Jameson necessarily invokes the developmental timeline that puts the First World "ahead" of the Third.

Postmodernism's decentered fragmentation, its transcendence of collective identities such as class- or nation-state membership, its global heterogeneity, and its less tacit, more explicitly "cultural" constitution, all mark it out as a decentering movement globally. But as avant-garde as Jameson's and Lash and Urry's descriptions of the postmodern style sound, and as reasonable as it seems to place such a social formation at the forefront of world development, these formulations still center the global system about a (paradoxically) decentered core. And they reinscribe the developmental timeline, not as a nationalist emergence of increasing self-sufficiency, of the increasing integrity of national development, but as the postnationalist unraveling of national coherence—as an advance into an era in which both national and class structures are of the past. Both elements were visible in comments that Jameson made in an interview with Anders Stephanson. Arguing that "the proletariat of the first world is now in the third world," he reaffirmed the global centrism of Wallerstein; commenting that "the control of national space may itself be an outmoded idea in a situation of multinationals," Jameson indicated that the preoccupation he has famously ascribed to Third World literature, the recurring creation of national allegories, marks it as "behind" the First in its development. Indeed, these subtle, but real biases are precisely what lies at the heart of the now-famous dispute between Jameson (1986) and Aijaz Ahmad (1987) about Jameson's article theorizing Third World literature as literature of national allegory.

In "Third World Literature in the Era of Multinational Capitalism," Jameson outlines two possible scenarios for using the term "Third World" as (faute de mieux) an analytic category for literary criticism. One approach, which he chose not to pursue in that essay, would have been to concentrate on the literary "backwardness" of what Jameson calls "non-canonical" Third World literature:

> Nothing is to be gained by passing over in silence the radical difference of non-canonical texts. The third-world novel will not offer the satisfac-

tions of Proust or Joyce; what is more damaging than that, perhaps, is its tendency to remind us of the outmoded stages of our own first-world cultural development and to cause us to conclude that "they are still writing novels like Dreiser or Sherwood Anderson." (Jameson 1986:65)

These are hard words, potentially offensive to Third World critics. Jameson's apparent lack of accommodation of such an audience is, of course, partly explained by the fact that the essay was originally a lecture given in the United States; still, the fact that the American academy was on its way to considerable pluralization, and that that process has influenced greatly its discourse about literature, marks out as important the "hardness" of both these words and the persistent "we"-"they" framework Jameson uses throughout the essay. Such considerations may be mitigated, although not effaced, by placing this fragment back in the context of the overall essay: Jameson's ultimate purpose is to express intelligent sympathy with "third-world literature" and to argue that it has something to teach, something to hold up against the comparative political unconsciousness of First World productions in the era of postmodernism.

As noted, Jameson makes it clear that he does not choose in this essay to explore the implications of the assertion that Third World literature seems to "remind us of the outmoded stages of our own first-world cultural development." Reserving this topic for later exploration, he picks a second focus, on hierarchy, not timeline. Analyzing Third World writing as a literature of "subalternity," he contends, will illuminate much that First World literature, by contrast, mystifies.

In choosing this focus, Jameson, like Wallerstein, sees the "Third World" as a construct of international power relations, not a set of autonomous cultures. Given this awareness, Jameson is cautious about retaining the term "Third World" at all. He does so only, he says, because there is no "comparable expression that articulates, as this one does, the fundamental breaks between the capitalist first world, the socialist bloc of the second world, and a wide range of other countries which have suffered the experience of colonialism and imperialism" (67). The reason for Jameson's caution was the difficulty created by the model of separate cultures that underlay the term: "Any articulation of radical difference—," he writes, "that of gender, incidentally, fully as much as that of culture—is susceptible to appropriation by that strategy of otherness which Edward Said . . . called 'orientalism'" (77). This defect—the conscious or unconscious reliance on Orientalist assumptions—does not, moreover, depend on whether "the radical otherness of the culture in question is praised or valorized" (77).

In short, Jameson knew he was walking a minefield. Presumably he did so in the hope that he would not append radical difference to positive or negative, colonialist or liberationist Orientalism, but keep it consciously foregrounded as a socioeconomic construct. The risk was worth taking, because "I don't see how a first-world intellectual can avoid this operation without falling back into some general liberal and humanistic universalism: it seems to me that one of our basic political tasks lies precisely in the ceaseless effort to remind the American public of the radical difference of other national situations" (77).

Jameson's retention of "radical difference" (as opposed to other sorts of difference) became part of an important dispute with Aijaz Ahmad. Jameson sought to transport the concept of radical difference out of Orientalism and into political economy, and to make it a reflection of power relations rather than primordial cultures. Maintaining that the difference is "radical," however—that there are a clearly demarcated "we" and "they," and that "national situations" differ rather than interrelate—led Jameson to make surprisingly culturalist comments in writing about specific literary traditions. For example, in commenting on Lu Hsün's story "Medicine," Jameson assembles a vision of Chinese culture that is not a "theory of Chinese culture," to be sure, but a "methodological example"; what makes it the latter, however, is not the impropriety of theories of national culture, but the fact that Jameson is not a "specialist" (72). Jameson then constructs a vision of "Chinese culture" as libidinously fixated on the oral stage, citing examples from sex manuals, culinary tradition, and language (the verb "to eat" in Chinese is, Jameson says, put to multiple uses). Although he does not ascribe this pattern to a primordial essence, he performs the same consolidative operations as those who do by discerning in heterogeneous evidence a single, buried pattern and making it representative of a whole culture, thereby valorizing the notion of cultural wholes.

But much more important than these lapses is the strictness of Jameson's we-they distinction, something that elicits sopisticated dismay from Ahmad. In the process, it creates a fascinating test case of how a smallish shift in models for the world might necessitate a rather large shift in cultural interpretation.

If what constitutes the term "third world" for Jameson is the historical experience of colonialism and imperialism—the experience of subalterneity—what differentiates different sites within that category depends basically on that history. Accordingly, Jameson theorizes that significant difference between Third World countries depends not so much on a concept of the survival of different indigenous traditions as on a particular version of the original colonial encounters. How a Third World area entered the capitalist world system was foundational and determinative, and this entrance is interpreted through Marxian mode-of-production analysis. The distinctions it authorizes are gross and strongly marked ones:

> The initial distinction that imposes itself has to do with the nature and
> development of older cultures at the moment of capitalist penetration,
> something it seems to me most enlightening to examine in terms of the
> marxian concept of modes of production. Contemporary historians
> seem to be in the process of reaching a consensus on the specificity of
> feudalism as a form which, issuing from the break-up of the Roman
> Empire or the Japanese Shogunate, is able to develop directly into cap-
> italism. This is not the case with the other modes of production, which
> in some sense must be disaggregated or destroyed by violence, before
> capitalism is able to implant its specific forms and displace the older
> ones. In the gradual expansion of capitalism across the globe, then, our
> economic system confronts two very distinct modes of production that
> pose two very different types of social and cultural resistance to its influ-
> ence. These are so-called primitive, or tribal society on the one hand, and
> the Asiatic mode of production, or the great bureaucratic imperial sys-
> tems, on the other. . . . Latin America offers yet a third kind of
> development—one involving an even earlier destruction of imperial
> systems now projected by collective memory back into the archaic or
> tribal. Thus the earlier nominal conquests of independence open them
> at once to a kind of indirect economic penetration and control—
> something Africa and Asia will come to experience only more recently
> with decolonization in the 1950s and 1960s. (Jameson 1986:68–69)

Given this interrelationship, what constructs the Third World today is
preeminently its legacy of interactions between capitalist Eurocolonialism
and different modes of production in the rest of the world: this is the
source of the radical difference that still exists. To be sure, this sort of
radical difference interconnects even as it separates. The study of Third
World culture "necessarily entails a new view of ourselves, from the outside" (60). But it is significant that this remains, for Jameson, a view from
the outside: Jameson keeps his boundaries in place and his "we" and
"they" still geographically separate, just as Eric Wolf does in asserting that
"our" history and "their" history are two sides of the same history
(1982:19).

Jameson then turns to the way these differences mark, even determine,
Third World literature. His specific focus is on the absence in the Third
World of psychologism as the West knows it. This is because of the absence
of "one of the determinants of capitalist culture," namely, "a radical split
between the private and the public, between the poetic and the political,
between what we have come to think of as the domain of sexuality and the
unconscious and that of the public world of classes, of the economic, and
of secular political power: in other words, Freud versus Marx" (69). By
contrast, private experience in the Third World is never finally private, but

reveals the public: since the defining experience of the Third World was subalternity, most private experience, as in Fanon, is constructed from that fact, and therefore private experience and personal psychology rest much more transparently in the Third World on public historical reality. Describing the notion of cultural revolution in the Third World, Jameson writes that it

> turns on the phenomenon of what Gramsci called "subalternity," name-ly the feelings of mental inferiority and habits of subservience and obe-dience which necessarily and structurally develop in situations of domination—most dramatically in the experience of colonized peoples. But here, as so often, the subjectivizing and psychologizing habits of first-world peoples such as ourselves can play us false and lead us into misunderstandings. Subalternity is not in that sense a psychological matter, although it governs psychologies; and I suppose that the strate-gic choice of the term "cultural" aims precisely at restructuring that view of the problem and projecting it outwards into the realm of objective or collective spirit in some non-psychological but also non-reductionist or non-economistic, materialistic fashion. When a psychic structure is ob-jectively determined by economic and political relationships, it cannot be dealt with by means of purely psychological therapies; yet it equally cannot be dealt with by means of purely objective transformations of the economic and political situation itself, since the habits remain and exer-cise a baleful and crippling residual effect. (76)

Given this close unity of psychological and political factors, a unity depen-dant on the experience of subalternity, Jameson asserts, with startling rigor, that "all third-world texts are necessarily, I want to argue, allegorical, and in a very specific way: they are to be read as *national allegories*" (69). The private and the public, Freud and Marx, opposed in the First World, are fused in the Third.

Jameson's sympathy for the category of Third World literature he con-structs should, from the above comments, be clear. Third World literature can teach the First World what it would otherwise be blind to, thanks to the mystification to which those at the top of a hierarchy are typically prone. Jameson quotes Hegel's grim aphorism about domination and ser-vitude: "The truth of the Master is the Slave; while the truth of the Slave, on the other hand, is the Master" (85). He does so to valorize the slave and the slave's perspective:

> In the end, only the slave knows what reality and the resistance of matter really are; only the slave can attain some true materialistic consciousness of his situation, since it is precisely to that that he is condemned. The Master, however, is condemned to idealism—the luxury of a placeless freedom in which any consciousness of his own concrete situation flees

like a dream, like a word unremembered on the tip of the tongue, a
nagging doubt which the puzzled mind is unable to formulate. (85)

For a First World Marxist critic, then, Third World literature offers the
painful, necessary challenge of seeing the process of domination and subalternity clearly, and of reconnecting what the First World, mystifyingly,
has set asunder, the private and the public, the individual and the collective, as well as theory and praxis. To do this, "we," as First World readers,
have to reconstitute ourselves, to unlearn old and uncover new ways of
reading texts, as well as to become aware of a novel sort of literary style. For
"us," then, Jameson concludes "such unaccustomed exposure to reality, or
to the collective totality, is often intolerable, leaving us in Quentin's position at the end of *Absalom, Absalom!,* murmuring the great denial, 'I don't
hate the Third World! I don't! I don't!'" (86).

Jameson's interview with Anders Stephanson suggests a similarly up-
beat, sympathetic final turn to the line of inquiry he does not pursue in his
controversial article, the notion of Third World literature, not defined in
terms of subalternity, but echoing "outmoded stages of our own first world
cultural development." In these terms, the Third World also represents
consciousness of a goal toward which a mystified First World is groping:
"Let's say that here the first world—if it does not revert back into third-
world realities—unexpectedly and in a peculiar dialectical reversal begins
to touch some features of third-world experience, perhaps another reason
third-world culture has lately become one of our passionate interests" (42).

Jameson cited contemporary Chinese literature as an example: "Chinese strings of episodic narratives" are not "realism," which was Western-
originated, but "an example of going back to the sort of storytelling which
one finds both in the third world's discovery of its own way of telling
stories *and* in a certain form of postmodernism" (49). "Third World" literature, conceived of in this way, reveals not only the West's past but also
something of its future; it is paradoxically both "an outmoded form of
cultural production" and an indicator of what Western postmodernity is
coming to. Jameson thus echoes many of the Third World appropriations
of postmodern culture noted above, but he does so cautiously. Rather than
the Third World revealing itself as always-already avant-garde, the First
World goes *back* to Third World sources for equivalents to its more advanced experience.

Jameson's conclusions about Third World literature seem sympathetic,
to put the point in its harshest form, because Third World literature is
useful to First World self-awareness when interpreted from the standpoint
of First World oppositional scholarly sophistication. It does not actually

create a conversation between the two, as the fuller sort of dialogism surveyed in chapter 9 desires; it provides, instead, the occasion for critical intelligences in the First World to tell the First World what it does not know. It is, in short, still part of what Trinh Minh-ha calls gossip between the Masters. A more sympathetic version of the same critique would be to say that Jameson's exercise of conscience and his participation in the circuits of metropolitan self-critiques expose him, in a changed globalist era, to an unintended problem: his sympathy for the other, in staying the property of the metropolitan power, replicates the boundaries that keep the "other" in its subordinate place. Jameson's article, one could argue from this perspective, falls into the lineage of European and American auto-criticism that presses the "other" into serving its own ends, from the *Travels* of John Mandeville to *Candide,* nineteenth- and twentieth-century literary primitivism, the school of ethnographic surrealism James Clifford analyzes, and previous, and often highly ambiguous, attempts by Marxists to yoke ethnic and national issues to the "larger" or "more fundamental" plots of anticapitalism and class conflict (Miller 1990:32–45). Every bit as much as oppositional Third World nationalism, metropolitan oppositional self-critique thus needs dramatic revision in light of recent alterations in the global order. It has to be subjected to an astringent critique of how it may replicate what it intends to resist, and it needs to be reshaped by the construction of new knowledge-circuits that enshrine dialogue, or polylogue, not the interrupted conversation of master and slave. Both metropolitan and marginal critic must speak with the awareness that they speak from heterogeneous positions to heterogeneous audiences within, not apart or against, a common intercultural conversation.

It was precisely on account of Jameson's assertion of radical difference between a First World "we" and Third World "they" that Ahmad (1987) attacked him. For Ahmad, Jameson's very use of the term "Third World," however he may seek to reinterpret its "radical difference," involves him in the legacy of Orientalism. The term "Third World" is, for Ahmad, "even in its most telling deployments, a polemical one, with no theoretical status whatsoever" (4). To use it as a basis for "a theory of the cognitive aesthetics of third-world literature" is to construct "ideal-types, in the Weberian manner, duplicating all the basic procedures which orientalist scholars have historically deployed in presenting their own readings of a certain tradition of 'high' textuality as *the* knowledge of a supposedly unitary object which they call 'the Islamic civilization'" (4).

The construction of such ideal types depends on institutional blindness that is akin to ignorance. Concretely, global patterns for the circulation of knowledge and literary texts means that the First World knows much less about the Third than vice versa.

> Rare would be a modern intellectual in Asia or Africa who does not know at least one European language; equally rare would be, on the other side, a major literary theorist in Europe or the United States who has ever bothered with an Asian or African language; and the enormous industry of translation which circulates texts among the advanced capitalist countries comes to the most erratic and slowest possible grind when it comes to translation from Asian to African languages. The upshot is that major literary traditions—such as those of Bengali, Hindi, Tamil, Telegu and half a dozen others from India alone—remain, beyond a few texts here and there, virtually unknown to the American literary theorist. (5)

Those Third World texts that do get through this barrier are not just overemphasized—even lionized—but turned, like model immigrants, into what they are not, ideal-types for a whole category: "The retribution visited upon the head of an Asian, an African, an Arab intellectual who is of any consequence and who writes in English is that he/she is immediately elevated to the lonely splendour of a 'representative'—of a race, a continent, a civilization, even the 'third world'" (5).

In arguing that Jameson's construction of ideal types is permitted by the thin sampling of "Third World" literature available in—and represented as such to—the First World, Ahmad argues for much more detailed, and much less totalizeable literary histories for traditions outside the First World. On the one hand, the "fecundity of real narratives in the so-called third world" would elude the attempts to metanarratives to encompass them, and

> conversely, many of the questions that one would ask about, let us say, Urdu or Bengali traditions of literature may turn out to be rather similar to the questions one has asked previously about English/American literatures. By the same token, a *real* knowledge of those other traditions may force U.S. literary theorists to ask questions about their own tradition which they have heretofore not asked. (9)

On the one hand, Ahmad rejects the packaging of differences as contemporary exoticism, the construction of them into ideal types; on the other, he does not advocate homogenization of difference, but interactivity. This interactivity allows "First World" questions to be put to "Third World" literatures and "Third World" literatures to suggest new questions to be put back to "First World" literatures. Further, Ahmad argues that Jameson's Orientalizing vice, the construction of an ideal type that homogenizes diversity into a single category, is a specifically First World problem. Thanks to the structure of the circulation of knowledge globally, the First

World was historically homogenized, while the Third, in sharp contrast, was both originally heterogeneous and subsequently heterogenized:

> The cultural logic of late capitalism is so strongly operative in these metropolitan formations; the circulation of cultural products among them is so immediate, so extensive, so brisk that one could sensibly speak of a certain cultural homogeneity among them. But Asia, Africa, and Latin America? Historically, these countries were never so closely tied together; Peru and India simply do not have a common history of the sort that Germany and France, or Britain and the United States, have; not even the singular "experience of colonialism and imperialism" has been in specific ways [the] same or similar in, say, India and Namibia. These various countries, from the three continents, have been assimilated into the global structure of capitalism not as a single cultural ensemble but highly differentially, each establishing its own circuits of (unequal) exchange with the metropolis, each acquiring its own very distinct class formations. Circuits of exchange among them are rudimentary at best; an average Nigerian who is literate about his own country would know infinitely more about England and the United States than about any country of Asia or Latin America or indeed about most countries of Africa. The kind of circuits that bind the cultural complexes of the advanced capitalist countries simply do not exist among countries of backward capitalism, and capitalism itself, which is dominant but not altogether universalized, does not yet have the same power of homogenization in its cultural logic in most of these countries, except among the urban bourgeoisie. (10–11)

In contrast to Jameson's heavy emphasis on radical difference as the result of how societies have been absorbed into capitalism, Ahmad, using the sociology of knowledge, finds that to be only one of many factors, part of an ongoing production of difference.

Ultimately, however, Ahmad's criticism of Jameson's construction of his ideal type rests on something more than an appeal to the sociology of knowledge. Jameson's construction is theoretically illegitimate:

> I find it significant [Ahmad argues] that first and second worlds are defined in terms of their production systems (capitalism and socialism, respectively), whereas the third category—the third world—is defined purely in terms of an "experience" of externally inserted phenomena. That which is constitutive of human history itself is present in the first two cases, absent in the third one. Ideologically, this classification divides the world between those who make history and those who are mere objects of it; elsewhere in the text, Jameson would significantly reinvoke Hegel's famous description of the master / slave relation to encapsulate the first / third world opposition. But analytically, this classification leaves the so-called third world in a limbo; if only the first world is capitalist and the second world socialist, how does one understand the

third world? Is it pre-capitalist? Transitional? Transitional between what
and what? (6–7).

In making this criticism, Ahmad in effect argues that Jameson practices an
Orientalism, not of "culture," but of political economy. Jameson's revised
version of radical difference has been created by his unequal definition of
the First and Second worlds in terms of production systems, and the Third
World in terms of its victimization, not its mode of production. To do this,
moreover, is to analyze the First and Second worlds in terms of present
circumstances, but to view the Third in terms of past colonial and imperial
penetration.

Perhaps the most illuminating point in the exchange between Ahmad
and Jameson comes when Ahmad locates his theoretical criticism in history, by invoking a profound recent change in models of world organization.
Here we can see at work the crucial change in paradigms of global cultural
order that I have been tracing throughout this book. Having attacked
Jameson for his use of the terminology of the three worlds theory, and for
the residues of Orientalism in its legacy, Ahmad asserts that the contemporary world system is more unified and less centrist (and everywhere more
contemporary) than Jameson allows it to be:

> One could start with a radically different premise, namely the proposi-
> tion that we live not in three worlds but in one; that this world includes
> the experience of colonialism and imperialism on both sides of Jam-
> eson's global divide (the "experience" of imperialism is a central fact of
> all aspects of life inside the U.S. from ideological formation to the utilisa-
> tion of the social surplus in military-industrial complexes); that societies
> in formations of backward capitalism are as much constituted by the
> division of classes as are societies in the advanced capitalist countries;
> that socialism is not restricted to something called the second world but
> is simply the name of a resistance that saturates the globe today, as
> capitalism does; that the different parts of the capitalist system are to be
> known not in terms of a binary opposition but as a contradictory unity,
> with differences, yes, but also with profound overlaps. (9)

The "one world" of this description defies clear divisions according to
geography. As Ahmad pictures it, it is everywhere heterogeneous and overlapping, a "contradictory unity." Thus, in cultural matters, no metanarra-
tive can encompass or totalize "all the fecundity of real narratives in the so-
called third world"; the global cultural system is one, not of exoticist,
disjunctive "radical difference," but of interpenetrating differences within
a common, but extremely complex, system.

The rhetoric of Ahmad's response is itself an example of this "contradictory unity." It both assumes commonality and manipulates difference.

Ahmad presents his essay as the response of one theoretical Marxist to another across the divide of imposed cultural difference. Crucial to Ahmad's response is his tone of wounded chagrin at having his alterity so roughly thrust upon him by Jameson—at finding himself, in an essay by a much-admired fellow-Marxist, cast in the alienating role of that person's "civilizational other." This initial chagrin, coupled with Ahmad's subsequent engagement with Jameson on both the field of literary theory and the field of Marxian thought, evokes a strong sense of his community with Jameson, something that renders Jameson's analysis still more alien and alienating: Jameson's emphatic maintenance of we-they boundary lines seems to inscribe Ahmad in his essay, not only as his civilizational other, but as a subaltern Third World intellectual doomed to / privileged with the limitations / advantages of subalterneity. Indeed, as Ahmad argues openly at the end of his response, neither he nor Jameson can be confined thus within geopolitical borders or be so locally determined in their self-constructions. Both they and their texts are marked by the "contradictory unity" of the globalist era; both are both cosmopolitan, exhibiting an international heterogeneity of influences and allegiances. Ahmad's awareness of cosmopolitanism—and his demonstration of it in his urbane rhetoric of chagrin—thus hints that Jameson's, by contrast, like First World Marxist internationalism generally, is provincial.

Replying thus as a slighted colleague, Ahmad equally strongly evokes his status as both expert on and member of the community of colonial and postcolonial Urdu literature. By invoking this insider knowledge, Ahmad also rhetorically benefits from the very position of alterity he has overtly deflated, a position that would legitimize him, not Jameson, as spokesperson for and expositor of Third World cultural traditions. Indeed, having noted how knowledge of language and tradition gave him an insider's access to Urdu literature, Ahmad goes on to argue that his Third World position gives him a privileged view on the contemporary world system.

What gives the world its unity, then, is not a humanist ideology but the ferocious struggle of capital and labor which is now strictly and fundamentally global in character. The prospect of a socialist revolution has receded so much from the practical horizon of so much of the metropolitan left that the temptation for the U.S. left intelligentsia is to forget the ferocity of that basic struggle which in our time transcends all others. The advantage of coming from Pakistan, in my own case, is that the country is saturated with capitalist commodities, bristles with U.S. weaponry, borders on China, the Soviet Union and Afghanistan, suffers from a proliferation of competing nationalisms, and is currently witnessing the first stage in the consolidation of the communist movement. (10)

Ahmad's description of contemporary Pakistan evokes a postmodern globalist landscape of extreme cultural heterogeneity; only such a landscape,
Ahmad argues, can reveal the contradictions of the current global system.
Citizenship in Pakistan thus provides a privileged view of the overall system, an up-to-the-minute view of its breaches, unevennesses, and
heterogeneities—a view denied First World intellectuals.

This privileged view is different from what Jameson seeks ultimately to
honor as demystified Third World knowledge. It does not represent a
slave's view of the master; rather, it is a sophisticated insider's view of the
common, heterogeneous, interpenetrating system. This system, moreover, should sponsor a conversation among participants, not the lack of
communication between master and slave; to that conversation, moreover, Third World positions have something particularly relevant to con-
tribute.

Ahmad has subsequently extended and sharpened his critique of metropolitan theory and further valorized his peripheral Marxist perspective
as crucial for cultural and political analysis of the contemporary period. *In
Theory* (1992) incorporates his criticisms of Jameson and adds an equally
sharp critique of Said. The book also offers a still broader analysis of metropolitan theory in the United States as politically vagrant and even reactionary, thanks to the lack of a vital Marxist movement and culture there, a
postwar obsession with cultural nationalism that resulted from the prominence of ethnic struggles at home and corresponding interest in worldwide revolutionary decolonization, and a highly ambiguous "empowerment" of immigrant Third World intellectuals in cultural nationalist
categories. The result, Ahmad argues, was that the American academic left
uncritically supported Third World nationalism in the 1960s, incapable of
distinguishing between bourgeois nationalist and socialist regimes, and it
equally uncritically embraced poststructuralism, which made nationalism
an object of attack once the dramatic expansion of capitalism globally had
led to the frustration of both socialist ideals and bourgeois aspirations in
the Third World. No "properly Marxist political or literary culture on any
appreciable scale" was therefore formed (1992:64).

In contrast, a peripheral position exposes most clearly the nature and
instability of the present capitalist system, one that is now "undergoing a
new phase of vast global restructuring." In the new hierarchically structured world system, the United States, Japan, and Germany preside over a
world of "subordinated backward capitalist countries" increasingly differentiated from each other according to "vast differences in demography,
sociohistorical formation, economic scale, levels of accumulation, and
modes of articulation into the world economy" (1992:312). In these coun-

tries, differences between classes and regions will only increase, signs of which will be their instability and "the devastating combination of the most modern technology and backward capitalist development" (315). Given the fact that the global capitalist system is now so interrelated, economic slowdowns in the core will not yield intra-imperialist war. But, in the periphery, such interrelationship, combined with intractable ecological limitations, means that capitalist transition of the European type (based on the use of colonies for exportation of surplus population and as sources of wealth and raw materials) is not at all feasible as a means of remedying the "structural inability of capitalism to provide for the vast majority of the populations which it has sucked into its own dominion" (316). Ahmad therefore foresees a revolutionary struggle to realize the socialist projects of redistributing wealth and restructuring production. This struggle should, he believes, be initiated by "producers in the backward formations" seeking revolutionary transformation of nation-states they inhabit (316).

Ahmad's book—with its criticism of Said and Jameson, its critique of poststructuralism as "*repressive* and *bourgeois*" (1992:36), and its severe portrait of Third World intellectuals in America—has been both buried in "silence and oblivion" (Ahmad 1993:144) and attacked with unusual vitriol in a recent forum on the book in *Public Culture* (for example, Dhareshwar 1993; Chatterjee 1993; van der Veer 1993; Levinson 1993). A good portion of the fury the book provoked doubtless came from anger at Ahmad's attack on institutional, intellectual, and professional commitments (Levinson castigates the book as a "harangue, jeremiad, flyting, ethnic cleansing: not to make a mystery of it, jihad" and an "insult to every familiar name in the field of study" [1993:101]). But, apart from goring oxen, Ahmad's wholesale dismissal of metropolitan theory allows no space for considering the forms of opposition that theory *has* sponsored and also ways in which the legacy of cultural nationalism cannot be so simply dismissed. Indeed, the transformation of cultural nationalism for a globalist era has as we have seen, produced a wide variety of practices, from the creation of a new generation of ethnic politics in the United States to the advocacy of strategic essentialism worldwide. Ahmad's assertion that "Third Worldism and poststructuralism . . . remain discrete and epiphenomenal, even though the most outlandish of the poststructuralists have tried to combine them" seems needlessly dismissive of a significant amount of recent scholarship (36), some of which we have examined in previous chapters. And one might take Ahmad to task for rejecting, as he does, all the progressive possibilities in Said's metropolitan contrapuntalism, however vulnerable it might be when proposed as an epochal change or a panacea. Ahmad styles it as merely a conversation between elites; surely, the reorientation of metropolitan thought is not a wholly insignificant goal. For Ahmad to argue that it is, moreover, is self-defeating to say the least, as is it is precisely this sort of conversation that Ahmad's own book (as we have seen in examining the article on Jameson) falls into. Finally, one might be impatient with Ahmad's (like Wallerstein's) postponement of real systemic change to the time of future catastrophe. The study of meaningful changes within the developing world system has been pursued much more fully by others working outside the Marxian tradition. As we turn to this material, we shall see how the notion of the world as a contradictory unity is articulated differently, depicting a far more complexly decentered system than Ahmad allows, and an awareness of heterogeneity is positively valorized, rather than remaining a sign of oncoming catastrophe as it is in Ahmad.

11

Outside the Marxian Tradition

PERHAPS THE MOST popular view of globalization has been that we have entered a new era of worldwide interaction and are, accordingly, witnessing the dawn of a truly "global" culture. According to this way of picturing the process, a new kind of culture, a "third" culture, has emerged on top of national and local formations, rather than in transformative relationship with them. What this culture has turned out to be has been speculated about at some length; most often, in recent opinion, it has been seen as the creation of media and multinationals, a global commercial culture that has spread satellite dishes, designer jeans, ethnic food, and automatic weapons around the world. This culture—which we have already seen described by Stuart Hall—has sent rock concerts through Africa and put CNN reporters in Baghdad, but the concerts consist of multicultural music, and television reporting has been so standardized that a Moscow newscaster and Dan Rather in New York clearly belong to the same tribe.

The similarity of such concepts to Jameson's description of postmodern culture should be clear. In both theories, the new culture is the dominant of a new era of global capitalism. Similarly, in both theories, the new culture is constructed out of the decontextualized fragments of regional, national, and local cultures. But in contrast to Jameson, theorists of global commercial culture see this construction, not as representing the decentering, and therefore death, of the subjects it comprises, but as the assembly of a new kind of noncatastrophic, globalized subject.

Ulf Hannerz's description of global cosmopolitans (1990) does not do justice to the full range of his thought about globalization, but it is a good illustration of such theories. Hannerz studies global cosmopolitans as a particular set of "types" and links the construction of these types to the formation of transnational networks. Global cosmopolitans represent a new breed of identities based on mobility. They were usually not èmigrès or exiles, and never migrants. Instead, they are "organization" people

(243), members of what James Field, in "Transnationalism and the New Tribe" (1971), dubs a new tribe for a new era. These transnational cultures tend "to be more or less clear-cut occupational cultures (and are often tied to transnational job markets)" (243). Included, then, among these "cosmopolitans" are intellectuals, "bureaucrats, politicians, and business people and . . . journalists and diplomats, and various others" (244).

Hannerz distinguishes among the members of this list by noting that some are "more marked by some territorial culture than" others; indeed, most transnational cultures are "in different ways extensions or transformations of western Europe and North America" (244). (Among the members of the more territorialized and least cosmopolitan of these cultures are the "accidental tourists" of Anne Tyler [1985], who need to know which restaurants in Tokyo offer Sweet n' Low, and corporate employees trained in IBM-conformist style.) Intellectuals (consumers of Tyler's ironies about the provinciality of her accidental tourists) are, however, at the other end of the spectrum: they are the most deterritorialized and most cosmopolitan. Hannerz quotes György Konrád's (1984) description of them:

> We may describe as transnational those intellectuals who are at home in the cultures of other peoples as well as their own. They keep track of what is happening in various places. They have special ties to those countries where they have lived, they have friends all over the world, they hop across the sea to discuss something with their colleagues; they fly to visit one another as easily as their counterparts two hundred years ago rode over the next town to exchange ideas. (244)

Writing skeptically about the new commercial global culture, Anthony Smith (1990) similarly focuses on the degree to which it is cosmopolitan and deterritorialized—the degree to which it constructs itself independently of ties to a former colonial center. He argues that contemporary global culture has neither been wholly separate from nor remains wholly tied to those former centers. Instead, it has come to represent a stage in the development of a tradition of "cultural imperialisms":

> There is an important difference from earlier cultural imperialisms. Earlier imperialisms were usually extensions of ethnic or national sentiments and ideologies, French, British, Russian, etc. Today's imperialisms are ostensibly non-national; "capitalism" and "socialism" and in a different sense "Europeanism" are by definition and intention, "supranational," if not universal. They are supported by a technological infrastructure which is truly "cosmopolitan," in the sense that the same telecommunications base will eventually erode cultural differences and create a genuinely "global culture" based on the properties of the media themselves, to which the "message" will become increasingly inciden-

tal. For the rest, tourism and museology alone will preserve the memory of an earlier era of "national cultures." (176)

The relationship between a worldwide, media-supported commercial culture and its imperial past is thus not direct, but still persists in an increasingly sublimated form. At its most transnational, it operates by what Deena Weinstein calls, in writing about the 1988 Amnesty International concert tour (a multinational concoction of commercial musical cultures sponsored by Reebok and Amnesty International—in other words, by both commercial and oppositional political organizations) "permissive unification." The concert altered its program, in a kind of modular multicultural manner, to suit the audiences it played for, while the underlying modular format, as well as its commercial sponsorship, remained the same. Material from widely disparate cultural contexts was thus extracted from those contexts or decontextualized, then recontextualized as commercial multiculturalism (1989:63). Smith, who remains skeptical of the significance of globalization as opposed to the persistence of national cultures, summarizes its mechanisms admirably:

> A global culture, so the argument runs, will be eclectic like its western or European progenitor, but will wear a uniformly streamlined packaging. Standardized, commercialized mass commodities will nevertheless draw for their contents upon revivals of traditional, folk or national motifs and styles in fashions, furnishings, music and the arts, lifted out of their original contexts and anaesthetized. So that a global culture would operate at several levels simultaneously: as a cornucopia of standardized commodities, as a patchwork of denationalized ethnic or folk motifs, as a series of generalized "human values and interests," as a uniform "scientific" discourse of meaning, and finally as the interdependent system of communications which forms the material base for all the other components and levels. (1990:176)

While Smith foresees a cosmopolitan, deterritorialized global culture that is, at bottom, standardizing, Hannerz pictures the new culture more subtly as a heightened skill in manipulating differences—as the cultivation of code-switching between local differences, not their anesthetization via incorporation. As such, he foresees a global culture that coexists with local structures, rather than overriding them. Previously, the elite of a society were locals.

> When locals were influential, Robert Merton found in his classic study, their influence rested not so much on what they knew as whom they knew. Cosmopolitans, in contrast, based whatever influence they had on a knowledge less tied to particular others, or to the unique community setting. They came equipped with special knowledge, and they

could leave and take it with them without devaluing it. . . . They are "the new class," people with credentials, decontextualized cultural capital. . . . Their decontextualized knowledge can be quickly and shiftingly recontextualized in a series of different settings. (Which is not to say that the transnational cultures consist of nothing but such knowledge—they may well evolve their own particularisms as well, of the kind which are elsewhere the special resource of locals: biographical knowledge of individuals, anecdotal knowledge of events and even of the constellations of locales which form the settings of these cultures.) What they carry, however, is not just special knowledge, but also that overall orientation toward structures of meaning to which the notion of the "culture of critical discourse" refers. This orientation, according to Gouldner's description, is reflexive, problematizing, concerned with metacommunication; I would also describe it as generally expansionist in its management of meaning. (246)

Such a description could include many of Hannerz's different kinds of figures. If accidental tourists may not really be covered by it, certainly their more sophisticated counterparts, who may instead read, not only the burgeoning literature of the culture-shock-prevention industry, but also the specialized literatures of cross-cultural communication (such as cross-cultural legal relations [Gessner and Schade 1990]), would be examples. And at the top end, it would include poststructuralist intellectuals, responsible for, among other things, the ferment of contemporary cultural studies.

Smith's view of global culture, as opposed to local, territorialized culture, and Hannerz's different perspective on cosmopolitan globalism as code-switching between persisting local differences both involve the conceptual separation of the global from the local. The former is a realm that has recently been constructed on top of prior local formations. But in contrast to both Smith and Hannerz, a more sophisticated line of inquiry into globalization has not opposed contemporary global cultures to the existence and/or persistence of older local cultures, but has seen the two phenomena united as two aspects of the same process. In this more subtle vein, globalization has been conceived of as a cultural process not just at work on top of, but more tellingly also (although much less transparently) at work everywhere within older social and cultural formations. As such, globalization has even been effectively read backward into histories of those formations, contradicting the view of it as a recent phenomenon.

Vytautas Kavolis presents a significantly different version of the transnational Smith and Hannerz describe. "To be sure," he writes, contemporary civilizations are (as perhaps the ancient Near Eastern civilizations were between 1,700 and 500 B.C.) in the process of self-reconstruction as a result of modernization and inter-civilizational encounters. The maintenance of their own identities has become problematic. This has the consequence that boundaries are blurred, contents interpenetrate, even central meanings become subject to contestations both within and outside of particular civilizational-traditions-in-transformation, alien genres suggest themselves for uncovering native experiences. Bicivilizational, multiethnic identities or identity diffractions arise, either functioning imaginatively as workshops in critical translation or dissolving into the waste products of "cosmopolitan" consumerism. While this is consciously grasped by a relatively small (though larger than during the preceding millennium or so) proportion of humanity and proves to be a weak force when it comes to matters as weighty and binding upon large populations as national interest, religion, or economic survival, it is the major worldwide spontaneous thrust of formation of cultural perceptions, against which other forces can only act defensively. (1991:129)

Kavolis depicts this contemporary cultural ferment—which would include both the emergence of international consumer culture and the new post-1968 oppositional movements—as a civilizational moment, part of a deeply traditional affair. He is less daring than William NcNeill in the way he revises the assumptions of great civilizationists like Spengler and Toynbee, but he pursues the same interesting strategy. Whereas McNeill radically refigures the civilizational inheritance as one that emphasizes "polyethnicity"—the heterogeneity within—rather than the coherence and wholeness of the civilizational system, Kavolis sees such heterogeneity as a phenomenon of transition periods produced by encounters between previously more coherent civilizational forms. Kavolis thus refuses to sanction contemporary ferment with as deeply civilizational an imprimatur as McNeill does. He finds his analogies to the present, not in the heart of great pre-European civilizations, but in still earlier times. But this traditionalizes the present nonetheless: its new is not new, but a version of something old. In short, Kavolis retrojects Ricoeur's drama of civilizational encounter in the postwar period into the archaic past; he makes it more centrally a part of the format of civilizational development, not primarily what might undo it.

The postmodern, global-cultural ferment Kavolis describes does not however, count, for as much as other underlying processes. It is a weak force compared to national interest, religion, and economic survival, one that galvanizes an elite, not the mass of mankind. The ferment itself does not represent the main vehicle of change; rather, it helps mediate change by being part of a deeper and slower process that affects the majority of humanity much more substantially. That deeper drama of tectonic, epochal, transformative change is not the postmodern heterogenization of social and cultural forms, but a polylogue between civilizations. Kavolis describes this civilizational polylogue as involving reciprocal acts of communication and criticism, and he conceptualizes these in much the same way Ashis Nandy imagines his "dialogue of cultures" (1987:55). "Within the globalizing frame of consciousness," Kavolis writes,

> mutual criticism acquires a two-way communicative structure. On the one hand, everyone is sooner or later constrained to seek *justification* of one's own behavior in a "universally understandable" idiom—that is, its explanation either in the manner of a globally accepted mode of discourse, such as the rhetorics of culture, nationalism, democracy, or human rights; or by some demonstration of the empirical consequences of accepting one or another set of premises. On the other hand, one is constantly engaged in *judging* the "universal understandings"—that is, the globally accepted modes of discourse and the assumptions of "empiricism"—by one's own (though not necessarily "traditional") values and in the light of one's own historical and current experience. (130)

The communicative structure thus embodies a "selection of meanings" that constitute a "universally understandable idiom," one "in which each particular culture is increasingly constrained, but to varying extents, in proportion to its involvement with the 'world system,' to justify itself" (131). Reciprocally, within each civilization, these meanings are themselves judged; they have to endure those "reality tests" to acquire "spontaneous world-wide appeal" in order to remain a part of the always "revisable selections of meanings" of the universal idiom (131). In this way, then, the weak force of global-cultural postmodern ferment becomes part of the deeper, strong interactions of civilizational polylogue: as today's "major worldwide spontaneous thrust of formation of cultural perceptions," the weak force of postmodern cultural ferment has become part of the idiom that constrains the polylogue of cultures and societies today.

In Kavolis's analysis, globalization is deeply at work in local cultural formations: local cultural units have always been produced in part by interaction with each other. The global culture of Smith's media culture and Hannerz's cosmopolitans—global culture as a new third culture, distinct from "local" culture, laid down on top of previous formations—and Kavolis's polylogue—globalization as a process intrinsically interrelated with its opposite, localization—thus form two distinct frames of reference. In the former, the global is separate from the local; in the latter, the two frames are interconnected and even help produce each other.

Clearly, while Hannerz's and Smith's assumptions may initially have been more popular, Kavolis's general frame of reference has not only emerged as the more powerful and academically legitimate mode of conceptualization, but has also gradually become more widely accepted. As the discourse of globalization has begun to replace the discourse of modernization in general public awareness, the subtleties of the later conceptual model have also to some degree been popularized. The modern cosmopolitan negotiating local provincialisms has been giving way in America to bumper stickers advocating "Think Globally; Act Locally"— stickers that have come as a result of the mainstreaming of previous radical discourses, such as eco-activism and reformulated populism—and, increasingly, contemporary globalization and localization have become widely viewed as a single, Janus-faced process.

As we have seen in discussing Ngũgĩ, this frame of reference has been made a basis for activism, for a new radical project tailored specifically for a postnational world. In the wake of disillusionment with oppositional nationalism, and gloom about the capacity of Third World industrialization to yield progressive social change, many political activists embrace localization as a means of oppositional activism, and economic analysts advocate localist micro-economic activity in the informal sector as the only remedy for basket-case regional and national economies. Thus, Peter Worsley notes:

> All across the globe, non-governmental popular organizations such as the Consumer's Association of Penang, or the Kerala Popular Science Movement (KSSP), or SEWA, the organization set up by illiterate Outcaste women workers in Ahmedabad, denied membership of male-dominated trade unions, who went on to establish their own bank, are constantly, day in and day out, fighting to change the world, and to improve their life-circumstances. (1990:93)

More generally, however, current emphasis on simultaneous awareness of the global and the local has yielded an important new view of world order. First, it presents a decentered, democratically egalitarian view of world organization: nations may be differentiated and rankable into a hierarchy, but no particular local-global perspective would seem to be so privileged. The terminology appears to suppress hierarchy, and the local-global frames available are too dizzyingly numerous to rank. Second, the new local-global conceptual framework vividly embodies a sense of waning faith in the importance of national systems. Thus, Worsley urges that we move beyond the nation-state to other formations for our models for world order, as well as for grounding our hope for change. We should think both more locally and more globally than we have done in the past:

> All the models we have discussed, even world-system theory, paradoxically take the nation-state as their unit of analysis. Yet all of us belong to communities which are both smaller and wider than the nation-state. Hence, as one anthropologist has put it, as long as there are "ten thousand societies inhabiting 160 nation-states" which refuse to recognize their cultural and political rights, minority peoples will continue to struggle to run their own affairs, by force of arms if need be.
>
> Conversely, the modern world has been shaped by cultural communities, from the Catholic Church and Islam to secular ideologies and movements like communism which transcend the boundaries of the largest and most centralized state. (94)

Focus on the global-local dyad has thus provided ways around nationalism's previous near monopoly on globally significant cultural differences. It has dramatically expanded the number of communities (or, more generally, "local sites") people are aware they belong to, and it has made these memberships and identities simultaneously global and local in significance. Thus, along with ending the near monopoly nationalism had on the production of global cultural difference, current emphasis on the global-local has also broken the stranglehold that the nation-state has had on managing worldwide relationships.

As Ngũgĩ and Worsley suggest, many of the differences produced by the new global-localisms (such as micro-populisms, tribal and ethnic movements, and some of the larger fundamentalisms) have remained territorialized, but have gone below and above the nation. More bewilderingly, though, a variety of global-"localisms" have gone above and below the nation, but have not remained attached to territory. These would include a host of other kinds of affiliations and identity positions, from gender to occupational culture, on the basis of which local groups and transnational relationships have been reciprocally constructed. Thinking globally and acting locally has thus become very complex, especially given the fact that any given person always exists and acts in a variety of different local-global contexts. With such awareness, the global map of nation-states—of national differences and international relationships—both fissures and is overdrawn with a multitude of new, increasingly decentered strategic boundaries: multitudes of overlapping, abutting, conflicting, more *and* less territorialized global-localisms appear.

But, as Kavolis's polylogue indicates, globalization-localization has not just been a process at work only in the brave new present; it was also active in the remote past. Roland Robertson's ongoing elaboration of his global-ization theory is one of the most sophisticated versions of the reciprocity of globalization and localization we now have. Like Smith, Robertson notes that few believe a global culture exists in a strong sense (i.e., as a body of values, ideas, etc., that are binding on a group)—only "those who strongly emphasize the force and significance of the homogenization of popular culture, global styles of consumerism, individual 'life-styles,' 'global information,' and so on" (1992c:399). Rather, he maintains, "we may best consider contemporary globalization in its most general sense as a form of institutionalization of the two-fold process involving universal-ization of particularism and particularization of universalism" (1991:80). The pretheoretical commitment of globalization theory, he elsewhere ar-gues, was to a recently intensifying, centuries-long production of global heterogeneity, not a recent production of increasingly homogenized uni-versality via the anesthetization of older, local cultures. Thus Robertson maintains "that the globalization process itself—the rendering of the world as what I call a single place—constrains civilizations and societies (including oppressed national-ethnic solidarities) to be increasingly ex-plicit about what might be called their *global callings* (their unique geo-cultural or geomoral contributions to world history) (1987:21).

Crucial to Robertson's globalization theory, then, is the assertion that the same processes that yoke nations, civilizations, and cultures together also stimulate their attempts to differentiate themselves from each other. And equally crucial is the fact that Robertson, like Kavolis, does not con-fine these processes to the present, but conceives of them as being of great historical age. Indeed, Robertson's comment comes from an exchange with Kavolis conducted prior to the appearance of the article by Kavolis discussed above. Civilizationalism, as Kavolis refigures it, disputes with and then finds an increasingly large interface with globalization. Corre-spondingly, globalization theory does not stay tinnily modern, but pre-sents an analysis of processes that have been operating for a long time. It revises history at the same time as it reveals a new present and future.

Robertson grounds the development of globalization theory in a genealogical critique of his own discipline, sociology:

> I consider it to be of the utmost importance for us to realize fully that much of the conventional sociology which has developed since the first quarter of the twentieth century has been held in thrall by the virtually global institutionalization of the idea of the culturally cohesive and sequestered national society during the main phase of "classical" soci-ology. Ironically, the global aspect of that phenomenon has received relatively little attention. (1992a:50)

As the last sentence suggests—and as I have noted previously—this institutional blindness is not merely blindness but also—paradoxically—part of the ongoing process of globalization: what Robertson calls the take-off phase, in which "conceptions of the 'correct outline' of an 'acceptable' national society" are increasingly globalized (1992a:59). But in fact, the globalization process in its most general form began long before this time. From the construction of early civilizational identities and the rise of the "great religiocultural traditions during what Karl Jaspers called the Axial Period" (1991:76), "civilizations, empires and other entities have been almost continuously faced with the problem of response to the wider, increasingly compressed and by now global, context" (1991:88). "It can be shown," Robertson argues, "that each distinct civilization possesses as part of its symbolic heritage a conception of the world as a whole" (1987:24).

Robertson is more interested, however, in "the temporal-historical path toward the present circumstance of a very high degree of *global density and complexity*" (1990:26)—the period that began in Europe in the early fifteenth century, which he divides into four phases. At that time, the form of globalization was developing that persists to this day, to which Robertson devotes his most specific attention as theorist. In tracing this development, however, Robertson is emphatically clear that this form of globalization was not the result of a totalizing evolutionary grand narrative:

> The world-as-a-whole could, in theory, have become the reality which it now is in ways and along trajectories other than those which have actually obtained. The world could, in principle, have been rendered as a "singular system" via the imperial hegemony of a single nation or a "grand alliance" between two or more dynasties or nations; the victory of "the universal proletariat"; the global triumph of a particular form of organized religion; the crystallization of "the world spirit"; the yielding of nationalism to the ideal of "free-trade"; the success of the world-federalist movement; the world wide triumph of a trading company; or in yet other ways. Some of these have held sway at certain moments in world history. Indeed, in coming to terms analytically with the contemporary circumstance we have to acknowledge that some such possibilities are as old as world history in any meaningful sense of that phrase and have, in fact, greatly contributed to the existence of the globalized world of the late twentieth century. (1990:21)

To fully describe Robertson's vision of the form in which globalization has actually proceeded in modern times, however, some grasp of his overall approach is necessary. At one extreme, he describes it as an objective development independent of human consciousness, which at the most comprehensive level he calls "globalization," or "the set of processes that yields a single world" (1992c:396). He most often pictures globalization as a form of compression—the effect of a world of separate civilizations and societies crunching together, becoming conscious of each other. He also, however, considers the opposite process of expansion, or dissemination. Balancing the two, he depicts a "process of globalization . . . involving, from one perspective, the implosion of the world and, from another perspective, the explosion of societally and civilizationally situated cultures, institutions, and modes of life" (1992c:395).

Although this process of globalization is the heart of Robertson's enterprise, what he has written still more about is "globality," which he defines as the consciousness of the process of globalization, the "perceived facticity of a single world" (1992c:396) and "extensive awareness of the world as a whole" (1992a:78). Since Robertson typically depicts varieties of consciousness of globalization as essential parts of the process itself, globality becomes an essential determinant of the process of globalization, driving it and, more important, determining the directions it takes. Seen from this perspective, the centuries-long process of globalization in its most general form comprises the "ways in which the world 'moved' from being merely 'in itself' to the problem or the possibility of its being 'for itself' (1992a:55).

Robertson has pictured these constitutive effects of globality—of consciousness of the "world as a whole"—in different ways at different times. He has written at different times of the global diffusion of ideas; of the penetration of local life by globally diffused ideas; of global valorization of particular local forms and social identities; of constraint placed on individual societies to be increasingly explicit about their global callings; of exacerbation of societal self-consciousness in reaction against globalization; of consciousness of interdependence; and of establishment of a context within which local entities can reassert themselves. The different formulations clearly involve different degrees and kinds of awareness by social actors; different degrees of freedom of action; different sorts of actions; different visions of the globalization process by the actors; and, of course, different actors, ranging from individuals to institutions to nation-states. If one fleshes out different versions of these formulations, one can develop a multiplicity of examples, ranging from a demogogic leader reacting against globalization by mobilizing archaic communal imagery in the service of maintaining a repressive system at home and promoting military expansionism abroad, to the implementation of "modern" (or postmodern) globally disseminated ideas simultaneously, but without conscious coordination, by different groups within a society, from museologists to trade negotiators. All of these would represent forms of globality;

globalization would be proceeding via them all. Responding to Robertson's emphasis on globality, Janet Wolff argues, with some truth, that his commitment is to a "voluntaristic world system theory" in which "it is primarily consciousness *of* and response *to* globalization which affects and permeates the lives of people and societies" (162). Or as Robertson puts it, "*globality*—defined as consciousness of the (problem of) the world as a single place—appears increasingly to permeate the affairs of all societies and multitudes of people across the world" (1987:23–24).

With these factors in mind, we can return to Robertson's historical narrative. The modern form of globalization actually emerged in the fifteenth and sixteenth centuries:

> As a form with its own dynamics it began to take shape during the period of the decline of feudalism in Europe. During that period there was an acceleration in the early shaping of the nationally organized society; the mounting thematization of the (primarily male) individual; the enhancement of the system of inter-state relations; and the beginnings of modern ideas of humanity, particularly in philosophy and in early international law. (1992a:182)

Conceived more narrowly thus in both structural and historical terms, globalization has four components that seem to be "the major dimensions of the global-human condition—namely societies, individuals, the system of intersocietal relations, and mankind" (1987:28). Elsewhere, perhaps more illuminatingly, he calls these the different ways in which globality has been thematized. Either way, he argues that a rigorous discussion has to detail "the shifting relationships between and the relative autonomization of each of the four major components" (1990:24), and he pictures these relationships as mutually constraining: "For example, individuals as such are increasingly constrained by being members of societies, members of an increasingly thematized and threatened human species and greatly affected by the vicissitudes of international relations" (1991:79–80).

Focus on these four loosely related, mutually constraining components of globalization (or thematizations of globality) allows Robertson to discuss a heterogeneous variety of topics as part of the same enterprise. For example, on the level of the individual, the dissemination globally of the idea of individualism, and the way this "globewide encouragement of individualism" operates "in association with increasing polyethnicity and multiculturality" (1991:80), has transformed the world into a large-scale version of the United States as depicted by Clifford Geertz. America is thus no longer the "main model of cultural fragmentation and ethnic tumbling" (Robertson 1991:70). Meanwhile, "mankind" has been increasingly thematized globally—recently, for example, when "concern with human life *per se*" arose "in connection with two major species-threatening phenomena—namely, nuclear annihilation and AIDS" (1987:25). Societal identities are similarly a product of consciousness of globalization, and Robertson emphasizes the increasing need for such entities to be explicit about their global callings. Finally, the international system is itself constructed as part of a changing consciousness of globalization: in a recent article (1992b), for example, Robertson summarizes work on the transformation of the standard for admission to the international community from "civilization" to "national self-determination" when the creed of European imperialism was modified by Woodrow Wilson at the end of World War I.

Tracing development of the four components of globalization since the fifteenth and sixteenth centuries produces a rough historical plot, but it is so multifactoral and aleatory (globalization could have proceeded along other trajectories) as to be untotalizeable. Robertson describes five phases of globalization, including a "germinal phase" from the early fifteenth to the mid eighteenth century; an "incipient phase" from the mid eighteenth century to the 1870s; a "take-off phase" from the 1870s to the mid 1920s; and a "struggle-for hegemony phase" from the mid 1920s to the late 1960s. The most recent of these phases, which he calls the "uncertainty phase," Robertson describes as follows:

> Phase V—*the uncertainty phase*, beginning in the 1960s and displaying crisis tendencies in the early 1990s. Inclusion of Third World and heightening of global consciousness in late 1960s. Moon landing. Accentuation of "post-materialist" values. End of Cold War and spread of nuclear weapons. Number of global institutions and movements greatly increases. Societies increasingly face problems of multiculturality and polyethnicity. Conceptions of individuals rendered more complex by gender, ethnic and racial considerations. Civil rights. International system more fluid—end of bipolarity. Concern with humankind as a species-community greatly enhanced. Interest in world civil society and world citizenship. Consolidation of global media system. (1990:27)

In this phase, as he elsewhere puts it, "the distinction between the global and the local is becoming very complex and problematic—to such an extent that we should now speak in such terms as the global institutionalization of the life-world and the localization of globality" (1990:19).

Or, to view the process another way, the global field has become increasingly more fragmented and complex. Where Kavolis sees a civilizational polylogue—in our postmodern present—a conversation in which persisting civilizational wholes are constrained by a continually evolving common idiom—Robertson sees rather an exponential multiplication of the conversation partners. More inclusive and au courant than Kavolis, Robertson sees how, in the contemporary world, not only civilizational wholes, but also other formations (from national societies to subnational and transnational movements and groups) conduct important global (and globalizing) conversations.

> The global field as a whole is a sociocultural "system" which has resulted from the compression of—to the point that it increasingly imposes constraints upon, but also differentially empowers—civilizational cultures, national societies, intra- and cross-national movements and organizations, sub-societies and ethnic groups, intra-societal quasi-groups, individuals, and so on. As the general process of globalization proceeds there is a concomitant constraint upon such entities to "identify" themselves in relation to the global-human circumstance. In addition, globalization also yields new actors and "third cultures"—such as transnational movements and international organizations—that are oriented, negatively or positively, to the global-human circumstance. (1992a:61).

Both through the logic of his approach and his conclusions about the present world, Robertson thus depicts a decentered/decentering and heterogeneous/heterogenizing contemporary world. With the example of world-systems theory before him, Robertson is sensitive to the possibility of Eurocentrism in a historical narrative that privileges the West by regarding the contemporary form of globalization as Western-originated. We have seen how this emerged as a problem in Marxian world history—even in Wallerstein's revision of Marxian theory and its narrativization by Eric Wolf. Although Robertson also privileges the European transformation and expansion, he seeks to avoid the difficulty both by pushing his globalization process back in time well before the rise of the West and by distinguishing globalization's more recent development from simple Westernization. Whereas Westernizing modernization calls on the Third World to imitate the First, globalization calls on the whole world to define itself:

> Present concern with globality and globalization cannot be comprehensively considered simply as an aspect of outcome of the Western "project" of modernity or, except in very broad terms, enlightenment. In an increasingly globalized world, there is a heightening of civilizational, societal, ethnic, regional and, indeed[,] individual, self-consciousness. There are constraints on social entities to locate themselves within world history and the global future. Yet globalization in and of itself also involves the diffusion of the *expectation* of such identity declarations. (1992a:27)

Finally, and most important, in emphasizing the importance of consciousness of globalization as a driving force of the process itself, Robertson
maintains a diffused, polycentric focus: globalization is a process operating at a wide variety of points throughout the whole system, not one
driven by "capitalism," a narrative that privileges the global core.

Robertson's theory shares with Wallerstein's the inclination and startling ability to find global factors at work everywhere—even in the formation of academic disciplines—where people had previously only seen local
determination. Like Wallerstein, Robertson rewrites history dramatically,
revealing global interactions in what were previously thought to be local
circumstances, finding globality where few had suspected it, and seeing
consciousness of the world as a whole as a constraining and creative force
in the construction of local cultures and social forms. Wallerstein has
made similar discoveries thanks to his perception of a common, yet highly
differential, economic system covertly at work everywhere. But although
his theory shares with Wallerstein's this focus on a demystifying rewriting
of world history by discovering the global hand at work in local events,
Robertson's emphasis on consciousness rather than economic determinism leads him to unmask these interactions in a wider variety of places
(from international systems to "sub societies") than Wallerstein.

At the same time, however, Robertson's globalization theory has not
gone to the extreme of decentering and heterogenization that some work
in cultural studies has advocated, and that Robertson has criticized as
diffuse and disorderly, not "connected to the general structural and ac-
tional features of the global system" (1990:19). Robertson's vision of an
increasingly complexly differentiated—even self-differentiating—field,
in which the number of actors has increased and the transactions between
local sites and the global-human circumstance have become more transparent, remains contained within his analytic/empirical framework of the
modern globalization process: a relatively autonomous process that, as we
have seen, has four components. With Euclidean orderliness, Robertson
pictures it as a rectangle whose four corners are dynamically interconnected by their diagonals and sides.

For others, as we shall see, the non-Euclidean (dis)order of contemporary cultural studies is not to be resisted, but is itself the basis on which a
new theory of local-global cultural interactions must be built. And, similarly, the present is, not a new step in the fourfold process of globalization
that has been going on since the fifteenth century, but the stage for a larger
rupture, the appearance of a new kind of world system, a postmodern,
even postnational, global system substantially distinct from the modern
one.

The sociology of nationalism and the sociology of ethnicity are also fields in which a shift in models of the world in the postwar period can be traced. This movement has occurred most forcefully on two main fronts: demystifying study of the origin and development of national and ethnic identity and examination of how both nationalism and ethnicity have been affected by the rapid recent development of global interconnectedness. I have previously referred frequently to studies of the former sort—to Eric Hobsbawm's work on nationalism, and to Benedict Anderson's argument that the national form—which he calls a "cultural artefact"—was historically constructed and globally disseminated. In discussing theories of ethnicity, I have also charted its construction in America. Here I shall focus on how these globally disseminated notions of national and ethnic culture have been stressed and disrupted by contemporary developments.

Anthony Tambiah (1989) analyzes one of the most prominent challenges to nationalism in the contemporary period: the tendency toward fissiparous ethnicity, the insurgence of ten thousand unrecognized nationalities within the much smaller number of actually constituted nations. This tendency has, of course, not been confined to very recent times. Indeed, its prominence in the headlines today is because it has been involved in many of the ills and horrors of the entire century, from both world wars to current local conflicts, and has come to represent, after the era of fascism in particular, the nightmarish underside of the nation-state form. But, as Tambiah argues, the tendency toward ethnic unrest worldwide has not only increased in the contemporary world, it has emerged in qualitatively new ways. It has come to represent no less than a new phase in world history, one that has fragmented and decentered the global map of postwar nationalism.

Like many recent theorizers about national cultural identity, Tambiah demystifies the phenomenon he studies. In his depiction of ethnicity, Tambiah shows clearly that it constructs untrue, invented, but nonetheless believed-in, primordialist claims in the service of practical ends. He describes the process of constructing ethnic identity as one that unites "the semantics of primordial and historical claims with the pragmatics of calculated choice and opportunism in dynamic contexts of political and economic competition between interest groups" (336). Ethnic identity is thus not a persistence of tradition, but a social construction, a "pseudo-speciation" according to which "collectivities in a certain sociopolitical space think of themselves as separate social kinds." Given the value to group-formation of primordialist faith, ethnic groups persistently seek to reify and naturalize their identities. What is much more crucial and innovative, however, is that Tambiah sees this process of mystification and group formation as something that is not local, but driven by the world system (336).

In the contemporary world, Tambiah notes, ethnic conflicts have intensified dramatically. The striking thing about

> ethnic conflict as a major reality of our time is not simply its ubiquity alone, but also its cumulative increase in *frequency* and *intensity* of occurrence. Consider these conflicts, by no means an exhaustive listing, that have occurred since the sixties (some of them have a longer history, of course): conflicts between anglophone and francophone in Canada; Catholic and Protestant in Northern Ireland; Walloon and Fleming in Belgium; Chinese and Malay in Malaysia; Greek and Turk in Cyprus; Jews and other minorities on the one hand and Great Russians on the other in the Soviet Union; and Ibo and Hausa and Yoruba in Nigeria; the East Indians and Creoles in Guyana. Add to these instances, upheavals, that became climactic in recent years: the Sinhala-Tamil war in Sri Lanka, the Sikh-Hindu, and Muslim-Hindu confrontations in India, the Chakma-Muslim turmoil in Bangladesh, the actions of the Fijians against Indians in Fiji, the Pathan-Bihari clashes in Pakistan, and last, but not least, the inferno in Lebanon, and the serious erosion of human rights currently manifest in Israeli actions in Gaza and the West Bank. That there is possibly no end to these eruptions, and that they are world-wide has been forcibly brought to our attention by a century-old difference that exploded in March 1988 between Christian Armenians and Muslim Azerbiajanis in southern USSR. (337)

Wallerstein ties this upsurge in contemporary ethnic conflict to the sorcerer's-apprentice logic of the capitalist world system. As the world system mobilized the nation-state as its essential superstructural form, it became clear

> that "nationalities" were not just there in some form that could be objectively delineated. Nationalities were rather the product of a complex process of ongoing social creation, combining the achievement of consciousness (by themselves and others) and socio-juridicial labeling. It followed that for every nation there could and would be sub-nations in what threatened to be an unending cascade. It followed that each transformation of some "minority" into a "majority" created new "minorities." There could be no cut-off of this process. (1991:73)

The problem is not just that old groups have still not made states for themselves—that primordial nations have not yet acquired armies and borders—but that new ones, thanks to the logic of nationalism, continue to be produced and invented. The "heritage politics" of nationalism is not an affair of the past:

> A civilization refers to a contemporary claim about the past in terms of its use in the present to justify heritage, separateness, rights.
> Chinese civilization, Western civilization, Indian civilization are such contemporary claims. These claims do not have to be based exclusively on verifiable empirical data. These claims are in any case based on contemporary choices about historical boundaries of inclusion. Apparently, neither Chinese "civilization" nor Indian "civilization" lays claim to a direct heritage from Central Asia but Western "civilization" lays claim to a direct heritage from Greece and perhaps even from ancient Israel. The reason for such claims cannot be located in what happened in the past but in what is happening in the present. These claims about historical boundaries of inclusion are not subject to empirical verification, except as current ideology. Studying the situation in the past will not throw light on the validity of regarding certain prior time-place structures as part of the "heritage" of a contemporary group. This is because a cultural heritage is non-material and can be appropriated by multiple groups. (1991:236)

Similarly, Robertson argues that there are now "estimated to be about five thousand 'nations,' in comparison to fewer than two hundred states" and that these movements recognize that "promotion of the local is only possible on an increasingly global basis" (1992a:172).

Tambiah, while constructing a similar analysis to Wallerstein's, echoes Robertson's commitment to multidimensional analysis by not presenting ethnic ferment so forcefully as a product of the logic of a singular, totalized system. He begins instead by considering a host of more specific, contingent historical factors. Prominent among them is the fact that war has been privatized, and the state no longer has a monopoly on force in many places. Similarly crucial is the fact that ethnicity and ethnic conflict have entered the computerized, electronic information age. In recent times, countless new techniques and sites have come into existence worldwide for the present construction of "past" ethnic identities.

> The awareness that collective ethnic identity can be used and manipulated in political action is of course related to the increasing possibilities of contact through the improvement of transport, of the quick adoption and deployment of modern media, and of the raised levels of education and literacy and the spread of what Benedict Anderson has called "print capitalism." Another explanation lies in the proliferation and popularization of street theaters and public arenas, occasions for collective massing of people, ranging from political rallies and elections and referendums to strikes, demonstrations, sit-ins, and mass protests. All these capabilities for large-scale political action have occurred in tandem with population explosions in third world countries, the migration of vast numbers of rural peoples to cities and metropolitan centers, and to loca-

tions where industries or where peasant resettlement schemes have been established. Another significant factor is the proliferation of schools, colleges and universities, which have provided sites, just as factories had done in the history of industrial development, for the mobilization and massing of activists for engaging in political action. (1989:343)

Ethnicity, then, no longer represents a "survival," a continuance of a social form not really contemporary with the West, but is—and is perceivable as—a present production: "the revolution in the media, their instant transmission of visual images and auditory messages, linking metropolitan centers and distant places, and their wide coverage of events, such that news broadcasts (whether by NBC, CBS or ABC) present diverse events occurring at diverse places as a single synchronic and simultaneously occurring reality" (338).

Even more crucial, however, is the fact that, with the increased technological, communicational, and societal compression of the world today, this present production of local identities is increasingly globally mediated. Not only have organizational techniques, information, and empowering structures been globally disseminated, "local" ethnic movements have established specific connections between themselves worldwide, exchanging "knowledge of guerrilla tactics and the art of resistance. Militant groups in Japan, Germany, Lebanon, Libya, Sri Lanka and India have international networks of collaboration, not unlike—perhaps more solidary than—the diplomatic channels that exist between mutually wary sovereign countries and the great powers" (338).

The presentness and globalization of localist ethnicity and ethnic conflict in today's world are not ultimately, however, a product of this wide variety of independent developments for Tambiah. Drawing on Wallerstein, he argues that they are an integral part of the development of the world system in the modern period. Tambiah and Wallerstein conceive of this system differently, however. Tambiah sees the contemporary situation as having been produced, not by a transformation within a single capitalist system, but by the collision of two relatively independent global formations—of the capitalist economic system and the continuing worldwide construction of the "imagined communities" of nation-states. What Wallerstein links together as base and superstructure, Tambiah, distinguishing Wallerstein's world-systems theory and Anderson's theory of nationalism, divides, and casts as interacting forces:

The politics of ethnicity is indeed a product of the interweaving and collision of the two global processes we mentioned earlier: world capitalism and its operation through multinational corporations, and widespread nation building by liberated colonies now ruled by elite intel-

ligentsias who, however, have to react to their divided civilian constituencies. These interacting global processes, while having certain homogenizing effects, have simultaneously spawned differentiation and opposition within the new polities, manifested as ethnic conflict. (341)

Tambiah sees this process as fueled especially by the tensions encoded
in the second of the two processes, nationalism. First, the historical legacies of nationalism did not go away, but piled one upon the other, in
layered form. Second, a variety of contemporary circumstances mean that
nationalism has come to shape itself in a dramatically new way: it has
entered a new phase. For Tambiah, the narrative of the twentieth century
runs as follows. Old colonial processes, which impressed alien boundaries
on diverse peoples and employed the technique of social homogenization
as a "double edged sword, used in the interest both of development and
progress and of divide and rule," produced varieties of plural societies
(341). Decolonization consolidated these territories in the hands of local
elite groups, introducing the phase of nation building which Fanon's *The
Wretched of the Earth* intervened, with its "programmatic celebration of
'national consciousness,' 'national culture' and 'national' literature in the
African States, newly delivered from the chains of colonialism" (342).
Following this hopeful, expansive phase, however, came an eruption of
ethnic conflicts, stimulated by the failure of the national project and the
series of heterogeneous developments reviewed above, developments in
contemporary media, travel, forms of political activism, demography, educational practice, and so on, that empowered localist ethnic groups orga-
nizationally by global exchanges of information, techniques, and strategies. These developments—products of the increasing integration of the
capitalist world system—spread rapidly to places all around the world, and
the enhancement of nationalism intersected with the evolution of the
world system to help produce fissiparous ethnic turmoil.

Tambiah concludes with several paradoxes of system-created
diversity—that "the time of becoming the same is also the time of claiming to be different" and "the time of modernizing is also the time of
inventing tradition as well as traditionalizing innovations" (348): although the conclusions echo Wallerstein, Tambiah clearly emphasizes a
greater fragmentation in the present. For Tambiah, Wallerstein's fundamental building block, the nation-state form itself, is presently under
siege; what Wallerstein relegates to the other side of the bifurcation point,
Tambiah sees as active now.

Tambiah thus foregrounds the global exchanges involved in the construction of local ethnic groups and, more generally, the fact that current ethnic

turmoil is the product of world history, not local processes. Despite doing so, however he still depicts ethnicity as basically localist because territorializing. Although he is clear that ethnicity uses constructed primordia, and is a present production of our present world and not a "survival" of the noncontemporary, he still sees ethnicity as fundamentally rooted in myths of past descent and primordial connection to place, and the contemporary ethnic groups he examines are, accordingly, ones that have staked claims to particular territories.

A radically different approach—one that, on the one hand, globalizes and deterritorializes ethnicity much more than Tambiah does, and, on the other, refigures it more strikingly as avant-garde than traditionalizing—is a recent movement to theorize ethnic cultures as transnational. Arjun Appadurai argues that contemporary ethnic nationalism has become increasingly transnational—that such "nationalisms actually contain transnational, subnational links and, more generally, nonnational identities and aspirations" (417) and that the "nationalist genie" has become increasingly "diasporic . . . , unrestrained by ideas of spatial boundary and territorial sovereignty" (1993:413). Accordingly, he suggests that exposing the actual transnationalism of contemporary ethnic nationalism may remedy the "incapacity of many deterritorialized groups to think their way out of the imaginary of the nation-state," something that has been "the cause of much global violence since many movements of emancipation and identity are forced, in their struggles against existing nation-states, to embrace the very imaginary they seek to escape" (418).

Once this is done, as Appadurai and others have shown, transnational ethnicity is freed to become a sign of the cosmopolitan and avant-garde, even of the postmodern. Marginalized Americans present themselves, for example, as the sophisticated insiders of the system, to whom the insights of contemporary deconstructionism and poststructuralism are readily available, and something similar has happened globally. Introducing the new journal *Diaspora*, Khachig Tölöyan, writes that "diasporas are the exemplary communities of the transnational moment"—or at least an exemplary form of community in a time when we "dwell" transnationally (1991:5).

Examining the challenges a changed world order presents anthropological theory and practice with, James Clifford has perhaps drawn the most arresting picture of ethnicity as transnational. In addition, he shows how changed global relationships have created an almost exponential increase in cultural heterogeneity, which strains the ability of existing theory (especially any totalizing theory) to encompass it. Thanks not only to migration, but also to travel and the imagined travel produced by the modern media, Clifford argues, "new 'spatial practices,' new forms of dwelling and circulating" have emerged in the contemporary world. Cultures (ethnic and national) are no longer clearly territorialized. Instead,

> more and more people "dwell" with the help of mass transit, automobiles, airplanes. In cities on six continents foreign populations have come to stay—mixing in but often in partial, specific fashions. The "exotic" is uncannily close. Conversely, there seem no distant places left on the planet where the presence of "modern" products, media, and power cannot be felt. An older topography and experience of travel is exploded. One no longer leaves home confident of finding something radically new, another time or space. Difference is encountered in the adjoining neighborhood, the familiar turns up at the ends of the earth. (Clifford 1988:13–14)

Such changes in the world and people's experience of it, along with the methodological challenges resulting from reappraisals of the past and the impact of contemporary cultural interventionism, have imposed a new task on ethnography. Cultural relativism responded to a previous crisis:

> with the breakdown of evolutionist master narratives, the relativist science of culture worked to rethink the world as a dispersed whole, composed of distinct, functioning, and interrelated cultures. It reconstituted social and moral wholeness plurally. If synecdochic ethnography argued, in effect, that "cultures" hold together, it did so in response to a pervasive modern feeling, linking the Irishman Yeats with the Nigerian Achebe, that "things fall apart." (64)

In the wake of the failure of synecdochic ethnography, Clifford has become fascinated with the way things have fallen apart: like Ashcroft, Griffiths, and Tiffin, he takes as representative the syncretic, ambiguous, increasingly "Caribbean" experience of our increasingly hybrid "urban archipelagoes" (15). In this way, cultural interpenetration and intermingling have become the global norm, and heightened awareness of cultural difference—the foregrounding of ethnic-national difference everywhere thanks to close juxtaposition of the exotic and the familiar—has become the mark of contemporary global culture. As a result, for Clifford, the present has not only has become increasingly centerless; more important, it has emerged as the result of a profound break with the recent past. In this world, Pico Iyer, a precocious student of startling, boundary-violating cultural intersections (and a student, moreover, with a tricultural identity) has become a sophisticated insider. The modern world system has ended, and a qualitatively different postmodern world order has been revealed.

In his essay, "Disjuncture and Difference in the Global Cultural Economy" (1990), Arjun Appadurai draws on an unusual variety of recent scholarship to achieve a series of ends: to extend the study of postnational ethnicity and nationalism beyond what has been done by Anderson and Tambiah; to make the notion of the transnationalization of culture central (as Clifford does not attempt to do), not just to a provocative description of contemporary cultural interactions, but to an overall theory of world relationships; to respond fully to the ferment of postcolonial and postmodern cultural studies; and to do this by radically revising Wallerstein's world-systems theory, bringing chaos back from the future and locating it as the explanation of the present.

In developing the concept of a postnational world of fragmented, localized "imagined communities," Appadurai argues that the development of global electronic media has created a vastly more complex pattern of deterritoralized imagined communities than Anderson and his successor, Tambiah, perceived. A new *kind* of imagined community has been created, an electronically mediated sort that is fundamentally transnational, qualitatively different from Benedict Anderson's print-based national form. From these developments, a new, fundamentally transnational world system has been produced: this contemporary system no longer has Wallerstein's visualizeable, Euclidean, center-periphery structure, but can only be described by an appeal to chaotics. The result is a comprehensive, complexly interacting system that is by definition not totalizeable or deterministic, one that is bewilderingly heterogeneous and heterogenizing at a multitude of sites.

Against the background of global history, Appadurai argues that our present era is a new phase in the progressive transformation of what he calls Wallerstein's "interactive" world system. This significant information-age characterization emphasizes the postmodern, decentering quality latent in Wallerstein's original conceptualization, just as dependency theory provides Wallerstein's theory with a centering, anticolonialist side. For Appadurai, the globalized present is marked by a foregrounding and intensifying of the latent interactivity theorized by previous formulations.

To highlight the way the present differs from the past, Appadurai sketches a brief global history. During most of human prehistory, cultural interactions involved long-distance transportation of commodities, warfare, and religious conversions (to which we could add long-term migrations). This era yielded to one characterized by the rise of cities, regional kingdoms, and then regional civilizations, which were subsequently reshaped into complex, overlapping Eurocolonial orders. Then, from traffic within these colonial orders in "complex ideas of peoplehood and selfhood," the "imagined communities of recent nationalisms throughout the world" that Benedict Anderson has described were formed. Crucial to these "imagined communities" according to Anderson, was print capitalism; with it "a new power was unleashed in the world, the power of mass literacy and its attendant large-scale production of projects of ethnic affinity that were remarkably free of the need for face-to-face communication or even of indirect communication between persons and groups. The act of reading things together set the stage for movements based on a paradox—the paradox of constructed primordialism" (2). Appadurai goes on, however:

> But the revolution of print capitalism, and the cultural affinities and dialogues unleashed in it, were only modest precursors to the world we live in now. For in the last century, there has been a technological explosion, largely in the domain of transportation and information, which makes the interactions of a print-dominated world seem as hard-won and as easily erased as the print revolution made earlier forms of cultural traffic appear. For with the advent of the steamship, the automobile and the aeroplane, the camera, the computer and the telephone, we have entered into an altogether new condition of neighborliness, even with those most distant from ourselves. (2)

World history and the world system it forms are always interactive, and they have been transformed, over the centuries, by the development of new mechanisms for new forms of that interactivity. The present situation, according to Appadurai, thus differs in degree (a vast increase in the amount of interaction) and kind (the interactions occur in new ways, mediated by new technologies). This present era is the one Clifford describes aspects of more restrictively: global difference is discovered everywhere right in one's neighborhood, even as one's own culture can be encountered at the ends of the earth.

Drawing on contemporary cultural studies, Appadurai argues that full recognition of these changed historical circumstances calls for theorizing a "new role for the imagination in social life." In this view, the imagination is no longer the superstructure of an economic base; it has become equally determinative with economic factors in a world that is now "a complex transnational construction of imaginary landscapes." In this world, imagination no longer represents transcendence or escape, but is a crucial—indeed, the most crucial—form of social construction, of productive work. Thus, Appadurai calls the system he describes the "global cultural economy," fusing the two terms. He attributes crucial significance to the notion of imagined communities—communities produced by the imagination functioning as productive work. In the postnationalist, electronic-media-based present, the concept of imagined community can be used to theorize all social, cultural, and political forms; or, as Raymond Williams (1982) envisioned, the "means of communication" can be conceptualized as a crucial "means of production" (Brantlinger 1990:192).

The transformation of an era of print-capitalism into an era of global media thus represents, not only a different, but, more forcefully, a dramatically enhanced role for the imagination as work. Following Walter Benjamin (1969), Lash and Urry (1987) and Jameson (1984) Appadurai sees contemporary "reality" as more thoroughly culture-constructed than ever before; capitalism penetrated one of the last enclaves to resist it—the imagination—when the technology of culture entered the electronic-media stage. As we have seen, Jameson, like Lash and Urry, argues that a prodigious expansion of culture throughout the social realm is part of the logic of late capitalism, which means that "everything in our social life— from economic value and state power to practices and to the very structure of the psyche itself—can be said to have become 'cultural' in some original and as yet untheorized sense" (1984:87). Acknowledging his debt to Jameson, Appadurai tries to fill the theoretical void Jameson sees by conceptualizing this encompassing "cultural" quality in a new fashion in the context of a variety of global and world-systems perspectives:

> The new global cultural economy has to be seen as a complex, overlapping, disjunctive order, which cannot any longer be understood in terms of existing center-periphery models (even those which might account for multiple centers and peripheries). Nor is it susceptible to simple models of push and pull (in terms of migration theory), or of surpluses and deficits (as in traditional models of balance of trade), or of consumers and producers (as in most neo-Marxist theories of development). Even the most complex and flexible theories of global development which have come out of the Marxist tradition (Amin 1980; Mandel 1978; Wallerstein 1974; Wolf 1982) are inadequately quirky and have failed to come to terms with what Lash and Urry have called disorganized capitalism. The complexity of the current global economy has to do with certain fundamental disjunctures between economy, culture and politics which we have only begun to theorize. (6)

Appadurai goes on to outline his intentionally "quirky" alternative:

> I propose that an elementary framework for exploring such disjunctures is to look at the relationship between five dimensions of global cultural flow which can be termed: (a) ethnoscapes; (b) mediascapes; (c) technoscapes; (d) finanscapes; and (e) ideoscapes. The suffix -scape allows us to point to the fluid, irregular shapes of these landscapes, shapes which characterize international capital as deeply as they do international clothing styles. These terms with the common suffix -scape also indicate that these are not objectively given relations which look the same from every angle of vision, but rather that they are deeply perspectival constructs, inflected by the historical, linguistic and political situatedness of

different sorts of actors: nation-states, multinationals, diasporic communities, as well as sub-national groupings and movements (whether
religious, political or economic), and even intimate face-to-face groups,
such as villages, neighbourhoods and families. (7)

Appadurai's global system is constructed out of a series of relational
"landscapes," which are themselves perspectival constructs by a series of
different localized, specifically situated "actors" (the more "traditional" of
which still seek, as a part of their self-invention, to attach themselves to
territories). Many of these localized "actors," from multinationals to diasporas, are, however, as little attached to territory with definite geographic
boundaries as the "landscapes" of the electronic global system are. Appadurai's theory thus presents us, first, with the most complete picture to
date of a global system composed not simply or perhaps even primarily of
nation-states, but of a multitude of deterritorialized globalist-localisms
that operate above and below the level of the nation-state. Second, Appadurai thereby describes a world system that is no longer unitary, but
rather both one and many (heterogeneous, conflicting, cooperating, overlapping) systems at the same time.

The astonishing, increasingly postnational fragmentation Appadurai
advocates can be pictured in a number of different ways. First, the flows
that comprise the system are plural, distinct, and disjunct from one another. Presumably, in a centered global system, these -scapes would be yoked
to one another by virtue of being anchored in a core: population would
flow to/from the core for work/colonization; media would emanate from
there, and technology, investment, and ideology likewise. Correspondingly, the different flows might be theorized as linked with each other
(objectively, not just perspectively) as parts of one process (for example,
imperialism). Imperial economic power would, therefore, be seen as yoked
with cultural domination via mediascapes and ideoscapes. These Newtonian certainties are disrupted radically in Appadurai; they appear, as the
Newtonian world appears through the complex lenses of quantum and
chaos theories, to be a very special island of apparent determinism afloat
in a fundamentally indeterminate, much weirder world.

Appadurai argues that in the contemporary world these flows are anything but centered or unified. In general, the polycentric dispersion of the
contemporary world has progressed so far that Americanization is no
longer the only cultural threat in town: "For the people of Irian Jaya,
Indonesianization may be more worrisome than Americanization, as Ja-
panization may be for Koreans, Indianization for Sri Lankans, Vietnamiza-
tion for the Cambodians, Russianization for the people of Soviet Armenia
and the Baltic Republics" (5–6). Like the ethnoscape, each flow is increas-

ingly decentered from global and regional metropolitan cores and complexly polymorphous: "Men and women from villages in India think not
just of moving to Poona or Madras, but of moving to Dubai and Houston,
and refugees from Sri Lanka find themselves in South India as well as
Switzerland" (7). Different flows operate separately from one another. The
finanscape presents a quite different kind of global mapping from, say, the
ideoscape: although relationships exist, they are "deeply disjunctive and
profoundly unpredictable, since each of these landscapes is subject to its
own constraints and incentives (some political, some informational and
some techno-environmental), at the same time as each acts as a constraint
and a parameter for movements in the others" (8). Such disjunctures are
not new, but recent history has made them crucial to the world system as
never before:

> People, machinery, money, images, and ideas now follow increasingly
> non-isomorphic paths: of course, at all periods in human history, there
> have been some disjunctures between the flows of these things, but the
> sheer speed, scale and volume of each of these flows is now so great that
> the disjunctures have become central to the politics of global culture.
> The Japanese are notoriously hospitable to ideas and are stereotyped as
> inclined to export (all) and import (some) goods, but they are also noto-
> riously closed to immigration, like the Swiss, the Swedes and the Saudis.
> Yet the Swiss and Saudis accept populations of guest-workers, thus creat-
> ing labor diaporas of Turks, Italians and other circum-Mediterranean
> groups. (11)

Increasingly disjunctures between the global flows have thus both more
dramatically fragmented and more complexly interconnected the contemporary world.

A second, and related, way of picturing the fragmentation Appadurai's
theory entails is to note that, as the flows are separated from each other,
they and what they contain are also pried loose from their anchors, not
just in the core, but in any delimited territory (from nation to community
to family) at all. The result is the nearly complete transgression of older •
territorial political, economic, and cultural boundaries. First, Appadurai
argues that ethnoscapes are routinely deterritorialized as homelands are
invented or kept alive by diasporic groups and primordia (whether of
language, skin color, neighborhood, or kinship) become globalized.
Ideoscapes and mediascapes are similarly transformed as ideology and
media images are severed from origins and the coherences of national
traditions meant for national consumption, and manufactured instead for
internationally dispersed and/or heterogeneous groups and interpreted
differently at different sites in the world. Finanscapes are also altered as

finance capital becomes multinational and "money managers seek the best markets for their investments, independent of national boundaries" (12). Second, disjunct, rapid global flows have "subverted the hyphen that links the nation and the state," putting the "states under siege,"

> especially where contests over the ideoscapes of democracy are fierce and fundamental, and where the radical disjunctures between ideoscapes and technoscapes (as in the case of very small countries that lack contemporary technologies of production and information); or between ideoscapes and finanscapes (as in countries such as Mexico or Brazil, where international lending influences national politics to a very large degree); or between ideoscapes and ethnoscapes (as in Beirut, where diasporic, local and translocal filiations are suicidally at battle); or between ideoscapes and mediascapes (as in many countries in the Middle East and Asia) where the lifestyles represented on both national and international TV and cinema completely overwhelm and undermine the rhetoric of national politics. (14)

Third, even the "transgenerational stability of knowledge" is disrupted, as the task of cultural reproduction, "even in its most intimate areas, such as husband-wife and parent-child relations, becomes both politicized and exposed to the traumas of deterritorialization," producing an often-violent politics of identity, exacerbated by "the effects of mechanical art," the media, as they intervene in this process (17–18).

A final way of depicting the fragmentation Appadurai's world system describes is perhaps the most dramatic. The complex and volatile plurality Appadurai theorizes is exponentially increased because the global system's relations are "not objectively given relations . . . but deeply perspectival constructs," which not only look but are different according to the "historical, linguistic and political situatedness of different sorts of actors." Among Appadurai's differently situated "actors" are "nation-states, multi-nationals, diasporic communities, as well as sub-national groupings and movements (whether religious, political or economic), and even intimate face-to-face groups, such as villages, neighborhoods and families." The list is not exhaustive: supranational religious groupings, civilizational identities, gender-identifying movements, occupational cultures (such as international societies of physicists), regional identities (the intermediate step between the nation and the outside world), fan clubs, and so on, could be added to it. These different "actors" constitute different imagined communities. The nation is now just one of a wealth of imagined communities—localized sites for the production of globally significant differences.

Each of these sites, Appadurai argues, constructs its own version of the global -scapes; each condenses a different version of the fundamentally polymorphic global system. Since every individual is a member of a number of these communities, each person is, of necessity, inhabiting / negotiating / being constructed through a variety of imagined communities and simultaneously inhabits / negotiates a number of different, disjunct global systems as well. Appadurai's system simultaneously fragments and pluralizes selves, localized sites, and the overall global order itself. Furthermore, since Appadurai enumerates these sites democratically, as a list, refusing to privilege any formation (like a nation) clearly as the mediator for others (like communities), this polymorphousness is heightened.

Clearly, experience in this world system is not what it used to be. Since each individual is a member of a variety of different imagined communities (and therefore involved in a variety of "different" global systems), representative individual lives in this contemporary world are distinctly postmodern; unitary subjects are dramatically denaturalized and dispersed. The individual is inserted into heterogeneous and potentially conflicting contexts—nation, ethnic group, occupational culture, gender, religion, class, and so forth—and thus participates in disjunctive, mutually interrupting imagined communities, each of which generates different mappings of the globe. No longer unitary subjects, inhabitants of this postmodern global system reemerge as baroque, syncretic constructions, each in him- or herself embodying some always-eccentric version of the cultural, social, economic heterogeneity of the whole system. As in Iyer, the ongoing production of startlingly novel, heterogenizing identity combinations is an essential, indeed routine, aspect of the world according to Appadurai. In Appadurai's theory, then, in a number of different ways, the world simultaneously becomes more comprehensively, interactively unitary and more decentered and multiplicitous.

Appadurai concludes his essay with some recommendations about how to evolve a full-blown "general theory of global cultural processes" from this model of bewilderingly fragmenting, yet interconnecting cultural flows (19). Arguing that "our very models of cultural shape will have to alter, as configurations of people, place and heritage lose all semblance of isomorphism" (20), Appadurai sees the deconstruction in anthropology of "the shackles of highly localized, boundary-oriented, holistic, primordialist images of cultural form and substance" as a positive step. But nothing has been set in place of those shackles aside from what Appadurai calls "a larger version of those images"—that is, the tradition of world-systems theory that Appadurai is a revisionist heir to. Conceptions of the systemacity of "world systems," then, are still too indebted, according to Appadurai, to the closed, isomorphic Euclidean shapes of anthropological structural-functionalism; the nature of the system has to be radically rethought. To do so, Appadurai proposes, first, that "we begin to think of the configuration of cultural forms in today's world as fundamentally fractal, that is possessing no Euclidean boundaries, structures, or regularities" (20). Benoit Mandelbrot's fractal shapes and geometry, he and Christopher Scholz argue, describe the nonlinear, random irregularities that really characterize the bulk of nature (Gleick 1987:103–7). As Jean-François Lyotard summarizes it, they respond to problems like "a precise measurement of the coast of Brittany, the crater-filled substance of the moon, the distribution of stellar matter, the frequency of bursts of interference during a telephone call, turbulence in general, the shape of clouds. In short, the majority of the objects whose outlines and distributions have not undergone regularization at the hands of man" (Lyotard 1984:58).

When shaped according to this model, a global cultural system will clearly not have the geometry of centered, bounded wholes (whether, as in cultural relativism, a juxtaposition of many, or, as in world-systems theory, a single large one). Its geometry will have to describe nonlinear, chaotically variable shapes, without a clear center or clear boundaries. Moreover, the fractal geometry that thus grounds Appadurai's perspectivism is, as Mandelbrot describes it, fundamentally nonobjective. It is dependent on the relation of object to observer.

Appadurai then turns to "pure mathematics (. . . set theory for example)" and "biology (in the language of polythetic classifications)" to argue that these cultural forms, "which we should strive to represent as fully fractal, are also overlapping"; this prospect dismays him as theorist, however, prompting him to ask "How are we to compare fractally shaped cultural forms which are also polythetically overlapping in their coverage of terrestrial space"? (20). Last, but not least, in opposition to both the primordialism of cultural relativism and the fatalism of world-systems theory, Appadurai argues that this global system is as unstable as it is complex:

> We will need to ask how these complex, overlapping, fractal shapes constitute not a simple, stable (even if large-scale) system, but to ask what its dynamics are: why do ethnic riots occur when and where they do? Why do states wither at greater rates in some places and times rather than others? Why do some countries flout conventions of international debt repayment with so much less apparent worry than others? How are international arms flows driving ethnic battles and genocides? Why are some states exiting the global stage while others are clamouring to get in? Why do key events occur at a certain point in a certain place rather

than in others? These are, of course, the great traditional questions of causality, contingency and prediction in the human sciences, but in a world of disjunctive global flows, it is perhaps important to start asking them in a way that relies on images of flow and uncertainty, hence "chaos," rather than older images of order, stability, and systemacity. (20)

Appadurai's situated actors are not Foucaultian subject positions, haplessly constructed out of discourses, but imagined communities; as such, they hold out more promise of agency. This fact, when coupled with chaos theory's emphasis on how small changes can cascade unexpectedly through a system to produce great ones, leads Appadurai to depict his system as catastrophically uncertain, even as he is able to retain the notion of individual agency. Local action can, just, upset the whole global system, despite the enormous disparity in size between the two frames. Traditional determinism does not apply to the perspectivism and indeterminacy of the new world system; just as quantum theory and chaotics have revised traditional physics, seeing it as embodying localist blindness to deeper, stranger forms of (dis)order, so social scientists must abandon traditional determinist assumptions. Whereas Wallerstein banishes chaotics to the far side of his bifurcation point—to the end of the capitalist world system as we know it—Appadurai locates it in the here and now, and Janet Abu-Lughod supplements his postmodern revision with a premodern challenge of her own. She argues, as we have seen, for the appropriateness of chaos theory to the medieval world system in particular, and to all world systems and world-systems conceptions in general. Asserting that "no system is fully integrated and therefore none can be completely controlled, even by the most powerful participants," Abu-Lughod claims that chaos theory is relevant to world-systems analysis because "the traditional 'same cause yields same effect' logic that underlies positivist social science seems sadly ill equipped to deal with systemic change. Instead, the theories of chaos (recently described by Gleick) may be pertinent" (369).

For both Appadurai and Abu-Lughod, then, a global system thus reconceived allows escape from the fatalism of Wallerstein's world system. Thanks to the butterfly effect, or what chaos theory calls sensitive dependence on initial conditions, small disturbances within a system may cascade catastrophically into great ones, depending on what else is happening throughout the system. Chaos theory, in short, privileges agency on the microlevel for them much more strongly and systematically than in Worsley's concept of localist resistances. If Worsley sees micro-resistance and organization as accomplishing real good in an era of disillusionment with nationalism, Appadurai and Abu-Lughod, using the analytic framework of world-systems theory, see the possibility of, not merely local, but even world-systemwide change resulting from it.

This synopsis of Appadurai's overall theory echoes fears that emphasis on interactivity may undermine the centeredness of theories of neocolonial order and anticolonial activism surprisingly closely. Like Mukherjee—and Suleri too, in the context of postcolonial scholarship—Appadurai extends cultural decentering well beyond the oppositional dramas of the colonial/anticolonial narrative. All three relocate cultural interactiveness in a global model so decentered and fragmented that anticolonialism threatens to lose its ideological bite. No longer are oppressor and oppressed so clearly bounded; indeed, boundaries are different for each context, and no one, in the interpenetrating complexity of the contemporary global system, truly inhabits only a single context. To try, on the one hand, to draw clear boundary lines to authorize a large-scale project would be to simplify world complexity and suppress many of the contexts in which one personally is also constructed. On the other hand, in Appadurai's fragmented world system, constructing heterogeneous alliances of microgroups authorizes a wealth of projects. The problem is that it is hard to confine this wealth, as JanMohamed, Lloyd, and Lowe seek to do, within a marginalized-mainstream opposition, given the disappearance in Appadurai of a unifying (neocolonial, racist) center to be resisted.

Critics like Benita Parry (1989) may feel that this emphasis on sociocultural fragmentation and interaction licenses a deceptive multiculturalism, one that masks persisting racial and geopolitical inequities with claims of cultural equality attained. Furthermore, a Marxian critic (like Fredric Jameson) may (and indeed does [1991:318–31]) suspect a mystifying function in claims of cultural decenteredness: in an era of multinational capitalism, cultural decenteredness can serve the capitalist system by constructing an international proletariat both fragmented and globalized, just as the new multinationals might wish. Like Mukherjee's cultural comedies, Appadurai's system does not encode insurgent resistance against a still-centered system, a pluralist attack on monoculture, or an *Orientalism*-inspired deconstruction of interrelationships between imperial domination and culture-construction that empowers Europe and afflicts its "others." It describes a world that no longer has a center to resist in the old way, one in which power is fragmented and diffused according to a wholly different geometry. Freed thus from Wallersteinian fatalism, Appadurai risks a different vulnerability: his extension of the radical project threatens to undermine that project. In a world so fragmented into disparate imagined communities, the old rationales for collective action disappear, and new, heterogeneous oppositional alliances are deprived of the cultural and political boundary lines upon which they depend.

Despite the above caveats, I believe that Appadurai's theory provides the most satisfying means to date for grasping what is specifically new about the present time. It focuses squarely on how globalization has proceeded to develop outside national and civilizational frames and, at the same time, to challenge these frames from within. Also, by evoking a historical narrative of interactiveness, Appadurai's theory shows, like Kavolis's, Wallerstein's, and Robertson's, that these mechanisms are civilizationally old. In pursuing these goals so fully, Appadurai has, to be sure, destabilized old progressive legacies; still, he has made a genuine, although uncertain and disruptive, opening for future work. By violating the sacred boundary line between colonial and anticolonial, his theory opens up the possibility, even as it has made it difficult, for new heterogeneous alliances that yoke together, more than Lowe's, JanMohamed's, and Lloyd's do, what formerly was held asunder. Like Anzaldúa's vision of crossing the border between Anglo and other, and Suleri's advocacy of cultural compassion, Appadurai's theory authorizes the creation of cultural alignments of genuinely new sorts. Appadurai has sought, with limited success, to describe one such project—the development of "cross-cutting alliances" in an American postnational context—in his essay "Patriotism and Its Futures" (1993:427). But even if, like Nandy's notion of dialogue, the possibility of unusual new global conversations between partners formerly ranked as antagonistic, but now equally decentered, is seen as utopian, it provides an opening from the uncertainty of the present onto a future that past nationalism could scarcely imagine.

After fifteen years of world-systems and globalization theory, we have constructed a model of the world very different from the one that emerged from the ruins of the colonial empire and the era of nationalism. Separate nations grouped geopolitically and culturally in a tripartite hierarchy have given way to a series of different versions of the world as a single system or place. In the process, we have learned to negotiate a changing world by inventing a multitude of maps for it, the most recent being the succession of world-systems and globalization theories we have just surveyed. Even these recent maps, moreover, are not transparencies on the world, innocent of involvement in the process they study; just as hindsight allows us to discover constitutive force and a variety of specific agendas in the hierarchical nationalism of the three worlds theory, so recently generated theory must be seen as politically implicated in contemporary globalism. "I suggest that world systems theory, in a diffuse sense, has also (and not undeliberately) become ideology, and one possible definition of the global situation, a 'party' in global cultural conflict," Robertson writes (1992a:72).

The political indebtedness of recent theories of globalization—the character of globalization theory as an emerging discourse—has yet to be defined. To date, the discourse has been more politically polymorphous than postmodernism, which has seemed radical to some, the opposite to others. If globalism in economics has fueled new considerations of gaining global hegemony (e.g., Japan as the information-age society, the current emphasis on the global economy in the United States), it is also strongly located in oppositional theory (the neo-Marxianism of world-system theory). And if globalism has yielded a new generation of cultural radicalism, it also has induced mainstream nationalism to try to reproduce itself in new forms.

In the preceeding chapters, I have organized my presentation of the ongoing development of new forms of global mapping as a historical narrative. I should, however, conclude this chapter by arguing that none of the models are out of date, that all are interpretatively necessary to us still. This necessity is perhaps easiest to understand as historical necessity, a function of either history's constraint upon the present or the constraint that the invention of culture shares with other creative activity—namely, its need to use the codes that are to hand in its attempts at transformation. Janet Abu-Lughod states the former argument well: "Successive systems reorganize in a somewhat cumulative fashion, the lines and connections laid down in prior epochs tending to persist even though their significance and roles in the new system may be altered" (1989:368).

Thus, to use Appadurai's terms, the situatedness of some contemporary "actors" has been traditionalizing, and has invoked the legacy of older colonial world systems; the situatedness of others is anticolonial, continuing the radical nationalism of the 1960s; the situatedness of others is postcolonial, invoking and criticizing the legacy of anticolonial nationalism in order further to dismantle imperial culture; and the situatedness of still others is global-postmodern, evoking a very different kind of model. Each kind exists; that each exists leads me necessarily to represent the contemporary world as still more heterogeneous than I have yet argued. For in circulation on contemporary knowledge circuits, we find not only theories of heterogenizing world systems, but also an increasing heterogeneity of world-systems theories themselves, all of which, from anticolonial to postmodern formulations, correspond to widely held perspectives on the contemporary globe. To the continued propagation of previous colonial and anticolonial versions of the three worlds theory, then, we must add the invention of a new multiplicity: a growing number of conceptions of the world as a single place.

12

Postmodernism and Globalization

CHARLES JENCKS dates the passage to the postmodern as 3:32 P.M. on July 15, 1972, "when the Pruitt-Igoe housing development in St. Louis (a prize-winning version of Le Corbusier's 'machine for modern living') was dynamited as an uninhabitable environment for the low income people it housed" (Harvey 1989:39). Thus ended modernism—its transformative rationalization and integration, processes that operated in the area of national culture, in the production of citizenry for modern nation-states, as well as architecture. Space was thereby opened up for the creation of Jencks's postmodern eclectic aesthetic style, a heterogenizing style that quotes material from the global *musée imaginaire* that, Jencks believed, all possess (Harvey 1989:87; Rose 1991:107–19).

As Craig Owens (1989) points out, however, Jencks's notion of the *musée imaginaire* was not original with him. It was presciently evoked earlier in the postwar period by Paul Ricoeur—in the essay analyzed in the first chapter of this book. What was for Ricoeur a vision of the melancholy end of national culture and civilization, if American vague syncretism were to triumph, became, for Owens, a prophecy of what postmodernism would proclaim as accomplished. Ricoeur wrote that the "discovery of the plurality of cultures is never a harmless experience":

> When we discover that there are several cultures instead of just one and consequently at the time when we acknowledge the end of a sort of cultural monopoly, be it illusory or real, we are threatened with destruction by our own discovery. Suddenly it becomes possible that there are just *others*, that we ourselves are an "other" among others. All meaning and every goal having disappeared, it becomes possible to wander through civilizations as if through vestiges and ruins. The whole of mankind becomes an imaginary museum: where shall we go this weekend—visit the Angkor ruins or take a stroll in the Tivoli of Copenhagen? We can very easily imagine a time when any fairly well-to-do person will be able to leave his country indefinitely in order to taste his own national death in an interminable, aimless voyage. (1965:278)

"Lately we have come to regard this condition as postmodern," Craig Owens (1989:58) comments. The postmodern pluralism Ricoeur evokes, which reduces "us to being an other among others," has rather extreme effects. In general, it undercuts all possibility of meaning; more specifically, as Owens adds, it undoes "not only the hegemony of Western culture, but also (our sense of) our identity as a culture" (58).

Following Fredric Jameson's now industry-standard view, however, Owens (like Jencks, Baudrillard, and Lyotard [Featherstone 1991:3]) sees postmodernism as an outgrowth of metropolitan-centered processes. For Jameson, it is the cultural dominant of late capitalism, and despite his invocation, following Ricoeur, of globalism, Owens likewise centers this process in the West, describing it as "a crisis of cultural authority, specifically of the authority vested in Western European culture and its institutions" (57). But the decontextualized eclecticism Ricoeur mourns and Jencks celebrates had clearly global sources and has subsequently resurfaced as a crucial component of contemporary global commercial culture. Furthermore, Pico Iyer demonstrates how this eclecticism reveals itself as decentered, once one recognizes how "others" consume and manipulate metropolitan culture, even as metropolitans wander through their imaginary museums. Indeed, the implications of Iyer's prose, like the prevailing analyses of Japanese Disneyland, are first, that peripheral participation in postmodernism is something to be reckoned with, and, second, that this participation is not severely constrained by either cultural dependency *or* the rather extreme metropolitan melancholy Ricoeur displays. Perhaps this important difference has something to do with the fact that the postmodern crisis for some has meant opportunity for others—that what evokes end-of-civilization gloom in Ricoeur means something quite different for peripheral figures and societies.

In place of First World melancholy, peripheral siting of the postmodern has, generally speaking, tended toward the revelation of an extravagant carnival, in which colonial and postcolonial history have been incorporated as catastrophe. But these peripheral carnivals, although catastrophic, have had a different kind of vigor as well—a vigor that has hinted at their cultures' increasing centrality to the contemporary world. Thus, for example, Antonio Benítez-Rojo (1992) has recently described the Caribbean from a postmodern perspective. Echoing Ashcroft, Griffiths, and Tiffin, he sees it as a site of cultural syncretism, and, like them, he takes this as a sign that the Caribbean provides a far clearer model for the postmodern world than First World cultures do. Indeed, he depicts the Caribbean as the locus, not just of cultural syncretism, but of supersyncretism, and asserts that these processes were civilizationally foundational (responsible for nothing less than classical Greek culture) as well as being central to the contemporary world. Benítez-Rojo delights in exemplifying his assertions with intentionally chaotic lists, full of unchartable complexity and boundary violation:

> Caribbean literature cannot free itself totally from the multiethnic society upon which it floats, and it tells of its fragmentation and instability: that of the Negro who studied in London or in Paris, that of the white who believes in voodoo, that of the Negro who wants to find his identity in Africa, that of the mulatto who wants to be white, that of the white man who loves a black woman and vice versa, that of the rich black man and the poor white man, that of the mulatto woman who passes for white and has a black child, that of the mulatto who says that the races do not exist. Add to these differences those that resulted—and still result in certain regions—from the encounter of the Indoamerican with the European and of the latter with the Asian. Finally, add to all of this the unstable system of relations which, amid uncompromising alliances and conflicts, brings together and separates the Native American and the Asian, the Asian and the African, but why go on with this? What model of the human sciences can predict what will happen in the Caribbean next year, next month, next week? (27)

The carnivalesque quality of Benítez-Rojo's description permeates his whole book, and the model that he settles on to explain confusing interactions like these is chaos theory. What Appadurai finds at work in the postmodern global ecumene, Benítez-Rojo finds privileged in both ancient Greece and the contemporary Caribbean.

Such developments have led me, throughout this book, to point out how peripheral cultures either have used or could use postmodernism as a means of claiming new kinds of centrality in the contemporary world system. They have done this most often by claiming that they have in some way been "always already" postmodern. The rationale for these interventionist claims—and the fact that what the ideology of postmodernism represents has been vastly more empowering for the Third World than the ideology of modernism, in which a Third World has always had to play catch-up—can be made clearer, I believe, if we alter the industry-standard base for the analysis of the postmodern. Appreciating peripheral postmodernism requires abandoning primary focus on the deconstruction of First World institutions, culture, and knowledge as a result of a transmutation in the narrative of capitalism. Peripheral postmodernism is best analyzed instead from the perspective of globalization, as a result of contemporary developments in what we have seen to be a centuries-long globalization process that links changes in the core and changes in the periphery explicitly together.

It will help to illustrate this point at the outset. In exactly this vein, Edward Said has criticized Lyotard's theory of the breakdown of grand narratives that legitimate knowledge in the postmodern period. For Said, Lyotard's First World knowledge critique, grounded as it is (paradoxically) in a narrative of First World postindustrial development, is "not an explanation but a symptom." It is this because, as Said writes, Lyotard "*separates* Western postmodernism from the non-European world, and from the consequences of European modernism—and modernization—in the colonized world" (1989:222). Said goes on:

> The striking thing about Lyotard's argument, and perhaps the very reason for its widespread popularity, is how it not only misreads but misrepresents the major challenge to the great narratives and the reason why their power may now appear abated. They have lost their legitimation in large measure as a result of the crisis of modernism, which foundered on or was frozen in contemplative irony for various reasons, of which one was the disturbing appearance in Europe of various Others, whose provenance was the imperial domain. (222)

In place of Lyotard's analysis for the breakup of master narratives, Said puts a postcolonial contrapuntal process, a history of increasing interaction between metropolitan power and colony/postcolony. Insurgence in the colonies, coupled with increasingly significant intervention by peripheral intellectuals in First World knowledge critique and construction, has shattered imperial assumptions about knowledge and representation that were dependent on metropolitan-controlled narratives. In short, Lyotardian metropolitan deconstruction found its deeper cause in peripheral contrapuntalism—the recent enhancement of global interactions that globalization theory has described. A similar change can be seen in Appadurai's use of catastrophe theory: whereas Lyotard cites it as part of the transformation of First World knowledge, Appadurai theorizes catastrophe as a feature of the postmodern interactive global system, in which the Third World is vastly more present than it was in the era of modernity.

If recent global interactiveness can be foregrounded as the cause of the dissolution of grand narratives, so it can upstage metropolitan self-deconstruction as cause for other topoi of postmodernism. Thus the fragmentation of centered cultures and identities, and the loss of both reality and history to the reign of simulacra have, as Ricoeur's lament indicates, involved a different kind of dramatically enhanced flow of cultural material between core and peripheral sites. But the fullest appreciation of the relevance of globalization theory for exploring the emergence of postmodernism in both the core and peripheral areas must include more than just a consideration of these recent transformations. It must consider them against the legacy of past phases of globalization, in particular the restructuring of the world effected by colonialism. Only thus can the peripheral claim to have been "always already" postmodern be really illustrated.

It is hard to imagine a more glaringly syncretic, code-mixing, carnivalesque, postmodern representation of a society than what Carlos Diegues's film *Bye Bye Brazil* (1980) does for contemporary Brazil. In this film, contemporary globalization seems to have fascinatingly transformed "backward" Brazil into a central site in the postmodern world system. But the film's explicitly postmodern landscape—Brazilian hinterlands of provincial poverty and an Amazon penetrated and increasingly despoiled by international capital—could easily have been the locus for a cultural production of a previous sort, a harsh satire of external neocolonial penetration and exploitation and internal social tumult and rapacity. Indeed, before this postmodern landscape could be spectacularly revealed, some preparation, some space clearing of past modes, was necessary.

The protagonists of the film—the Gypsy Lord and his consort, Salomé, who run a traveling carnival show with the help of their black mute assistant, Swallow—pick up a young accordionist and his pregnant wife in a small town they pass through: the naive, but ambitious, young accordionist and his more wholesomely provincial wife leave home charmed with the romance that the carnival represents. Soon, the wonders of the carnival show—in which locals are awed by a simulated snowfall, while Bing Crosby sings "White Christmas" and the Gypsy Lord proclaims that snow now falls in Brazil, as it does in Europe, the United States, and all the civilized countries of the world—are qualified somewhat by the fact that the carnival is also a brothel. The Gypsy Lord is pimp, and Salomé the hooker. He thus appears to be, symbolically, an agent of neocolonialism, someone who exploits his own people's cultural dependency, and the opening of the movie seems to be a sharp satire of cultural dependency à la Herbert Schiller.

This theme is further developed when the Gypsy Lord meets an amusing comeuppance. When he fails to lure an audience at a town that has served him well in the past, he discovers that the whole community is gathered in a hall staring zombielike at a TV set it has purchased. No one is interested any more in carnival tricks or carnival sex. As neocolonial agent, the Gypsy Lord and his carnival are clearly obsolete: a greater neocolonialism has swallowed them up. Realizing that his tricks have lost their magic in an era of the stupefying, American-modernist technology of television, he decides to head inland, and back in time, to the jungle, where the modern world may not have penetrated, and where the extermination of the Indians seems to open up all sorts of more traditional, imperial possibilities. If outdone by modern American neocolonialism, the Gypsy Lord will seek to participate as internal colonialist in an earlier and more brutal world of territorial expansion.

In the earlier mode, this quest would only have heightened the film's condemnation of colonialism and neocolonial cultural dependency in "backward" Brazil. But what would have been critique in that analytic-stylistic universe is thoroughly transformed in the film into postmodern spectacle. The jungle does not turn out to be a primitive enclave independent of encroaching, TV-standardized American modernism, where at least the ruins of authentic Brazilian national culture might be found. It is instead thoroughly postmodern, a futuristic landscape of international capital at work. The carnival's travels in the jungle become a picaresque trip through the postmodern hyperreal: the domain of mixed codes, jarring cultural heterogeneity, and social disintegration. In this setting, the Gypsy Lord, rather than standing forth as a manipulator of dependency, reveals his truer identity. His new surroundings seem to be a reflection of him. If he runs a carnival, Brazil is simply a much bigger one, filled with simulacra—which is congenial to the Gypsy Lord, who is an impressario of simulacra. As Tokyo Disneyland does, the Gypsy Lord in the Brazilian jungle thus exposes the postmodern truth that Brazil (and, indeed, the whole contemporary world) is itself unreal, a fantastic, illegitimate construct.

The most outrageous and vivid segments of the film come when the troupe journey to Altamira along a highway cut in the disastrously penetrated jungle, torn up by bulldozers, decimated by chain saws. Altamira turns out to be crowned with hundreds of what the Gypsy Lord calls "fishbones"—TV antennas. More startlingly, the troupe meet a small group of Indians. One is dressed in a polyester jumpsuit. Another carries a transistor radio, which at one point plays the Everly Brothers' "Bye Bye Love," the source of the movie's title. Revealing the incompleteness and artificiality of Brazilian nationalism, the Indians ask if the carnival group is from Brazil, a country they have heard about and are in search of. Eventually, several, lured in Altamira by the prospect of riding in a plane, which they have always wanted to do, sign up to work on an enormous Amazon paper project financed by North American capital. As the labor recruiter says, no one ever returns from that plane trip: it is a no-hassle, easy, gringo deal.

The Amazon landscape echoes the implication of the title: a parody of the song "Bye Bye Love" (part of a North American nostalgia boom), rather than a genuine lament for a lost culture, it does not indicate the disappearance of old Brazil, but instead offers Brazil as a sign of the disappearance of the real—of the reality of both the present and its hitherto stipulated past—in postmodern pastiche and simulacra. An apparent satire of neocolonialism thus masks something different, the presentation of postmodernity. A similar message is contained in the adventures of the carnival troupe: in search of a preserve not yet incorporated into American neoimperial modernism—a place that Herbert Schiller's bane has not yet touched, and one still undergoing a more traditional colonial assault on people and territory, in which the carnival group hope to participate—they find nothing of the kind. Instead, they discover a catastrophic carnival, something beyond Schiller's imagining. It is not a zombification of an old and original culture, but a wholly new state, an expression of catastrophic vigor. Social critique became picaresque spectacle; a penetrated Brazil becomes Brazil as pastiche. And the jump-suit-clad, sartorially avant-garde Indian reveals that the Brazilian national pastiche is a fictional construction in origin as well as in postmodernity. In its foundation a fantastic invention, which the Indian has recently heard about and wants to see for himself, Brazil is in the present a fantastic spectacle, in which the postmodern and premodern have merged.

The end of the movie underscores this postmodern message. Thanks to hard times and gambling losses, the carnival is disbanded in favor of hardcore whoring. The faithful mute colonial servant, Swallow, leaves in remorse, as it was his failure at arm-wrestling contests that led to the gambling losses, and the Gypsy Lord joins the larger carnival explicitly as a pimp and smuggler. Then, in a last dramatization of its central theme, the movie suggests that some may attain an enclave within postmodernism's unreality. Just when Dasdó, the accordionist's wife, is to become a prostitute like Salomé, the Gypsy Lord and Salomé pack them off on a bus to Brasilia, where they eventually find regular jobs as entertainers. But rather than implying that Brasilia (a city that is in many ways the epitome of Third World modernization) will provide them with bourgeois shelter from the postmodern, the film reveals it to be yet another testimony to the complete postmodernization of the world. The camera records the modern facade of Brasilia as an extension of the illusionary Brazil hitherto presented. Indeed, in some ways, it is the most bizarre Brazilian fantasy of all. Its social service bureaucracy is far less human than the picaresquely sleazy Gypsy Lord, and, as an island of instrumental rationality in the midst of a total absence thereof, it is more fictional a creation than anything else in the film. Brasilia becomes an example of Jameson's observation that, in postmodernism, subjects are inserted "into a multidimen-

sional set of discontinuous realities, whose frames range from the still surviving space of the bourgeois subject all the way to the unimaginable decentering of global capital itself" (1988:351). Modernism becomes one
more code afloat in the hyperreal sea of codes that the postmodern sponsors.

The young family become domesticated in Brasilia's bourgeois modernist postmodern simulacrum, becoming successful and happy in their new
work. In the film's last scenes, however, they encounter the carnival again:
reappearing with a new, outrageously refurbished carnival truck, with its
logo flashing on and off in garish neon, the Gypsy Lord and Salomé invite
their former companions to join them on a trip deeper still into the back-
lands. Their offer is affectionately refused, and they drive off in one of the
movie's most comically transgressive scenes. The truck lights up the jungle
dark with flashing neon, while Frank Sinatra croons "Brazil" over the
loudspeakers. The postmodern postreferential dereification of Herbert
Schiller ("Brazil" is hyperreal fantasy) thus voyages on; the Gypsy Lord
and Salomé drive off toward the sunrise (parodying, along the way, Marcel
Camus's *Black Orpheus* [1959] another foreign-made simulacrum of "Brazil"). As the Gypsy Lord remarks, they are off to do shows for the Indians,
who have never seen anything like them. But, recollecting the Indians
who have appeared in the movie, one might think instead that they are
merely traveling to the audience who will best appreciate what they have
to display. They are journeying, not to a premodern enclave, but to the
place where the truest aficionados of the postmodern are to be found.

The Brazil of *Bye Bye Brazil* is thus to postmodernism as Aijaz Ahmad's
depiction of the contemporary landscape of Pakistan is to Marxism: a
place that reveals the astonishment of the postmodern more vigorously
than anything in the First World. And *Bye Bye Brazil*'s characters are, every
bit as much as postmodern ethnics in North America, "others" who are
not backward, but cutting-edge, even (as with the Indians) "always already" postmodern. These circumstances are, as we have seen, indebted to
the contemporary globalization of Brazil—to its deep penetration by international capital. But what is crucial also to investigate is how the
sources of such peripheral postmodernism lie, aesthetically and sociologically, not only in the transgressive changes of contemporary globalism,
but in recent reinterpretations of colonial history as well. For the peripheral postmodern claim to being "always already" postmodern ultimately
looks back, in both particular and general ways, to colonial experience as it
has been re-seen through the lens of globalizing theories—theories committed to revealing colonialism as a worldwide process of differential cultural invention.

First of all, the film looks back to a particular colonial tradition. Like magical realism, to which it bears some resemblance, *Bye Bye Brazil* draws on a reworking of discovery myth—or what one might, remembering Christopher Miller's economy of Orientalisms, label a Latin American "Orientalism." As Gabriel García Márquez writes:

> Daily life in Latin America shows us that reality is full of extraordinary things. In this respect, I usually mention the North American explorer F. W. de Graff, who at the close of the last century made an incredible voyage through the Amazonian world in which, among other things, he saw a stream of boiling water and a place where the mere sound of a human voice provoked torrential downpours. (Quoted in Brennan 1989:67)

When John Smith wrote, in his advertisement for settlers for New England, that the great staple of that region was the "mean" and "base" commodity of fish ("never could the Spaniard with all his mines of gold and silver pay his debts, his friends, and army half so truly as the Hollanders still have done by this contemptible trade of fish"), he underscored a foundational difference between two traditions of "Americanism." The fabulous splendor of Mexico City, undone by Cortés, but depicted by Bernal Díaz in the imagery of romance, was not to be the ideological province of North Americans, who constructed themselves as more pragmatic and domesticating. Exotic quest-romance was, however, to resurface in the numerous fabulous jungles depicted in magical realism, from Alejo Carpentier's *The Lost Steps* (1953) to García Márquez's *Hundred Years of Solitude* (1967).

Brazilian interest in the region, sparked by the Nordestino movement in literature and exemplified in many of the novels of Jorge Amado, is less "magical" in quality, but, in many ways, equally fantastic in its creation of a distinctive epic-picaresque style. In *Bye Bye Brazil,* as in Márcio Souza's extravagant mock history *The Emperor of the Amazon* (1977), epic-picaresque yields to picaresque farce; the central character is, like the Gypsy Lord, a trickster, a cunning, disenchanted master of the spectacular. But the postmodern landscape *Bye Bye Brazil* reveals remains as marvelous as anything contained in the early discovery literature that fascinates García Márquez, and the movie is thus, in part, a reflection on and of this particular form of colonial discourse, a Latin American Orientalism. Survival into the postmodern present of the particular features of this colonial discourse are underscored if one notes, for example, that magical realism in Latin America and magical realism in Asia (as in Salman Rushdie) are strongly differentiated, and that the survival of a specific colonial discourse is the cause. In García Márquez, the discovery tradition is crucial, whereas in

Rushdie's *Midnight's Children* (1980), the master trope, as Timothy Brennan calls it, is the old, civilizationally Orientalist East Indian one of uncontainable multiplicity.

More generally, though, colonial history—a history of penetration, pluralism, and explicitly simulationist cultural invention—has made such sites, not just in Latin America, but throughout the world, "always already" postmodern. Writing of the imperial durbar in Delhi in 1877 to proclaim Queen Victoria empress of India, Bernard Cohn describes the construction of the viceroy's dais:

> Over the dais was a large canopy. The shafts holding the canopy were festooned with laurel wreaths, imperial crowns, gargoyle-like eagles, banners displaying the Cross of St. George and the Union Jack. There was an embroidered frieze hanging from the canopy displaying the Rose, Shamrock and Thistle with the Lotus of India. Also hanging from the shafts supporting the canopy were shields with the Irish Harp, the Lion Rampant of Scotland, and the Three Lions of England. . . . Along the backposts were mounted the large silken banners with the coats of arms [newly invented by the British] of the [Indian] princes and chiefs. Not all observers were impressed. Val[entine] Prinsep, a painter who had been commissioned to paint a picture of the scene, was aghast by what he thought to be a display of bad taste. On seeing the site he wrote "Oh Horror! What have I to paint? A kind of thing that outdoes the Crystal Palace in hideosity. . . . Never was such a brummagem ornament, or more atrocious taste. . . . They have been heaping ornament on ornament, colour on colour. . . . The size [of the whole collection of structures] gives it a vast appearance like a gigantic circus and the decorations are in keeping." (Cohn 1983:33)

Shiva Naipaul's Trinidad, portrayed as a copy of a distant original, is similarly almost prototypical of the postmodern condition. Indeed, any site first colonized by an imperialism that sought to import into it, not only its language, values, manners, and culture, but even its ecology (Crosby 1986) has had abundant previous experience with code-mixing, global heterogeneity, and simulacra, especially if this was followed up by a neoimperialism that flooded it with advertisements for foreign consumer goods and media iconography. Strongly reinforcing these insights, the "invention of invention," as Gaurav Desai (1993) has dubbed it, has of late become so widespread in recent scholarship that it has almost emerged as a discourse of its own. Situated in clefts between First World knowledge critiques, postcolonialism, and postmodernism, this discovery of invention at the root of previous cultural givens has yielded such work as Allan Hanson's "The Making of the Maori: Cultural Invention and Its Logic" (1989), Adam Kupfer's *The Invention of Primitive Society* (1988), and a collection of essays edited by Werner Sollors, *The Invention of Ethnicity* (1989), as well as a number of studies cited above, such as the collection by Hobsbawm and Ranger, books by Mudimbe and Miller, and the essay by Patrick Wolfe.

From a postmodern perspective, then, colonial and neocolonial penetration makes more explicitly transparent than Disneyland ever could the fact that "reality" is a construct and artifice; the same applies, as *Bye Bye Brazil's* quick shift from satire of neocolonialism to postmodern spectacle indicates, to subsequent neocolonial absorption of materials from a foreign cultural core. Just as Yoshimoto sees Disneyworld as more foundationally postmodern in Japan than in America, watching "I Love Lucy" in a remote district in India, as Richard Schweder did (1993:286), seems more essentially postmodern than an equivalent metropolitan hour of MTV. Crucial to all of these examples is, not just the attempt of colonialism and neocolonialism to reshape the peripheral world, but the fact that this attempt parallels the ongoing invention of the "otherness" of peripheral cultures, keeping the "other" "othered." Only via this simultaneous creation and violation of cultural boundary lines are the postmodern effects of clashing cultural universes, the consequent annihilation of referentiality, and the revelation of culture as manipulable simulacrum created.

One further circumstance sociologically endorses peripheral cultures' claim to exemplary postmodernity. Contrary to Jameson's argument that First World postmodernism reflects the fact that everything has finally been modernized—that modernization is at last utterly completed— peripheral postmodernism thrives on incomplete modernization, the result of modernization from the top down. Peripheral sites thus produce cultural situations in which distinct time frames (artifically) constructed by colonialism and Orientalism, and powerfully separated by developmentalism's evolutionary narrative, circulate together. Once the ethos of modernization has lost its hold and grand evolutionary narratives are no longer credible, the soup of codes in the Third World becomes, if anything, richer than the metropolitan version. Dissonant temporal realities abut on each other, interact with each other, and transgress each other's spheres, producing a startlingly vital, not civilizationally melancholic, brand of loss of reality.

To be sure, Jean Franco (1988) disputes Brian McHale's (1987) claim that magical realism is truly postmodern, arguing that traits like its penchant for pastiche (which reflects its "dissolution of any universal system of meaning or master discourse" [1988:211]) seem to be, but are not, in fact, postmodern. On the contrary, recent Latin American fiction, Franco maintains, uses "pastiche and citation . . . as correlatives of the continent's uneasy and unfinished relationship to modernity" (211). But the category of the "postmodern" ought not, I believe, to be as strictly regulated as Franco would have it. Seen as one of the styles evoked by ongoing globalization, rather than *the* cultural dominant of late capitalism, it will understandably be inflected differently at different sites. Peripheral postmodernity will thus deconstruct the idea of the grand narrative from a different position than metropolitan postmodernity, by making postmodern use of its unfinished relationship to modernity; it will then create its hyperreal from the startling juxtapositions of incomplete modernization, even as metropolitan hyperreality is created by the total commodification of reality.

The startling cultural juxtapositions produced as a result of incomplete modernization ground many of the postmodern effects achieved in *Bye Bye Brazil,* even as they do much of the carnival of syncretism Pico Iyer describes. Something similar is involved in many of the entries in the file Richard Schweder kept of postmodern truths that seem stranger than fiction. For example, Schweder records this transgression of professional and cultural boundaries:

> A "symbolic anthropologist" . . . sought official research permission to do work among the Maori people of New Zealand. As part of the official procedure he found himself interrogated by a "native," a Maori with an Oxford Ph.D. in anthropology, who was a gatekeeper for the tribe and who had some doubts about the "Chicago school" of symbolism as a way to represent the beliefs and practices of "others." (1993:284)

What Schweder casts in a too-flippant postmodern form is a fruit of the "voyage in" to the metropolitan core Said more earnestly describes as part of a postcolonial project. But in either frame, postcolonial or postmodern, the clash of differently encoded temporalities discoverable in the peripheries startlingly reveals that the global order has changed, and that cultural theory and practice have to hurry to catch up.

By way of summary, one essential, underlying truth must be pointed out. Most of these peripheral postmodern effects and claims I have been recording stem directly from decomposition, under the pressure of the contemporary phase of globalization, of the two fundamental assumptions of the three worlds theory discussed in chapter 1. The cultural borders authorized/enforced under that theory yield to perception of cultural interpenetration and transgression as the normal state in both the demystified past and the avant-garde present. And the evolutionary timeline along which the three worlds theory ranks cultures is cut up into discontinuously segmented, free-floating "realities," with even more transgressive an effect, making the primitive postmodern, and startlingly juxtaposing, not only different cultures and life-styles, but even distinct epochs.

As Anthony Appiah (1991) points out, postmodernism clears space in the wake of the series of the First World discourses it challenges. It is, in short, ever "post-," disrupting metropolitan narratives and foregrounding metropolitan critiques. The globalization process offers a perspective from which these metropolitan doings can be seen as the effects of a worldwide reorganization of barriers and borders, an alteration in geopolitical and geocultural maps, a restructuring of global interactiveness. Accordingly, the analysis of the postmodern from the perspective of globalization theory may lead to openings as well as space-clearing. In its analysis of the disruption of narratives of development and knowledge, the loss of reality and history, and the decentering of societies and selves, globalization theory has heightened our awareness, even more complexly than Said's postcolonialism, that culture and knowledge are a globally interactive construction that hinges on patterns of circulation. Enhancing awareness of the geocultural complexity of the interactions involved, and dismantling barriers to them, is a radically transformative project, authorizing more profound (although also less certain) futures than even Said's recent continuation of the anticolonial tradition can promise.

The underlying argument of this book is that the theorization and representation of culture has changed in the postwar period in response to a succession of geopolitical and geocultural shifts. The emergent communicational model of globalization theory suggests that one of the chief symptoms and causes of these developments has been the rapid alteration in the circulation of knowledge. World-systems theory suggests that the geocultural, national, and temporal barriers of the three worlds theory (and the legacy of colonialism they have incarnated) are breaking down, and both world-systems and globalization theories show an increasing emphasis on complex, decentered interactiveness. Wallerstein's emphasis on the exploitation of the periphery by the core—a relatively conservative drama of refused and regulated communication—changes into Robertson's analysis of actors defining identities by becoming conscious of their global callings—a notion that is both defensive and incipiently communicational. The communicational model then emerges as the primary driving force of Appadurai's interactive, perspectival global system.

In these transformations, old notions about bounded, territorially rooted civilizations and national cultures are utterly broken down. The very notion of cultural boundaries is drastically changed. Formerly, thanks to the hard work of the era of high imperialism and Herderian nationalism, cultural boundaries seemed simply referential, apparently marking natural boundary lines. The sharpest of these was the colonial-racial boundary line Said comments on: the absolute ontological difference stipulated between metropolitan peoples and cultures and those of colonized racial "others." As this ideology was attacked, however, these borders increasingly appeared to be sociocultural constructions, not things in nature perceived by an objective social science. One had to see that these boundaries were less markers of geographical/racial differences than ways of regulating complex patterns of flow between and within nations and regions. Circulating in these "flows," as Appadurai calls them, are a variety of kinds of material: for the student of culture, information (cultural, intellectual, social, ideological) is perhaps the most important, but factors like demographic movement (or dwelling), economic investment and trade, dissemination of technology, and so forth, are also crucial.

From this perspective, familiar stories of the past can be rewritten in interesting new ways. Out of the interactions between these different flows, a multitude of feedback loops created apparently stable patterns in colonialism and postwar nationalism, but since World War II, these patterns have proven more and more rapidly variable; similarly, recent scholarship has shown that, even in the past, the regulation of their boundaries was often extremely inefficient. In the act of establishing the older colonial global system—a system that constructed itself by means of the codes of referential knowledge—"the world's spaces," as David Harvey puts it, "were deterritorialized, stripped of their preceding significations, and then reterritorialized according to the convenience of colonial and imperial administrations" (1989:264). In that process, the center was strongly bounded and the peripheries were splintered in order each to be linked separately with that core, in circuits as exclusive as possible. Aijaz Ahmad underscores the fact that Third World peoples came to know vastly more about their metropolitan centers than they did about their immediate neighbors, and Gunnar Myrdal describes similarly exclusive economic relationships as "enforced bilateralism" (Stavrianos 1981:260). The flow between colony and core was, moreover, highly unbalanced. Patterns of subordinating, selective inclusions and exclusions—as in Ngũgĩ's description of the forced Europeanization of Africans and Benedict Anderson's analysis of colonials' interrupted pilgrimages to the metropolitan center—were typical ways of regulating many sorts of flow, from culture to economics.

As World War I proved, the center of the colonial world system was dramatically unstable; similarly, the emergence of strong internal dissent within metropolitan cultures disrupted the unity of the core. Neither, however, undid the strong boundary line between core and periphery; seen from that perspective, metropolitan disputes were still disputes between the masters. Those patterns were most significantly disrupted next by anticolonial nationalism when it reached its worldwide peak in the post–World War II era. Then the older colonial world system was quickly dismantled, and the United States became the center of an altered, more genuinely global order, dominated by indirect rather than direct control. Although numerous separate culture circuits were now formed, as national-cultural self-determination was emphasized, the ghost of empire remained, inasmuch as these cultures were separated according to the spatial hierarchy of the three worlds theory and positioned along a developmental timeline. In the process, a paradoxical tension between centering and globalization, neocolonial penetration and the integrity of national circuits, actual global hegemony and supposed "freedom" of international flows of information, money, trade, and so on, emerged. Herbert Schiller is thus able to describe U.S. insistence on "the free flow of information" and "worldwide access to news" (1976:26) as part of a concerted and successful attempt to wrest control of the worldwide communications network from the main colonial powers, Britain and France.

Following Edward Said, I believe that the most important instability resulting from this system was the unforeseen legacy of oppositional nationalism, which achieved something different from its explicit aim. In the American century, revolutionary nationalism yielded few of the internal and external gains it had promised. Its more enduring legacy was not making new borders but inciting a new generation to transform old ones. In the process, it increasingly undermined and refigured the strong "ontological" border regulating the flow of knowledge between core and periphery, between the developed "First" and the undeveloped "Third" worlds, that Said has drawn attention to in colonialism. With the disillusionment with oppositional nationalism that followed on its early successes, the world's spaces—to use David Harvey's (1989) formulation—were, for a third time, again deterritorialized; but this time they were not to be so clearly reterritorialized in a new form. A globalism that emphasized a multitude of sub- and supranational interactions, as well as a reformulation of the meaning of the borders of existing nations, was born.

The new patterns of the circulation of knowledge now emerging on top of the older ones are very much still in the process of formation, and consequently the subject of considerable debate. But several things seem clear. First, by significantly refiguring the borders within metropolitan societies, between metropolitan and peripheral societies, and between peripheral societies themselves, they have more completely transformed colonial patterns than before. The metropolitan nations have been increasingly heterogenized, and changed regulation of metropolitan-peripheral borders has empowered peripheral positions in new peripheral-metropolitan dialogues and altered the nature of metropolitan cultural dispute. Barriers created between peripheral societies under colonialism have grown even more porous than the three worlds theory made them when coalitions like the nonaligned movement were formed. Clearly, old regimes are very much still in force, as information disparities and economic inequities throughout the world indicate. But under the influence of globalization, considerable work has been done culturally, not to erase, but to reformulate borders to allow new patterns of circulation to emerge.

Second, as overall patterns of circulation have changed, so have the kinds of conversations permitted and empowered along global circuits. The question of who may address whom is now quite different from what it was only a decade ago, as a variety of new subject positions in cultural discourses have been created. Said has written, for instance, of the new subject position of the exile and migrant, arguing that "liberation as an intellectual mission, born in the resistance and opposition to the confinements and ravages of imperialism, has now shifted from the settled, established, and domesticated dynamics of culture to its unhoused, decentered, and exilic energies, whose incarnation today is the migrant, and whose consciousness is that of the intellectual and artist in exile, the political figure between domains, between forms, between homes, and between languages" (1993:332). He has also, like many multiculturalists, celebrated the foregrounding of ethnicity and cultural difference as crucial to the creation of a new kind of reader and writer of literature who "no longer need be tied to an image of the poet or scholar in isolation, secure, stable, national in identity, class or profession, but can think and experience with Genet in Palestine or Algeria, with Tayeb Salih as a Black man in London, with Jamaica Kincaid in the white world, with Rushdie in India and Britain, and so on" (317).

More inclusively, like Gyan Prakash, Ngũgĩ, and many others, Said has argued that "a cultural coalition [is] now being built between anti-imperialist resistance in the peripheries and oppositional culture of Europe and the United States" (261). And, most inclusively, and perhaps most originally, he has argued that "though the grand, nourishingly optimistic narratives of emancipatory nationalism no longer serve to confirm a community of culture . . . a new community of method—more difficult and astringent in its demands—arises instead" (255).

But if Said's recent book is littered with so many different new positions and alliances from which to speak, the pages of this one are too. From

Anzaldúa's mestiza to Mukherjee's cosmopolitan, from Ngũgĩ's indigenous activist to Ashcroft, Griffith, and Tiffin's postcolonialist, from Iyer's au courant Asian, to Benítez-Rojo's postmodern Caribbean, the invention of new, boundary-violating subject positions from which to speak to (and of) a new heterogeneous, globally compressed world has proceeded apace. And it is again crucial to observe that in the construction of these positions, old boundaries have *not* been effaced but reassembled in fluid, strategic, situational ways. In fact, the new positions from which one can speak have increasingly evoked, not erased, the borders they have transformed: but they have done so *not* to divide, to exclude, but to interface and construct. Thus, for example, when the Third World outsider becomes the new global cosmopolitan, two very diverse, even opposed, legacies are evoked and yoked together, and a new constitutive, not exclusionary, logic of orders is at work. Similarly, a use of borders, not to separate, but to connect has become the basis for assembling new coalitions to negotiate the postnationalist fragmentation and restructuring of the world system—to negotiate a set of global patterns so complex that chaos theory has had to be invoked to describe it.

Ralph Linton reacted against the anti-immigrant American chauvinism of the early twentieth century by writing an amusing satire of the "Hundred Per-Cent American." This self-satisfied individual is anything but what he thinks he is: completing his toilette in the morning,

> he puts on his feet stiff coverings made from hide prepared by a process invented in ancient Egypt and cut to a pattern which can be traced back to ancient Greece. Then he makes sure that they are properly polished, also a Greek idea. Lastly he ties about his neck a strip of bright-colored cloth which is a vestigal survival of the shoulder shawls worn by seventeenth-century Croats. He gives himself a final appraisal in the mirror, an old Mediterranean invention, and goes downstairs to breakfast.
>
> Here a whole new series of foreign things confronts him. His food and drink are placed before him in pottery vessels, the popular name of which—China—is sufficient evidence of their origin. His fork is a medieval Italian invention. His spoon is a copy of a Roman original. He will usually begin the meal with coffee, an Abyssinian plant first discovered by the Arabs. . . . Whereas the Arabs took their coffee straight, he will probably sweeten it with sugar, discovered in India; and dilute it with cream. Both the domestication of cattle and the technique of milking originated in Asia Minor. . . .
>
> Breakfast over, he sets out for work. If it looks like rain, our patriot puts on outer shoes of rubber, discovered by the ancient Mexicans. He will also take an umbrella, invented in India. He then sprints for the train—

the train, not sprinting, being an English invention. At the station he pauses for a moment to buy a newspaper, paying for it with coins invented in ancient Lydia. (1937:428–29)

In Linton's revelation of the global connections concealed by American nationalism, polyculturality is diachronic. Today, thanks to increased global compression and increased emphasis on the transparency of global relationships, it is more and more transparently synchronic. In the current phase of globalization, we no longer suppress, but seek out and highlight such interactions. Thus, refiguring the past, Hugh Trevor-Roper (1983) has pointed out how, as a part of a wholesale invention of the Highland traditions of Scotland, English industrialists originated the clan tartans; and Jonathan Friedman has written that "African cloth was, virtually in its entirely, made in certain European countries like Holland, a distinct pattern for every group and none of it for sale in Europe" (1988:459). Today, highlighting these formerly buried illegitimacies—what Linton, Trevor-Roper, and Friedman have to underscore in bold type against the faiths of the past—has become an important route to reconfiguration of culture globally. Thus, Friedman goes on to note that today, "Western clothing is in large part imported from the newly industrializing zones of the periphery, to say nothing of our transistors"; and today, others have pointed out, we not only manufacture our present cultures in closer relationship with each other than before, but also more and more overtly commingle the inventions of our memories and pasts. Thus, Burma becomes to Iyer's eye a museum of his colonial English past; American movie audiences find the 1950s, not just in *Grease,* but in the Amazon; and Japanese audiences recently underwent a nostalgia boom, in which they looked back to *their* experience of the American 1950s.

Increasingly, then, instead of culture unifying us in groups divided from one another, it promises to disaggregate us from those centered unities and interconnect us in more ways than we can easily conceive. That cultural workers—through paintings, novels, reportage, theory, methodological as well as political critiques, and so on—should seek to help us imagine and promote this difficult complexity seems to me not only reasonable but exciting. Vastly more than eighteenth-century concepts of universal citizenship, these developments represent an attempt to form a global civil culture (or, in Appadurai's words, a "postnational imaginary" [1993:428]) that foregrounds, rather than suppressing, cultural and historical differences. To be sure, the formation of such a culture may, to use Vytautas Kavolis's terminology, be only a weak force in the world today. First, the political valency of the globalization of culture is hotly debated. As described in previous chapters, Benita Parry sees contemporary celebration of syncretism as regressive, while Bill Ashcroft, Gareth Griffiths, and

Helen Tiffin find in it the basis for a valuable ethical project. Bharati Mukherjee's interventionist global cosmopolitanism is eyed balefully by Timothy Brennan. Third World postmodernization—the fact that "a Quechua from the Andes . . . [now] works on a computer, a Shuar from the Ecuadorian Amazon . . . [holds] a doctorate in pedagogy, a Kuna from Panama . . . is a doctor, a Tukano from Brazil . . . [has] a pilot's license, an Aymara or a Zapotec . . . writes books on sociology and history" (Varese 1991:16)—has been seen as having very different significances. Varese celebrates recognition of these changes and the creation of multinational organizations of indigenous peoples to press their claims in a "freer" transnational economy. Faye Ginsburg, while also seeing that possibility, warns against *Time* magazine's cover photo of a "Kayapo man in full Amazonian regalia holding a video camera to his eye." As she comments,

> Even in this postmodern era of the ironic pastiche, there seems to be a moment of pure modernist shock for many westerners at the seemingly incongruous combination of two different modes of life. Such images contrast with those of natives presented in traditional settings (the noble but exoticized savage) or as victims (the vanishing race) that are now problematic for Euro-Australian (and other) consumers who are increasingly aware of and uncomfortable with their own implication in the lives and historical circumstances of these "Others." Conversely, I would argue, there is a pleasure for these consumers in regarding the image of the indigenous photographer as a kind of bush cosmopolitan, at ease with both tradition and western technology; such an image evokes a kind of futuristic nostalgia, even as it masks inequality and responsibility. (1993:562)

If students of culture are divided about the progressive possibilities of contemporary postnational culture, students of globalization in other areas are more pessimistic about ongoing changes. Against similar enhancements of global interactiveness in other areas—such as the persistence and (if analysts as different as Fredric Jameson [1991], Robert Reich [1991], and Paul Kennedy [1993] are to be believed) the probable worsening of present economic inequities, and the possibility of future ecological catastrophe—cultural interventions appear to count for little. Not for nothing does Appadurai's model of the contemporary world system embody catastrophic uncertainty. Still, the exploration of global interactiveness provides cultural workers with a viable, even urgent, ethical project for our altered world, however limited it may be. And such exploration is a fascinating, and occasionally startling, means of revising our picture of the past—our received pictures of things as they supposedly were, but decidedly were not.

Works Cited

Abu-Lughod, Janet L. 1989. *Before European Hegemony: The World System, A.D. 1250–1350.* New York: Oxford University Press.

Abu-Lughod, Lila. 1993. "Editorial Comment: On Screening Politics in a World of Nations." *Public Culture* 5 (3): 465–67.

Achebe, Chinua. 1959. *Things Fall Apart.* New York: Astor Honor.

———. 1973. "The Novelist as Teacher." In *African Writers on African Writing,* edited by G. D. Killam. Evanston, Ill.: Northwestern University Press.

Ahmad, Aijaz. 1987. "Jameson's Rhetoric of Otherness and the 'National Allegory.'" *Social Text* 17 (Fall): 3–26.

———. 1992. *In Theory: Classes, Nations, Literatures.* London: Verso.

———. 1993. "A Response." *Public Culture* 6 (1): 143–91.

Alavi, Hamza. 1986. Review of *The Politics of the World Economy,* by Immanuel Wallerstein. *Race and Class* 27 (4): 87–90.

Amin, Samir. 1989. *Eurocentrism.* New York: Monthly Review Press.

Anderson, Amanda. 1992. "Cryptnormativism and Double Gestures: The Politics of Post-Structuralism." *Cultural Critique* 21: 63–96.

Anderson, Benedict. 1983. *Imagined Communities: Reflections on the Origin and Spread of Nationalism.* London: Verso.

Ang, Ien. 1985. *Watching Dallas: Soap Opera and the Melodramatic Imagination.* London: Methuen.

Angelou, Maya. 1986. *All God's Children Need Traveling Shoes.* New York: Random House.

Antin, Mary. 1912. *The Promised Land.* Boston: Houghton Mifflin.

Anzaldúa, Gloria. [1987] 1989. "*La conciencia de la mestiza:* Towards a New Consciousness." In *Making Face, Making Soul* = haciendo caras: *Creative and Critical Perspectives by Women of Color.* San Francisco: Aunt Lute Foundation Books.

Appadurai, Arjun. 1990. "Difference and Disjuncture in the Global Cultural Economy." *Public Culture* 2 (2): 1–24.

———. 1993. "Patriotism and Its Futures." *Public Culture* 5 (3): 411–30.

Appiah, Kwame Anthony. 1991. "Is the Post in Postmodernism the Post- in Postcolonial?" *Critical Inquiry* 17 (Winter): 336–67.

———. 1992. *In My Father's House: Africa in the Philosophy of Culture.* New York: Oxford University Press.

Archdeacon, Thomas J. 1983. *Becoming American: An Ethnic History.* New York: Free Press.

Arguedas, José Mariá. 1978. *Deep Rivers.* Translated by Frances Horning Barraclough. Austin: University of Texas Press.

Arlen, Michael. 1975. *Passage to Ararat.* New York: Farrar, Straus & Giroux.

Asad, Talal. 1986. "The Concept of Cultural Translation in British Social Anthropology." In *Writing Culture: The Poetics and Politics of Writing Ethnography,* edited by James Clifford and George Marcus, 141–64. Berkeley: University of California Press.

Ashcroft, Bill, Gareth Griffiths, and Helen Tiffin. 1989. *The Empire Writes Back: Theory and Practice in Post-Colonial Literatures.* New York: Routledge.

Bagai, Leona B. 1967. *The East Indians and the Pakistanis in America.* Minneapolis: Lerner Publications.

Baker, Houston A., Jr. 1986. "Caliban's Triple Play." *Critical Inquiry* 13 (1): 182–96.

Baldick, Chris. 1983. *The Social Mission of English Criticism, 1848–1932.* New York: Oxford University Press.

Barth, Fredrik. 1969. *Ethnic Groups and Boundaries: The Social Organization of Culture Difference.* Boston: Little, Brown.

Benítez-Rojo, Antonio. 1992. *The Repeating Island: The Caribbean and the Postmodern Perspective.* Durham, N.C.: Duke University Press.

Benjamin, Walter. 1969. "The Work of Art in the Age of Mechanical Reproduction." In *Illuminations,* edited by Hannah Arendt, translated by Harry Zohn, 217–51. New York: Schocken Books.

Bennett, David H. 1988. *The Party of Fear: From Nativist Movements to the New Right in American History.* Chapel Hill: University of North Carolina Press.

Bernal, Martin. 1987. *Black Athena: The Afroasiatic Roots of Classical Civilization.* New Brunswick, N.J.: Rutgers University Press.

Betz, Hans-Georg. 1992. "Postmodernism and the New Middle Class." *Theory, Culture and Society* 9 (2): 93–114.

Bhabha, Homi K. 1983. "Difference, Discrimination, and the Discourse of Colonialism." In *The Politics of Theory: Proceedings of the Essex Conference on the Sociology of Literature,* edited by Francis Barker et al., 197–211. Colchester: University of Essex Press.

———. 1984. "Of Mimicry and Man: The Ambivalence of Colonial Discourse." *October* 28, 125–33.

———. 1985a. "Sly Civility." *October* 34: 71–80.

———. 1985b. "Signs Taken for Wonders: Questions of Ambivalence and Authority under a Tree Outside Delhi, May 1817." In *Europe and Its Others,* edited by Francis Barker et al., 1: 89–106. Colchester: University of Essex Press.

———. ed. 1990., *Nation and Narration.* New York: Routledge.

Bodnar, John. 1985. *The Transplanted: A History of Immigrants in Urban America.* Bloomington: Indiana University Press.

Boelhower, William. 1987. *Through a Glass Darkly: Ethnic Semiosis in American Literature.* New York: Oxford University Press.

Bohannan, Laura. 1966. "Shakespeare in the Bush." *Natural History,* Aug.–Sept., 87–92.

Boyeson, Hjalmar Hjorth. [1877] 1969. *Tales from Two Hemispheres.* New York: Books for Libraries Press.

Brannen, Mary Yoko. 1992. " 'Bwana Mickey': Constructing Cultural Consumption at Tokyo Disneyland." In *Re-made in Japan: Everyday Life and Consumer Taste in a Changing Society,* edited by Joseph J. Tobin, 216–34. New Haven: Yale University Press.

Brantlinger, Patrick. 1990. *Crusoe's Footprints: Cultural Studies in Britain and America.* New York: Routledge.

Brennan, Timothy. 1989. *Salman Rushdie and the Third World: Myths of the Nation.* New York: St. Martin's Press.

———. 1990. "The National Longing for Form." In *Nation and Narration,* edited by Homi K. Bhabha, 44–70. London: Routledge.

Breuilly, John. 1982. *Nationalism and the State.* New York: St. Martin's Press.

Bright, Charles, and Michael Geyer. 1987. "For a Unified History of the World in the Twentieth Century." *Radical History Review* 39: 69–91.

Buell, Lawrence. 1989. "American Pastoral Ideology Reappraised." *American Literary History* 1 (1): 1–29.

———. 1992. "American Literary Emergence as a Post-Colonial Phenomenon." *American Literary History* 4 (3): 411–42.

Bull, H. 1984. Foreword to *The Standard of "Civilization" in International Society*, by G. W. Gong. Oxford: Clarendon Press.

Bulosan, Carlos. 1943. *America Is in the Heart*. New York: Harcourt, Brace.

Cahan, Abraham. 1898. *The Imported Bridegroom and Other Stories of the New York Ghetto*. New York: Houghton, Mifflin.

Capra, Fritjov. 1977. *The Tao of Physics: An Exploration of the Parallels between Modern Physics and Eastern Mysticism*. New York: Bantam Books.

Carby, Hazel V. 1987. *Reconstructing Womanhood: The Emergence of the Afro-American Woman Novelist*. New York: Oxford University Press.

Carpentier, Alejo. 1956. *The Lost Steps*. Translated by Harriet de Onis. New York: Knopf.

Césaire, Aimé. 1969. *Une Tempête: D'apres "La Tempête" de Shakespeare: Adaptation pour un théatre nègre*. Paris: Editions du seuil.

Chaterjee, Partha. 1993. "The Need to Dissemble." *Public Culture* 6 (1): 55–64.

Cliff, Michelle. 1987. *No Telephone to Heaven*. New York: Random House, Vintage Books.

Clifford, James. 1988. *The Predicament of Culture: Twentieth-Century Ethnography, Literature, and Art*. Cambridge, Mass.: Harvard University Press.

Clifford, James, and George Marcus, eds. 1986. *Writing Culture: The Poetics and Politics of Writing Ethnography*. Berkeley: University of California Press.

Cohn, Bernard. 1983. "Representing Authority in Victorian India." In *The Invention of Tradition*, edited by Eric Hobsbawm and Terence Ranger, 165–209. New York: Cambridge University Press.

Conrad, Peter. 1980. *Imagining America*. New York: Oxford University Press.

Creighton, Millie R. 1992. "The *depato*: Merchandising the West." In *Re-Made in Japan: Everyday Life and Consumer Taste in a Changing Society*, edited by Joseph J. Tobin, 42–57. New Haven: Yale University Press.

Crèvecoeur, St. Jean de. [1782] 1957. *Letters from an American Farmer*. New York: E. P. Dutton.

Deleuze, Gilles, and Felix Guattari. 1986. *Kafka: Toward a Minor Literature*. Minneapolis: University of Minnesota Press.

Derrida, Jacques. 1978. "Structure, Sign, and Play in the Discourse of the Human Sciences." In *Writing and Difference*, translated by Alan Bass, 84–92. London: Routledge & Kegan Paul.

Desai, Gaurav. 1993. "The Invention of Invention." *Cultural Critique* 24: 119–42.

Dhareshwar, Vivek. 1991. "Marxism, Location Politics, and the Possibility of Critique." *Public Culture* 6 (1): 41–54.

Díaz del Castillo, Bernal. 1956. *The Discovery and Conquest of Mexico*, edited by Genaro García, translated by A. P. Maudslay. New York: Farrar, Straus & Giroux.

Dike, K. Onwuka. 1956. *Trade and Politics in the Niger Delta, 1830–1885*. Oxford: Clarendon Press.

Dirks, Nicholas. 1990. "History as a Sign of the Modern." *Public Culture* 2 (2): 25–32.

Dirlik, Arlif. 1991. "Culturalism as Hegemonic Ideology and Liberating Practice." In *The Nature and Context of Minority Discourse*, edited by Abdul R. Jan-Mohamed and David Lloyd, 394–431. New York: Oxford University Press.

Dorfman, Ariel, and Armand Mattelart. 1975. *How to Read Donald Duck: Imperialist Ideology in the Disney Comic*. New York: International General Editions.
Eagleton, Terry. 1983. *Literary Theory: An Introduction*. Minneapolis: University of Minnesota Press.
———. 1990. "Nationalism: Irony and Commitment." In *Nationalism, Colonialism, and Literature*, 23–42. Minneapolis: University of Minnesota.
Ellison, Ralph. 1952. *Invisible Man*. New York: Random House.
Enloe, Cynthia. 1989. *Bananas, Beaches and Bases: Making Feminist Sense of International Politics*. Berkeley: University of California Press.
Fabian, Johannes. 1983. *Time and the Other: How Anthropology Makes Its Object*. New York: Columbia University Press.
Fanon, Frantz. [1963] 1968. *The Wretched of the Earth*. New York: Grove Press.
Farah, Nuruddin. [1979] 1992. *Sweet and Sour Milk*. Saint Paul: Greywolf Press.
———. [1981] 1992. *Sardines*. Saint Paul: Greywolf Press.
———. [1983] 1992. *Close Sesame*. Saint Paul: Greywolf Press.
Featherstone, Mike. 1991. *Consumer Culture and Postmodernism*. London: Sage.
Fernandez-Retamar, Roberto. 1989. *Caliban and Other Essays*. Translated by Edward Baker. Minneapolis: University of Minnesota Press.
Field, James. 1971. "Transnationalism and the New Tribe." *International Organization* 25: 353–62.
Fox-Genovese, Elizabeth. 1991. *Feminism without Illusions: A Critique of Individualism*. Chapel Hill: University of North Carolina Press.
Franco, Jean. 1988. "The Nation as Imagined Community." In *The New Historicism*, edited by H. Aram Veser, 204–12. New York: Routledge.
Frank, André Gunder. 1966. "The Development of Underdevelopment." *Monthly Review* 18: 17–31.
———. 1991. "A Plea for World System History." *Journal of World History* 2 (1): 1–28.
Fraser, Antonia. 1985. *Oxford Blood*. New York: Norton.
Friedman, Jonathan. 1988. "Cultural Logics of the Global System: A Sketch." *Theory, Culture & Society* 5 (2–3): 447–60.
Fröbel, Folker, Jürgen Heinrichs, and Otto Kreye. 1980. *The New International Division of Labor*. New York: Cambridge University Press.
Gabler, Neal. 1988. *An Empire of Their Own: How the Jews Invented Hollywood*. New York: Crown Books.
Gates, Henry Louis, Jr. 1986. "Talkin' That Talk." *Critical Inquiry* 13 (1): 203–10.
———. 1988. *The Signifying Monkey: A Theory of African-American Literary Criticism*. New York: Oxford University Press.
———. 1991a. "Authority, (White) Power and the (Black) Critic." In *The Nature and Context of Minority Discourse*, edited by Abdul R. JanMohamed and David Lloyd, 72–101. New York: Oxford University Press.
———. 1991b. "'Authenticity,' or the Lesson of Little Tree." *New York Times Book Review*, Nov. 24, 1991, 1, 26–30.
Geertz, Clifford. 1983. *Local Knowledge: Further Essays in Interpretative Anthropology*. New York: Basic Books.
———. 1988. *Works and Lives: The Anthropologist as Author*. Stanford: Stanford University Press.
Gellner, Ernest. 1983. *Nations and Nationalism*. Ithaca, N.Y.: Cornell University Press.
Gessner, Volkmar, and Angelika Schade. 1990. "Conflicts of Culture in Cross-Border Legal Relations: The Conception of a Research Topic in the Sociology of Law." *Theory, Culture & Society* 7 (2–3): 253–78.

Ghosh, Amitav. 1989. "The Diaspora in Indian Culture." *Public Culture* 2 (1): 73–78.

Ginsburg, Faye. 1993. "Aboriginal Media and the Australian Imaginary." *Public Culture* 5 (3): 557–78.

Giroux, Henry A. 1992. "Post-Colonial Ruptures and Democratic Possibilities: Multiculturalism as Anti-Racist Pedagogy." *Cultural Critique* 21: 5–40.

Glazer, Nathan. 1964. "Ethnic Groups in America: From National Culture to Ideology." In *Freedom and Control in Modern Society,* edited by Monroe Berger, Theodore Abel, and Charles H. Page, 158–73. New York: Octagon Books.

Glazer, Nathan, and Daniel P. Moynihan. 1963. *Beyond the Melting Pot.* Cambridge: MIT Press.

Gleason, Philip. 1980. "American Identity and Americanization." In *The Harvard Encyclopedia of American Ethnic Groups,* 31–58. Cambridge, Mass.: Harvard University Press, Belknap Press.

Gleick, James. 1987. *Chaos: Making a New Science.* New York: Penguin Books.

Gluck, Carol. 1985. *Japan's Modern Myths: Ideology in the Late Meiji Period.* Princeton: Princeton University Press.

Gold, Mike. 1930. *Jews without Money.* New York: Horace Liveright.

Haley, Alex. 1976. *Roots: The Saga of an American Family.* Garden City, N.Y.: Doubleday.

Hall, Stuart. 1991a. "The Local and the Global: Globalization and Ethnicity." In *Culture, Globalization and the World-System,* edited by Anthony D. King, 19–40. Binghamton: Department of Art and Art History, State University of New York at Binghamton.

———. 1991b. "Old and New Identities, Old and New Ethnicities." In *Culture, Globalization and the World-System,* edited by Anthony D. King, 41–68. Binghamton, State University of New York at Binghamton.

Handler, Richard. 1987. "Heritage and Hegemony: Recent Works on Historic Preservation and Interpretation." *Anthropological Quarterly* 60: 137–41.

Hannerz, Ulf. 1990. "Cosmopolitans and Locals in World Culture." *Theory Culture & Society* 7 (2–3): 237–52.

Hanson, Allan. 1989. "The Making of the Maori: Cultural Invention and Its Logic." *American Anthropologist* 91 (4): 890–902.

Harootunian, H. D. 1989. "Visible Discourses / Invisible Ideologies." In *Postmodernism and Japan,* edited by Masao Miyoshi and H. D. Harootunian, 63–92. Durham, N.C.: Duke University Press.

Harper, Frances Ellen Watkins. 1857. "Free Labor." In *The Heath Anthology of American Literature,* vol. 1, edited by Paul Lauter et al., 1921–22. Lexington, Mass.: Heath.

Harris, Nigel. 1987. *The End of the Third World: Newly Industrializing Countries and the Decline of an Ideology.* New York: Penguin Books.

Harvey, David. 1989. *The Condition of Postmodernity: An Enquiry into the Origins of Cultural Change.* Oxford: Basil Blackwell.

Henderson, Stephen. 1973. *Understanding the New Black Poetry.* New York: Morrow.

Higham, John. 1955. *Strangers in the Land: Patterns of American Nativism, 1860–1925.* New York: Atheneum.

Hijuelos, Oscar. 1983. *Our House in the Last World.* New York: Washington Square Press.

Hobsbawm, [Eric] J. 1990. *Nations and Nationalism since 1780: Programme, Myth, Reality.* Cambridge: Cambridge University Press.

Hobsbawm, Eric, and Terence Ranger, eds. 1983. *The Invention of Tradition.* New York: Cambridge University Press.

Horowitz, Tony. 1991. *Baghdad without a Map and Other Misadventures in Arabia.* New York: Dutton.

Howells, William Dean. 1890. *A Hazard of New Fortunes.* New York: Harper & Brothers.

Ito, Ken K. 1991. *Visions of Desire: Tanizaki's Fictional Worlds.* Stanford: Stanford University Press.

Ivy, Marilyn. 1989. "Critical Texts, Mass Artifacts: The Consumption of Knowledge in Postmodern Japan." In *Postmodernism and Japan,* edited by Masao Miyoshi and H. D. Harootunian, 21–46. Durham, N.C.: Duke University Press.

Iyer, Pico. 1988. *Video Night in Kathmandu.* New York: Knopf.

Jameson, Fredric. 1984. "Postmodernism, or, The Cultural Logic of Late Capitalism." *New Left Review* 146: 53–92.

———. 1986. "Third-World Literature in the Era of Multinational Capitalism." *Social Text* 15: 65–68.

———. 1988. "Cognitive Mapping." In *Marxism and the Interpretation of Culture,* edited by C. Nelson and L. Grossberg, 347–56. Urbana: University of Illinois Press.

———. 1991. *Postmodernism, or, The Cultural Logic of Late Capitalism.* Durham, N.C.: Duke University Press.

JanMohamed, Adbul R. 1983. *Manichean Aesthetics: The Politics of Literature in Colonial Africa.* Amherst: University of Massachusetts Press.

Johnson, Paul 1991. *Modern Times: The World from the Twenties to the Nineties.* Rev. ed. New York: HarperCollins.

Kammen, Michael. 1973. *People of Paradox: An Inquiry Concerning the Origins of American Civilization.* New York: Random House.

Kane, Cheikh Hamidou. 1986. *Ambiguous Adventure.* London: Heinemann.

Kaplan, Amy, and Donald E. Pease, eds. 1993. *Cultures of United States Imperialism.* Durham, N.C.: Duke University Press.

Karatani Kōjin. 1991. "The Discursive Space of Modern Japan." *boundary 2* 18 (3): 191–219.

Kavolis, Vytautas. 1991. "Nationalism, Modernization, and the Polylogue of Civilizations." *Comparative Civilizations Review* 25: 124–43.

Kennedy, Paul. 1993. *Preparing for the Twenty-First Century.* New York: Random House.

Kim, Elaine H. 1982. *Asian American Literature: An Introduction to the Writings and Their Social Context.* Philadelphia: Temple University Press.

———. 1991. "Defining Asian American Realities through Literature." In *The Nature and Context of Minority Discourse,* edited by Abdul R. JanMohamed and David Lloyd, 146–70. New York: Oxford University Press.

King, Anthony D. 1990a. *Urbanism, Colonialism, and the World Economy: Cultural and Spatial Foundations of the World Urban System.* New York: Routledge.

———. 1990b. *Global Cities: Post-Imperialism and the Internationalization of London.* New York: Routledge.

———. ed. 1991. *Culture, Globalization and the World-System: Contemporary Conditions for the Representation of Identity.* Binghamton: Department of Art and Art History, State University of New York at Binghamton.

Kingston, Maxine Hong. [1975] 1976. *The Woman Warrior: Memoirs of a Girlhood among Ghosts.* New York: Random House.

———. 1989. *Tripmaster Monkey: His Fake Book.* New York: Random House.

Klein, Marcus. 1981. *Foreigners: The Making of American Literature, 1900–1940.* Chicago: University of Chicago Press.

Konrád, György. 1984. *Antipolitics: An Essay.* Translated by Richard E. Allen. San Diego: Harcourt Brace Jovanovich.

Kuhn, Thomas S. [1963] 1970. *The Structure of Scientific Revolutions.* Chicago: University of Chicago Press.

Kupfer, Adam. 1988. *The Invention of Primitive Society: Transformations of an Illusion.* London: Routledge.

Kureishi, Hanif. 1986. *My Beautiful Laundrette.* Boston: Faber & Faber.

Laclau, Ernesto, and Chantal Mouffe. 1985. *Hegemony and Socialist Strategy: Towards a Radical Democratic Politics.* London: Verso.

Lambert, Michael. 1993. "From Citizenship to *négritude:* 'Making a Difference' in Elite Ideologies of Colonized Francophone West Africa." *Comparative Studies in Society and History* 35 (2): 239–62.

Lamming, George. 1960. *The Pleasure of Exile.* London: Michael Joseph.

Lash, Scott, and John Urry. 1987. *The End of Organized Capitalism.* Madison: University of Wisconsin Press.

Lawall, Sarah. 1985. "Yukio Mishima." In *The Norton Anthology of World Masterpieces,* 5th ed., edited by Maynard Mack et al., 2062–68. New York: Norton.

Layoun, Mary N. 1990. *Travels of a Genre: The Modern Novel and Ideology.* Princeton: Princeton University Press.

Lazarus, Emma [1883] 1967. *Emma Lazarus: Selections from Her Poetry and Prose,* edited by Morris U. Shappes, New York: Emma Lazarus Federation of Jewish Women's Clubs.

Levinson, Marjorie. 1993. "News from Nowhere: The Discontents of Aijaz Ahmad." *Public Culture* 6 (1): 97–132.

Lewis, L. Michael. 1991. "The Meeting of Worlds: Migration, Displacement, and World Literature." Paper presented at International Society for the Comparative Study of Civilizations conference, Santo Domingo, Dominican Republic.

Linton, Ralph. 1937. "One Hundred Per-Cent American." *The American Mercury* 50: 427–29.

Loomba, Ania. 1989. *Gender, Race, Renaissance Drama.* New York: Manchester University Press.

Lowe, Lisa. 1991. "Heterogeneity, Hybridity, Multiplicity: Marking Asian American Differences." *Diaspora* 1 (1): 24–44.

Lyotard, Jean-François. 1984. *The Postmodern Condition: A Report on Knowledge.* Translated by Geoff Bennington and Brian Massumi. Minneapolis: University of Minnesota Press.

Mandel, Ernest. 1978. *Late Capitalism.* London: Verso.

Marcus, George, and Michael M. J. Fischer. 1986. *Anthropology as Cultural Critique: An Experimental Moment in the Human Sciences.* Chicago: University of Chicago Press.

Márquez, Gabriel García. [1967] 1970. *One Hundred Years of Solitude,* Translated by Gregory Rabassa. New York: Harper & Row.

Marx, Karl. 1904. *A Contribution to the Critique of Political Economy.* Translated by N. I. Stone. Chicago: Charles H. Kerr.

Matthews, Fred H. 1970. "The Revolt against Americanism: Cultural Pluralism and Cultural Relativism as an Ideology of Liberation." *Canadian Review of American Studies* 1 (1): 4–31.

McHale, Brian. 1987. *Postmodernist Fiction.* New York: Methuen.

McNeill, William H. 1985. *Polyethnicity and National Unity in World History.* Toronto: University of Toronto Press.

———. 1990. *"The Rise of the West* after Twenty-Five Years." *Journal of World History* 1 (1): 1–22.

Mead, Margaret. 1948. *And Keep Your Powder Dry.* New York: Morrow.

Miller, Christopher L. 1985. *Blank Darkness: Africanist Discourse in French.* Chicago: University of Chicago Press.

———. 1990. *Theories of Africans: Francophone Literature and Anthropology in Africa.* Chicago: University of Chicago Press.

Mishima Yukio. 1966. "Patriotism." In *Death of Midsummer and Other Stories,* 93–118. New York: New Directions.

Mittelman, James H. 1988. *Out from Underdevelopment: Prospects for the Third World.* New York: St. Martin's Press.

Miyoshi, Masao. 1991. *Off Center: Power and Culture Relations between Japan and the United States.* Cambridge, Mass.: Harvard University Press.

Mo, Timothy. 1985. *Sour Sweet.* New York: Random House, Vintage Books.

Moore, Sally Falk. 1989. "The Production of Cultural Pluralism as a Process." *Public Culture* 1 (2): 26–48.

Mudimbe, V. Y. 1988. *The Invention of Africa: Gnosis, Philosophy, and the Order of Knowledge.* Bloomington: Indiana University Press.

Mukherjee, Bharati. 1985. *Darkness.* New York: Penguin Books.

———. 1988a. *The Middleman and Other Stories.* New York: Fawcett Crest.

———. 1988b. "Immigrant Writing: Give Us Your Maximalists." *New York Times Book Review* 93 (Aug. 28): 1, 28–29.

Murayama, Milton. 1975. *All I Asking for is My Body.* San Francisco: Supra Press.

Myrdal, Gunnar. 1944. *Am American Dilemma: The Negro Problem and Modern Democracy.* New York: Harper & Brothers.

Naipaul, Shiva. 1986. *Beyond the Dragon's Mouth.* New York: Penguin Books.

Najita, Tetsuo. 1989. "On Culture and Technology in Postmodern Japan." In *Postmodernism and Japan,* edited by Masao Miyoshi and H. D. Harootunian, 3–20. Durham, N.C.: Duke University Press.

Nandy, Ashis. 1983. *The Intimate Enemy: Loss and Recovery of Self under Colonialism.* New Delhi: Oxford University Press.

———. 1987. *Traditions, Tyranny and Utopias: Essays in the Politics of Awareness.* New Delhi: Oxford University Press.

———., ed. 1988. *Science, Hegemony, and Violence: A Requiem for Modernity.* New Delhi: Oxford University Press.

New York State Social Studies Review and Development Committee. 1991. *One Nation, Many Peoples: A Declaration of Cultural Interdependence.* Albany: New York State Education Department.

Ngũgĩ wa Thiong'o [James Ngugi]. 1967. *A Grain of Wheat.* London: Heinemann.

———. 1986. *Decolonising the Mind: The Politics of Language in African Literature.* Portsmouth, N.H.: Heinemann.

———. 1990. "Return of the Native Tongue." *Times Literary Supplement,* September 14–20, 972, 981.

Nicholas, Ralph. 1991. "Cultures in the Curriculum." *Liberal Education* 77 (3): 16–21.

Novak, Michael. 1971. *The Rise of the Unmeltable Ethnics: Politics and Culture in the Seventies.* New York: Macmillan.

Ōe Kenzaburō. 1989. "Japan's Dual Identity: A Writer's Dilemma." In *Postmodernism and Japan,* edited by Masao Miyoshi and H. D. Harootunian, 189–214. Durham, N.C.: Duke University Press.

Okada, John. [1957] 1979. *No-No Boy.* Seattle: University of Washington Press.

Olney, James. 1973. *Tell Me Africa: An Approach to African Literature.* Princeton: Princeton University Press.

Orleck, Annelise. 1987. "The Soviet Jews: Life in Brighton Beach, Brooklyn." In *New Immigrants in New York,* edited by Nancy Foner, 273–304. New York: Columbia University Press.

Owens, Craig. 1983. "The Discourse of Others: Feminists and Postmodernism." In *The Anti-Aesthetic: Essays on Postmodern Culture,* edited by Hal Foster, 57–82. Seattle: Bay Press.

Palencia-Roth, Michael. 1992. "*Quarta orbis Pars:* Monologizing the New World." *Comparative Civilizations Review* 26 (Spring): 4–42.

Parker, Andrew, Mary Russo, Doris Sommer, and Patricia Yeager. 1992. "Introduction." In *Nationalisms and Sexualities,* edited by Andrew Parker et al., 1–18. New York: Routledge.

Parry, Benita. 1989. "Problems in Current Theories of Colonial Discourse." *Oxford Literary Review* 9 (1–2): 27–58.

Pincus, Leslie. 1991. "In a Labyrinth of Western Desire: Kuki Shuzo and the Discovery of Japanese Being." *boundary 2* 18 (3): 142–56.

Prakash, Gyan. 1990. "Writing Post-Orientalist Histories of the Third World: Perspectives from Indian Historiography." *Comparative Studies in Society and History* 32 (2): 383–408.

———. 1992. "Can the 'Subaltern' Ride? A Reply to O'Hanlon and Washbrook." *Comparative Studies in Society and History* 34 (1): 168–84.

Prebisch, Raul. 1950. *The Economic Development of Latin America and its Principal Problems.* New York: United Nations.

Prigogine, Ilya, and Isabelle Stengers. 1984. *Order Out of Chaos: Man's New Dialogue with Nature.* New York: Bantam Books.

Rabinow, Paul. 1986. "Representations Are Social Facts: Modernity and Post-Modernity in Anthropology." In *Writing Culture: The Poetics and Politics of Writing Ethnography,* edited by James Clifford and George Marcus, 234–61. Berkeley: University of California Press.

Ranger, Terence. 1983. "The Invention of Tradition in Colonial Africa." In *The Invention of Tradition,* edited by Eric Hobsbawm and Terence Ranger, 211–62. New York: Cambridge University Press.

Rao, Raja. [1938] 1963. *Kanthapura.* New York: New Directions.

Ravitch, Diane. 1990. "Multiculturalism: *E Pluribus Plures.*" *American Scholar* 59 (3): 337–54.

Reed, Ishmael. 1972. *Mumbo Jumbo.* Garden City, N.Y.: Doubleday.

Reich, Robert. 1991. *The Work of Nations: Preparing Ourselves for Twenty-First-Century Capitalism.* New York: Knopf.

Rhys, Jean. [1966] 1982. *Wide Sargasso Sea.* New York: Norton.

Ricoeur, Paul. 1965. "Universal Civilization and National Cultures." In *History and Truth,* 271–87. Evanston, Ill.: Northwestern University Press.

Roberts, J. M. 1987. *The Pelican History of the World.* New York: Penguin Books.

Robertson, Roland. 1987. "Globalization Theory and Civilizational Analysis." *Comparative Civilizations Review* 17: 20–30.

———. 1990. "Mapping the Global Condition: Globalization as the Central Concept." *Theory, Culture & Society* 7 (2–3): 15–30.

———. 1991. "Social Theory, Cultural Relativity and the Problem of Globality." In *Culture, Globalization and the World System: Contemporary Conditions for the Representation of Identity,* edited by Anthony D. King, 69–90. Binghamton: Department of Art and Art History, State University of New York at Binghamton.

———. 1992a. *Globalization: Social Theory and Global Culture.* London: Sage Publications.

———. 1992b. "'Civilization' and the Civilizing Process; Elias, Globalization and Analytic Synthesis." *Theory, Culture & Society* 9 (1): 211–28.

———. 1992c. "Globality, Global Culture and Images of World Order." In *Social Change and Modernity,* edited by Hans Haferkamp and Neil J. Smelser, 395–411. Berkeley: University of California Press.

Rose, Margaret A. 1991. *The Post-Modern and the Post-Industrial: A Critical Analysis.* New York: Cambridge University Press.

Roseberry, William. 1989. *Anthropologies and Histories.* New Brunswick, N.J.: Rutgers University Press.

Rostow, W. W. 1960. *The Stages of Economic Growth: A Non-Communist Manifesto.* London: Cambridge University Press.

Rouse, Roger. 1991. "Mexican Migration and the Social Space of Postmodernism." *Diaspora* 1 (1): 8–24.

Rushdie, Salman. 1980. *Midnight's Children.* New York: Penguin Books.

Said, Edward W. 1978. *Orientalism.* New York: Random House.

———. 1985. "Orientalism Reconsidered." *Cultural Critique* 1 (Fall): 89–107.

———. 1986. "Intellectuals in the Post-Colonial World." *Salmagundi* 70–71 (Spring–Summer): 44–64.

———. 1989. "Representing the Colonized: Anthropology's Interlocutors." *Critical Inquiry* 15 (Winter): 205–25.

———. 1990. "Figures, Configurations, Transfigurations." *Race and Class,* 32 (1): 1–16.

———. 1993. *Culture and Imperialism.* New York: Knopf.

Sakai, Naoki. 1989. "Modernity and Its Critique: The Problem of Universalism and Particularism." In *Postmodernism and Japan,* edited by Masao Miyoshi and H. D. Harootunian, 93–122. Durham, N.C.: Duke University Press.

———. 1991. "Return to the West/Return to the East: Watsuji Tetsuro's Anthropology and Discussions of Authenticity." *boundary 2* 18 (3): 157–90.

Sassen-Koob, Saskia. 1982. "Recomposition and Peripheralization at the Core." *Contemporary Marxism* 5 (Summer): 88–100.

Schiller, Herbert I. 1969. *Mass Communications and American Empire.* New York: A. M. Kelley.

———. 1976. *Communication and Cultural Domination.* New York: International Arts and Sciences Press.

Schlesinger, Arthur. 1991. *The Disuniting of America: Reflections on a Multicultural Society.* New York: Norton.

Schweder, Richard A. 1993. "'Why Do Men Barbecue?' and Other Postmodern Ironies of Growing Up in the Decade of Ethnicity." *Daedalus* 122 (1): 279–308.

Sheldrake, Rupert. 1989. *The Presence of the Past: Morphic Resonance and the Habits of Nature.* New York: Random House.

Smith, Anthony D. 1983. *Theories of Nationalism.* 2d ed. New York: Holmes & Meier.

———. 1990. "Towards a Global Culture?" *Theory, Culture & Society* 7 (2–3): 171–93.

Sollors, Werner. 1978. *Amiri Baraka / Leroi Jones: The Quest for a "Populist Modernism."* New York: Columbia University Press.

———. 1986. *Beyond Ethnicity: Consent and Descent in American Culture.* New York: Oxford University Press.

———., ed. 1989. *The Invention of Ethnicity.* Oxford: Oxford University Press.

Souza, Márcio. [1977] 1980. *The Emperor of the Amazon.* Translated by Thomas Colchie. New York: Avon Books.

Soyinka, Wole. 1975. "Neo-Tarzanism: The Poetics of Pseudo-Tradition." *Transition* 48: 30–45.

Spivak, Gayatri Chakravorty. 1987. *In Other Worlds*. New York: Routledge.

———. 1990. *The Post-Colonial Critic: Interviews, Strategies, Dialogues,* edited by Sarah Harasym. New York: Routledge.

Stavrianos. L. S. 1981. *Global Rift: The Third World Comes of Age*. New York: Morrow.

Suleri, Sara. 1992. *The Rhetoric of English India*. Chicago: University of Chicago Press.

Sullivan, Nancy. 1993. "Film and Television Production in Papua New Guinea: How Media Become the Message." *Public Culture* 5 (3): 533–55.

Tagg, John. 1991. "Globalization, Totalization and the Discursive Field." In *Culture, Globalization and the World-System,* edited by Anthony D. King, 155–60. Binghamton: Department of Art and Art History, State University of New York at Binghamton.

Tambiah, Anthony. 1989. "Ethnic Conflict in the World Today." *American Ethnologist* 16 (2): 335–49.

Tan, Amy. 1989. *The Joy Luck Club*. New York: G. P. Putnam's Sons.

Tanizaki Jun'ichiro. [1924] 1985. *Naomi*. Translated by Anthony H. Chambers. New York: Knopf.

———. [1928] 1981. *Some Prefer Nettles*. Translated by Edward Seidensticker. New York: Perigee Books.

———. [1948] 1981. *The Makioka Sisters*. Translated by Edward Seidensticker. New York: Perigee Books.

Theroux, Paul. 1991. "The Wizard of Kansas." *New York Times Book Review* (Oct. 27): 1, 25–26.

Thistlewaite, Frank. 1991. "Migration from Europe Overseas: Postscript." In *A Century of European Migrations, 1830–1930,* edited by Rudolph J. Vecoli and Suzanne M. Sinke, 51–57. Urbana and Chicago: University of Illinois Press.

Tobin, Joseph J. 1992. "Introduction." In *Re-Made in Japan: Everyday Life and Consumer Taste in a Changing Society,* edited by Joseph J. Tobin, 1–41. New Haven: Yale University Press.

Todorov, Tzvetan. 1986. "'Race,' Writing, and Culture." *Critical Inquiry* 13 (1): 171–81.

Tölölyan, Khachig. 1991. "The Nation-State and Its Others: In Lieu of a Preface." *Diaspora* 1 (1): 3–8.

Tomlinson, John. 1991. *Cultural Imperialism*. Baltimore: Johns Hopkins University Press.

Trevor-Roper, Hugh. 1983. "The Highland Tradition in Scotland." In *The Invention of Tradition,* edited by Eric Hobsbawm and Terence Ranger, 15–41. New York: Cambridge University Press.

Trinh T. Minh-ha. 1989. *Woman, Native, Other*. Bloomington: Indiana University Press.

Tyler, Anne. 1985. *The Accidental Tourist*. New York: Knopf.

Urry, John. 1992. "The Tourist Gaze and the Environment." *Theory, Culture & Society* 9 (3): 1–26.

Van Deburg, William L. 1992. *New Day in Babylon: The Black Power Movement and American Culture, 1965–1975*. Chicago: University of Chicago Press.

Van der Veer, Peter. 1993. "No Nations, but Classes." *Public Culture* 6 (1): 77–82.

Varese, Stefano. 1991. "Think Locally, Act Globally." *Report on the Americas* 15 (3): 13–17.

Viswanathan, Gauri. 1989. *Masks of Conquest: Literary Study and British Rule in India*. New York: Columbia University Press.

Visnawathan, Shiv. 1988. "On the Annals of the Laboratory State." In *Science, Hegemony and Violence; A Requiem for Modernity,* edited by Ashis Nandy, 257–88. New Delhi: Oxford University Press.

Vogel, Ezra. 1979. *Japan as Number One: Lessons for America.* Cambridge, Mass.: Harvard University Press.

Van Laue, Theodor. 1987. *The World Revolution of Westernization: The Twentieth Century in Global Perspective.* New York: Oxford University Press.

Wakabayashi, Bob Tadashi. 1986. *Anti-Foreignism and Western Learning in Early Modern Japan.* Cambridge, Mass.: Harvard University Press.

Wallerstein, Immanuel. 1974. *The Modern World System.* New York: Academic Press.

———. 1984. *The Politics of the World Economy.* New York: Cambridge University Press.

———. 1990. "Culture as the Ideological Battleground of the Modern World System." *Theory, Culture & Society* 7 (2–3): 31–57.

———. 1991. *Geopolitics and Geoculture: Essays on the Changing World-System.* Cambridge: Cambridge University Press.

Weber, Eugen. 1976. *Peasants into Frenchmen: The Modernization of Rural France, 1870–1914.* Stanford: Stanford University Press.

Weinstein, Deena. 1989. "The Amnesty International Tour." *Public Culture* 1 (2): 60–65.

West, Cornel. 1990. "The New Cultural Politics of Difference." *October* (53): 93–109.

Williams, Raymond. 1982. *Problems in Materialism and Culture.* London: Verso.

Wolf, Eric R. 1982. *Europe and the People without History.* Berkeley: University of California Press.

Wolfe, Patrick. 1991. "On Being Woken Up: The Dreamtime in Anthropology and in Australian Settler Culture." *Comparative Studies in Society and History* 33 (2): 197–224.

Wolff, Janet. 1991. "The Global and the Specific: Reconciling Conflicting Theories of Culture." In *Culture, Globalization and the World-System,* edited by Anthony D. King, 155–60. Binghamton: Department of Art and Art History, State University of New York at Binghamton.

Worsley, Peter. 1964. *The Third World.* Chicago: University of Chicago Press.

———. 1984. *The Three Worlds.* Chicago: University of Chicago Press.

———. 1990. "Models of the Modern World System." *Theory, Culture & Society* 7 (2–3): 83–96.

Yamamoto, Hisaye. [1949] [1979] 1988. *Seventeen Syllables and Other Stories.* Latham, N.Y.: Kitchen Table / Women of Color Press.

Yezierska, Anzia. 1920. "The Fat of the Land." In *Hungry Hearts.* Boston: Houghton Mifflin.

Yoshimoto, Mitsuhiro. 1989. "The Postmodern and Mass Images in Japan." *Public Culture* 1 (2): 8–25.

Young, Robert. 1990. *White Mythologies: Writing History and the West.* New York: Routledge.

Zangwill, Israel. 1909. *The Melting Pot.* New York: Macmillan.

Index

x

Williams, William Carlos, 145
Wolf, Eric, 40, 84, 128–29, 280, 304
Wolfe, Patrick, 252–54, 335
Wolff, Janet, 266–67, 276, 302
world-systems theory, 1, 34, 40, 43,
    123–30, 136–37, 141, 164, 323, 337;
    antisystemic movements in, 266,
    268–70; on the contemporary
    world, 265–71; criticized and re-
    vised, 136–37, 259–62, 313, 319–22;
    in *El Norte,* 131–33
Worsley, Peter: on colonialism in the
    Third World, 36; on the conceptual-
    ization and reconceptualization of
    the Third World, 11, 18–21; on the
    geneology of world-systems theory,
    123–24; on globalization, 115, 118;

on transnationalism, 297–98,
    321

Y

Yamamoto, Hisaye, 178–79, 184–85,
    187, 189, 191
Yezierska, Anzia, 159, 181, 200
Yoshimoto, Mitsuhiro, 66–69, 192,
    335
Young, Al, 156
Young, Robert, 38, 221–25, 231–33

Z

Zangwill, Israel, 161